Carving Animals

Bunnies and Chipmunks

Rosalyn Leach Daisey

Schiffer Publishing Ltd®
4880 Lower Valley Road Atglen, Pennsylvania 19310

Other Schiffer Books by Rosalyn Leach Daisey

Songbird Carving, 256 pp.
ISBN 978-0-88740-057-5, hard cover, $45.00
Songbird Carving II, 270 pp.
ISBN 0-88740-119-8, hard cover, $45.00
Shorebird Carving, 256 pp.
ISBN 0-88740-219-4, hard cover, $49.95
Upland Game Bird Carving, 240 pp.
ISBN 0-88740-349-2, hard cover, $49.95
Baby Bird and Chick Carving, 208 pp.
ISBN 0-88740-590-8, hard cover, $49.95

Library of Congress Control Number: 2011931895

Designed by "Sue"
Type set in PhylisD/NewBskvll BT

ISBN: 978-0-7643-3885-4
Printed in China

Schiffer Books are available at special discounts for bulk purchases for sales promotions or premiums. Special editions, including personalized covers, corporate imprints, and excerpts can be created in large quantities for special needs. For more information contact the publisher:

Published by Schiffer Publishing Ltd.
4880 Lower Valley Road
Atglen, PA 19310
Phone: (610) 593-1777; Fax: (610) 593-2002
E-mail: Info@schifferbooks.com

For the largest selection of fine reference books on this and related subjects, please visit our website at:
www.schifferbooks.com
We are always looking for people to write books on new and related subjects. If you have an idea for a book, please contact us at the above address.

This book may be purchased from the publisher.
Include $5.00 for shipping.
Please try your bookstore first.
You may write for a free catalog.

In Europe, Schiffer books are distributed by
Bushwood Books
6 Marksbury Ave.
Kew Gardens
Surrey TW9 4JF England
Phone: 44 (0) 20 8392 8585; Fax: 44 (0) 20 8392 9876
E-mail: info@bushwoodbooks.co.uk
Website: www.bushwoodbooks.co.uk

This is the best part of doing any book. I get to say in written print, for all to see, who is important to me. In previous texts, I have dedicated a book to my wonderful parents, another one to my amazing sister and brothers, another one specifically to honor my father who passed away, and two other books to my glorious children, Jason and Jenna.

Since my last book, I have had the wonderful experience of becoming a grandmother! I am a person of words, but for this experience, I simply do not have the words to express the depth of this new development in my life!

I dedicate this book to Olivia Kate Holden, my Grand-Daughter, another bright light in my life! Oh my gosh, what a captivating human being—Livie Kate lights up a room like a 1000-watt light bulb, just as her mother and my mother do! She brings new dimensions to the world and certainly to my life! I knew this baby, born on October 1, 2008, would change the world and my life—I simply had no idea about the magnitude of that change!

Here's to you, Livie Kate!

Contents

Acknowledgments 4

Introduction 5

Helpful Hints 6

- *Carving grips* 6
- *Primary types of wood for these projects* 7
- *Roughing out bits* 7
- *Ruby carvers* 8
- *Cleaning bits and burrs* 9
- *Stones for sanding* 9
- *Compass tricks and measuring* 11
- *Burning pens* 14
- *Super-glue and accelerator* 16
- *Building bases* 17
- *Repair Materials* 27
- *Safety* 28
- *Whiskers* 29
- *Paintbrushes* 30
- *Paint* 31
- *Paint set-up* 32
- *Reference pictures* 33
- *How to find tools and stuff* 33

Sleepy Bunny 34

Sitting Bunny 80

Bunny Painting 139

Sitting Chipmunk 152

Scratching Chipmunk 192

Chipmunk Painting 236

Acknowledgments

My never-ending appreciation goes to all of my students from over thirty years of teaching classes! You have taught me as well! Thank you!

I wish to thank Pete, Doug, and Team Schiffer for the magic they work on the material that I supply them, as well as their support through the process. I am so fortunate to be associated with this publishing firm!

My son-in-law, Ken Holden, was especially helpful to me in doing this project. You see, he is my computer geek who keeps my Macs in tip-top shape whenever I screw them up! He lent me a Mac laptop that I could dedicate just for use in this book. He made sure that everything I wrote and every picture I took was backed up multiple times, so that there was NO way that anything would be lost. He was there at the ready for any problems I had! Thank you, Ken!

As always, I am grateful for my friend and mentor, Bill Veasey. Bill and I have been friends for over 32 years, and I value this relationship a great deal! He is always available for consultation and guidance. Thank you, Bill!

More than 32 years ago, I spent a week with Avis Brown, in upstate New York, carving my first animals. I was hooked! Thank you, Avis, and I wish you continued success in your carving career!

During any long-term project, it is especially helpful to consult with someone, who understands the projects and the process and who offers valuable insights. For this project, that person is Susan Dorsch! Thank you, Susz, for all of your support and insight!

For help in solving Nikon and picture problems, I want to thank Bob Rutan. Bob is very knowledgeable about photography and about photography software, and I called on him several times for help. Thank you, Bob!

Writing any book requires much effort and many hours, and this one is no exception. Throughout the process, my children, Jason, Jenna, and now my son-in-law, Ken, have been very supportive in this process. All of them understand that I need the space and time to work. While all of them are there if and when I need them, for the most part, they just let me "hole" up and absorb myself in the project! They are the best cheerleaders and supporting cast that anyone could wish for! Thank you, Jason, Jenna, and Ken!

Introduction

Writing and photographing the animal projects for this book has truly been a labor of love. This is the first book that I have ever done digitally. This time it was very exciting to use strobes to light my pictures, instead of hot lights, and then to see the picture pop up on the computer screen in about 2 seconds, instead of waiting several months for custom processed prints to return. I could see right away if I captured exactly what I wanted! I have always loved learning new things, and learning this new way of writing and photographing was really exciting! It is truly the learning of all kinds of new things that has kept me engaged in this amazing art form for more than 32 years!

Carving animals is something I have enjoyed even longer than I have enjoyed carving birds. Animals offer even more latitude in creating expression than birds. You have a tail, ears, face, and paws that you can animate to create feeling and attitude! Also creating fur is fun and can be a wonderful change of pace from feathers. If I have spent a stretch of time in carving and painting birds, I will delve into an animal project with gusto for a wonderful change of pace! I am particularly excited and enthusiastic to share this book and these projects with you!

As in my previous five books, the format is a step-by-step process through each procedure in completing four projects. There are two rabbit and two chipmunk projects with painting instructions for both species. The informational text follows each picture. I will lead you through each project in this way, one step at a time.

I would suggest that you read the "Helpful Hints" chapter first, where I offer many insights into techniques, tools, and materials. This will give you the basic background information for the carving, texturing, painting, and mounting procedures.

Let's get started and have some fun!

Rosalyn Leach Daisey
Newark, Delaware
www.rozdaisey.com

We must be the change we wish to see in the world.
—Mahatma Gandhi

Helpful Hints

Carving grips

Figure 1. The roughing out grip is done by holding the flexible shaft machine hand piece in the palm of your hand, putting the thumb of that hand on the carving, and pulling toward the thumb. This is a similar motion to pealing an apple or potato. Of course, you DO NOT bring the whirring bit all the way to the thumb!

Figure 2. When using a smaller hand piece and when carving details, hold the hand piece as you would a pencil, and pull the whirring bit downward and backward toward you. Note that my little finger of that hand is braced on the carving. You will find that you need to be anchored on the piece you are carving or on the table/bench. You want to be in control of the hand piece and bit and not the other way around! If you are not anchored, the whirring bit will take you where it wants you to go, and you will not have good control.

Primary types of wood for these projects

Figure 3. The chunk of wood on the left is tupelo and on the right is basswood. I have used tupelo for all of the projects in this book. You could do these projects in basswood, but you are going to have many more repairs with different parts breaking. Even though tupelo is lighter in weight, it is much stronger cross-grain. When you are doing animals, there are ears, tails, and paws—some things are just going to be cross-grain, and there is a possibility that some vital part is going to break, especially using basswood. To find a supplier for tupelo (if you don't go to the shows where tupelo suppliers sell) go to your bookstore and purchase a carving magazine. There are many wood and tool suppliers advertising in most carving magazines. You can also Google tupelo wood and find a supplier on line.

Roughing out bits

Figure 4. These bits are Typhoon carbide bits. The blue ones on the left are the fine grit and are the ones I use on tupelo. The cylinder in the middle of the two bright blue ones is still a blue/fine bit but one that has been used extensively with the blue color being worn off. The two red ones on the right are the coarse grit and are ones that I seldom use when carving tupelo. All of the bits have 1/4" shanks and fit in the larger capacity hand pieces.

Figure 5. These bits are Kutzall carbide bits. The gold ones on the left are fine and are the ones I use on tupelo. The bright and worn silver ones on the right are the coarse grit and are ones I use when carving basswood.

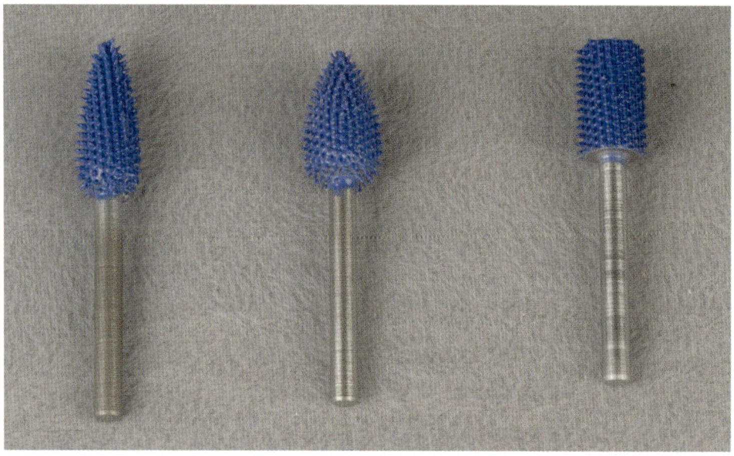

Figure 6. These are the smaller Typhoon roughing out bits that have 1/8" shanks and fit in the smaller hand piece or in the larger capacity hand piece with the appropriate size collet. The blue/fine grit bits work best on tupelo.

Ruby carvers

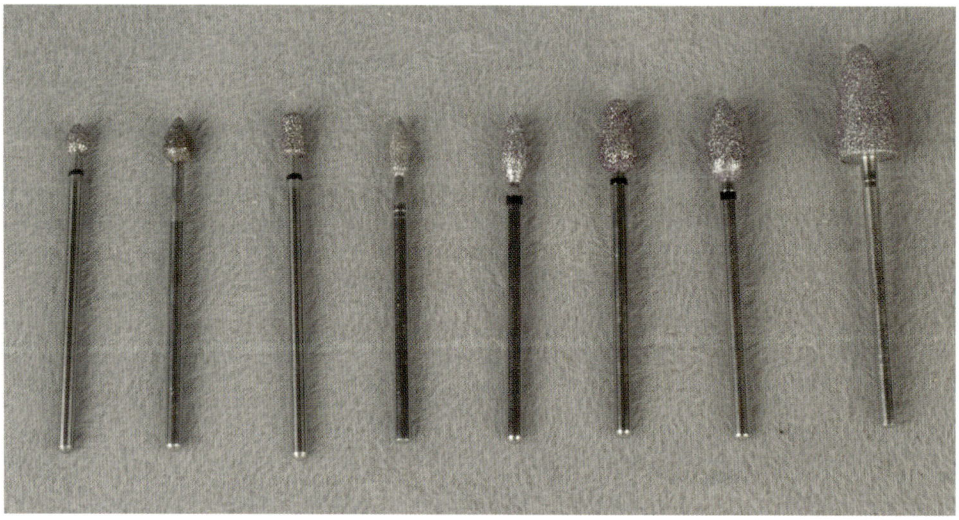

Figure 7. These are the ruby carver bits that I use when carving animals. From left to right, they are the small pointed ball (RC-16), the large pointed ball (RC-17), the slightly domed cylinder (RC-18), the #1 flame (RC-19), the #2 flame (RC-20), the pear shape (RC-23), the #3 flame (RC-25) and the large bullet (RC-30). Notice that most of the ruby carvers have black bands on the shafts. Some of the black bands have come off from use/wear or from being cleaned so many times. The black bands signify a super-coarse grit which I prefer. No colored band signifies a fine grit and a green band signifies a medium grit. Ruby carvers will last for quite awhile, depending on their use, but eventually they will need to be replaced. Rubies are primarily used for carving soft wood, and they will wear out more quickly if used on harder woods. As the burr encounters hard wood or grain, the burr heats up, and the adhesive, holding the little chips to the shape, melts, throwing the ruby chips off the bit.

Cleaning bits and burrs

Figure 8. All roughing out, ruby carver, and diamond bits will need cleaning periodically. If a bit is just slightly clogged, a brushing with a brass brush will get rid of the built up debris in the bit. If the bits are heavily encrusted, you will need to clean them out with bit cleaner (obtainable from most carving supply retailers) or oven cleaner. If you are using the oven cleaner, put the clogged bits in a glass jar, spray them with the oven cleaner, allow the spray to bubble up and then recede, and spray again. Soaking in oven cleaner overnight usually softens the crusty stuff. Rinse them off with water and dry thoroughly. Most often a light brushing with the brass brush will get rid of any build-up remaining. If you are using the bit cleaner, place the clogged bits in the plastic basket inside the container, and allow soaking for an hour or two. Pull the basket up and dry all the bits thoroughly. If necessary, lightly brush them with the brass brush.

Stones for sanding

Figure 9. These are some of the stones that I use for smoothing or sanding both birds and animals. The color of the stone or the coarseness/fineness does not seem to matter as much on tupelo as it does on basswood. I seldom use sandpaper to sand anything on birds or animals. I can't seem to make the sandpaper go around on the carved shapes without flattening them, and power sanding with stones seems to work so well.

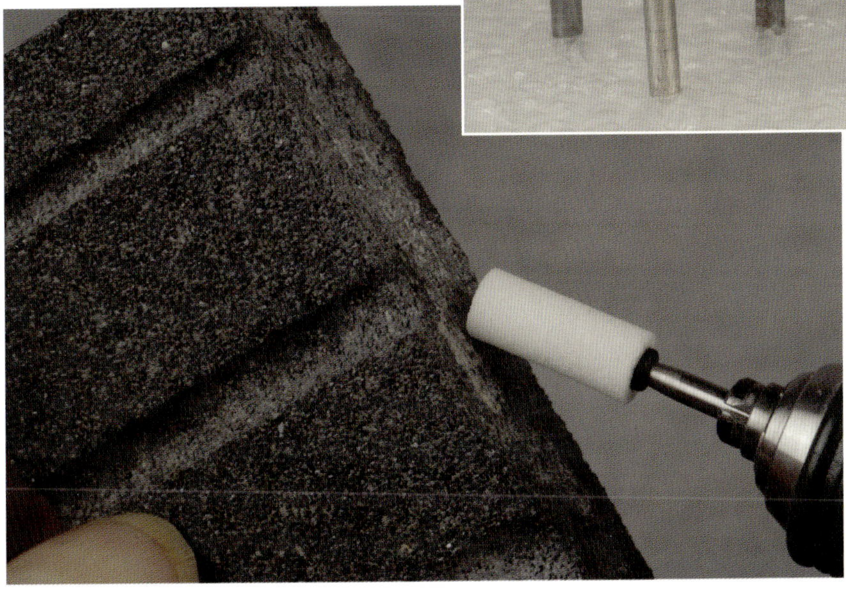

Figure 10. It is not always easy to find exactly the shaped stoned you need for a particular area. To change the shape, you can use a dressing stone that can be purchased from most of the carving supply retailers. Make sure that you have safety glasses or goggles on when doing this. Chuck up the stone in your flexible shaft or micro motor tool, which should be run at approximately half-speed.

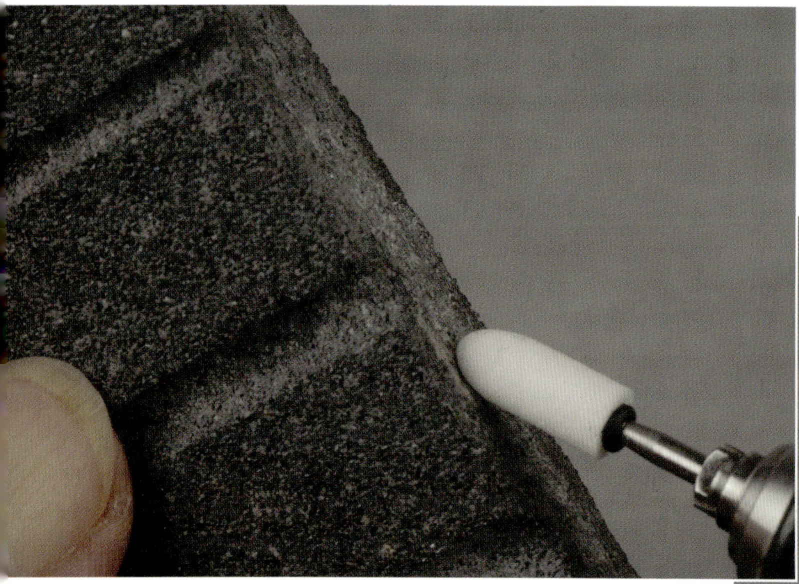

Figure 11. Hold the stone to the surface of the dressing stone, and keep grinding the whirring stone until you have the desired shape.

Figure 12. Hold the shape stone on a diamond file to further smooth the stone's surface.

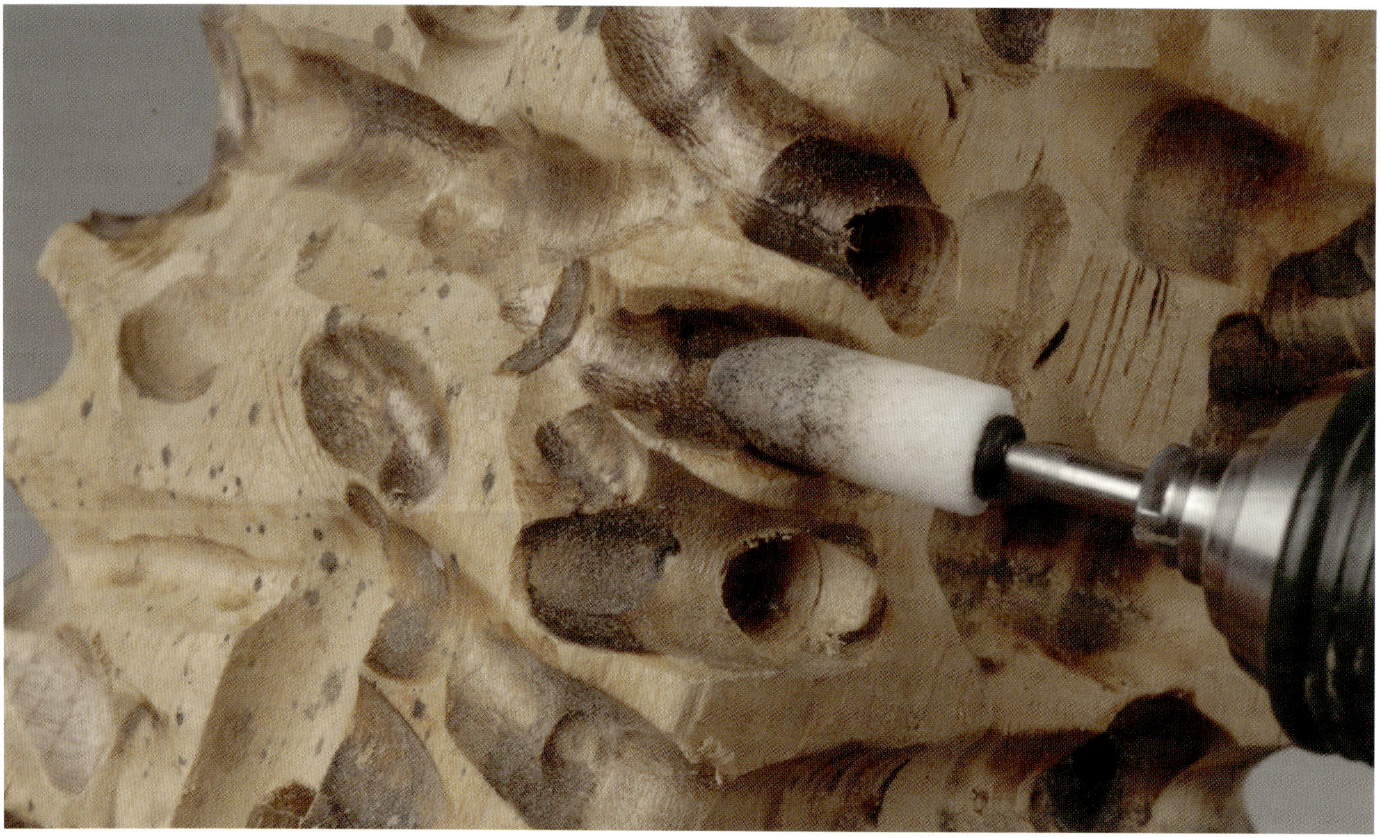

Figure 13. So that the stone will smooth the wood finely, fill it up by holding the whirring stone to a piece of basswood. You can see that the chunk of wood I'm using here has been used for just this very procedure many times! The more clogged the stone is, the smoother your carved area with be. I seldom clean stones unless they aren't cutting/smoothing at all. If necessary, you could regrind the stone to expose fresh grit.

Compass tricks and measuring

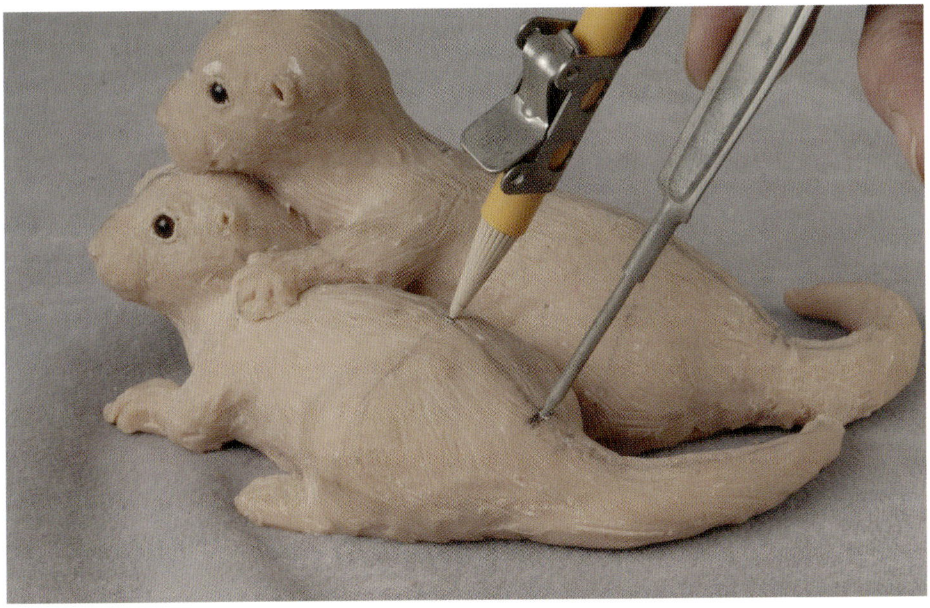

Figure 14. You can use a compass to transfer a particular measurement from a model to the carving.

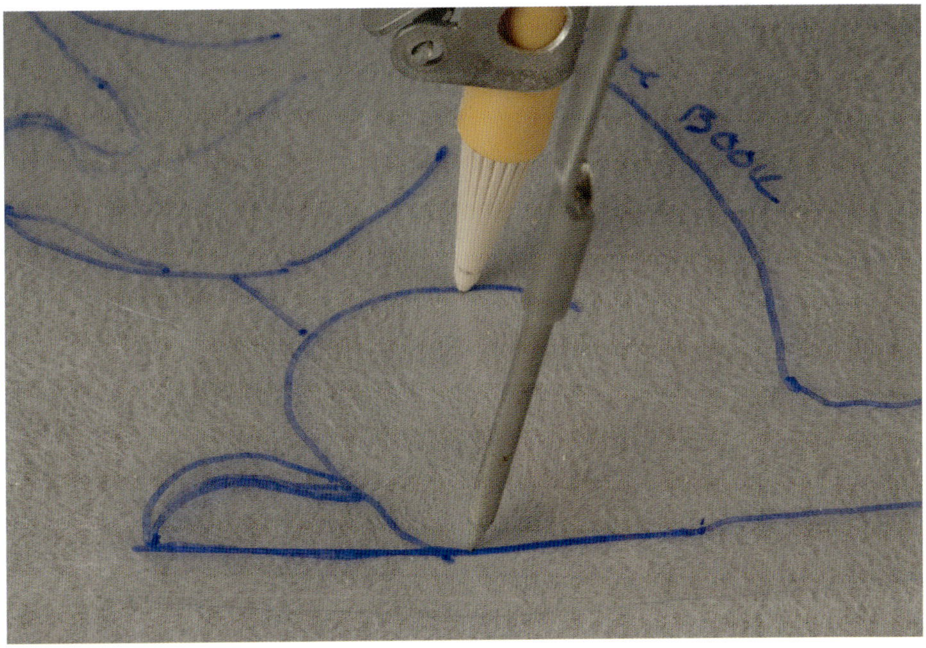

Figure 15. You can also use a compass to transfer a particular measurement from a drawing or acetate to the carving.

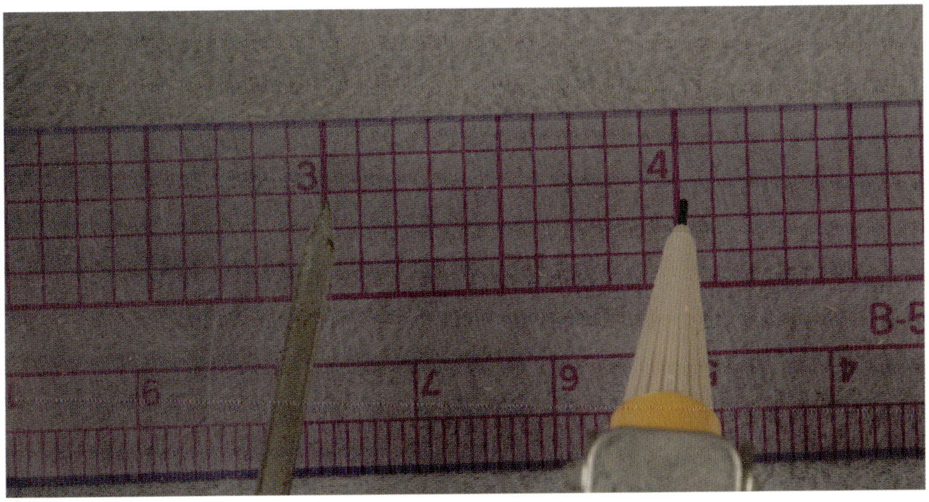

Figure 16. You can set a compass to a particular dimension and transfer that to the carving. One of the metal rulers works a little easier than a plastic ruler, since the grooves in the metal will keep the point of the compass from moving or tracking along its surface.

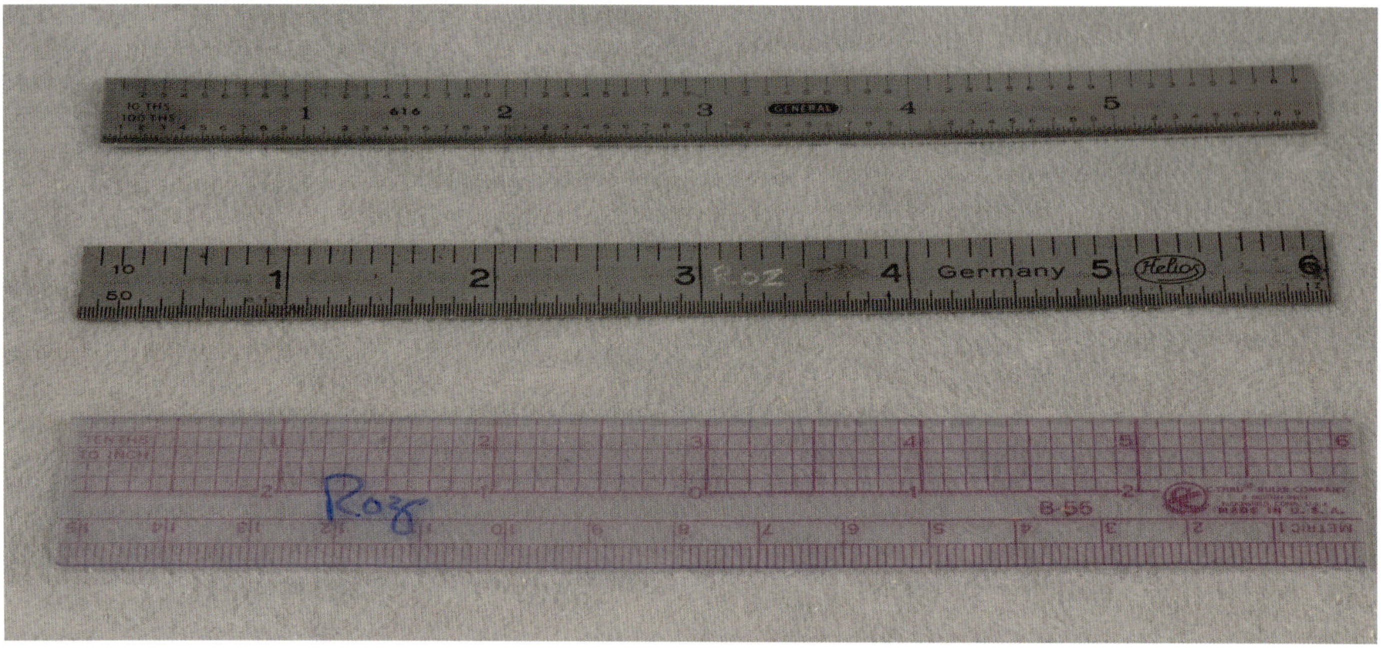

Figure 17. Yes, I measure in tenths of an inch. Once you get a ruler and a caliper that measures in tenths, you are good to go. Most of your carving retailers carry the tenths measuring devices. Even Lowes and many hardware stores carry General Tools, which make rulers and calipers in tenths. If you are having trouble finding them, try Googling "rulers and calipers in tenths." Why do I measure in tenths? The fellow who taught me to measure bird dimensions was a chemical engineer, and I am told that engineers use tenths in most of their drawings. And it is an easy system to use. Try dividing 27/64" equally across a centerline! Our money is in tenths, why not our linear dimensions? Fractions are great for building houses and such, but tenths are infinitely easier in measuring carvings.

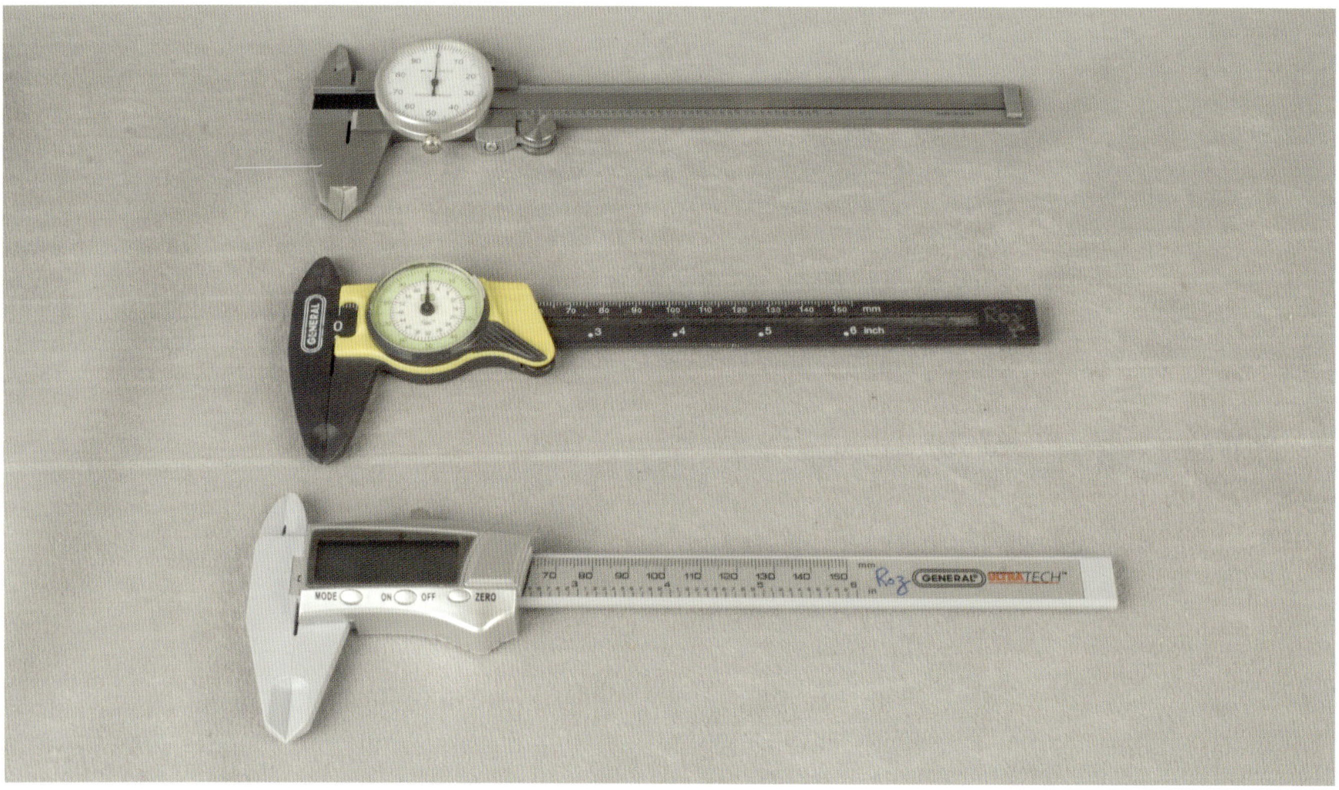

Figure 18. These are calipers that measure in tenths. General Tools makes the bottom one, and I found it at Lowe's recently. It has a button where you can toggle between tenths, fractions, and millimeters! If you have a metal caliper, be careful not to squeeze it too hard if you are working in tupelo. It can actually depress the wood and leave an indentation where you don't want one.

Figure 19. One way to use calipers is to measure an outside dimension. Measure whatever dimension you are checking by squeezing gently, and reading the dial.

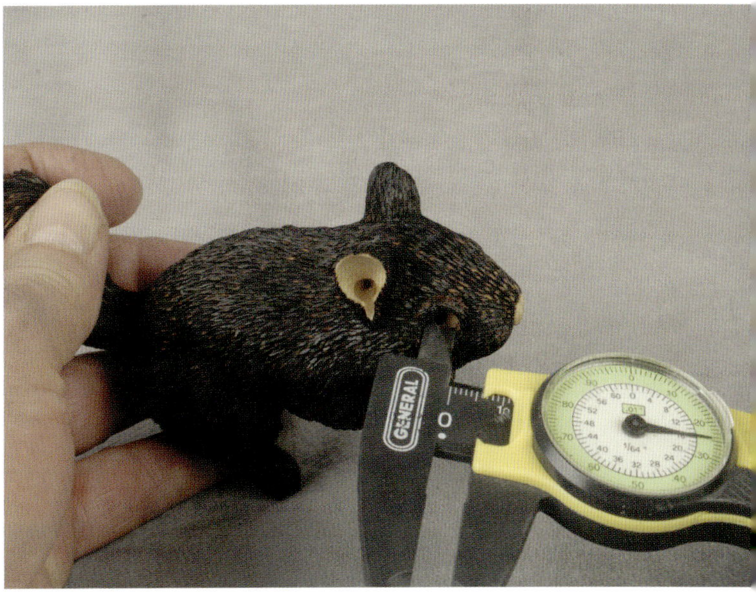

Figure 20. To measure an inside dimension, use the prongs on top of the caliper spread to the inside surfaces of whatever you are measuring, and then read the dial.

Figure 21. To measure depth, use the protruding slide part at the bottom of the caliper. Put the end down into whatever you are measuring, and where the bottom end of the calipers meets the surface determines the measurement on the dial.

Burning pens

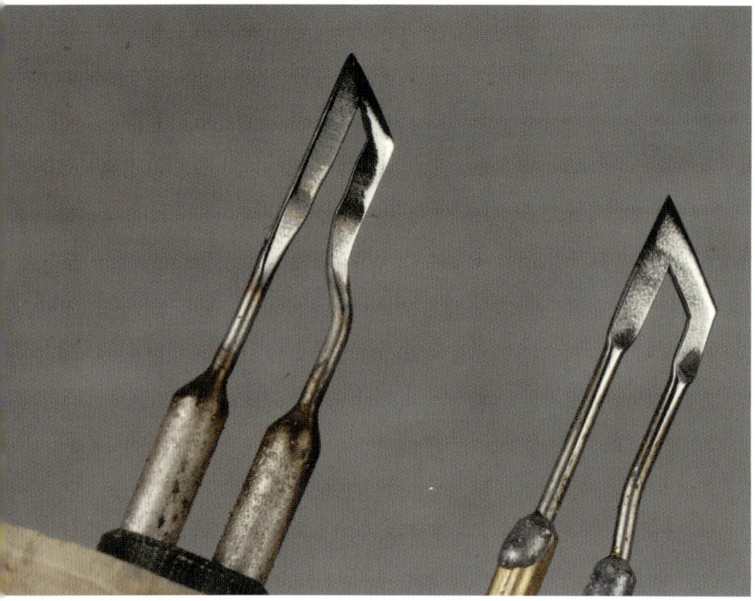

Figure 22. A medium skew burning pen tip is the primary one for burning fur. When sculpting fur, a burning pen with the pen tip wire silver-soldered into the pen is far superior to a pen with a replaceable tip. When you have a mechanical connection of the replaceable tip, there is much more heat that builds up in the pen handle.

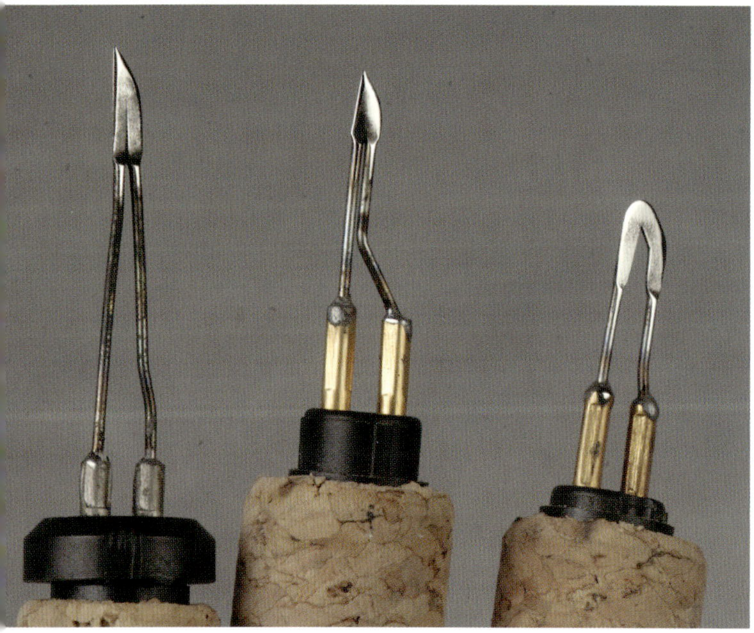

Figure 23. These are some other pen tip shapes that can be used on the animal projects. The long-pointed tip on the left is useful in reaching into deep recesses. The shorter pointed one is useful in tight, but less deep areas. The rounded tip is useful in concave areas.

Figure 24. Even with the silver soldered pen tips, the pen handles of some burning pens still get too hot to hold. In burning fur, you will need much higher heat than in doing feathers or other types of burning. The heat can be so high that in a dimly lit room, you can even see the reddish glow of the pen tip. To prevent the pen handle from burning your hand, you will need a barrier of some sort between the pen handle and your hand. Some people prefer to wear a thick leather glove on their hand to prevent blisters. I prefer to put something on the pen handle itself. The plastic mesh (most of the carving retailers sell these) on the top pen handle is one solution. The middle pen has a piece of plastic tubing that can be bought in different diameters in home improvement or hardware stores. Some of the carving retailers sell the rubber sleeves that will fit on the burning pen handles.

*__Safety note:__ when burning fur, hold the project out in front of you so that you do NOT inhale the smoke/fumes or wear a mask!

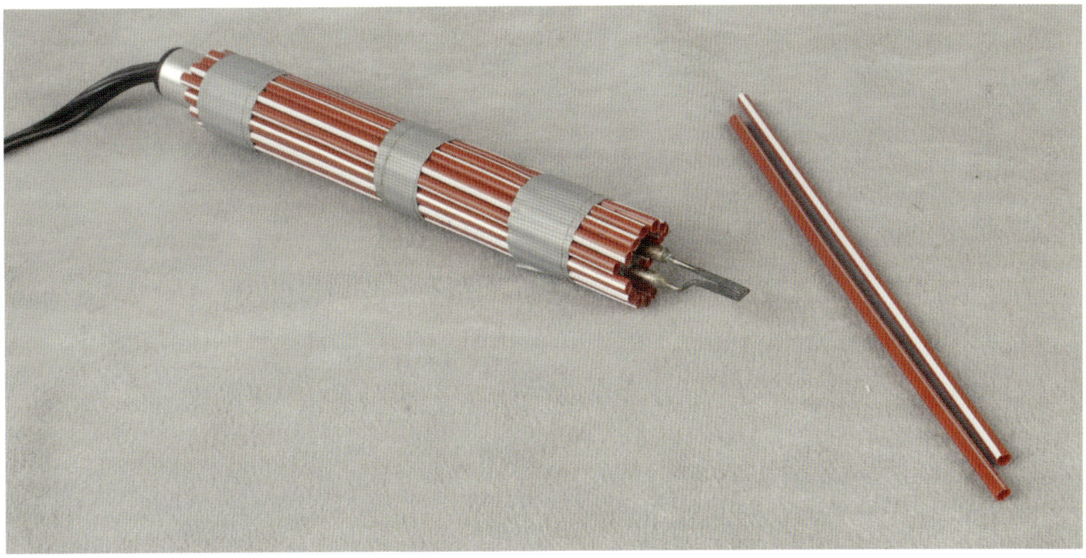

Figure 25. Some people prefer to tape coffee stirrers to the pen tip handle. The openings of the tubes dissipate the heat.

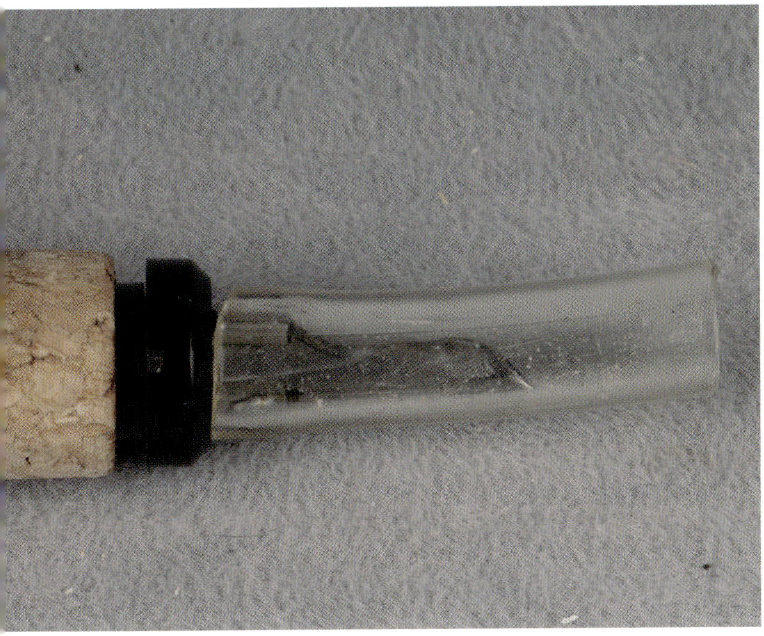

Figure 26. The clear plastic tubing can also be bought to cover and protect the tip of each of your burning pens. When traveling to teach classes, I use these to protect my pen tips.

Figure 27. In the previous pictures of burning pens, note that all the pen tips are shiny. I buff my pen tips 3 or 4 times a year. A shiny, buffed pen tip slides through the wood more easily and also collects less carbon. I never use any kind of sandpaper or abrasive cloth to clean or sharpen my pens. If you sharpen or clean the carbon off your pen tip by dragging it across sandpaper, the scratches and the burrs on the scratches allow the carbon a place to grab onto. Cleaning a burning pen on sandpaper, even a very fine grit, will also shorten the life of the pen, since you are basically grinding the metal away. The burning tip I am currently using has lasted at least ten years, and I do much burning of both birds and animals!

Figure 28. To buff a burning pen, use either a rock hard felt bob on a mandrel in a flexible shaft hand piece or a hard felt wheel on a grinding machine. Load the felt bob or wheel with buffing rouge by running it and holding the rouge against it. You will be able to see the rouge loading onto the felt. If you are using the flexible shaft machine, you will need to use a slower speed than you would in carving. As in the previous picture, hold the tip of the burning pen against the felt bob or wheel until it is shiny, and there are no scratches.

Super-glue and accelerator

Figure 29. Here you see three bottles of super-glue: thin, medium, and thick. Thin is used to soak into the wood to harden a particular area. Medium viscosity is useful when gluing two parts together that have a tight fit. Thick viscosity is helpful in gluing two parts together that may have voids or gaps in the connection. I keep all three viscosities on hand, and I store them in the freezer. The thick or gap-filling viscosity on the right was bought and opened in April 1997 (I always date each container when I open it)! Keeping them in the freezer greatly extends the shelf life! Carving retailers sell several sizes of the different viscosities.

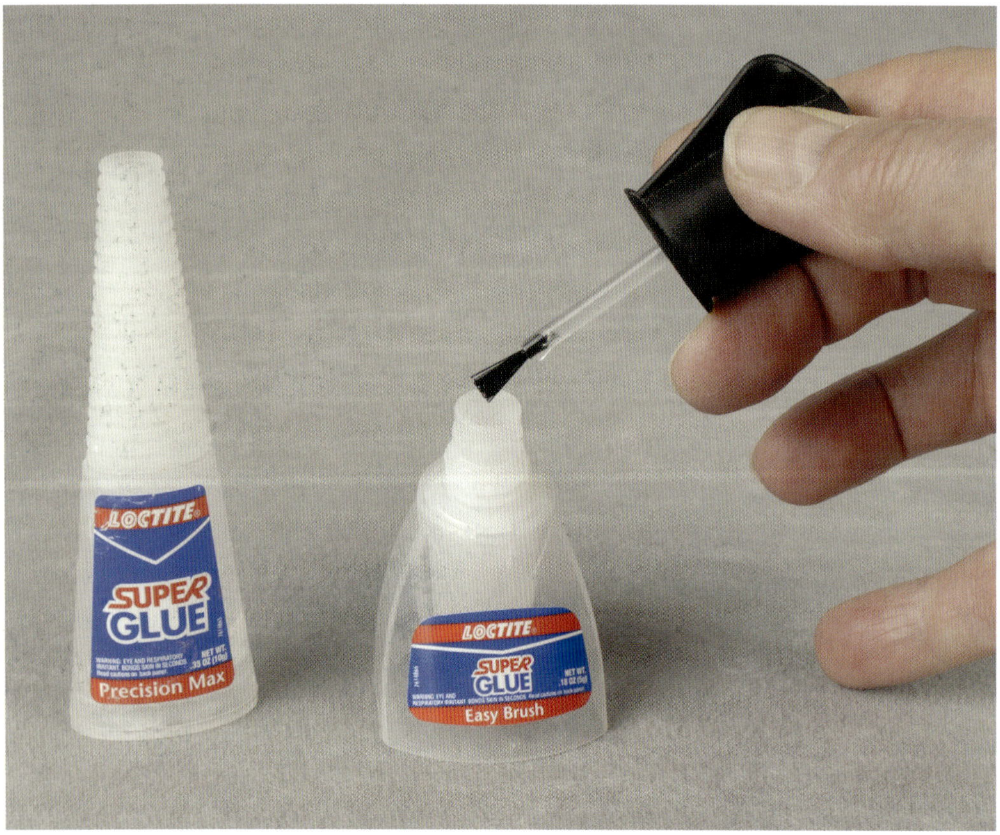

Figure 30. At some of the home improvement and hardware stores, you can find Loctite super-glue. It is medium-viscosity super-glue. The container on the right comes with a small brush, which is very useful in super-gluing a specific part without it running over unnecessary areas.

Figure 31. Accelerator is very useful for instantly hardening all three viscosities of super-glue. It can be bought from most carving retailers and some hobby stores.

Building bases

Figure 32. Since all of the projects in this book can fit on a flat base, here you see some examples of what can be used. To the left is a slice of a log, which I call a "cookie." In the middle is a slice of a Manzanita root. To the right is a slice of a piece of driftwood that I found along the bay front or river somewhere in my travels. Looking in obvious places for driftwood is one of my favorite nature pursuits! When I am working on a piece, I often will search my stash of driftwood looking for the perfect piece. When considering one, I want the fragile part of the carving (such as the tails in these pieces) to be protected, and yet I don't want the base to dwarf the carving.

Figure 33. For the scratching chippy piece, I want to do a base with some "dirt" on it. I pick out a pork-chop shaped base (www.blueribbonbases.net). Take a slightly larger piece of plain white paper, and press the edge of the base into the paper around its entire perimeter.

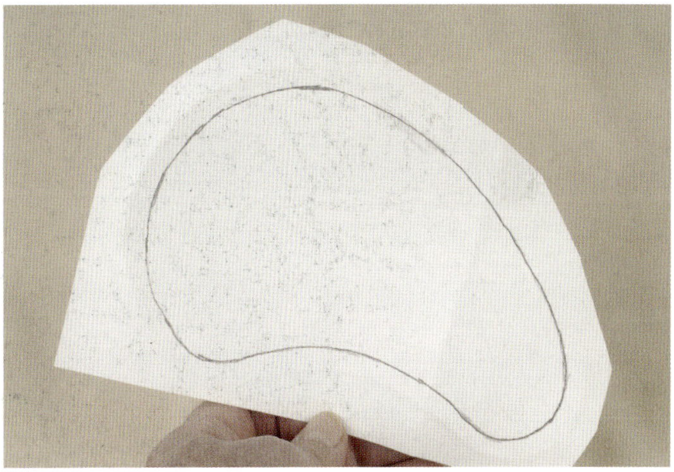

Figure 34. Draw a corresponding shape 0.25" inside the embossed edge indentation. Cut this shape out with scissors.

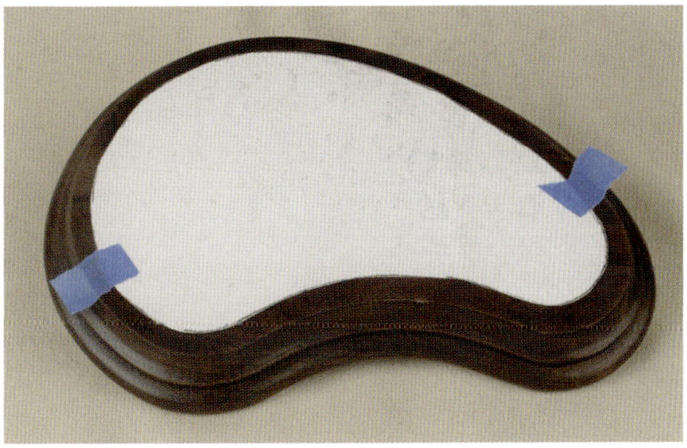

Figure 35. Masking tape the cutout paper pattern to the base to make sure that it is symmetrical with the base.

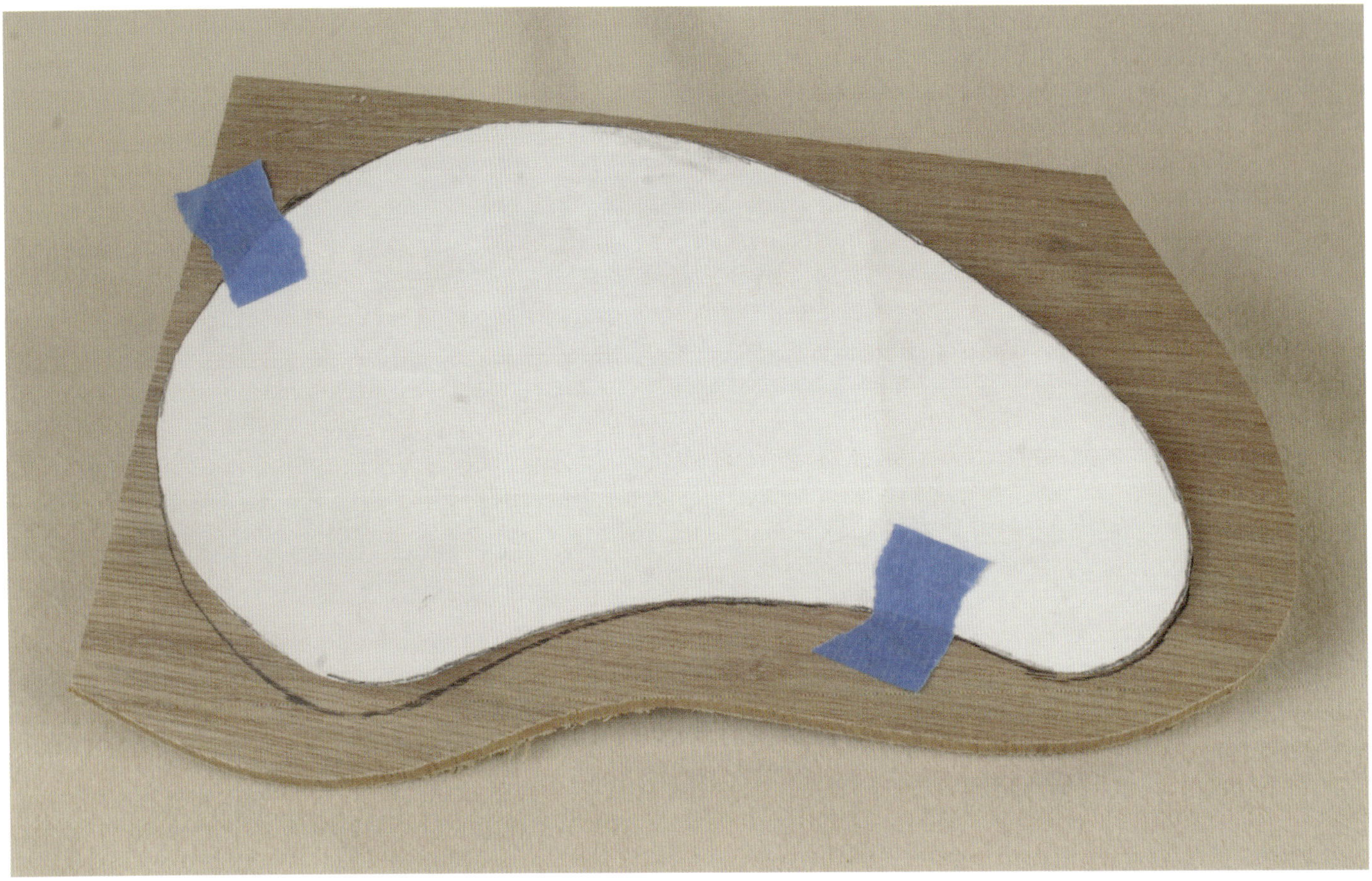

Figure 36. Now masking tape the pattern to an appropriate sized piece of 1/4" luan plywood. Cut this shape out with a coping saw or band saw.

Figure 37. Try the plywood on the base to make sure that is symmetrical around the perimeter.

Figure 38. Using a medium sized taper, Typhoon carbide cutter, angle the top edge of the plywood.

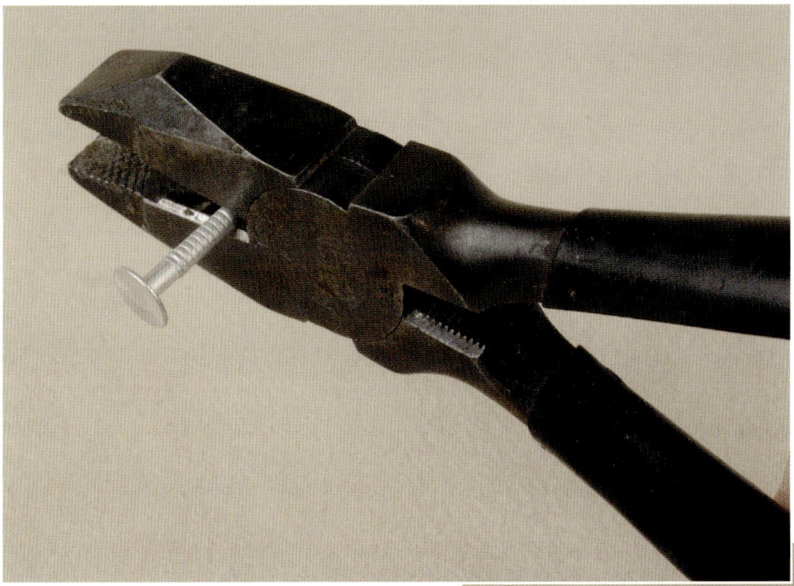

Figure 39. I use some type of big-headed aluminum nails for the next part because they can be cut by hand with linemen's pliers. Cut the nails slightly more than 1/2" from the nail head.

Figure 40. Clamp the plywood to the base using some type of clamp that won't mar the base in any way. Determine what size drill bit you need to be slightly larger diameter than the diameter of the nail's shank. Mark the length of the cut off nail on the drill bit with masking tape, and drill a hole that depth on each end of the plywood, not too near the edge.

Figure 41. Thoroughly mix equal amounts of 5-minute epoxy right on the plywood and cover the nail heads. Allow time for the glue to harden. Then you can remove the plywood from the base, which you can place out of the way for the time being.

Figure 42. On a plastic or heavy paper plate, thoroughly mix a quantity of modeling paste, raw or burnt umber paint, and a quantity of sand.

Figure 43. Use a palette or putty knife to frost the mixture on the plywood. Now, don't be chintzy with this! You need, at least, 1/4" of the goopy stuff to be able to do the next step.

Figure 44. Dry the mixture with a hair dryer on high heat for a minute or two. The outside of the modeling paste mixture will begin to dry and harden. Those of you who are "mature" might remember eating cake with old-fashioned frosting where the outside was kind of firm but the inside was mushy. This drying of the modeling paste mixture reminds me of that.

Figure 45. After the drying, take a palette knife or screwdriver and begin to "chunk" up the surface of the partially dried mixture. Repeat the drying and "chunking" up procedure several times until you see the irregularities begin to develop on the surface of the modeling paste mixture. Then put this aside to dry for 10-12 hours. Even after that length of time, deep in the mixture may still be pliable.

Figure 46. Use a 1/16" diameter drill bit to drill into the down front leg of the chipmunk, while supporting that leg. Make sure that the drill bit is aimed in the direction of the leg. You do NOT want the drill bit to exit the leg on any side. If you have not already done so, drill a 1/16" diameter hole in the flat bottom rump of the chipmunk.

Figure 47. Super-glue a piece of 16 gauge galvanized wire into each hole. While carefully supporting the front leg, bend the wire so that it is 90 degrees to the bottom of the carving. Do the same on the other wire.

Figure 48. After the modeling paste mixture has hardened to the touch on the surface (but still soft underneath), hold the chippy over the top where you want him to sit, and push the wires down into the mixture. Take an awl and widen out these holes a little. You want to make the holes with the wires and not have to drill these holes. Nothing ruins a drill bit faster than drilling through the modeling paste with sand in it! Now, give the mixture time to harden thoroughly (another day or so).

Figure 49. Do a heavy burnt umber wash over the entire base. While this is still wet, darken the perimeter with straight black dabbed and blended toward the center. Use a large, old brush for this since the modeling paste/sand mixture is such an abrasive surface. The sand in the modeling paste will sand away the tips of the bristles of any brush!

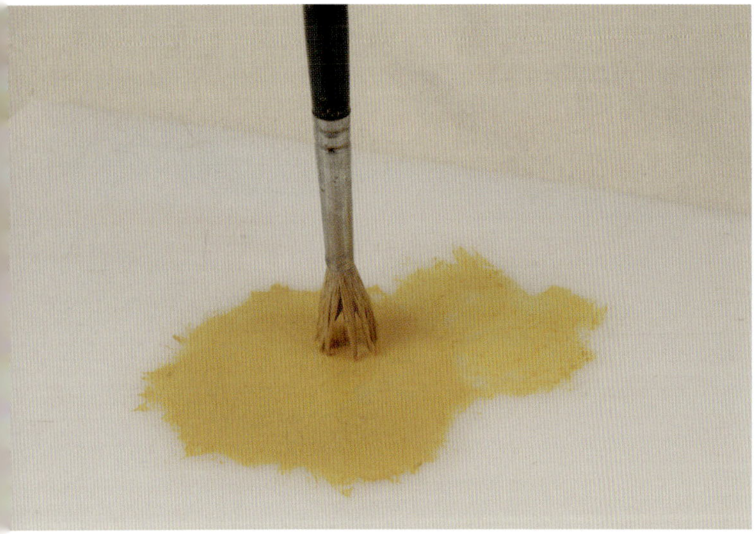

Figure 50. Take a small glob of yellow oxide paint, and mash the brush up and down until the spread out brush is filled with the paint.

Figure 52. Here is what mine looks like after I have gotten all the different shades randomly speckled all over the base.

Figure 53. Thoroughly mix a little puddle of equal amounts of the 5-minute epoxy glue, stuff it down into the drilled holes, and put the painted base in place. Allow time for the glue to harden.

Figure 51. Take the spread out brush loaded with yellow oxide, and apply the paint to the base with the brush 90 degrees to the surface—this is an irregular dabbing motion. The effect will be a random mottling of applied paint. Do this same dabbing technique with multiple colors: yellow oxide and white, raw sienna, raw sienna and white, burnt sienna, burnt sienna and white, raw umber, and raw umber and white. You will need to use the hair dryer to dry in between applications. You want many shades of the colors in random spots on the irregular surface. If the applications become too light, throw on a burnt umber wash to darken it. When you are happy with all the shades and all the colors, stop!

Figure 54. To mount a project directly onto a cookie or flat piece of wood, drill a 1/16" diameter hole about 1/4" into the bottom of the carving.

Figure 55. Hold the carving on the top of the base and twist slightly while lightly pressing the wire into the surface of the base.

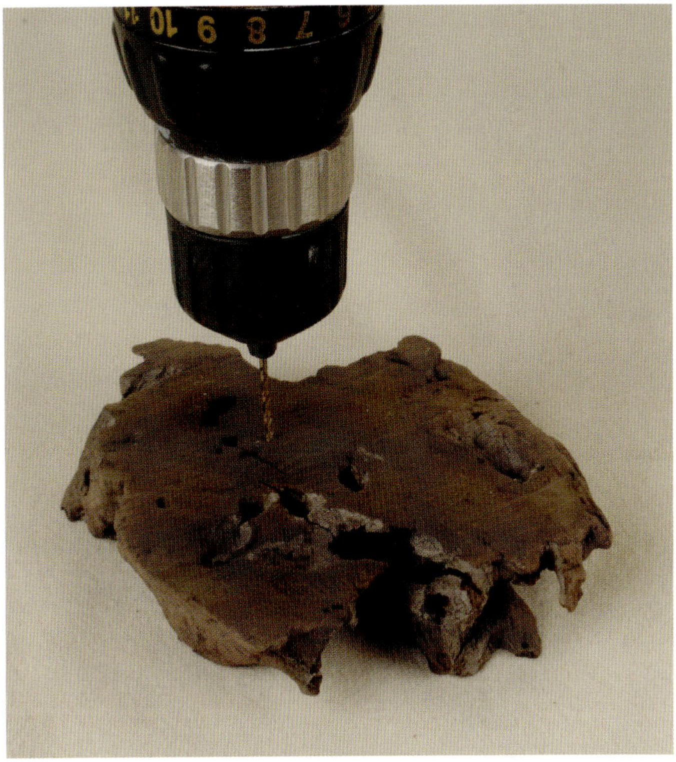

Figure 56. Drill a 5/64" diameter hole slightly longer than the protruding wire length.

Figure 57. Put super-glue down into the hole, and glue the project in place.

Figure 58. Put super-glue down in the holes in the ground mixture, and put the chippy in place. Allow the glue to harden.

Repair Materials

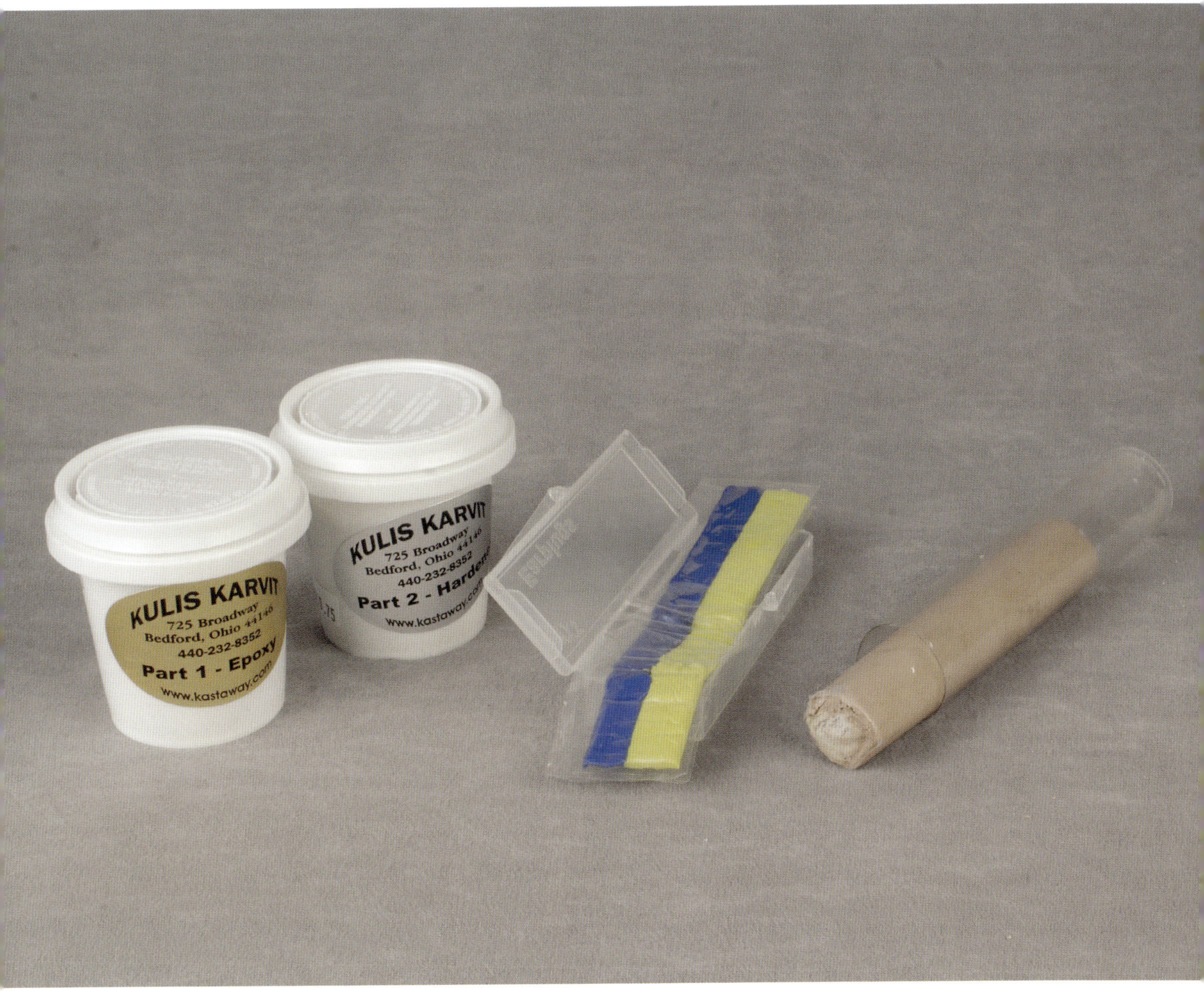

Figure 59. These are some of the materials available to make repairs and can be bought from most of the carving retailers.

Kulis Karvit (on the left) is a two-part epoxy compound. Thoroughly mix equal amounts of Part 1 and Part 2 until blended. Initial shaping can be accomplished before it hardens. Depending on the amount of hardener added, the mixture usually firms up in a hour or two, and thoroughly hardens in several hours. Once hardened, you can carve, sand, and stone it, but it cannot be burned easily as it tends to melt.

To use the ribbon epoxy (in the middle), cut the ribbon straight across at whatever width you think you will need, and then cut out the middle where the two colors are touching and have already chemically bonded. Knead it thoroughly until you can see no streaks or bits of either color. Apply it to whatever area needed, and shape and texture as necessary. After it has hardened, you can do a little touch-up shaping or texturing, but I have found that it is better to do that beforehand. It firms up in an hour or so, and thoroughly hardens in approximately 4 hours. To keep the tool end from pulling the epoxy off the carving as you are working it, it will need to be dunked in oily, non-hardening modeling clay.

On the right is a roll of QuikWood. To use this epoxy, cut straight across the roll, and thoroughly mix and knead until both colors are blended. Apply to the carving and do some initial shaping before it hardens, which takes approximately 30 minutes. Once hardened, it can be carved, sanded, and stoned, but not burned.

I would suggest trying all of these several types of repair materials to determine which one works best on different parts of carvings. All three compounds take some practice, and experience is the best teacher.

Safety

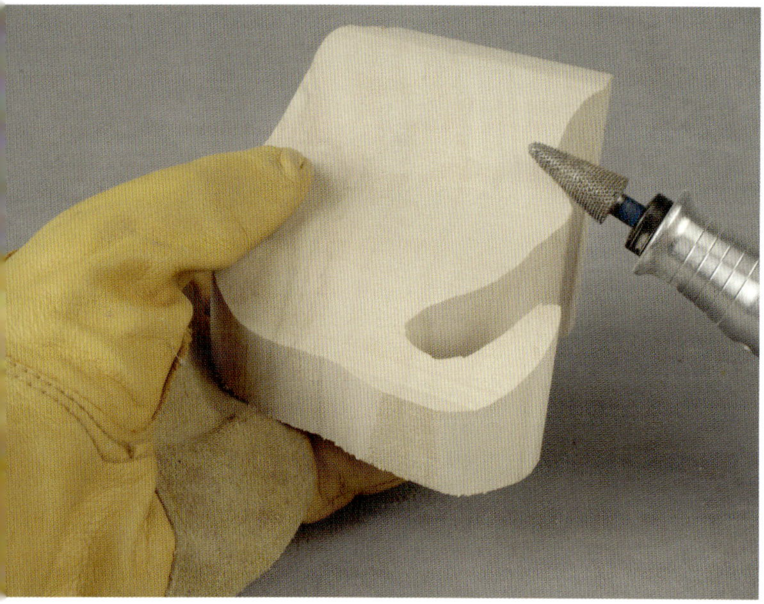

Figure 60. Wearing a leather garden glove will protect the hand holding the project from getting dinged up, especially with any roughing out bits.

Figure 61. Wearing safety glasses will protect your eyes. Many styles, such as these, will even fit over glasses. Many pairs of new glasses (considered stylish) have very small lenses that may not sufficiently cover and protect the eye area. Wear safety glasses/goggles over these new smaller lenses/glasses.

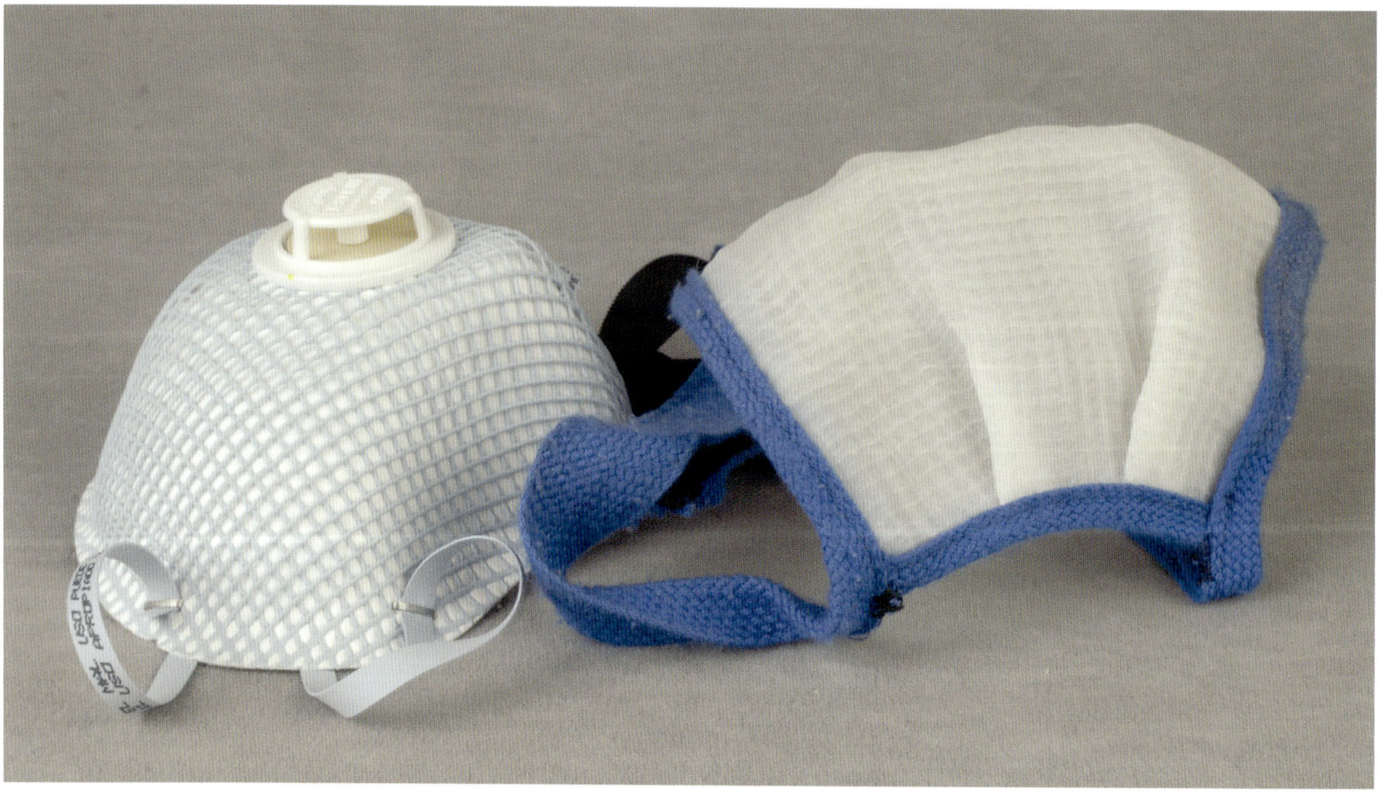

Figure 62. In addition to using some kind of dust collection, it is still necessary to wear a dust mask to prevent inhaling the dust released with grinding. You can find disposable paper masks at many hardware and home improvement stores, but I do not recommend these. There is too much air leakage around the edges. You will need a mask that fits snugly against your face.

If you insist on hanging your head over the carving while burning, wear a mask to prevent inhaling the smoke/fumes, or you can hold the carving out in front of you so the fumes do not waft in your face.

Whiskers

Figure 63. Paint brushes made with natural hairs can be used for whiskers. You can use a natural china bristle brush (left), a black china bristle brush (middle), or a badger hair paintbrush (right).

Figure 64. Even hair from actual animal hides can be used. The top row, from left to right, is a portion of the hind leg of a porcupine, and two kinds of deer hide. The bottom row, from left to right, is a piece of black bear hide, moose hide, and a piece of hide from an albino moose. You may be able to get swatches of actual animal hides from a local taxidermist, fly-tying shop, or hunters.

Paintbrushes

Figure 65. I seldom use any other kind of paintbrush than natural hairs. I find that they hold and let go of the paint in a wonderful way that makes painting easier. The white brush on the left is a stiff bristle brush used to apply gesso. The brushes in the middle are various sizes of sable rounds. By the way, there is no standardization of brush sizes and numbers. A #6 in one brand will not likely be the same size as a #6 from another brand or even another style in the same brand! The two brushes on the right are two Kolinsky sable liners of different sizes. Anytime you use a liner brush, add a drop or two of flow medium to your paint mixture. It will enable the paint to slide ride off the tip of the brush more easily. Flow medium breaks the viscosity of the water or liquid, making the paint more slippery.

I urge you to buy the best brushes you can afford and take extraordinary care of them. If you are painting all day, go to the sink several times during the day, and wash your brushes out with soap and water. At the end of the day, wash them again thoroughly using a good brush soap that can be bought in most art or hobby stores. The brush soap has natural oils and lubricants in it that will be absorbed into the natural hairs, and keep them painting well longer.

Paint

Figure 66. There are many brands of acrylic paint available. I have used Liquitex jar paints for 30 years, and I find they are wonderful pigments that mix, apply, and wear very well. If you are using another brand of paint, you will need to formulate your mixtures to match the ones in the book with different colors. There is NO standardization of paint between paint manufacturers. In other words, a burnt umber from one manufacturer is not the same shade of brown as one from another manufacturer.

Paint set-up

Figure 67. There are many different paint set-ups that can be used. You can use palette paper, white Styrofoam plates, tin foil, and/or a round palette with little cups around the circumference. My favorite is freezer paper masking taped to the table with the shiny side up. Because I am right-handed, I prefer my rinse water container on the right with a dry folded paper towel underneath the edge. On the upper left of the freezer paper is a folded paper towel that I have thoroughly saturated with water from the laboratory squirt bottle in the upper middle. As long as I keep the wet paper towel saturated, the paints will stay workable and usable. Acrylics on a firm surface or palette paper will dry out quickly, and you will need to keep putting out new blobs. The square plastic container lid at the top is used to cover the wet paints when I am finished painting for the day. They will still be usable the next day.

I dip into the blobs of paint on the wet paper towel and then mix my colors on the remainder of the freezer paper. The nicest thing about this paint set-up is the clean up—just wad the freezer paper up and throw it away. There is nothing to scrub but the rinse water container.

Reference Pictures

For years, I have collected books with pictures of birds and animals to use for reference. While I still use them often, I now use the Internet to search for me and gather them in one place.

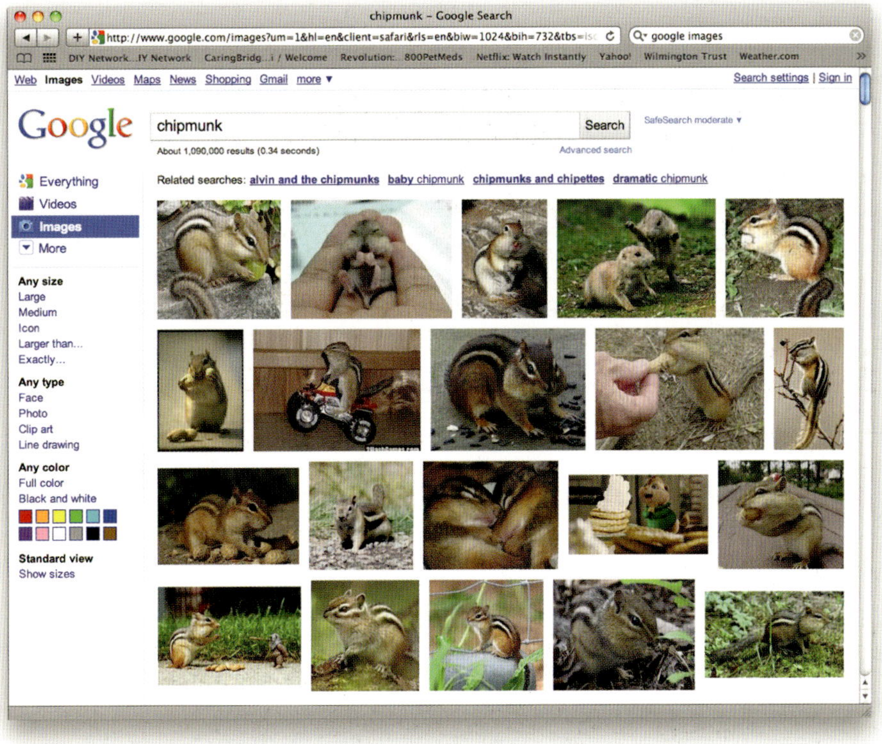

Figure 68. There are several search engines that can be used to obtain reference photographs. I generally use Google Images. After typing the species in the search box, hit the return or the search button. This is the screen that you will see. To the left of the pictures are two categories that you want to click. Find the "Any Size" category and choose "large." The screen will refresh with just large images. Next, find the "Any Type" category and choose "Photo." The screen will refresh again, this time with just large photos. Now click on any picture that you want to save—this action takes you to the place on the web where the image resides. If you are using a PC or a Mac, click on the image and drag it to your desktop. From there you can store it where you choose. Make sure that you go to the large image wherever it is stored on the web. Do not just click on the thumbnail and save that, as it will be too small to be of much value if printed. There will be some images that are copyrighted, and you will not be able to save them.

How to find tools and stuff

There are several ways to finds wood, tools, and carving supplies. Go to your local library or magazine store, and pick up a woodcarving magazine. You will find all kinds of suppliers, and you may even want to subscribe to the magazine. There are several very good ones being published.

Go online and Google "woodcarving supplies." There are a bazillion suppliers listed, from which you can order directly or request a catalog.

You should go online and join NWCA (www.chipchats.org/)—National Wood Carvers Association. You can download a membership form. Fill it out, send a check to the address listed, and sit back and wait for your first glorious issue of "Chip Chats," the best bargain in the carving market! You will get an issue every other month with listings of shows and classes. In the March/April issue, there is a section on suppliers of everything needed for all kinds of woodcarving. There are articles by world famous carvers about all kinds of things relating to many types of carving. You will also see many pictures from current shows of the carvings displayed there. You can probably find a carving club nearby that you can participate in and find kindred spirits! Just do it!

Sleepy Bunny

Tools & Supplies
- Band saw or coping saw
- Flexible shaft machine
- Micro motor machine helpful
- Variety of Kutzall/Typhoon carbide roughing out bits
- Variety of ruby carver bits and mounted stones
- Calipers and ruler, measuring in **tenths** of an inch
- Compass, pencil
- Knife
- Wire cutters, needle nose pliers, awl
- Drill and bits (1/16" and 5/64")
- Toothbrush (preferably natural bristle)
- Burning pen (rheostat type) and several burning pen styles
- Straight pin, hatpin, or fine dissecting needle
- Permanent ink marker (such as a fine point Sharpie)
- Dust mask, leather gloves, and safety glasses or goggles
- Optivisor or some type of magnification
- Clear acetate sheet (preferably .005 thickness)
- 4" piece of 16 gauge galvanized wire
- Super-glue and accelerator
- 50/50 lacquer/lacquer thinner mixture or Krylon Crystal Clear Spray
- Yellow carpenter glue
- Reference pictures

Materials
- 5.7"L x 3"W x 2.2"H tupelo block for sleepy bunny
- 6mm black eyes
- Medium colored China bristle paintbrush (to use for whiskers)
- Ribbon epoxy putty (preferably blue/yellow) or Kulis Karvit
- Oily, non-hardening modeling clay
- Flat base or piece of driftwood for mount

Painting Supplies
- Hair dryer
- Freezer paper and masking tape
- Brushes
- Water container and paper towels
- Flow medium
- Paints: (preferably Liquitex jar acrylics) white gesso (W), mars black (B), burnt umber (BU), raw umber (RU), yellow oxide (YO), raw sienna (RS), and burnt sienna (BS).
- Note: In color swatches, *denotes little bit
- Testor's Dull Cote Spray

Sleepy Bunny

5.7″

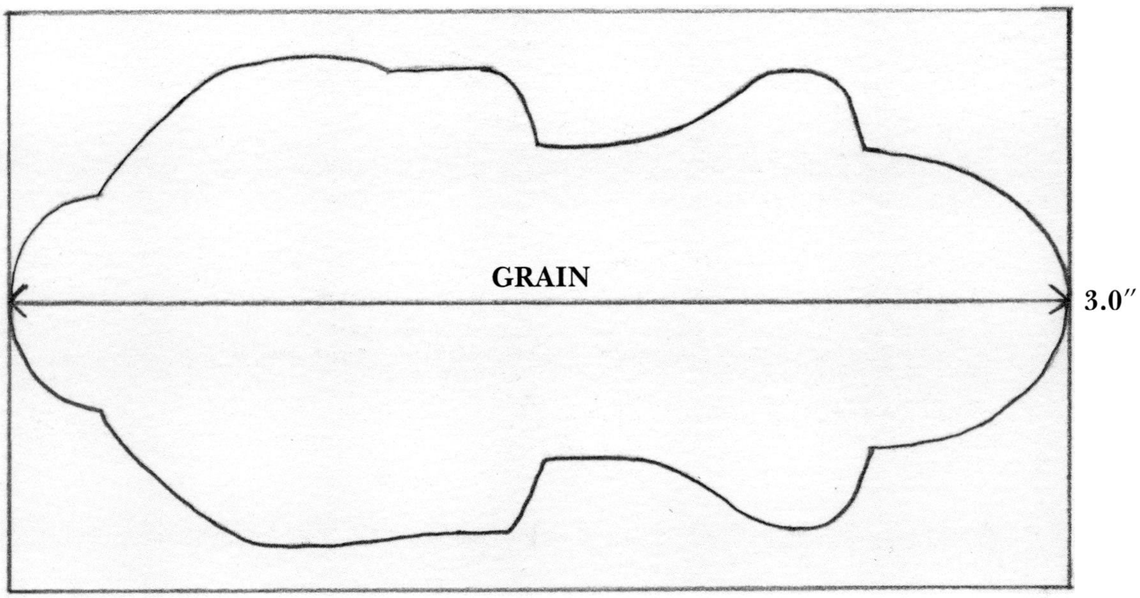

Top Plan View

Sleepy Bunny

5.7″

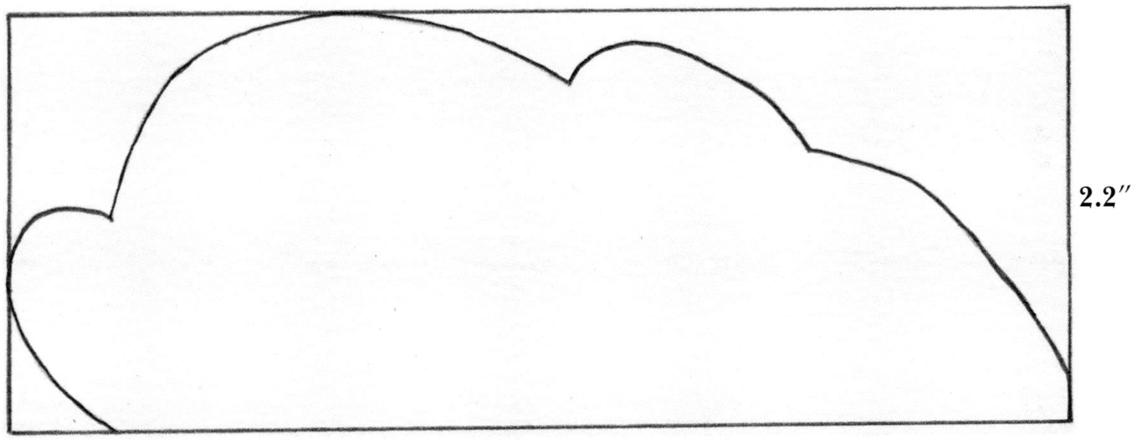

Profile View

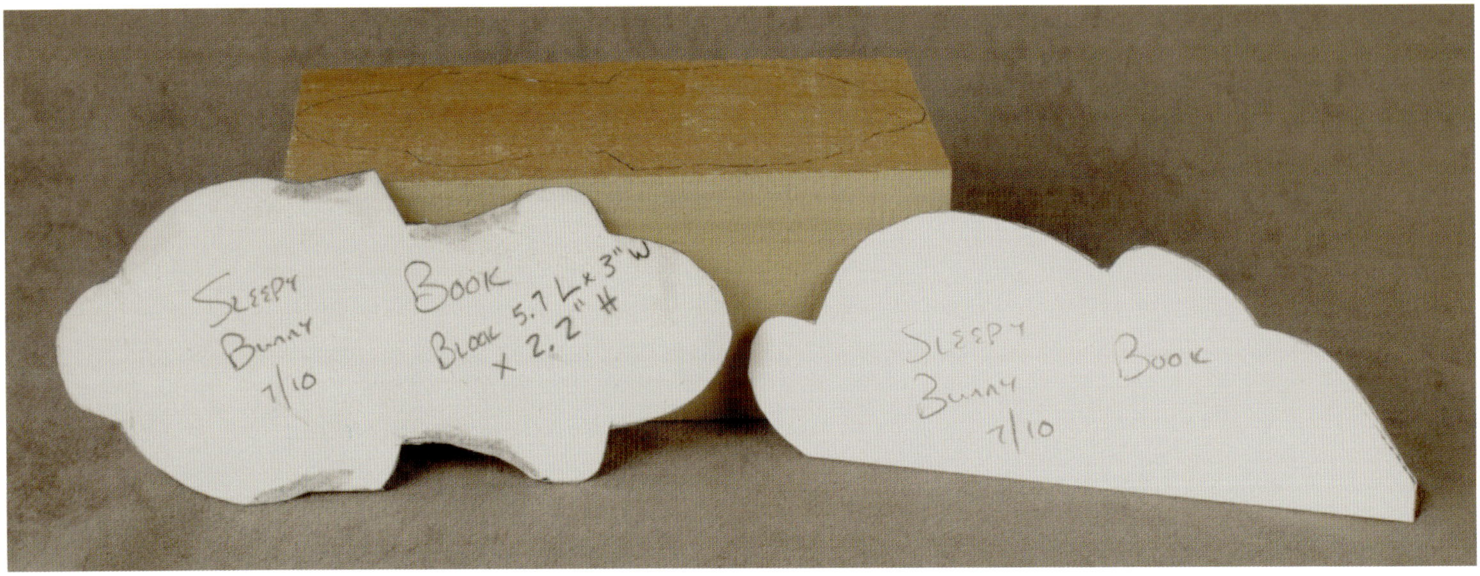

Figure 1. Transfer the profile and plan view patterns to stiff paper or cardboard. You will need a block of wood (preferably tupelo) that is 5.7"L x 3"W x 2.2"H.

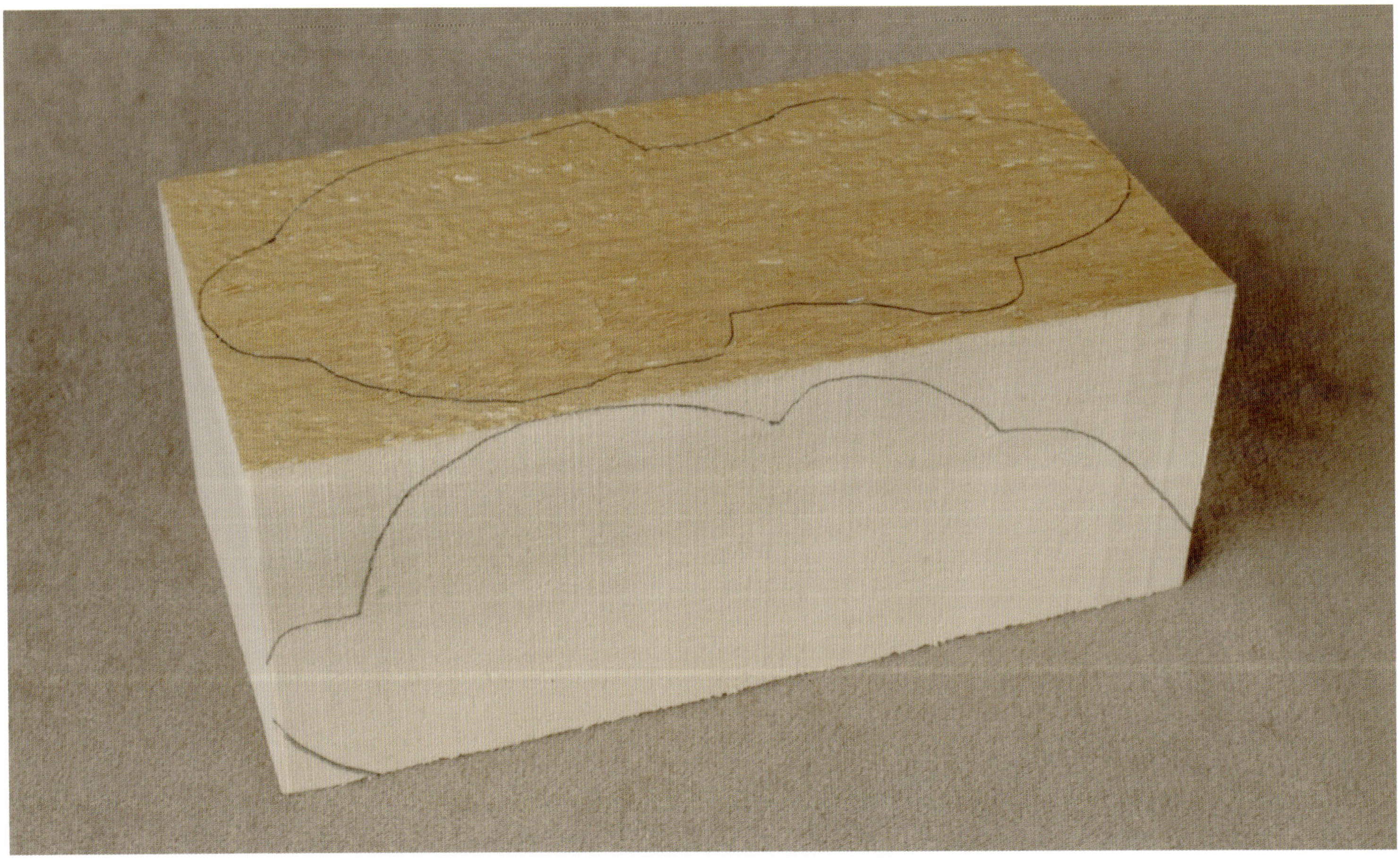

Figure 2. Trace the profile and plan view patterns on your block.

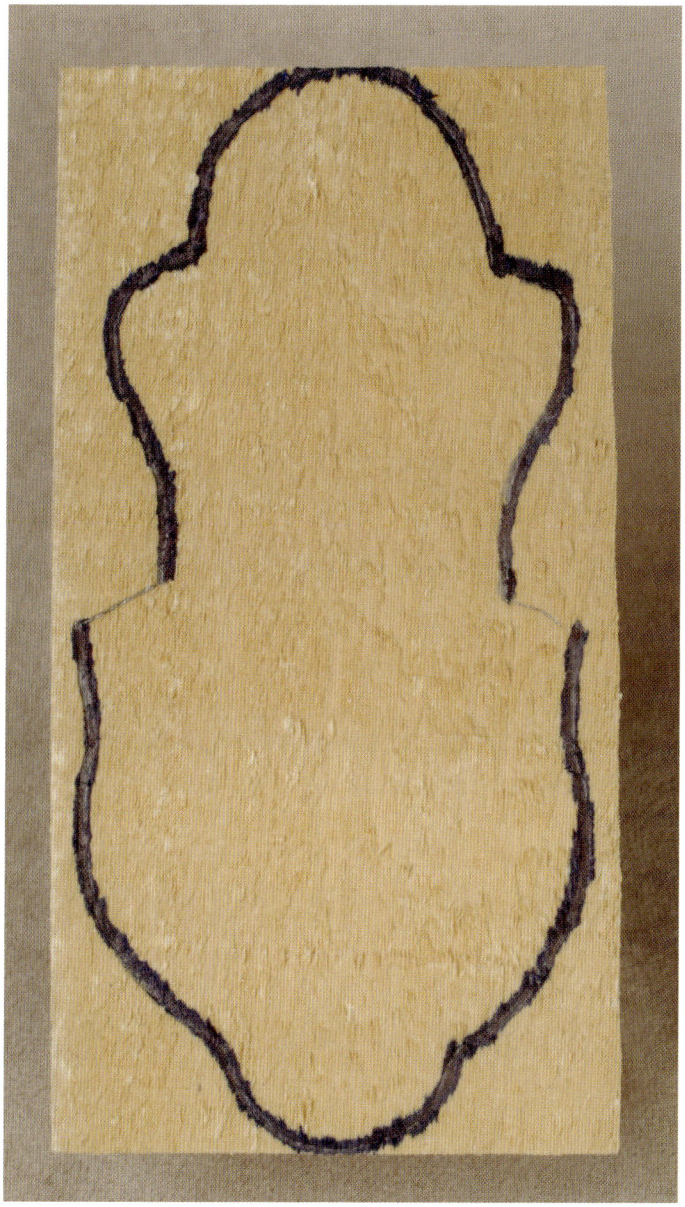

Figure 3. First carefully band saw the darkened lines. Start from each side of the nose and go back to the inside edge of the hind paws, carefully backing the band saw blade out of each cut. Then cut from the end of the block at the tail, and carefully back the band saw blade out of each cut there—make sure that you stop these cuts at the outside of the hind paws, leaving the front of the hind paws un-cut. If you are inexperienced with the bandsaw, ask an experienced woodworker to cut out this blank.

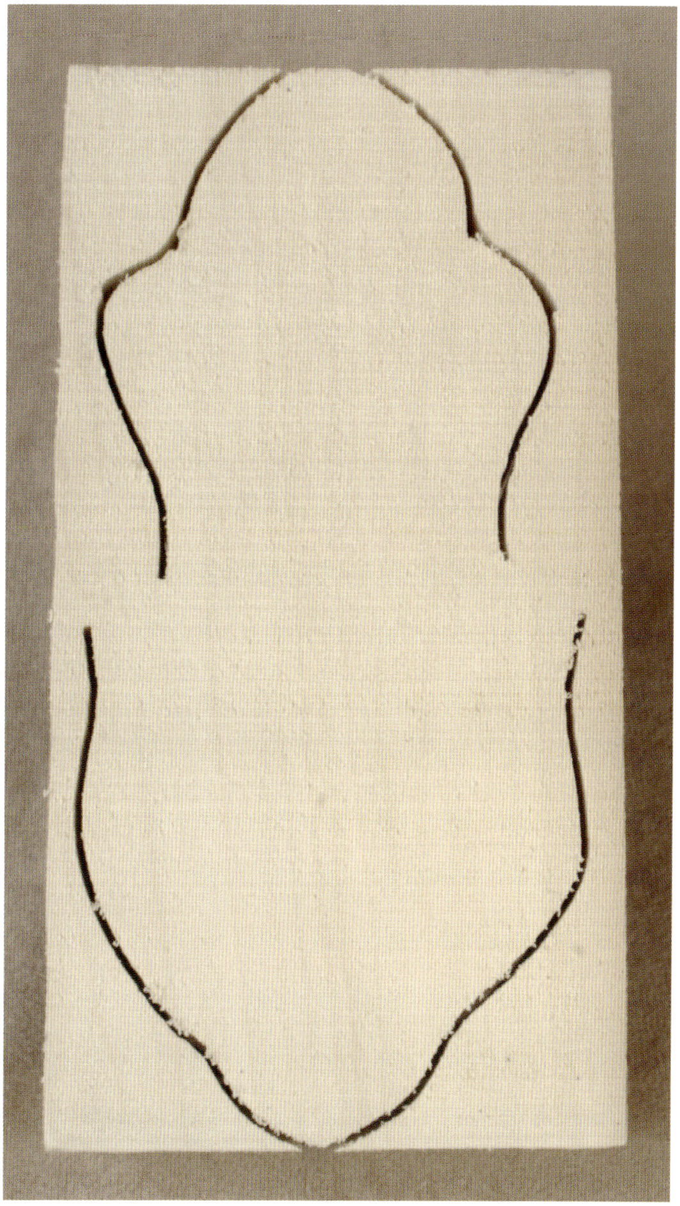

Figure 4. Here's what the bottom of the blank looks like after these cuts. Sometimes while making these cuts, you might have to back up the band saw blade to widen the cut in order to cut a small sliver to be able to make a turn.

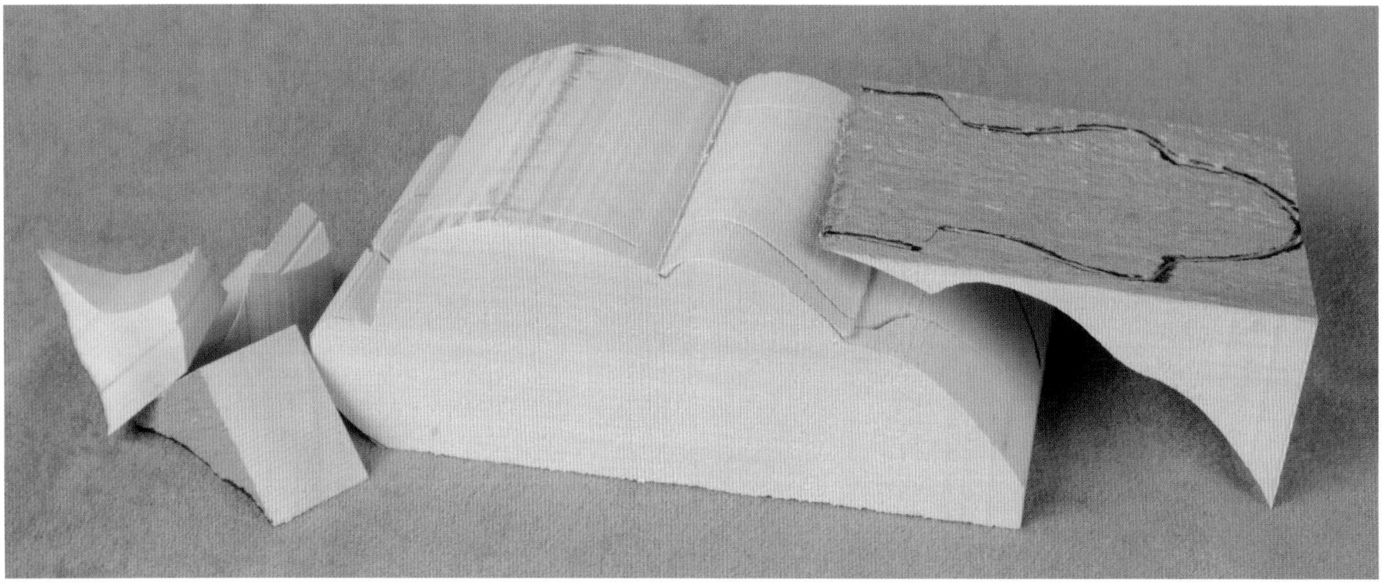

Figure 5. Now cut the profile view, letting the pieces fall away from the bunny.

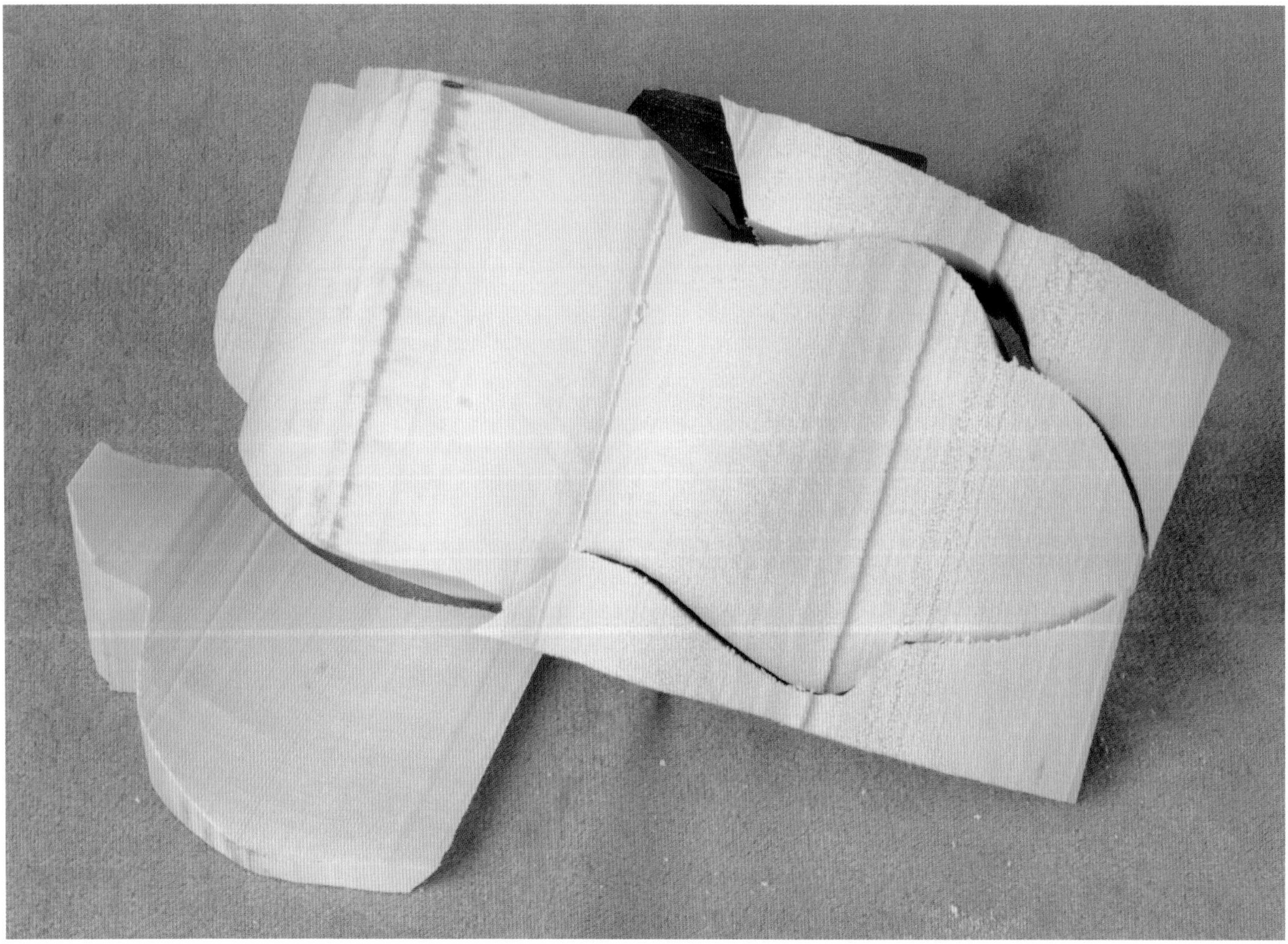

Figure 6. Place the bunny (bottom side down) flat on the band saw table and cut the angles in front of each back paw.

Figure 7. Sand the saw cuts off of the bottom. You can put a large piece of sandpaper on a flat table/workbench or rig up one of the sanders in the picture. Often when I do traveling seminars, I need my belt-sander to flatten whatever we are working on. My big 6" belt-sander does not fit very well in my little Subaru Forester—so I "built" a portable one. I cut a piece of 1/2" plywood 4" wide by about 10-12" long and another small piece (4" wide by about 1" high) to fit over the edge of a table. I glued and nailed these two pieces together at a right angle. After the glue was dry, I glued a piece of 4" wide cloth-backed abrasive 100-150 grit to the top. When that is dry, my portable sander is ready to be used to flatten whatever I need.

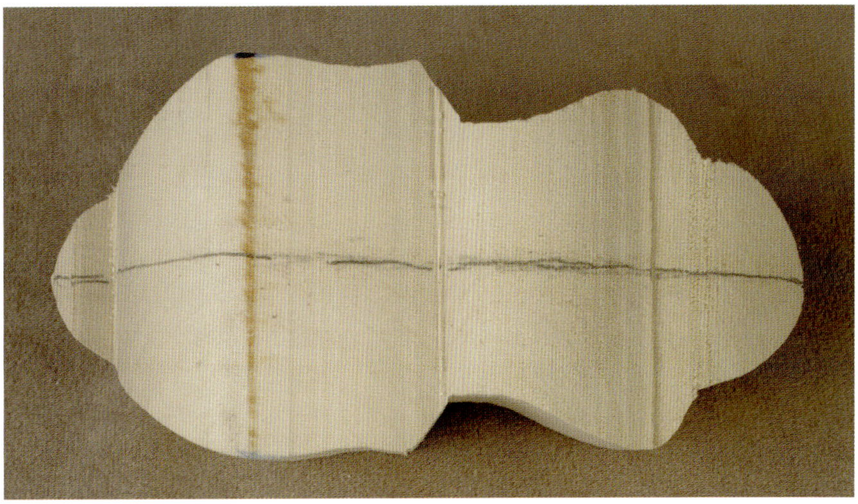

Figure 8. Draw a centerline all the way around the entire bunny, even on the bottom. This will help you to gauge balance and symmetry when carving. I try not to cut away the centerline when carving, unless I need to alter the band-sawed profile shape.

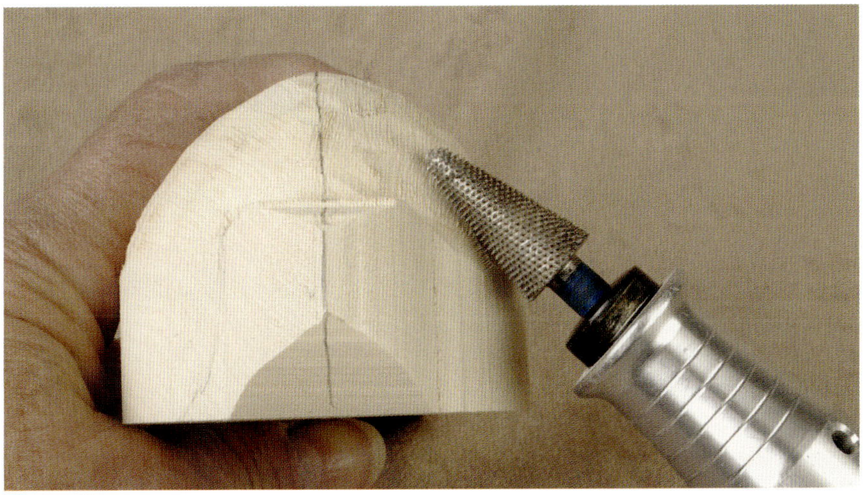

Figure 9. Using a medium size roughing out bit, round over the back and haunches areas about halfway down the height on both sides. A medium sized taper works nicely for this step. Work from just behind the tips of the ears to the top and sides of the tail.

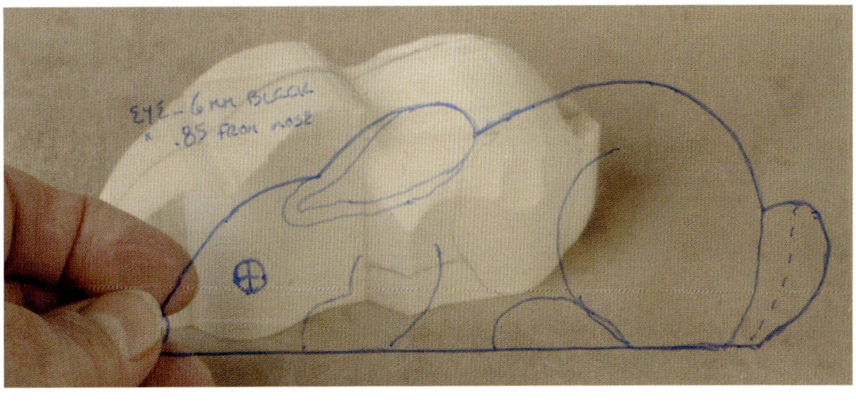

Figure 10. Trace the profile pattern on clear acetate with an ultrafine permanent marker such as a Sharpie. You can use 0.003" to 0.005" thick acetate. The 0.005 is a little thicker and a little more user-friendly than the thinner 0.003. You can usually purchase the clear acetate at your local art supply store, or you can order it online.

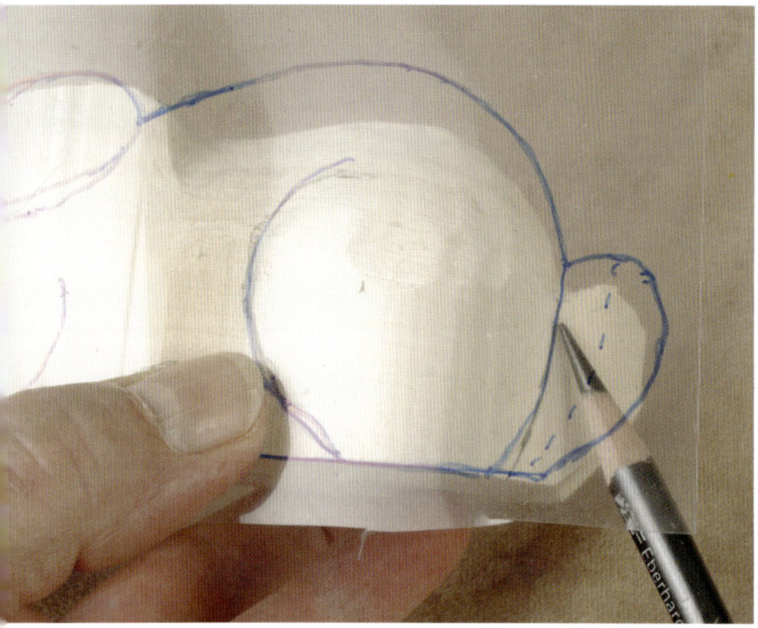

Figure 11. Holding the stiff acetate flat against the side of the hind paw, close one eye, sneak a pencil under the acetate and on the blank, trace the line separation between the tail and the back, the haunch line and the back/rear paws. Do this on both sides of the bunny. When using a drawing on the acetate, which is two-dimensional, you must be careful not to bend the acetate on the bunny's three-dimensional surface. Bending the acetate will foreshorten the line drawings, and thus, misshape the bunny's contour. Flip-flop the acetate in order to do both sides.

Figure 12. Draw in the oval shape of the tail.

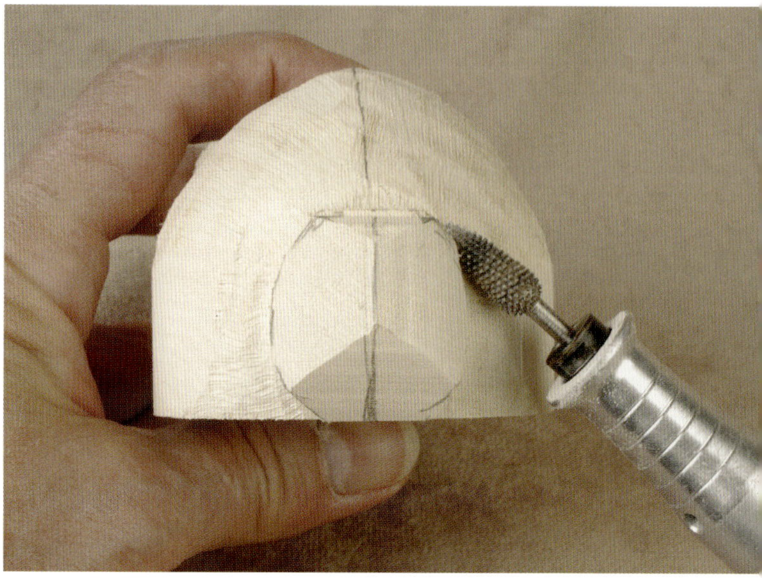

Figure 13. Using a blue/fine Typhoon bud (1/8" shaft is safer for roughing out), cut a shelf around the oval tail. Do not under-cut. For right now, you just want to delineate the back end view of the tail.

Figure 14. You want to follow your lines on the back of the haunches, curving the blank down and following your line.

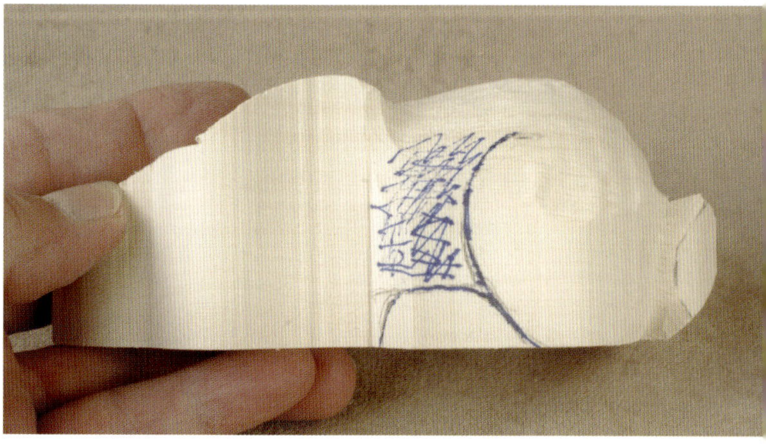

Figure 15. The area that is crosshatched in front of the haunch needs to be removed.

Figure 16. Using the bud Typhoon carbide bit, cut a channel around the front of the haunch including at the base of the hind paw and on top of the paw itself. Do the other haunch as well.

Figure 17. Round over the haunch itself, including its base. Do this on both haunches.

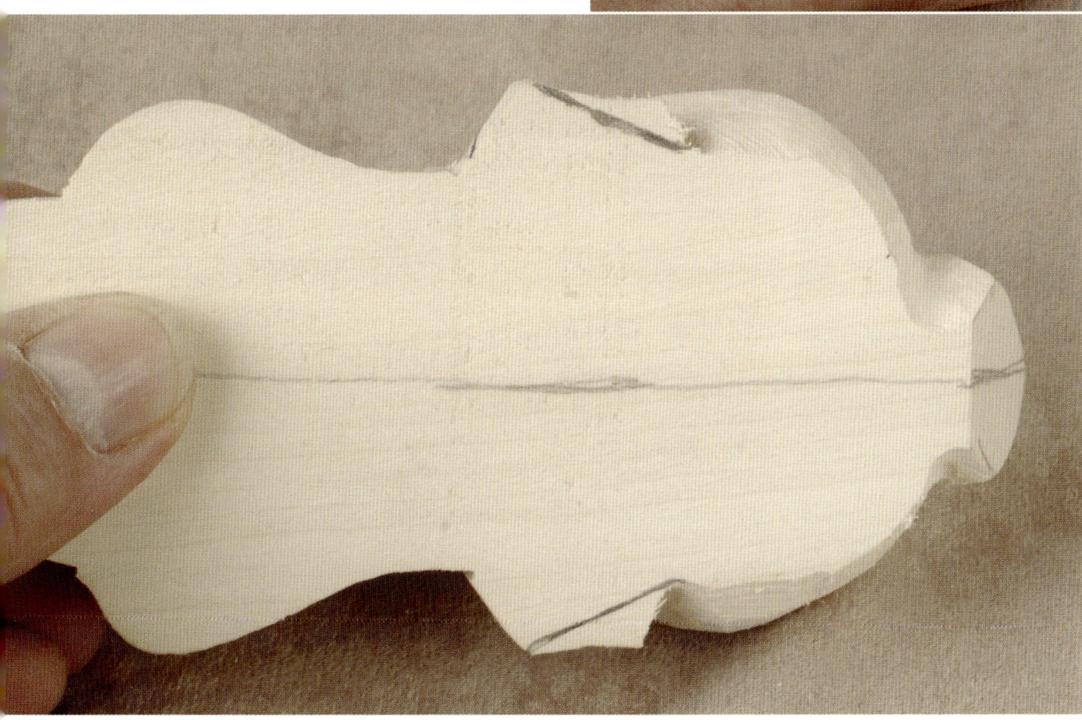

Figure 18. On the underside of the hind paws, draw lines from the outside front of the paw back to where the channel around the haunches is.

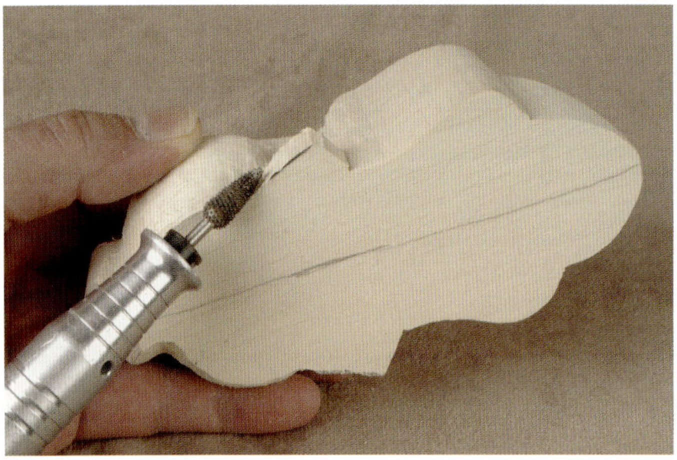

Figure 19. Using the bud again, trim the outside of the paws so that the sides go straight up.

Figure 20. Note that there is NO flat on the haunch. From the center, the shape goes down in every direction. Make sure that each haunch is sufficiently round and both are symmetrical and even.

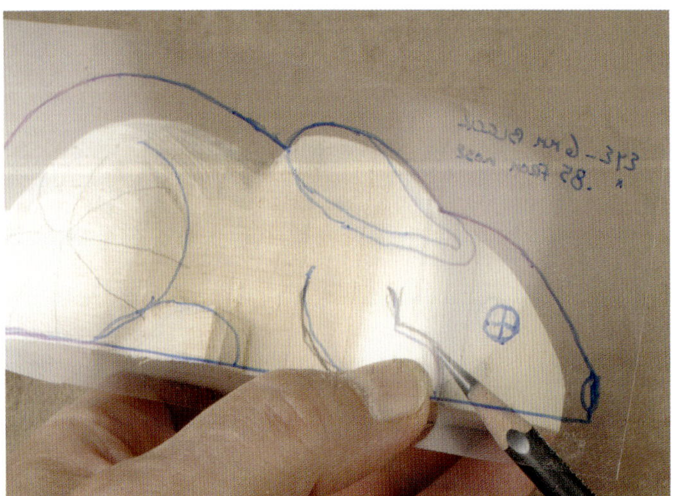

Figure 21. Holding the acetate flat on the outside of the front paw area, sneak a pencil underneath the acetate, and trace the front and back lines of the legs and paws. Flip-flop the acetate in order to do the other side.

Figure 22. Draw the front line and the back line of both paws around the corner to the underside of the blank. From the bottom view, check to make sure that the lengths are equal.

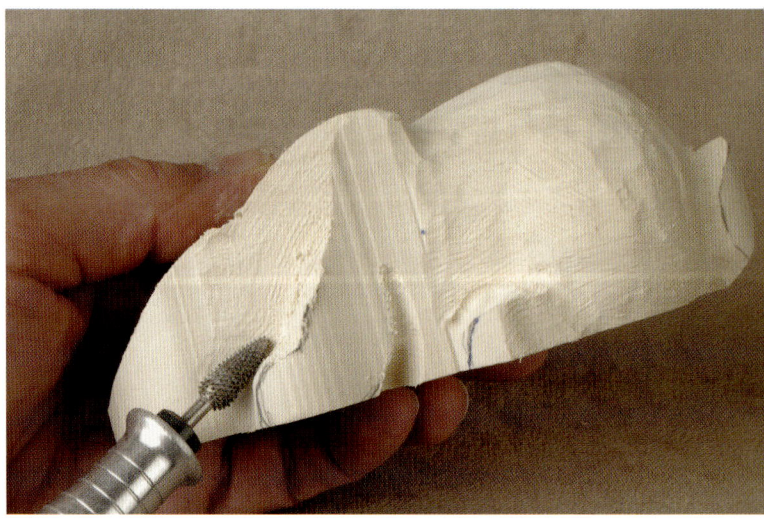

Figure 23. Cut around the front legs and paws with the blue Typhoon bud.

Figure 24. Roll the flank/side of the body between the hind and front paws underneath towards the underside belly, as you can see on the project's right side. Make sure that you complete the other side as well.

Figure 25. Draw in the nose, paying particular attention to its shape. The bottom of the nose is 0.1" from the bottom of the blank. The width and height both are 0.24". Note the angular bottom outside—this is not a sharp "V" but a rounded one. The top of the nose is slightly rounded.

Figure 26. Using a #2 flame ruby carver (RC-20), cut around the nose and level the area out on all sides. The top of the nose channel is shallower than the sides and bottom tip.

Figure 27. Using a flame stone, sand/smooth the end of the nose and round over the edges. The same flame stone is used to carve the slit on the centerline under the nose down to the bottom of the blank. Hold the tool handle at a 45-degree angle and just slide it down the centerline. If it's not deep enough the first time, just do it again.

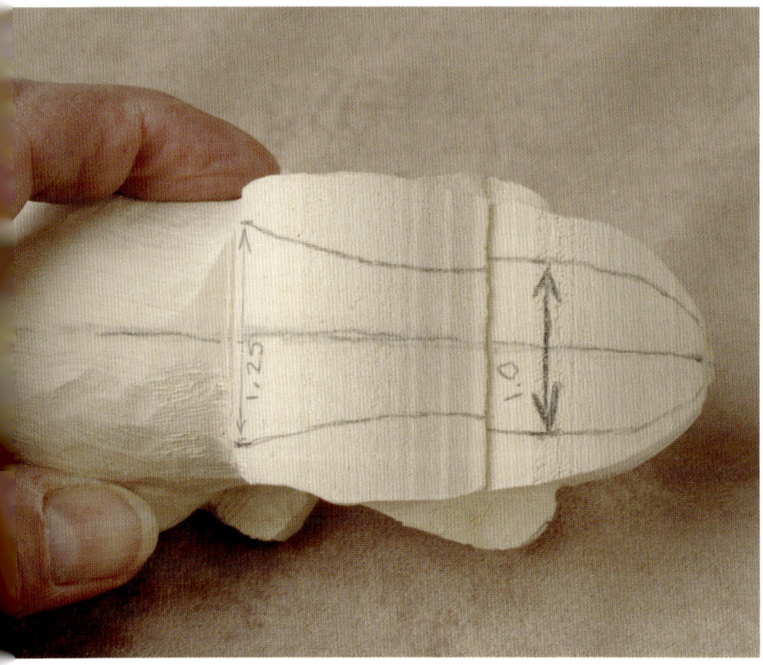

Figure 28. Measure and mark 1.0" centered across the centerline in front of the ears (0.5" on each side of the centerline). Arc the line along the top plan view of the head to the sides of the nose. Measure and mark 1.25" centered across the centerline (0.625" on each side of the centerline) at the tips of the ears. From just inside the 1.0" line at the front of the ears, draw an arced line to the measurement marks at the tips of the ears.

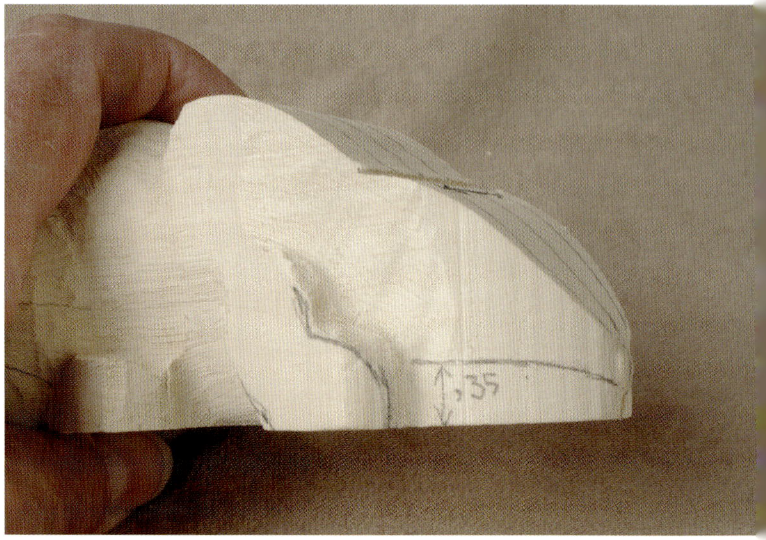

Figure 29. Just in front of the front paws, measure and mark 0.35" on both sides. Draw an arcing line to the bottom of the nose.

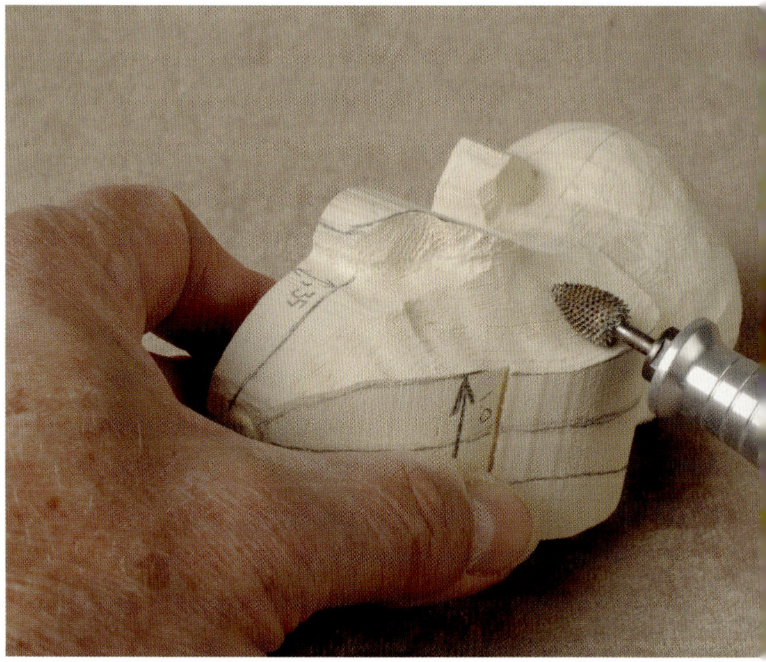

Figure 30. Use the 1/8" shank Typhoon flame to begin removing the wood to narrow up the ears and the sides of the head. Cut the ear height (use your profile view acetate to check the height of the ears) and cut the sides of the head down to the 0.35" line we put just in front of the front paws.

Figure 31. Keep removing wood on the outsides of the ears and head.

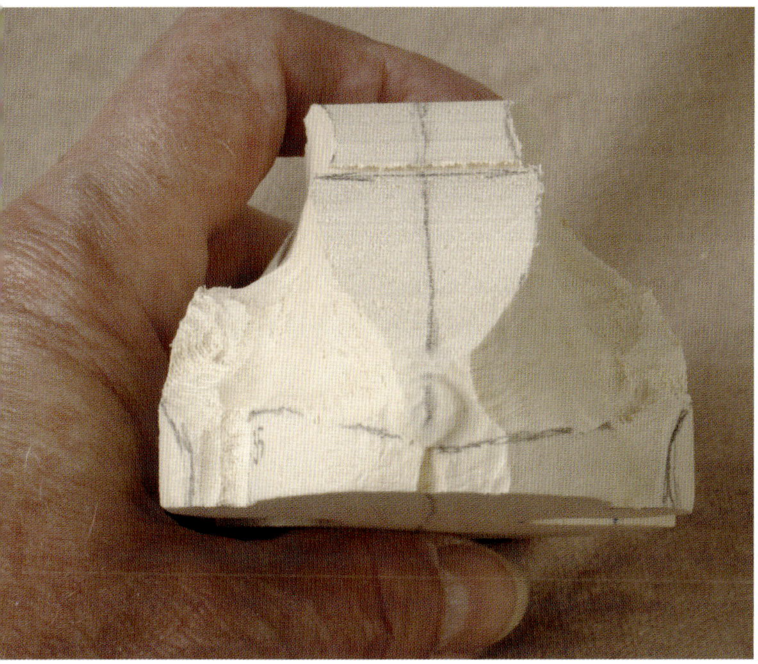

Figure 32. Here's what the bunny's head should look like when you have removed sufficient wood.

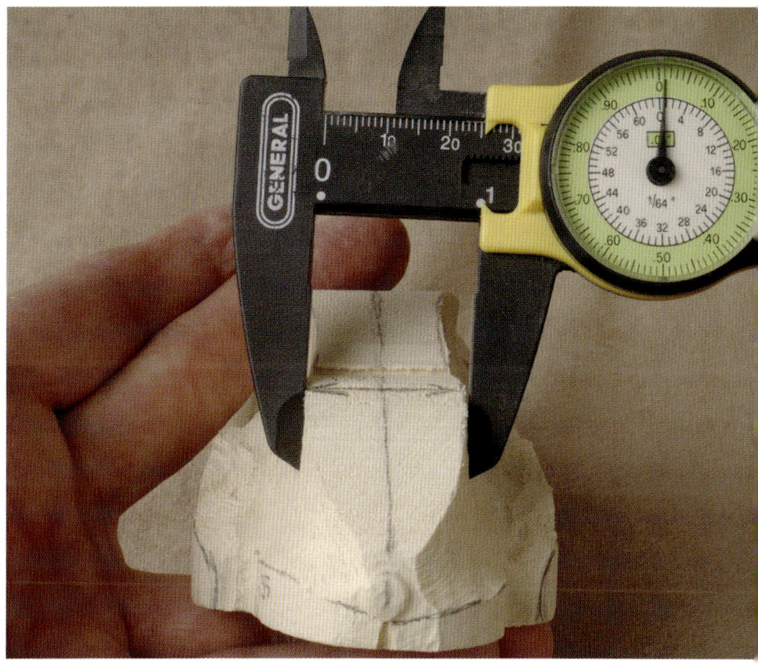

Figure 33. You should remove enough wood until the width of the head at approximately the eye position measures 1.0" about 0.5" from the top.

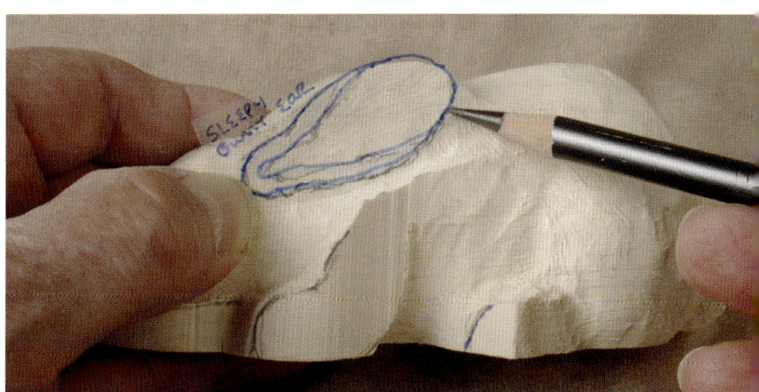

Figure 34. It is helpful to make a smaller acetate of just the bunny's ear from the profile bunny line drawing. Hold the acetate over the ear area, sneak a pencil on the wood under the acetate, and trace/mark the exterior and interior shapes of the ears on both sides of the bunny's head.

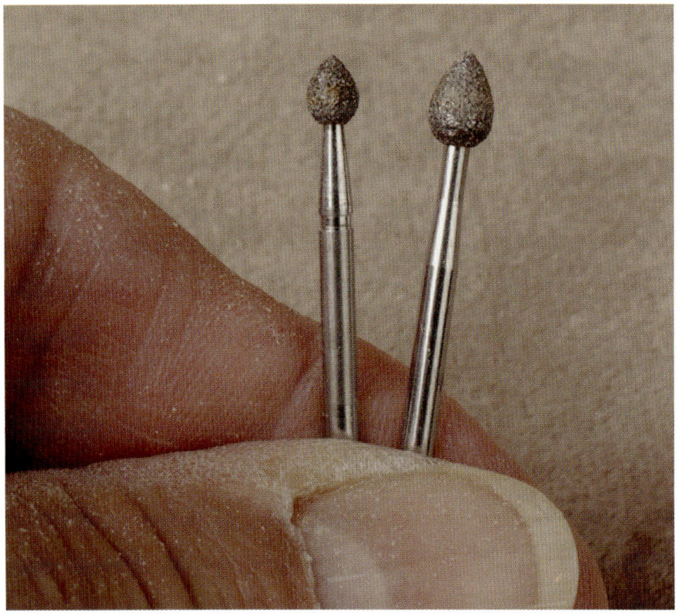

Figure 35. Ruby carver bits come in two sizes of what I call "the pointed ball." I use both of these often when carving animals. You can use the point to carve a shape or lay the bit down and use the rounded diameter. Learning to use these bits in different ways can ease the challenge of imparting different shapes on a particular carving.

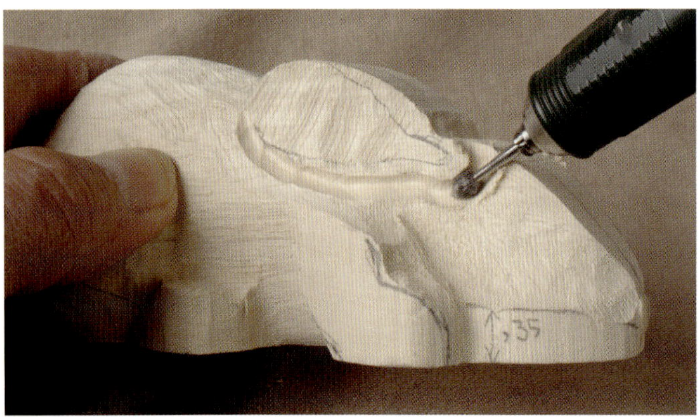

Figure 36. Using the larger pointed ball ruby carver (RC-17), cut around the bottom edge of the ears slightly less the depth of the bit's diameter.

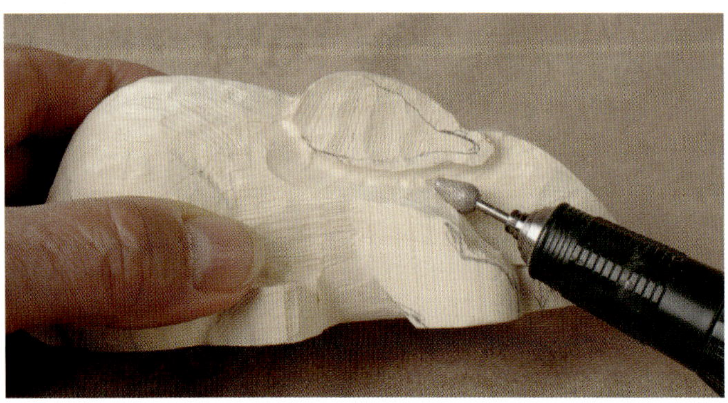

Figure 37. Flow the channel out and blend the bottom of the channel into the surrounding area. I used a small pear-shaped ruby carver (RC-23). Cutting in the channel and flowing the channel out raises the level of the ear flange itself so that it protrudes out further than the sides of the head and shoulders.

Figure 38. Use the pear-shaped ruby (RC-23) to round the head from the sides all the way to the centerline and from the base of the ears to the nose. Depending on the grain in the wood, you may have to grind at different angles to avoid the washboard effect that you sometimes get with tupelo. Using a larger bit/ burr and cutting at different angles are two ways to minimize any unevenness that you can get with tupelo.

Figure 39. Turning a carving upside down can help you to see balance and symmetry in a piece. As you can see, I've marked a couple of places where the bunny's head is not quite symmetrical.

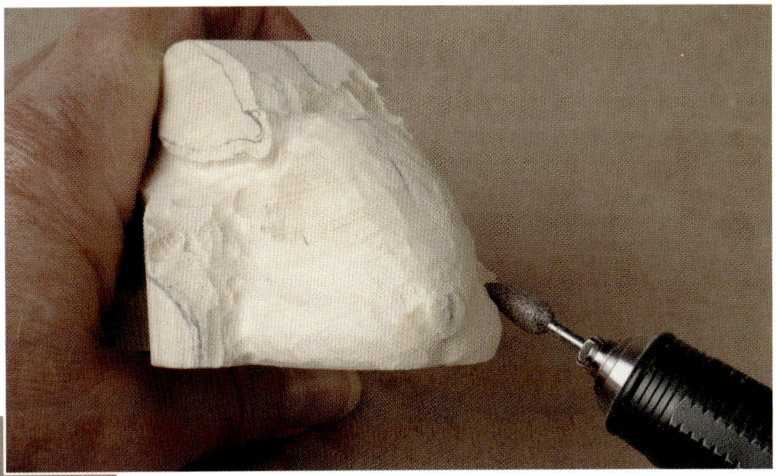

Figure 40. Round over the cheeks and roll them underneath.

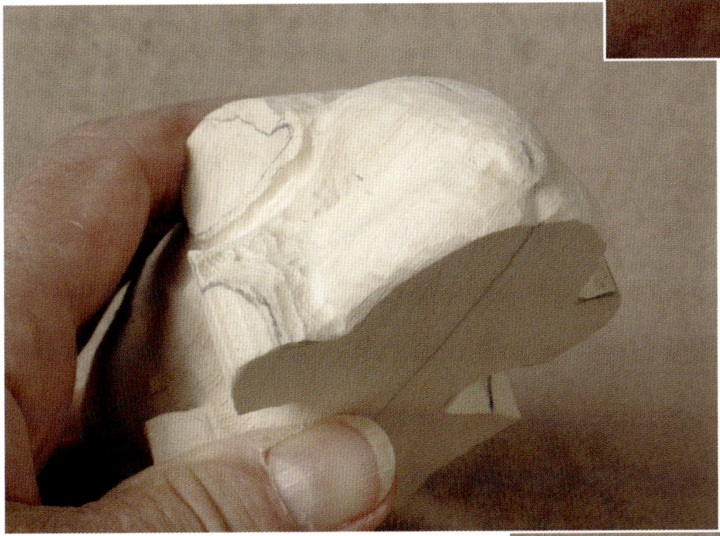

Figure 41. Round the edges of the little slit under the nose so that the sharp angles/ corners of the original cut are blended.

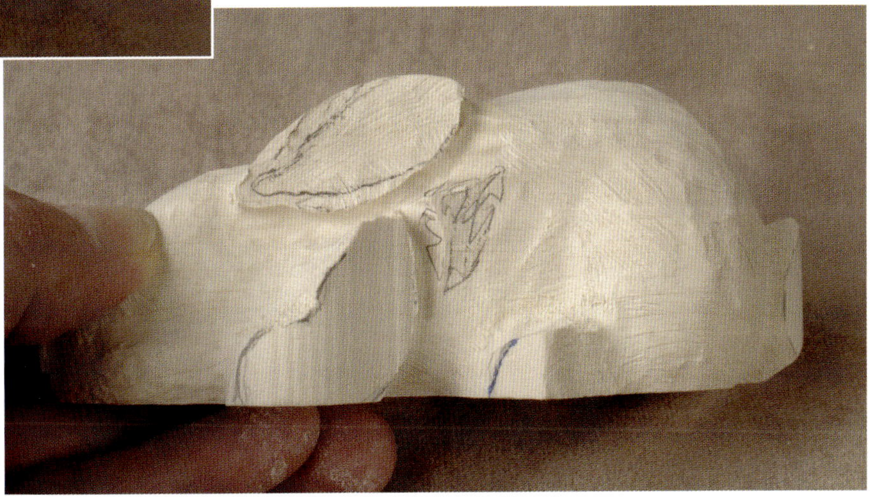

Figure 42. Cut a deeper channel behind the front legs and remove the area pencil-marked.

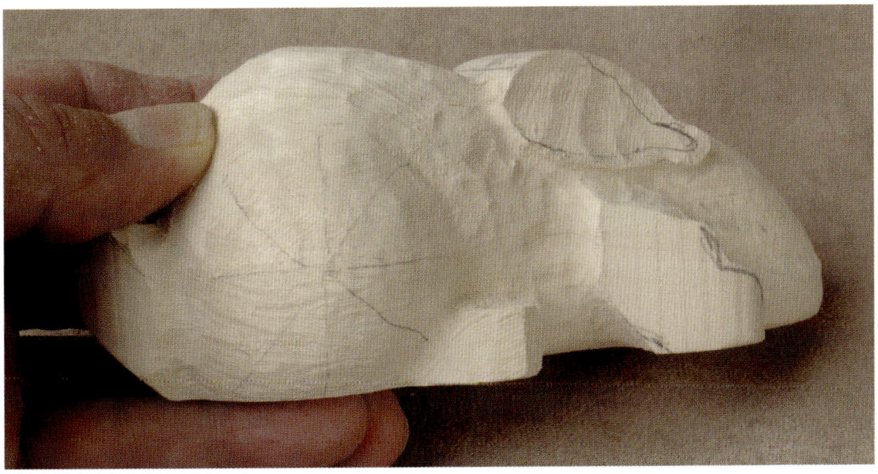

Figure 43. Here you can see the excess wood has been removed, and the area behind the front leg blends with the flank.

Figure 44. Thin the height of both front paws to 0.4" at the bend and 0.2" at the tips.

Figure 45. Draw an angled line from the outside of the front leg at the paw to the shoulder area underneath the ear.

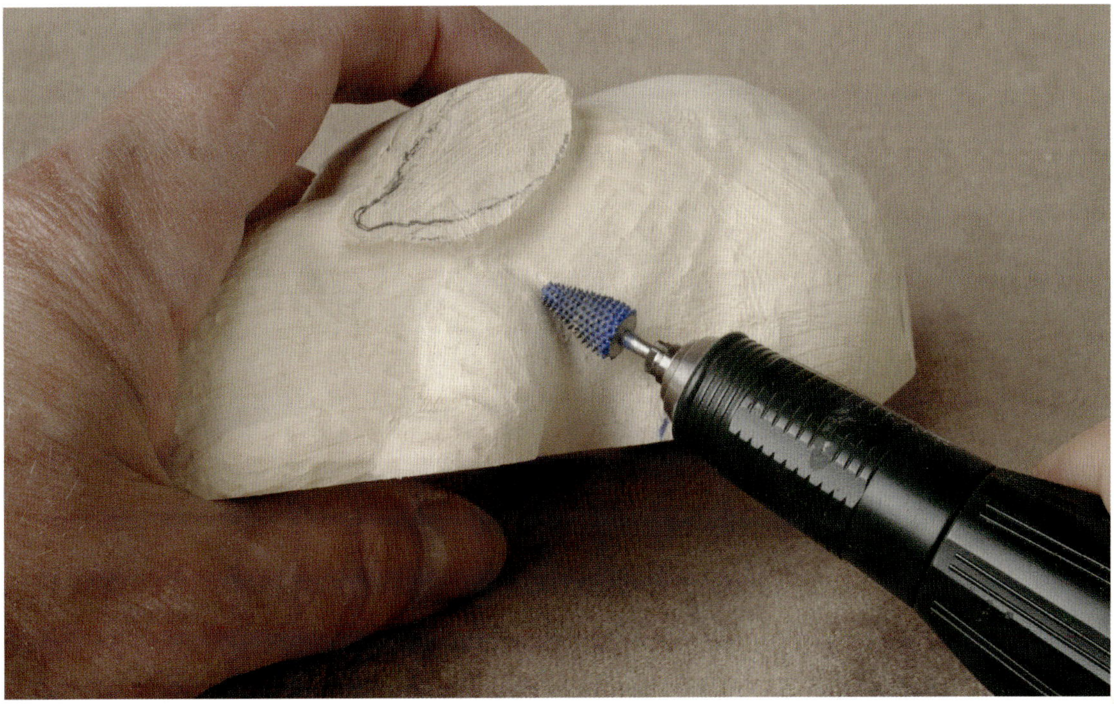

Figure 46. Use a small Typhoon taper to angle the outside of the paw to the shoulder and round over the front and back of the front leg and paw. Do both sides.

Figure 47. Note the angles of the front legs towards the shoulders and the area below the ears.

Figure 48. With a pointed flame ruby, cut the inside corner of the front paws (where the pencil marks are) so that they are slightly rounded. Note how the front legs and paws are NOT straight on but are splayed outwards.

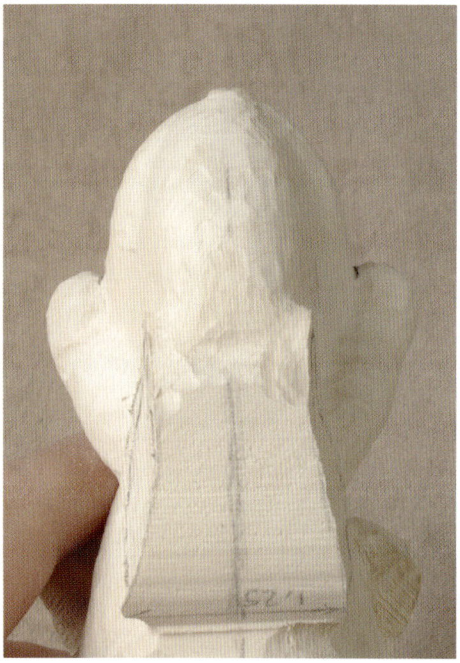

Figure 51. Round over the hind paws from the base to the tip and from the inside edge to the outside.

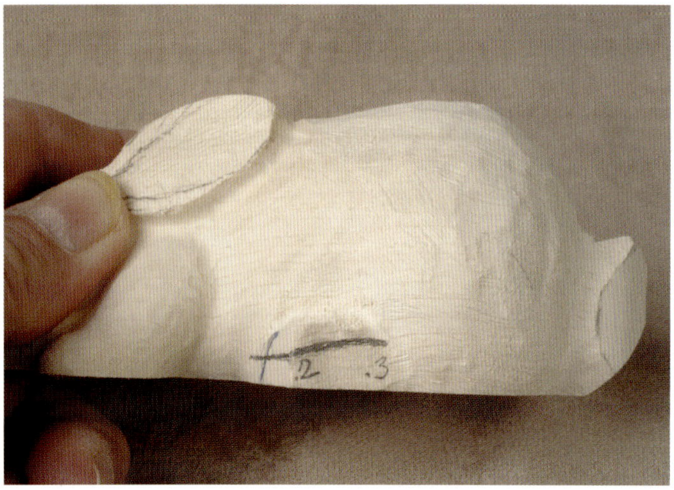

Figure 49. Measure and mark in 0.3" at the base of the hind paws, and measure and mark 0.2" of the tips of the hind paws. Draw a slight arc from the base of each hind paw to the tip.

Figure 52. Mark the inside edge of the hind paws, and using a pointed ruby, cut the inside edge, which rounds the tip of the paw.

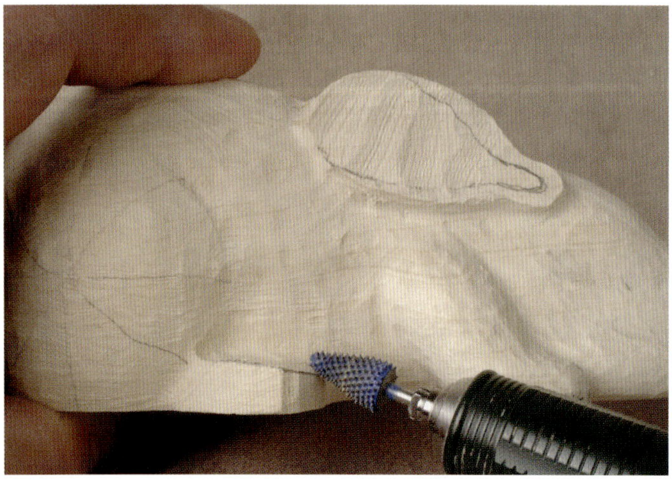

Figure 50. Remove the excess wood above the line, thus thinning the height of the hind paws.

Figure 53. Note that the hind paws are pointed outward as are the front paws. Check for balance and symmetry from the underside view.

Figure 54. Draw in the toe lines. A bunny has 5 toes on each front paw and 4 on each hind paw. In this piece, you will not see all of the toes, as some are tucked in under the cheeks and the flanks. When you have 4 toes on any particular paw, first draw a line down the center, and then divide each side of the paw in half. In other words, three lines will give you four toes. In the case of five toes, "guesstimate" the width of a toe and draw that toe smack-dab in the middle of the paw. Then divide what is left on each side in half. In other words, four lines will give you five toes.

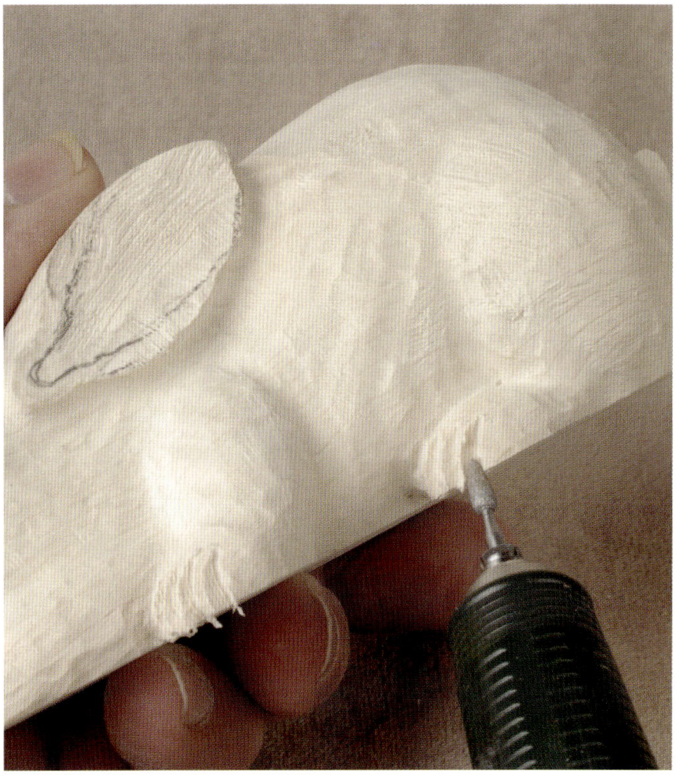

Figure 55. Slide the smallest flame ruby carver (RC-19) down each of the toes lines.

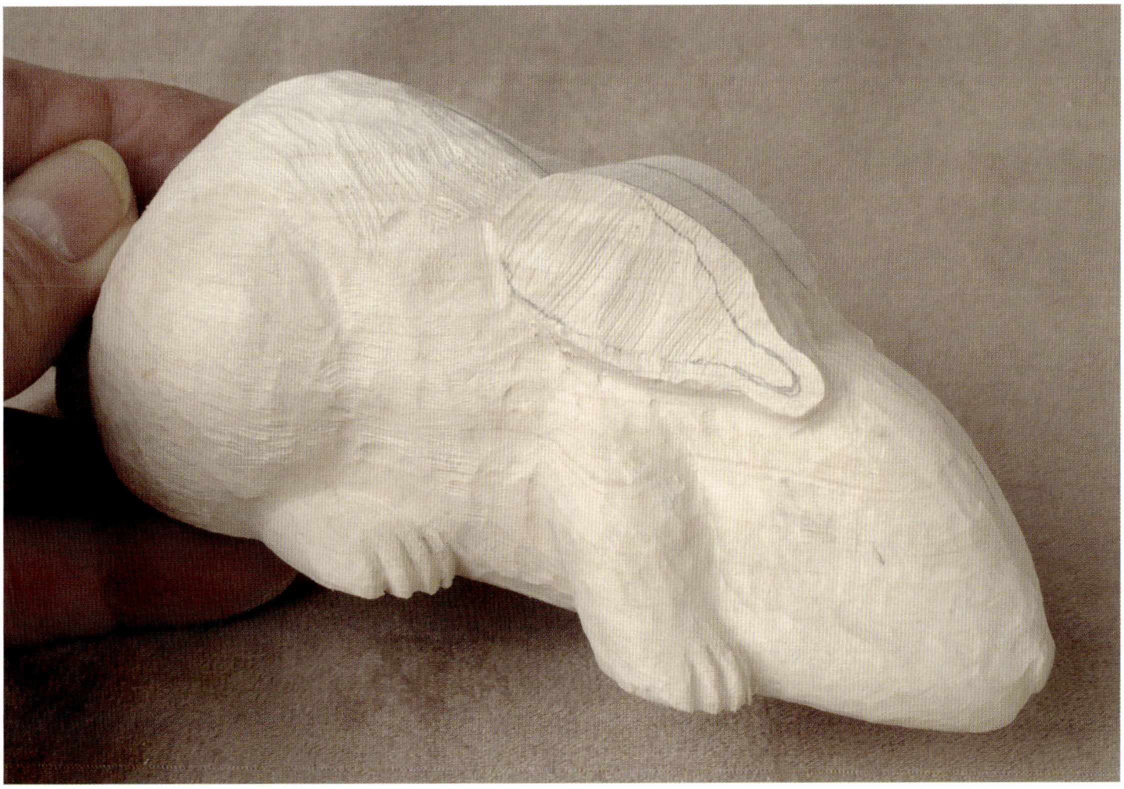

Figure 56. Using the smallest flame ruby carver again, round over each of the front and hind paw toes.

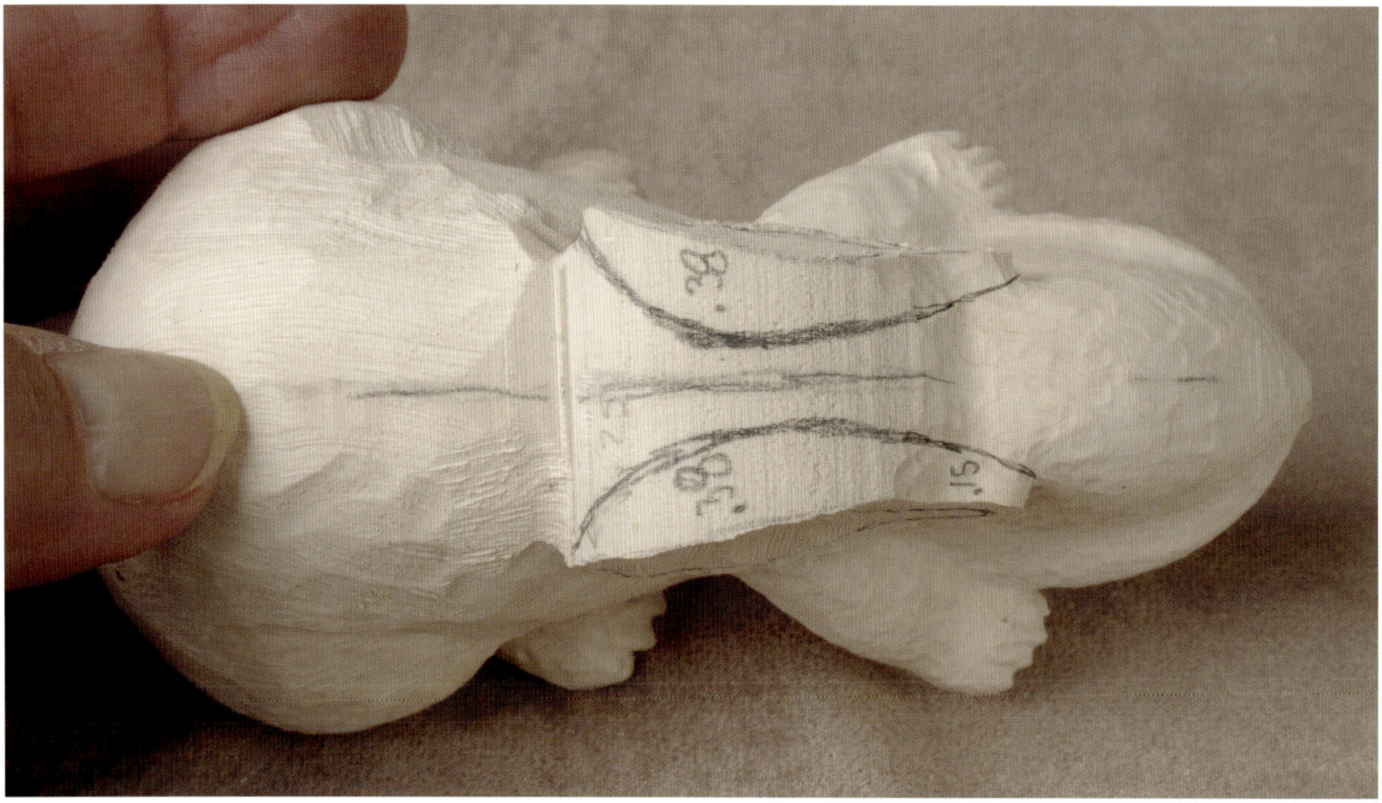

Figure 57. Measure and mark 0.38" on the widest part of the ears. Draw the contour of the outside of the ears from the tips, through the measurement marks, and on to the shelves on the bases of the ears.

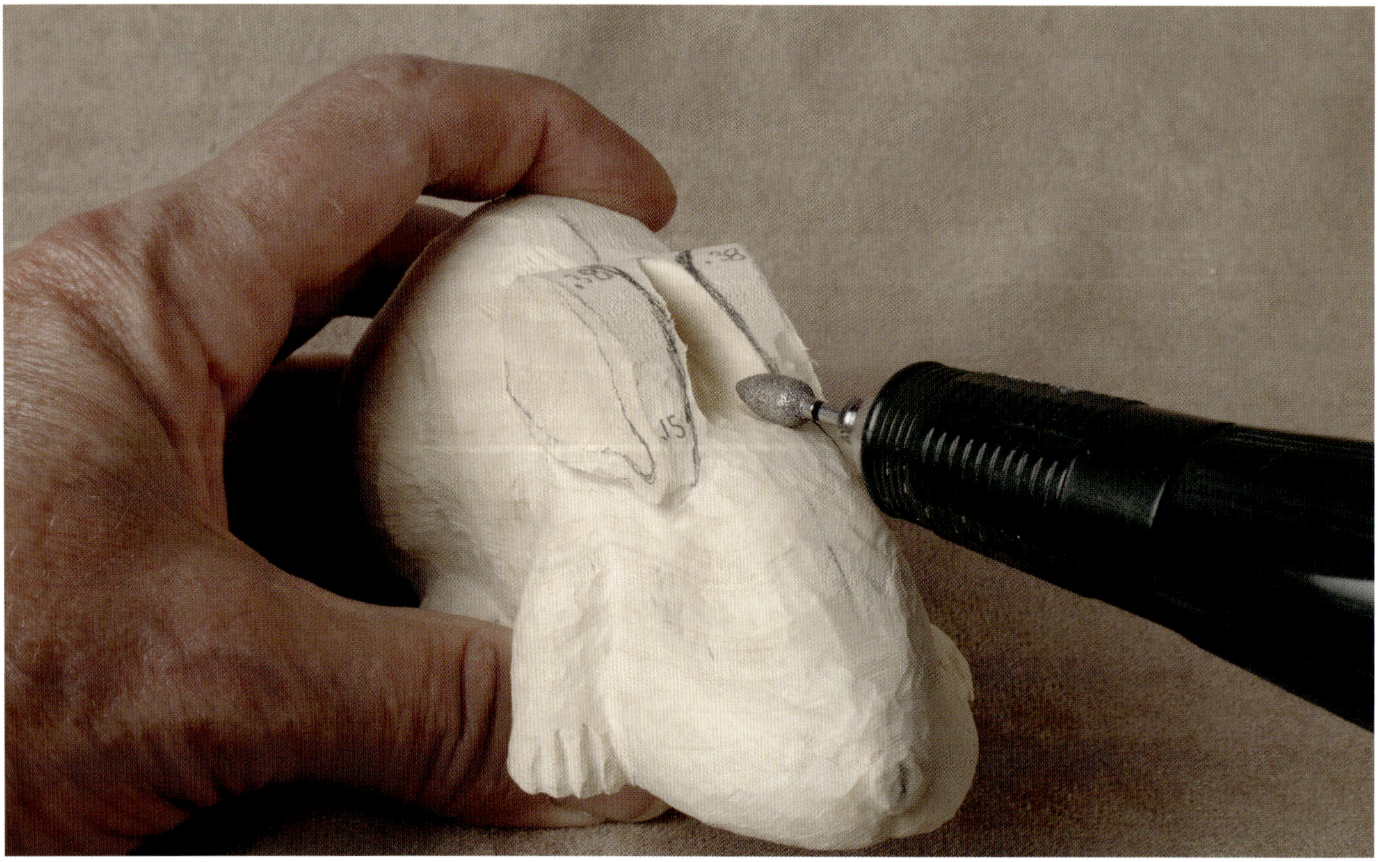

Figure 58. Start dividing the outside of the ears with a #3 ruby carver (RC-25). Narrow the ears until they measure 0.38" just before they round to the tips.

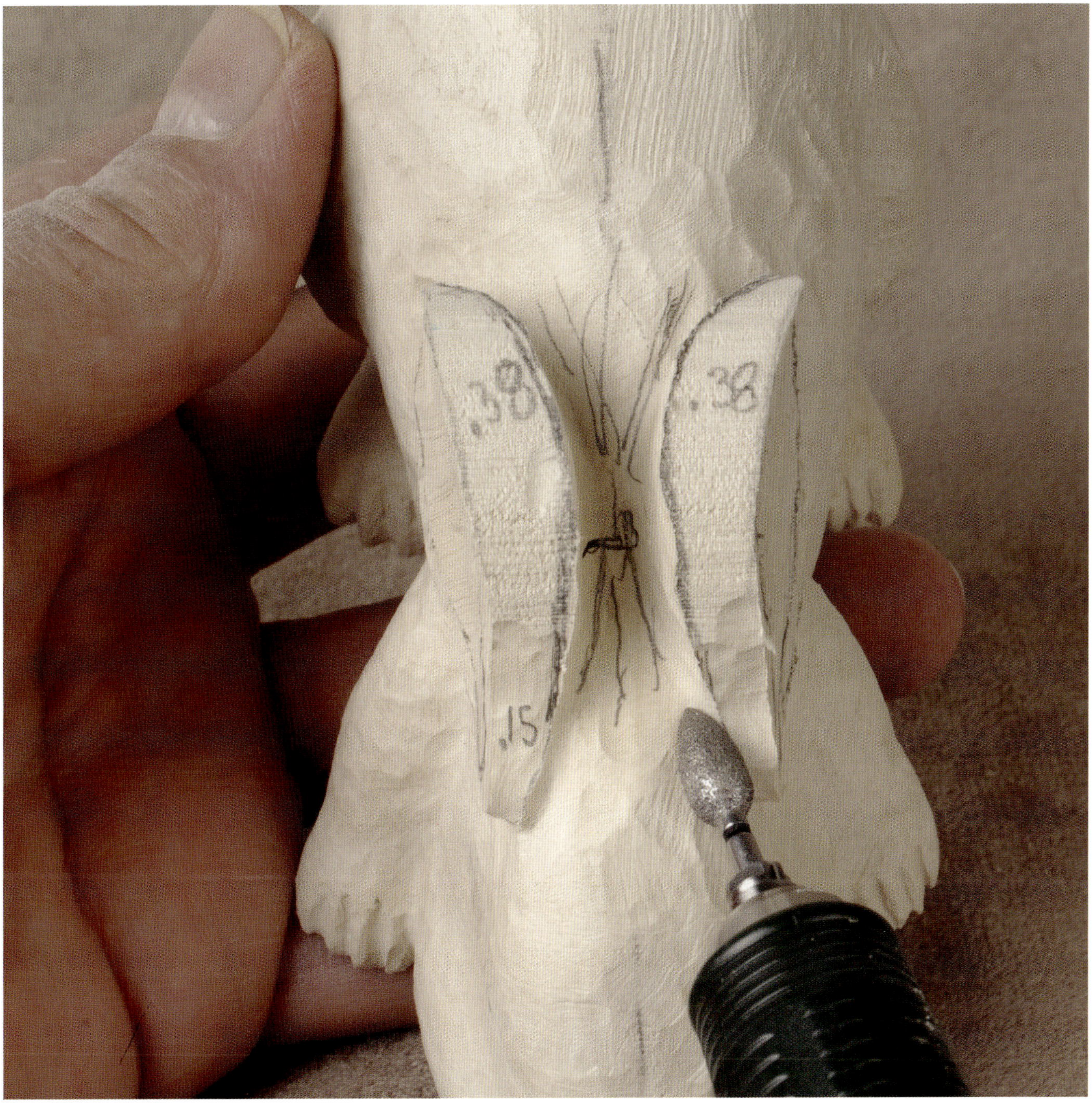

Figure 59. Continue cutting out the excess wood until you have the 0.38" wide ears as they near the tip. The contour of the back of the head is deeper than the top of the head, and then rises to blend into the back, which also rises.

Figure 60. Set the calipers to measure 0.36".

Figure 61. Use the bottom-protruding end of the caliper to insert in between the ears to get an inside/depth measurement.

Figure 62. Holding the bottom outside against the top of the ear, measure and mark the thickest part of the outside of the ear (0.36").

Figure 63. When using a dial caliper, you can measure three different ways. First, between the inside of the bottom prongs is the measurement you set on the dial. This is useful in measuring an outside dimension. Second, on the top prongs, the distance between the outside of the prongs is the measurement you've set. This is useful for measuring the inside of a diameter of a surface/circle or the distance between two different surfaces.

Figure 64. The third is the depth measurement that is helpful in measuring how deep something is.

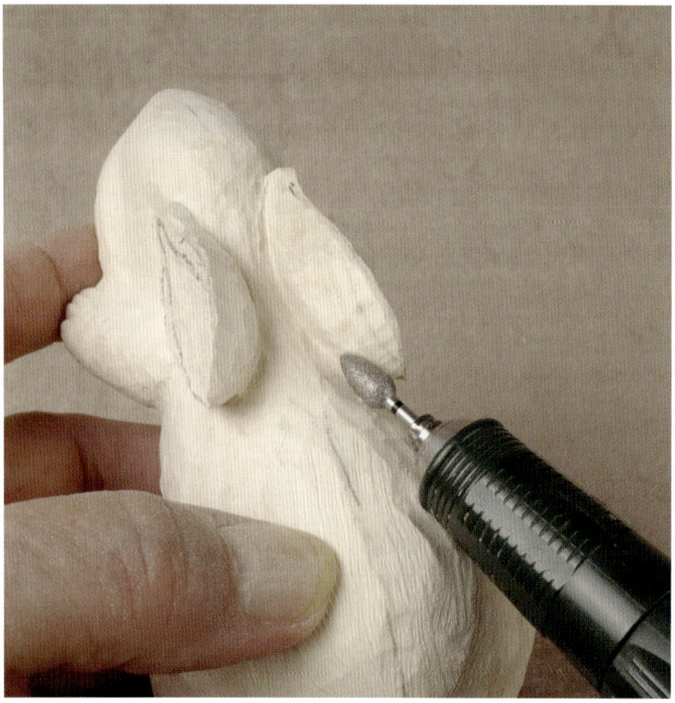

Figure 65. Continue separating the inside/outside of the ears until you get down to surface of the upper back, neck, and back of head, making sure that the head flows down to the neck and then gradually up to the upper back.

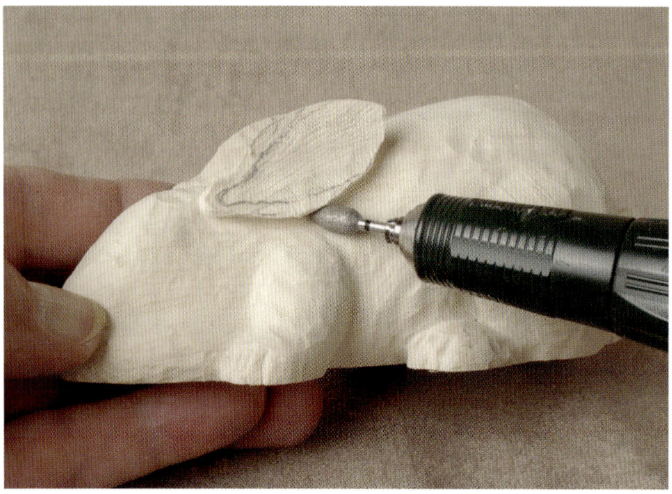

Figure 66. Lightly undercut the entire circumference of the ear.

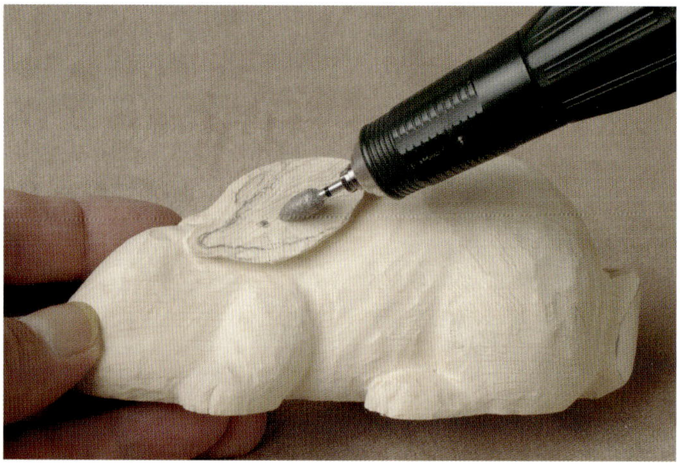

Figure 67. The pencil mark dot marks the spot where you need to start hollowing out the inside of the earflap.

Figure 68. Using the #3 ruby carver (RC-25), cut away the inside of the ear leaving the surface concave, but being careful not to cut too much. Holding the ear up to a bright light will show you how thin or thick the wood is. If it's too thin, you'll be able to see bright light through the wood. If there's more wood, you will not be able to see much light. When you think you are getting close, hold the ear up to the light and check, and then go back to taking away more wood if needed.

Figure 69. Use the #1 ruby carver flame (RC-19) to cut away the thinner parts of the base of the ear. Make sure the bit/burr is pointed inward towards the head, checking the angle frequently to make sure you not getting to close to the outside of the ear. Hold the ear up to the light to check the thickness of the wood left.

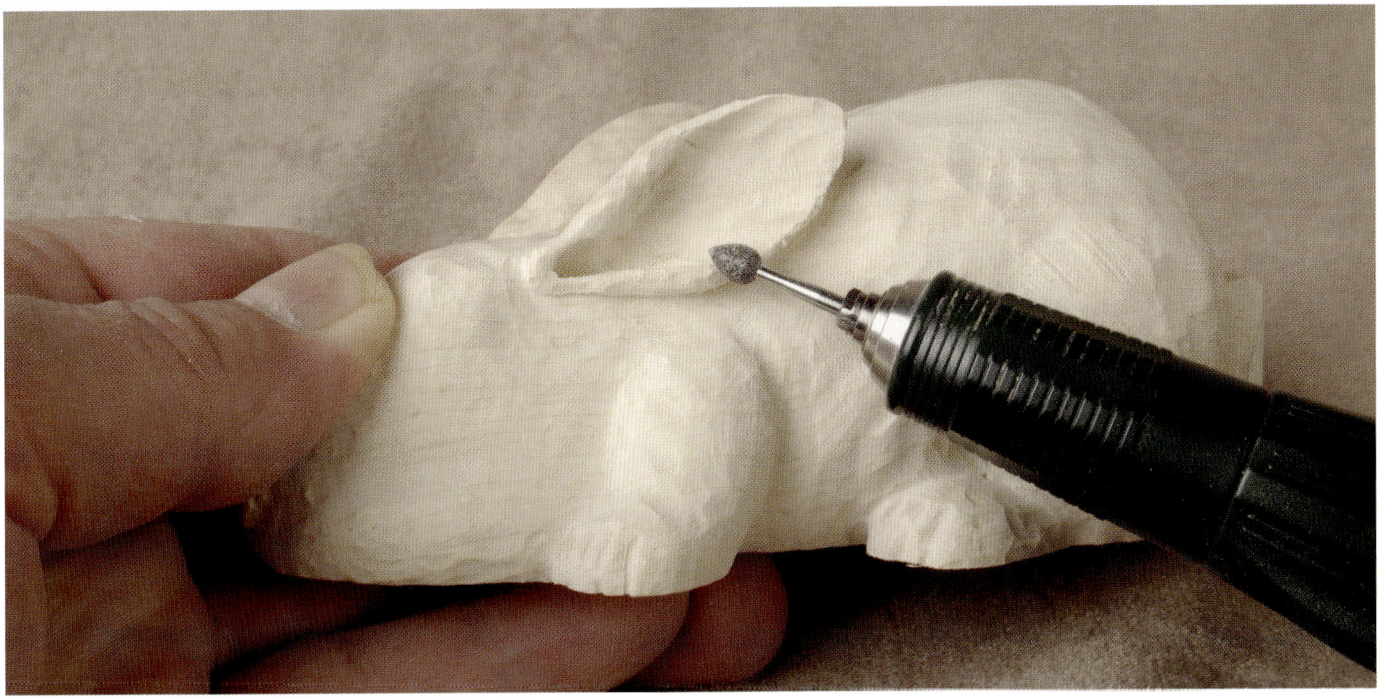

Figure 70. Use the larger pointed ball to round over the perimeter of the ear flange. You may need to taper it closer to the head.

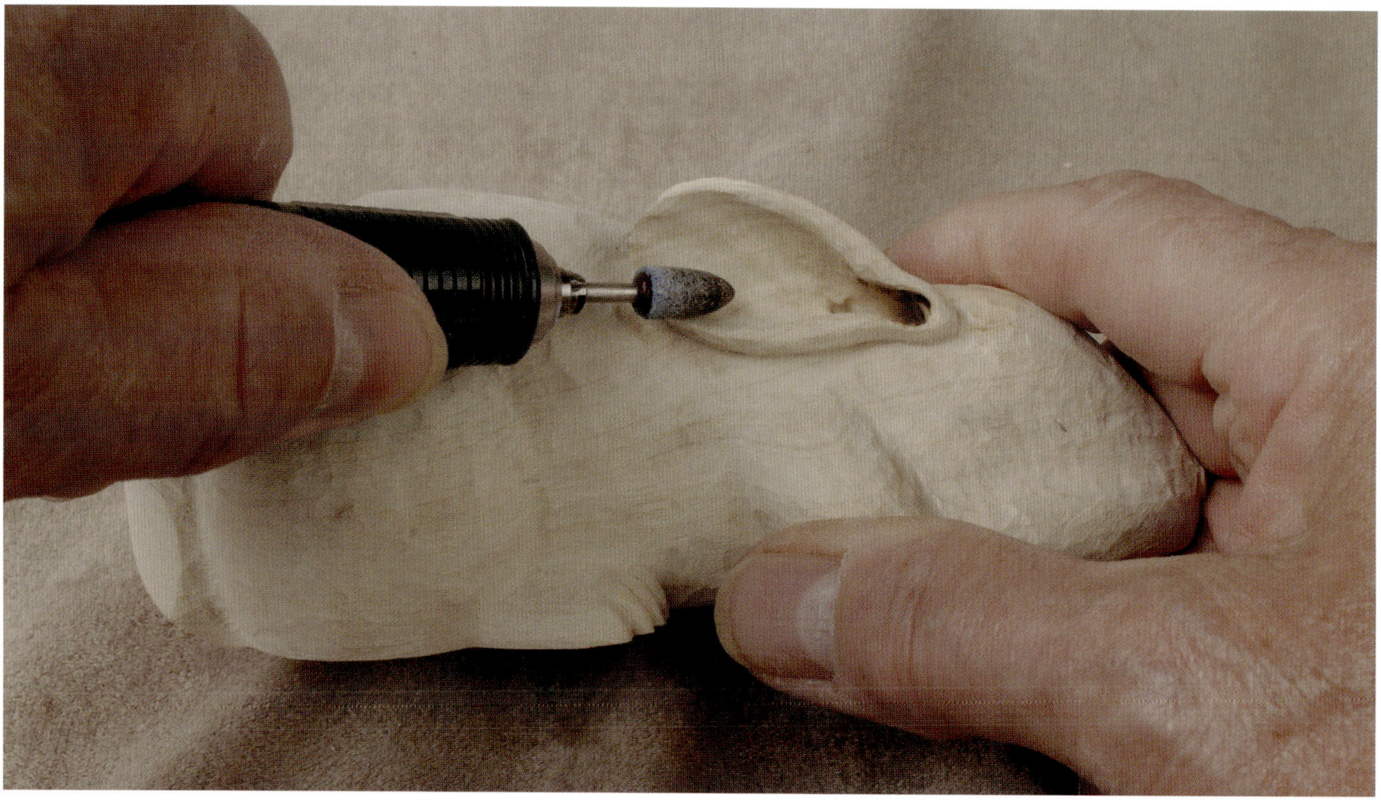

Figure 71. Sand/smooth the inside of the flap with a bullet stone.

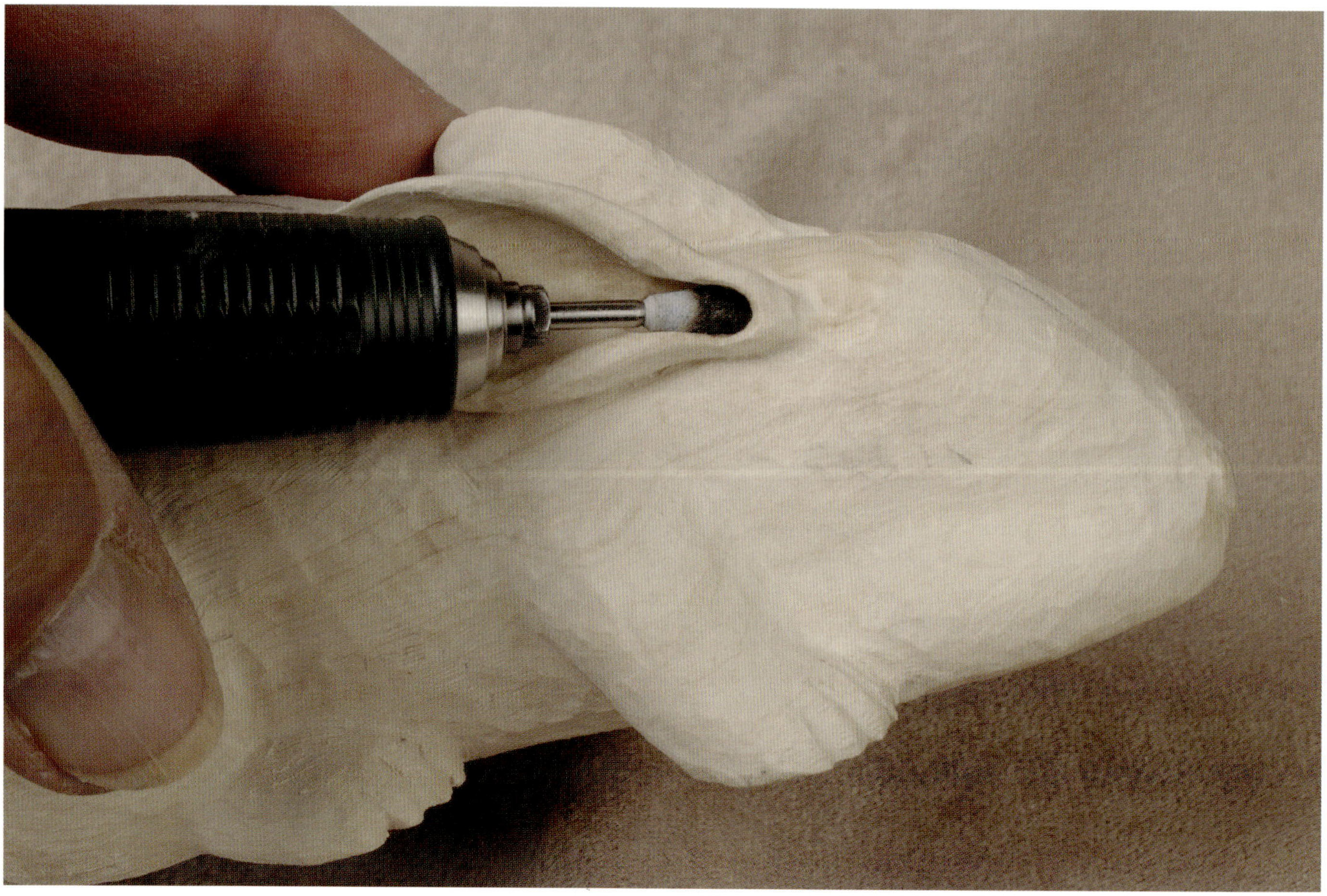

Figure 72. Use a pointed flame stone to sand/smooth the deeper parts of the ear.

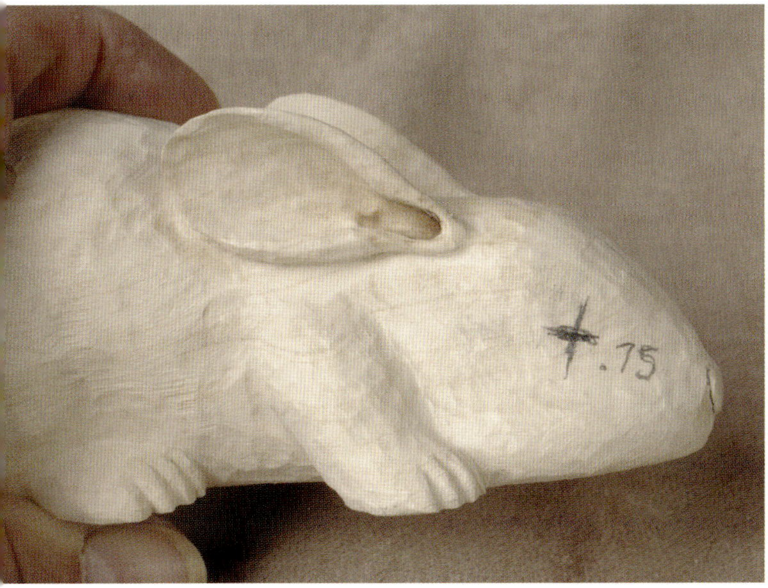

Figure 73. Measure halfway between the base of the ear and the back of the nose, and divide that in half. I mark the vertical line at 0.75" from the back of the nose. I just eyeball where I think the eye must go on the side of the head. Studying bunnies out in the yard and studying photographs will help you place the eyes correctly.

Figure 74. Turning the bunny and looking at him/her head-on and holding it level, I, then, mark the left eye.

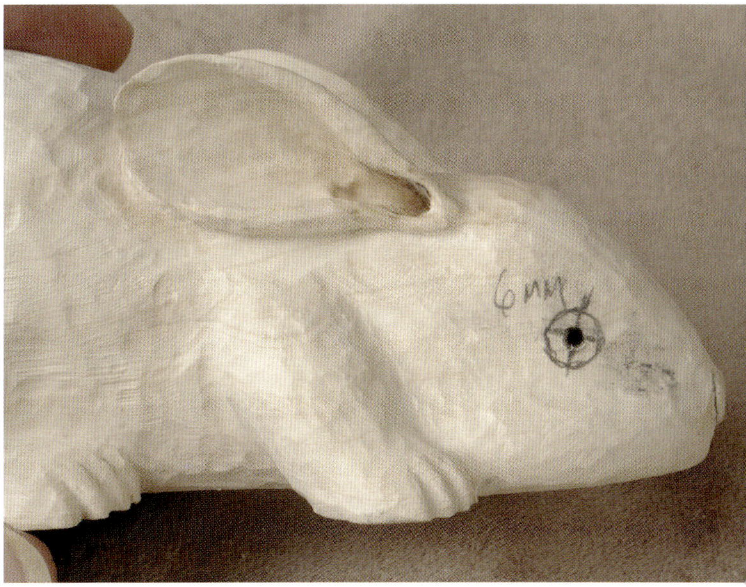

Figure 75. This bunny pattern requires 6mm eyes. Now, I understand we are going from measuring in tenths of an inch to millimeters. Glass eyes are hand-blown in Germany, and they are done in millimeters. Draw a 6mm circle around the cross hairs.

Figure 76. Again, check from the head-on view that everything is symmetrical and balanced.

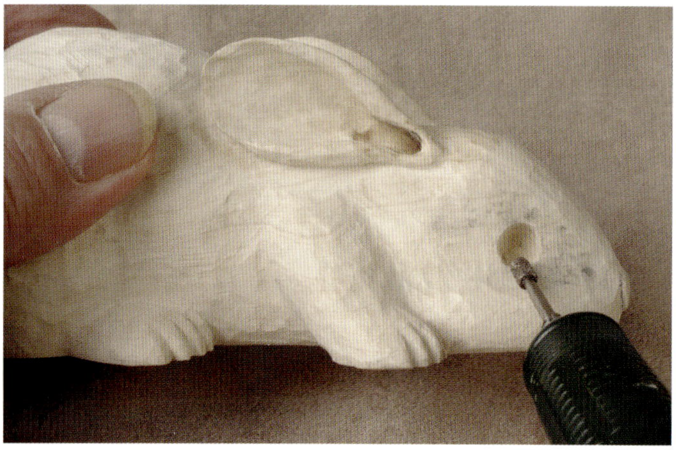

Figure 77. I use the slightly domed straight-sided cylinder ruby carver (RC-18) to drill the eyes. Just as in marking the eyes, I drill the right one first, and then, head-on, I drill the bunny's left eye. I drill the center first, getting my depth, and then I ream/ wiggle the bit in a circle to get the circumference for a 6mm eye.

Figure 79. Draw little slits in front and behind the eye—this angled slit/dash goes toward the nose and is the point at which the upper and lower eyelids meet.

Figure 80. Draw in the lower semi-circular lid smaller than the larger upper lid. Note how the upper lid is also longer in the back.

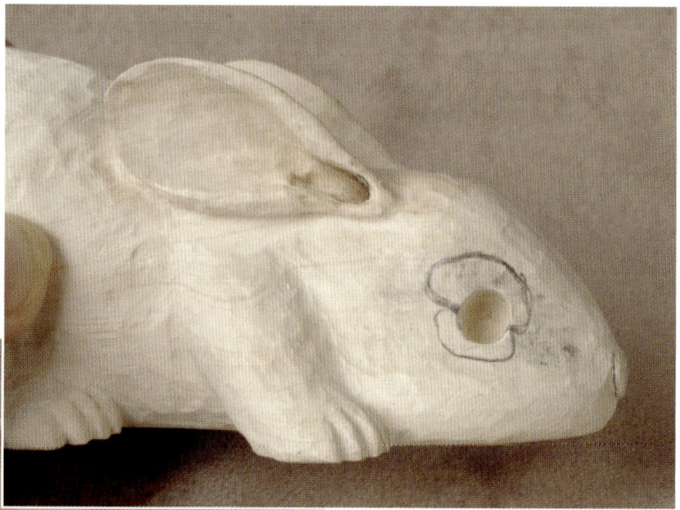

Figure 78. Make sure that the eyehole is sufficiently deep so that you don't have to re-drill it when you go to set the eyes. Ream out the holes slightly larger than the diameter of the eye, which allows you some room to stuff epoxy putty in there when setting the eyes. Make sure that each eye will fit into both holes. There is usually just a fraction of a difference in eyes on the same wire!

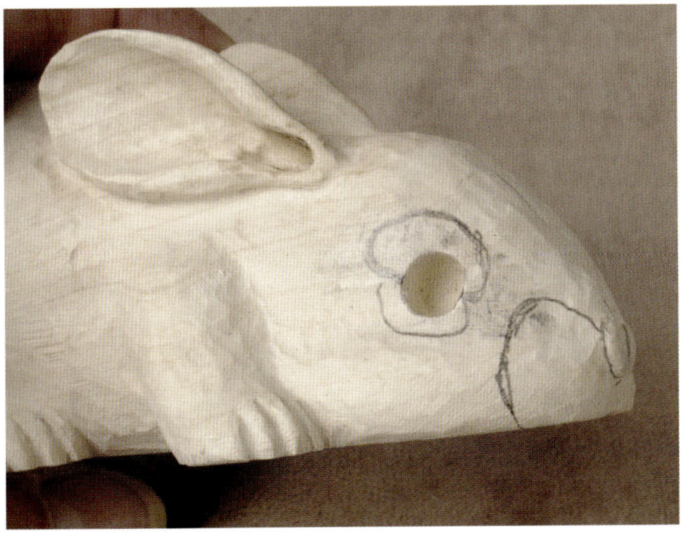

Figure 81. Draw in the whisker pad from the upper back of the nose and sweeping in an arc around the muzzle. Make sure that both of the whisker pads are symmetrical and even from every view.

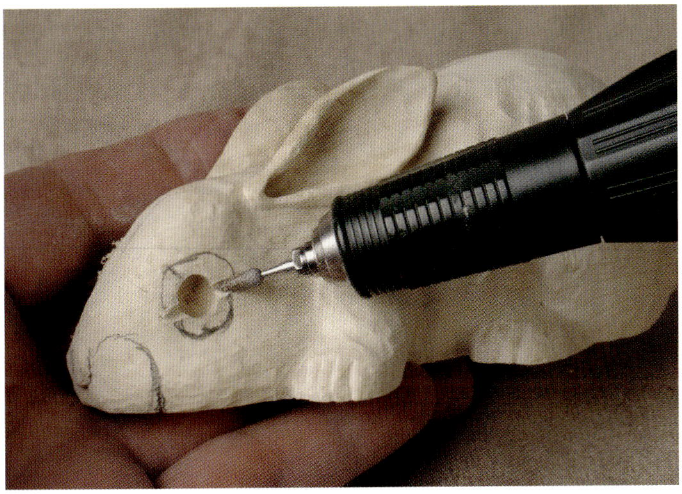

Figure 82. Using the smallest of the pointed flame ruby carvers (RC-19), cut the slits/dashes right into the eyehole on both sides.

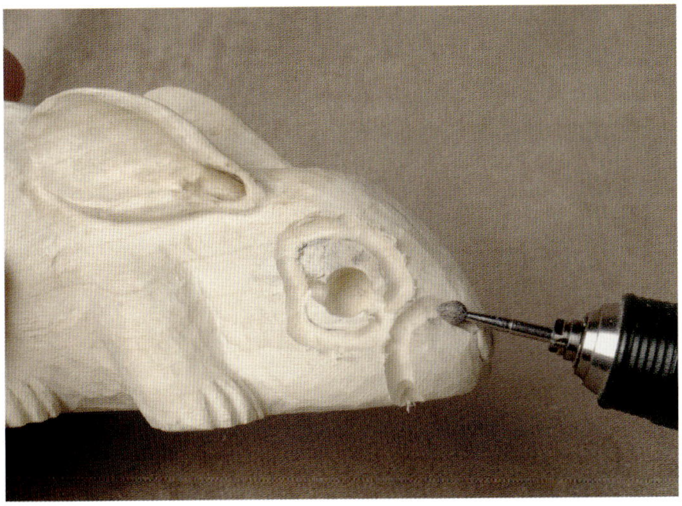

Figure 83. Cut a channel around the eyelids and the whisker pad on both sides using the smaller pointed ball (RC-16).

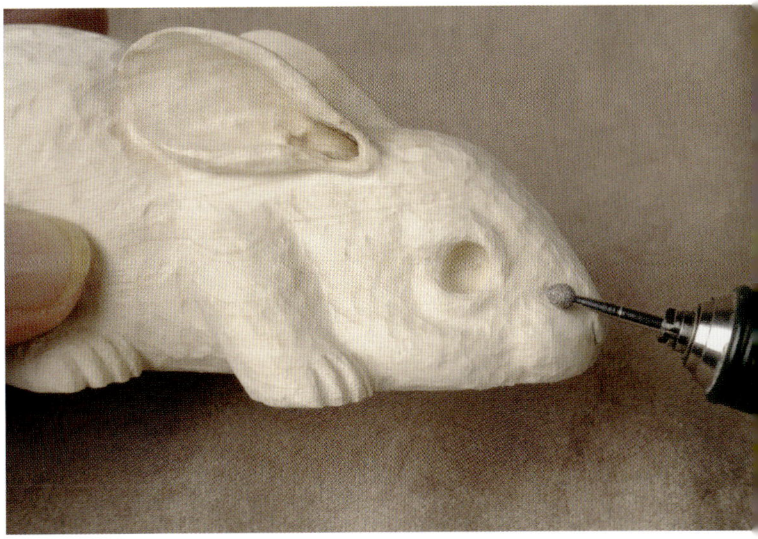

Figure 84. Round over the upper and lower eye lids and whisker pads on both sides. Make sure that everything blends together symmetrically on both sides of the head.

Figure 85. Make sure you check the symmetry from the top plan view and make any adjustments necessary.

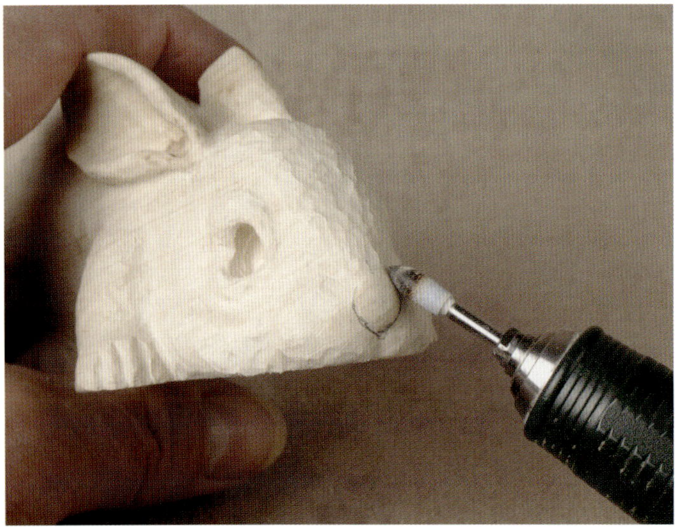

Figure 86. Sand/smooth any scratches off the nose.

Figure 88. Using the #2 flame ruby carver (RC-20), separate the tail from the hindquarters. Taper the inside edge to the centerline around the circumference.

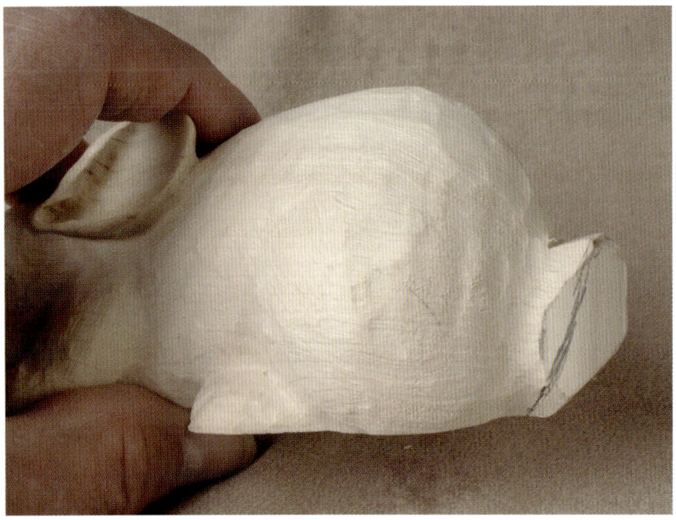

Figure 87. Draw in the centerline on the profile and top view of the tail.

Figure 89. Blend the body towards the tail attachment points, making sure that there is no bulge.

Figure 90. Check the top plan view for symmetry and balance.

Figure 91. Check the profile view to make sure that everything blends together.

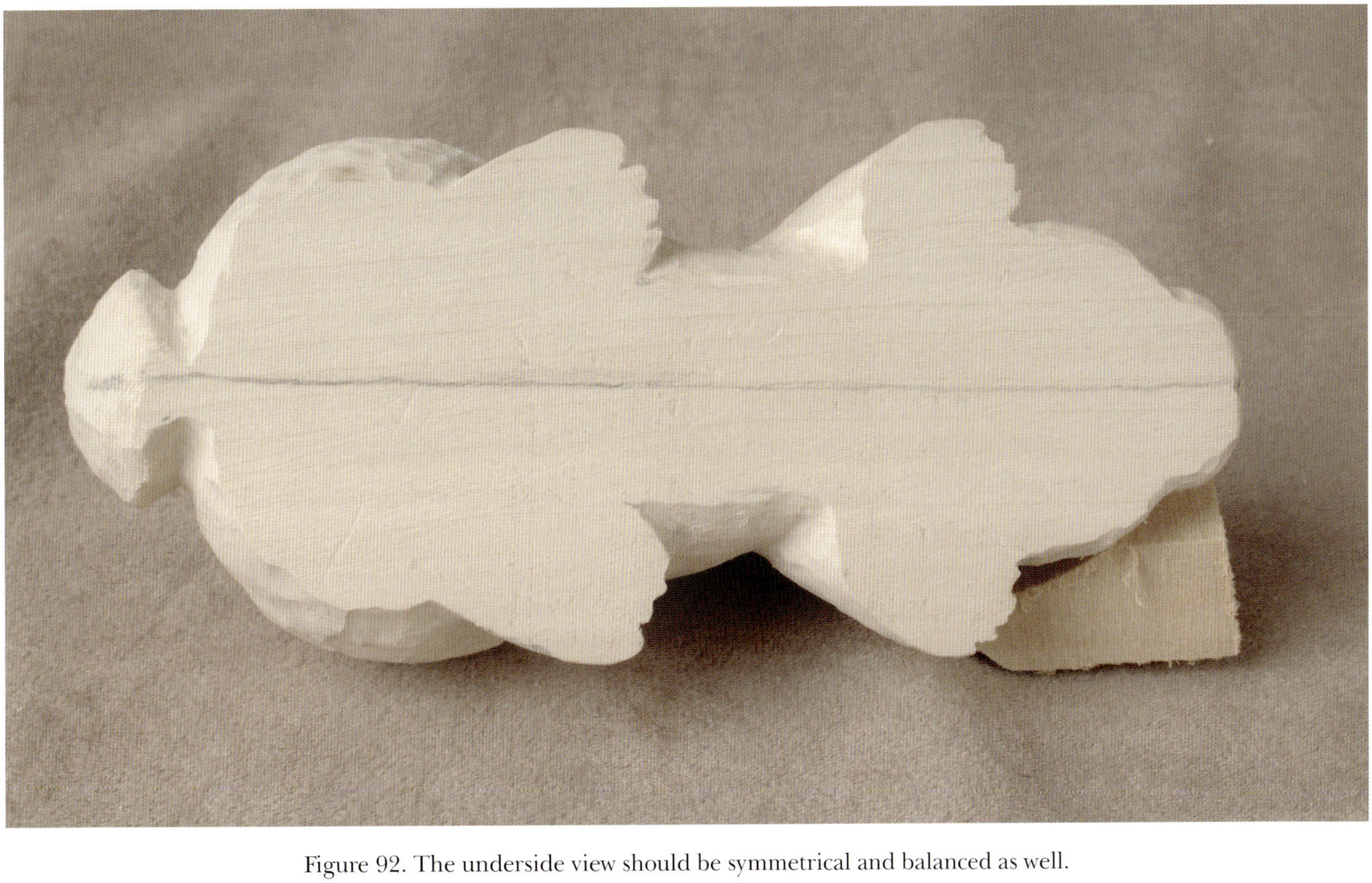

Figure 92. The underside view should be symmetrical and balanced as well.

Figure 93. The end view from the tail should look balanced and symmetrical.

Figure 94. Here is the head-on view.

Figure 95. Studying the picture carefully, draw in the flow lines for the fur. On most animals, fur flows from the head to the tail. Look at the way the hair on your body grows. It is the same for most mammals. With longer furred animals, gravity will affect the direction of the hair.

Figure 96. The other side fur/hair flow goes in the same direction. Note the direction of the hair flow on the upper and lower eyelids. It starts in the front corner of the eye and progresses back toward the back eye corner following the rounded shape of the eyelids.

Figure 97. Here is the top plan view of the flow lines.

Figure 98. You can see how the fur flows towards the tail on the back of the haunches. The flow on the tail itself is from the bottom to the tip and outward towards the edges.

Figure 99. This is the bit/burr that I use to do the first step in making fur. It is a ruby carver that is a straight-sided cylinder with a slightly domed top (RC-18). It is the same bit/burr that I use for drilling all eyeholes in animals and birds.

Figure 100. When doing fur or hair, you need multiple levels in the wood. Study up-close pictures of fur and notice all the different levels and directions that the hair flows in. To get that same effect on wood, we need to create the multiple levels first with a ruby carver, and then refine it with the burning pen. The texturing is the first step in creating fur. **Do not texture the nose, eyelids, paws, or ears**. Starting out around the nose and following the flow lines, hold the ruby carver at an angle so that you are just using the corner to create the texture, and do short strokes, leaving no flat areas in between. You want the entire surface textured. Texture lightly on the head, slightly deeper on the body, and deepest on the tail. You can do one stroke at a time, or do as I do, let the burr ride across the surface with a scribbling stroke. Do the scribbling stroke as you used to color in a picture when you were a kid! Doing the scribbling or scrubbing stroke covers a large area more quickly as the bit will be cutting in both directions. You need to do the texturing at different angles and not all straight inline strokes. You still need to follow the flow lines, but just not in a straight line.

Figure 101. Continue on the side of the head towards the front leg. To facilitate the turn at the top of the front leg, shorten your strokes and work around the corner. Continue down the front leg and stop on the bend of the paw.

Figure 102. Continue down the flank and over the haunch with slightly longer and deeper strokes. Do not do the hind paws or toes.

Figure 103. Note the deeper texturing and longer strokes on the haunch approaching the tail. The top of the tail (the part of the tail adjacent to the back) gets textured at angles from the base out toward the edges.

Figure 104. Note the depth of the texturing on the underside of the tail. I pressed hard on the bit to get the depth that I wanted and needed.

Figure 105. Okay, let's make us some fur! I use a medium skew tip burning pen to create most of the fur. Note that the pen tip wire is silver-soldered into the pen. I think this is critical. In many classes that I've taught over the years and across the nation, many students have had pens with the interchangeable tips or wire. When you have a mechanical connection such as the replaceable tips or wire, you have a great deal more of a heat build up that transfers to the pen handle itself, making it VERY hot to hold. Some burning pens seem to heat up so much that many students got blisters on their fingers from holding the burning pen while burning an animal. The pen needs to be much hotter for burning fur than for burning feathers. If your pen is heating up to the point of discomfort, there are several th ings you can do: buy a fixed-tip pen, wear a leather glove to insulate your hand, or wrap a barrier around your burning pen to insulate it.

Figure 106. In some places on most animals, a rounded tip is essential to burning in the fur in concave places.

Figure 107. Sometimes it is helpful to have a longer, skinny tip to reach areas that the regular skew tip cannot reach.

Figure 108. Start burning around the nose, radiating around the carved shape. Note that each burning stroke is so close to the previous one that there is no white, unburned wood in between. Make sure the nose is symmetrical when you finish going all the way around it. Each stroke should be short and at different angles. The biggest mistake that most carvers make is that there is not sufficient angle change between each stroke and that the strokes are all the same length. For this bunny, the strokes need to be shortest on the head, medium length on the body, and longest on the tail. Taking time to do the texturing and burning well will make the painting substantially easier. With the tops of the burning at different levels, it is easy to dry-brush highlights across the irregular surface and bring the fur to life! Look carefully at the bunny that has had gesso applied to it, and study the burned strokes carefully.

Figure 109. Continue burning back towards the eye. I usually leave the eyelids unburned until I burn the area around them.

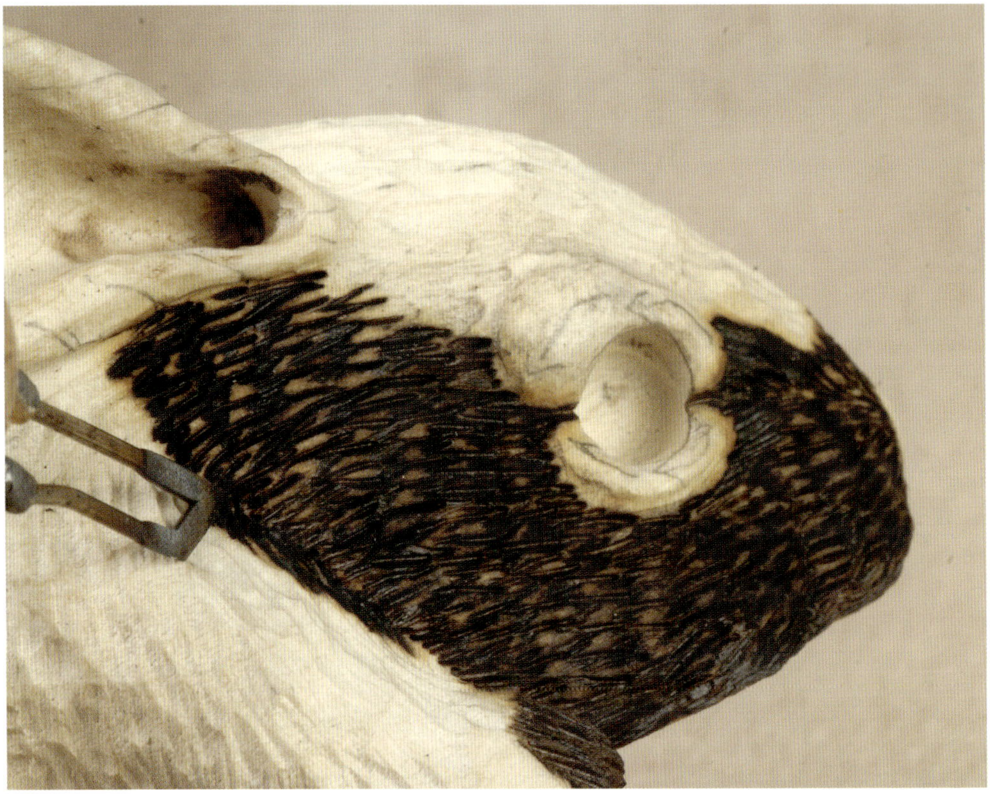

Figure 110. To make the turn at the shoulder/end of cheek/upper forearm, make the burning strokes shorter and curve them around until they are running down the front inside of the leg. To burn each of the toes, burn out at an angle from the bottom of the "v" separating each toe.

Figure 111. Because you are burning so hot, carbon will form on the surface of the burned lines. Clean the carving with a toothbrush. I find that a natural bristle toothbrush will clean much better than a synthetic one. Natural bristle toothbrushes can usually be found at online suppliers, as well as natural food stores. Because you are burning much hotter than you do with birds, you need to be careful not to work right over the top of the project so that you inhale the fumes. Try holding the carving out in front of you so that you are not right over top of it.

As with the eyelids, I burn around the ear circumference and then come back and burn the fur on them.

Figure 112. To burn the eyelids, start in the front corner and follow the contour on the upper and lower lids with little short strokes, working your way to the back corner.

Figure 113. After you get the front legs and paws done, proceed to the flanks and then on to the haunches and hind paws.

Figure 114. Here you see how to burn the flanges of the ears at an angle.

Figure 115. Fill in the burning with many strokes so that no unburned wood can be seen.

Figure 116. Burn the outside of the ear with strokes starting at the base and working towards the edge. There are some very fine hairs on the perimeter of the inside of the ears, but I do not burn them. I prefer to paint them. The fur on the outside of the ears is not burned as deeply as the body contour hair/fur—you certainly would NOT want to burn any strokes through to the inside!

Figure 117. Burn the hair/fur on the tail by starting at the base and working upward, towards the tip. Use longer and slightly deeper strokes than on the haunches.

Figure 118. Burn the topside part of the tail nearest the back of the body by working from the base crevice toward the outer edge.

Figure 119. The burning is now finished. Brush all of the burned areas with the toothbrush to get rid of any loose carbon. Blow off any carbon residue with an air compressor or canned air.

Figure 120. Either dip the bunny in 50/50 brushing lacquer and lacquer thinner or spray several coats of Krylon Clear Acrylic Spray 1301, waiting 10 minutes in between applications. For animals, I prefer the 50/50 lacquer/thinner mixture since I feel sure that it gets on every surface of the fur, ears, nose, and all of the other parts. For the dipping solution, I buy a gallon of gloss brushing lacquer and an extra empty gallon can. I pour half of the lacquer into the empty can, and add a half-gallon of lacquer thinner to each can. And ta-da, you have a perfect dipping solution that soaks into all the corners and hard to reach places. You can attach a wire or screw mandrel into the bottom of the bunny or other carving to hold the piece. When dipping, I usually hold the piece in the lacquer until most of the little air bubbles stop rising to the surface, allowing the mixture to soak deeply into the piece. Allow the spray or the dip to dry before setting the eyes.

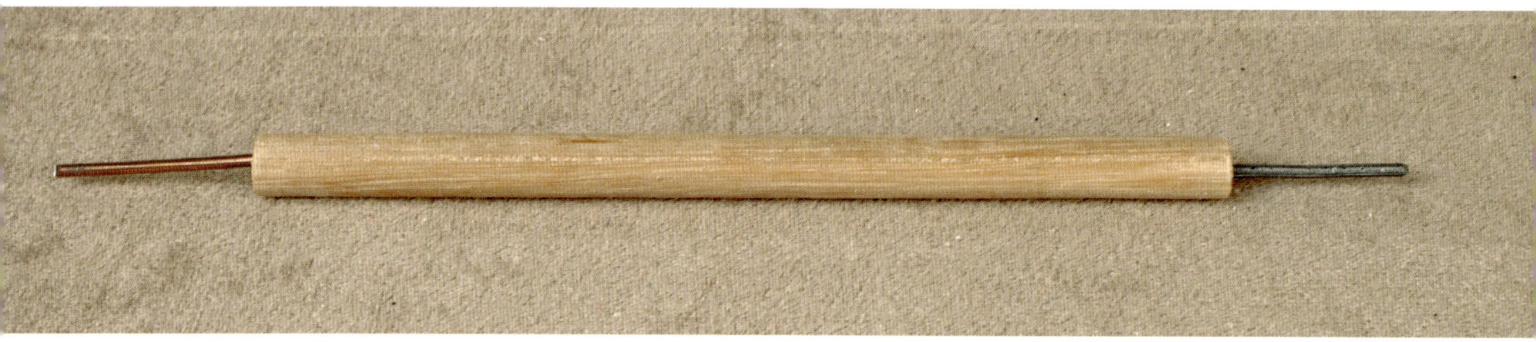

Figure 121. Thirty-one years ago when I started teaching carving classes, few students had dental tools, which could be used to model the epoxy putty we use around the eyes, on feet and legs, and in habitat applications. In the early classes, we fashioned Popsicle sticks or used whatever we could find to manipulate the putty to get the effects we needed. I had made my own "eye" tool and decided that I would make and give one of these tools to every student the first class he/she took from me. It is an easy tool to make.

Figure 122. Cut a small diameter dowel (I use one 5/16" in diameter) about 4.5" long. Drill a 1/16" diameter hole about 0.3" deep in both ends. Super-glue a piece of 16 gauge galvanized wire and shorten it to 1" long. In the other end, super-blue a piece of 1/16" diameter copper-covered gas-brazing rod and shorten to 1" long. If your local welding supply shop does not sell the gas-brazing rod, you could use a very stout needle, breaking the base so that the pointy end protrudes at least 1".

Figure 123. Using a hammer and an anvil, flatten the galvanized wire end so that it is the shape of a spatula. It will take several blows with the hammer to flatten it.

Figure 125. On a grinding wheel, sharpen the brazing rod to a long point. You could also use the sander to do this. Buff the scratches off both ends on a buffing wheel or a felt bob on a mandrel (loaded with polishing rouge) on your flexible shaft machine until you get a mirror finish.

Figure 124. Using a sandpaper cartridge roll sander or split-mandrel sander, refine the spatula shape and thin the end edges a little.

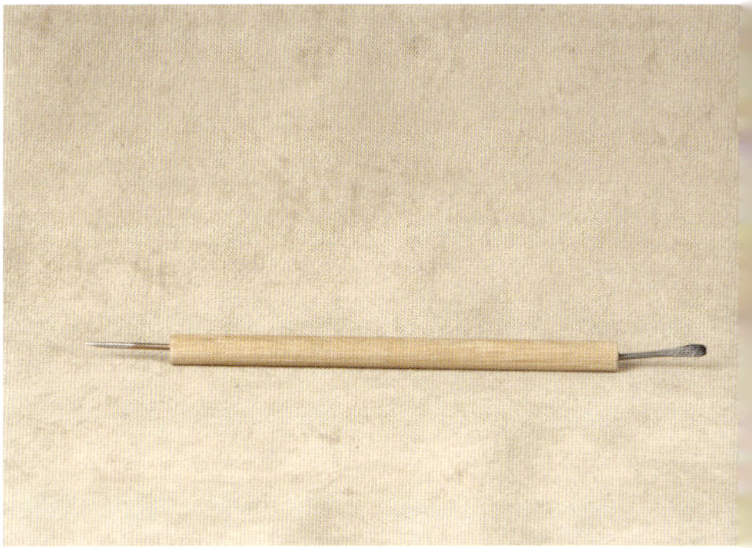

Figure 126. You now have a wonderful eye tool!

Figure 127. Before starting the eye setting procedure, recheck the eyeholes for fit and depth. If the holes are deep and wide enough, fill the holes with oil-based modeling clay, almost but not quite full. Most arts and crafts stores will sell the oil-based modeling clay.

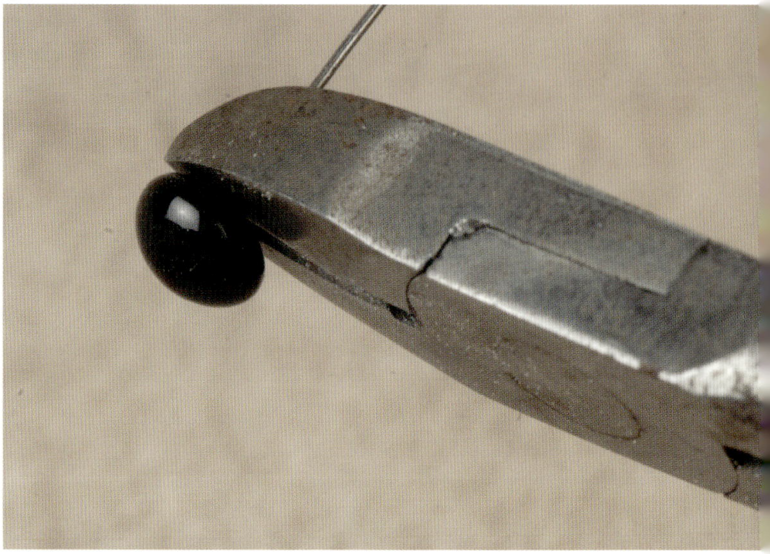

Figure 128. Cut the eye wire right up close to the back of the eye. Place an eye in the clay in each hole. Use the end of a dowel or the end of a pencil eraser to push the eyes in place. Do not use anything that might scratch the surface of the glass!

Figure 129. Make sure the eyes are even and set in the eyeholes deep enough.

Figure 130. Check the eyes for evenness from the head-on view and the top plan view. When looking straight down on the top of the head, you should be able to see just a little bit of the outside curvature of each eye.

Figure 131. A needle or pin super-glued into the end of a dowel is a great tool for cleaning out the excess clay in the crevice around the eye.

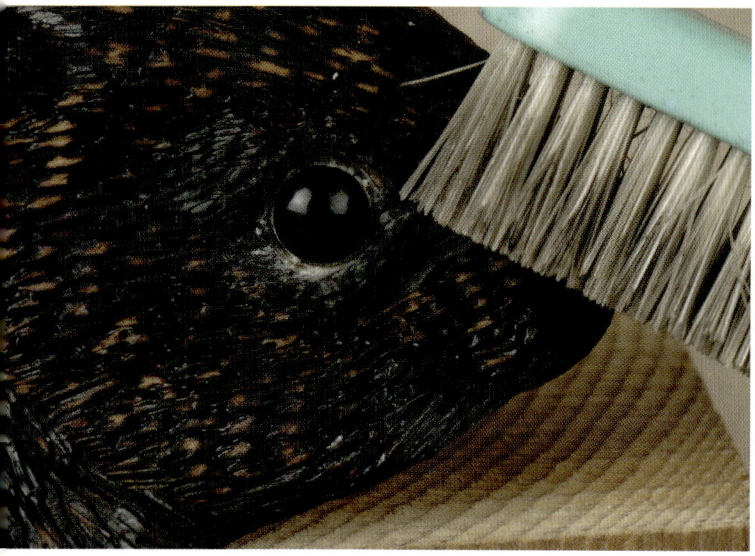

Figure 132. Use the natural bristle toothbrush to clean any excess clay from the texturing around the eyes. If any clay is left there, the epoxy putty will not stick to the wood.

Figure 133. Cut a small width of the epoxy putty straight across, and then cut a small section out of the middle. The part where the two colors meet has already chemically bonded, and you do not want the hard bits found there in your mix.

Figure 134. Mix the two colors until you can see no streaks of blue or chartreuse, and until you have an even green color.

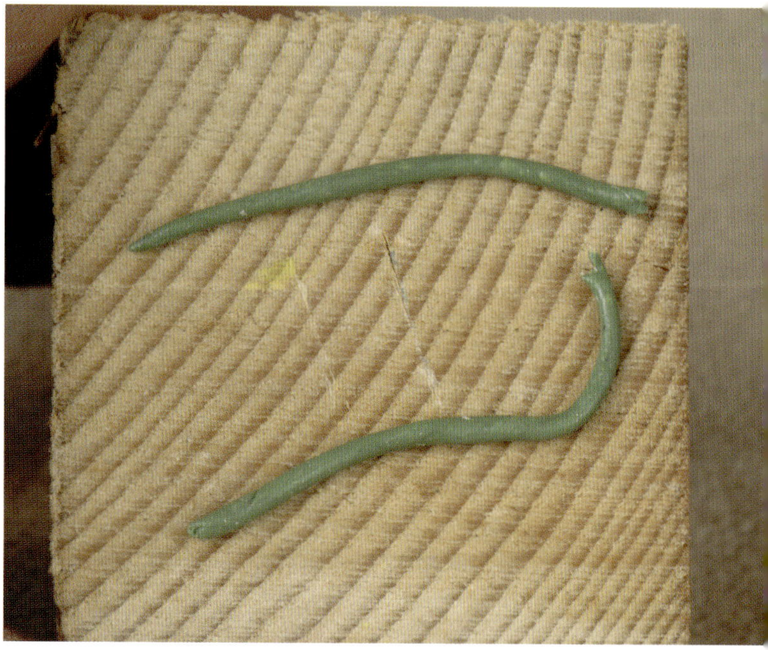

Figure 135. On a clean surface, roll out a small diameter worm and cut in half. Make sure that the diameter is not too big. It is easier, I think, to bunch it up to fill in the crevice around the eye than it is too stretch it out or remove the excess.

Figure 136. Pick up a piece of the worm with the spatula end of the eye tool, and push it down into the eye crevice. By pulling down and back, you can crimp the putty into the crevice and get it to stick.

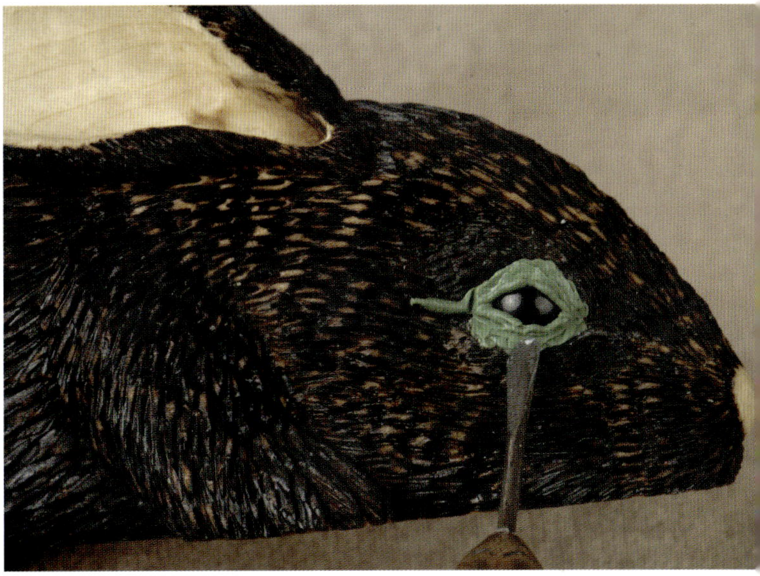

Figure 138. Work the putty around the eye. You will need extra putty left above and below the eye to do the "sleepy-eyed" look. Remove the excess at the end. Note that I left a little ridge bulging right at the inner edges. I will use this ridge to form the actual eye ring. You have approximately 45 minutes of working time with this ribbon epoxy putty.

Figure 137. Leave your clay out on your workbench. You will need to stick the end of the eye tool periodically in the clay to keep the putty from sticking to the tool. As you are working, you will hear a little smacking sound of the putty sticking to the tool, after you manipulate it 3 or 4 times. As soon as you hear that sound, dunk your tool end in the clay to impart an oily covering to keep the putty from sticking.

Figure 139. Blend the perimeter of the putty into the surrounding texturing on the eyelids. Remove any excess if needed. Note the sharp corners in front of and behind the eye. These corners should fall right at the slit divisions between the upper and lower lids. The point of a knife is useful in effecting these corners. When one eye is finished, then proceed to the other one. Pay attention that you do not smash the first one when working on the second one. When both eyes are finished, check from the head on view that you have similar closure/openness on both eyes. Allow the putty 4-6 hours to totally harden before starting to paint!

Sitting Bunny

Tools & Supplies

- Band saw or coping saw
- Flexible shaft machine
- Micro motor machine helpful
- Variety of Kutzall/Typhoon carbide roughing out bits
- Variety of ruby carver bits and mounted stones
- Calipers and ruler, measuring in **tenths** of an inch
- Adjustable clamp for sitting bunny project
- Compass, pencil
- Knife
- Wire cutters, needle nose pliers, awl
- Drill and bits (1/16" and 5/64")
- Toothbrush (preferably natural bristle)
- Burning pen (rheostat type) and several burning pen styles
- Straight pin, hatpin, or fine dissecting needle
- Permanent ink marker (such as a fine point Sharpie)
- Dust mask, leather gloves, and safety glasses or goggles
- Optivisor or some type of magnification
- Clear acetate sheet (preferably .005 thickness)
- Super-glue and accelerator
- 4" piece of 16 gauge galvanized wire
- 50/50 lacquer/lacquer thinner mixture or Krylon Crystal Clear Spray
- Yellow carpenter glue
- Reference pictures

Materials

- 5.2"L x 3.9W x 2.4"H tupelo block for sitting bunny
- 6mm black eyes
- Medium colored China bristle paintbrush (to use for whiskers)
- Ribbon epoxy putty (preferably blue/yellow) or Kulis Karvit
- Oily, non-hardening modeling clay
- Flat base or piece of driftwood for mount

Painting Supplies

- Hair dryer
- Freezer paper and masking tape
- Brushes
- Water container and paper towels
- Flow medium
- Paints: (preferably Liquitex jar acrylics) white gesso (W), mars black (B), burnt umber (BU), raw umber (RU), yellow oxide (YO), raw sienna (RS), and burnt sienna (BS).
- Note: In color swatches, *denotes little bit

SITTING BUNNY: PROFILE VIEW

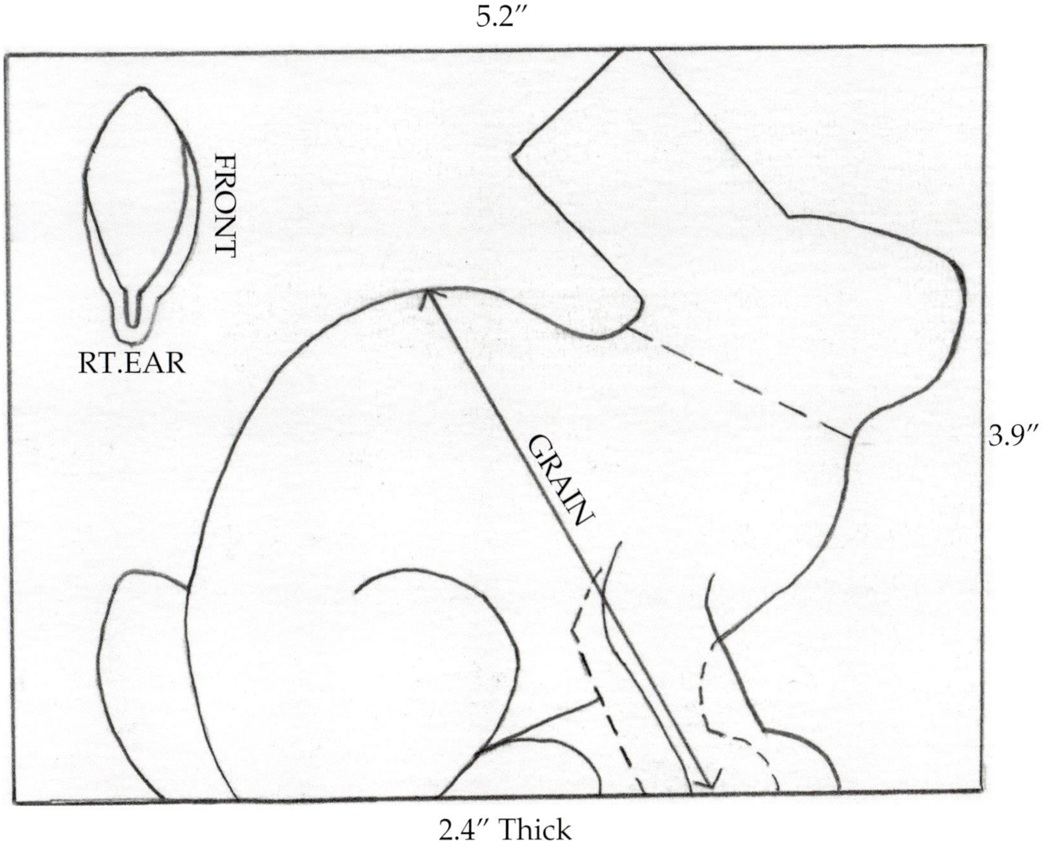

Figure 1. Cut out the upright bunny profile pattern from a block that is 5.2"L x 3.9"W x 2.4" thick. Run the grain from the front neck to the ears—because of running the grain this way, the block will be at an angle on a regular plank of tupelo. Draw a straight line from the front neck to the hind neck, and cut this line on the band saw. On the head part of the blank, note that the nose/muzzle part is rounded, and the ears part has corners. You could even write those on the head part itself so that when you glue the head to the body that you have the nose/muzzle heading forward and the ears in the back of the head where they belong. It is easy to get the parts backwards if you are not careful!

Figure 2. Find the centers of the bottom of the neck on the head block and the top of the neck on the body block piece by holding a ruler from corner to opposite corner and making a line in the middle and doing the same thing from the other corners. The "x" in the middle is the center of each block. Make sure that you do the bottom of the neck when working on the head block since it is easy to get it turned around and end up doing the wrong part. At the "x" on both pieces, drill a 1/16" diameter hole about 1/4" deep. Superglue a short piece of 16 gauge galvanized wire into the body block. After the super-glue is dry, dry fit the head to the body block to make sure you have a nice fit. If you cut the neckline perfectly straight, there should be no gaps in the joint. If not, after the carving and texturing/burning are complete, you can always go back and fill any vacancy with ribbon epoxy putty or some type of epoxy repair product.

Figure 3. Put wood glue on the neck parts of both blocks and clamp from the top of the muzzle to the bottom of the front paws and legs with a non-marring clamp.

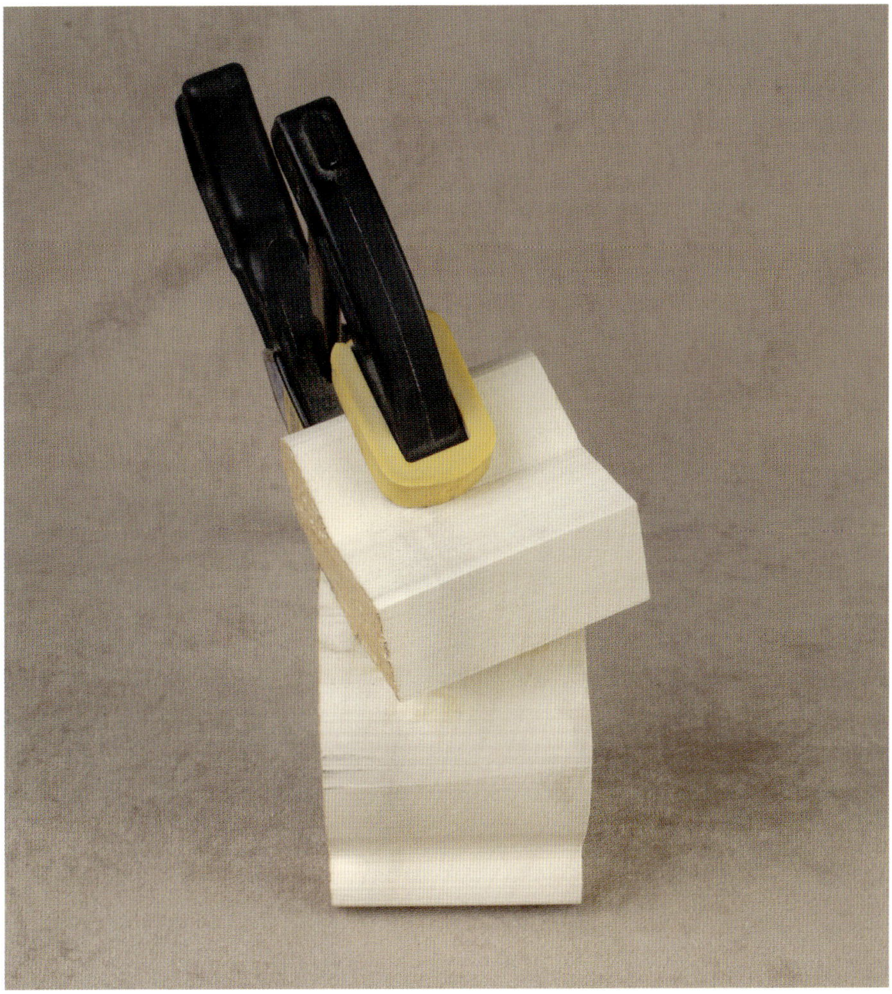

Figure 4. Turn the head about 25-35 degrees. Let the glue dry overnight before you start carving.

Figure 5. After the glue on the neck joint has hardened, flatten the bottom of bunny.

Figure 6. Draw in the separate head and body centerlines all the way around.

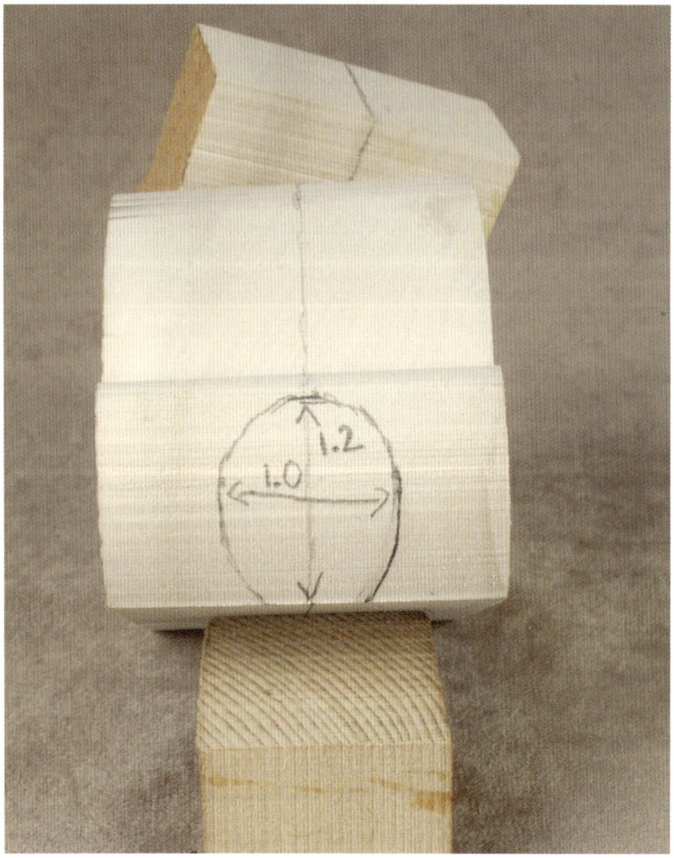

Figure 7. Measure the height of the tail at 1.2". Evenly divide 1.0" across the centerline (0.5" on both sides). Draw in the oval shape of the tail.

Figure 8. Draw in the continuation of the back/haunches to the bottom of the blank.

Figure 9. Use a small flame fine-cut Typhoon with a 1/8" shaft to cut around the tail. Do not undercut the tail at this point, and do keep the shelf around the tail straight up and down.

Figure 10. Using a medium-size Typhoon taper, round over the back from the base of the neck to the bottom of the haunches.

Figure 11. Note the rounding all the way to the bottom of the blank.

Figure 12. Trace the profile pattern onto a piece of acetate with a permanent ink marker. Hold the acetate over the hind haunch and back paw, sneak a pencil under the acetate, and trace the haunch and paw. Do both sides of the bunny. Do not mark in the front legs and paws just yet. The shoulders and outside the front legs and paws need to be narrowed first—coming up shortly.

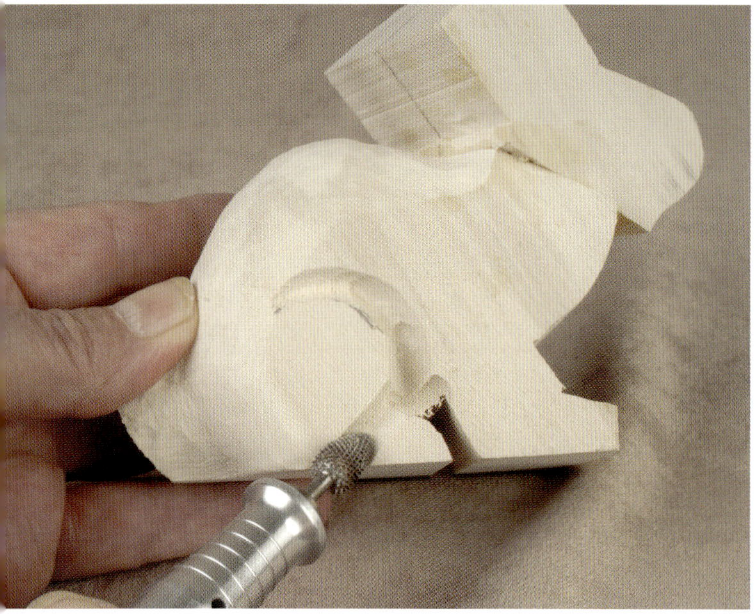

Figure 13. Using the fine flame Typhoon carbide burr, cut around the entire haunch and the top of the hind paw. Do both sides.

Figure 14. Measure and mark 0.9" on both sides of the centerline on the chest and front legs and paws. This gives you 1.8" width on the shoulders and outsides of the front legs and paws. This 1.8" shoulder measurement will not be the final measurement, just a roughing out one. When we do the front leg and chest details, we will be decreasing the shoulder width a little more.

Figure 15. Using a medium-sized flame or taper roughing-out bit, cut away the excess from the shoulders and front legs and paws.

Figure 16. Check your shoulder measurement so that you verify that the width is 1.8" across. Most animals are narrower in the shoulders than they are in the haunches.

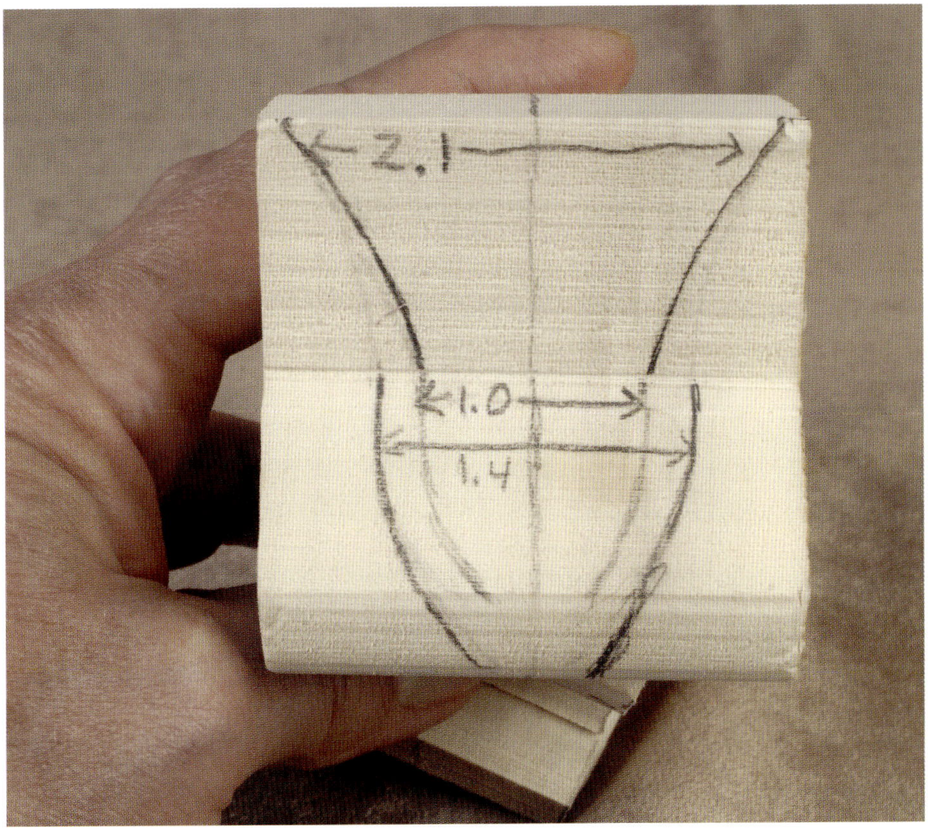

Figure 17. Before going on to rough out the front legs and paws, let's knock this head down to a more realistic size—it's driving me kinda nuts! At the base of the ears, measure and mark 0.7" on both sides (give us 1.4" all the way across). From the base of the ears at the measurement mark on both sides draw in the top plan view of the head, arcing the line towards the end of the muzzle. Measure and mark 0.5" on both sides (giving us a total of 1.0" here) at the base of the ears/back of the head. Starting at these measurement marks, draw lines from the back of the head towards the nose. These differing measurements give us more room for the cheek width than for the crown. At the top of the ear blank, measure 1.05" on each side of the centerline. This is the roughing out measurement for the tips of the ears. Draw a slightly curve line from the tip of the ear to the 0.5" mark on both sides, as shown.

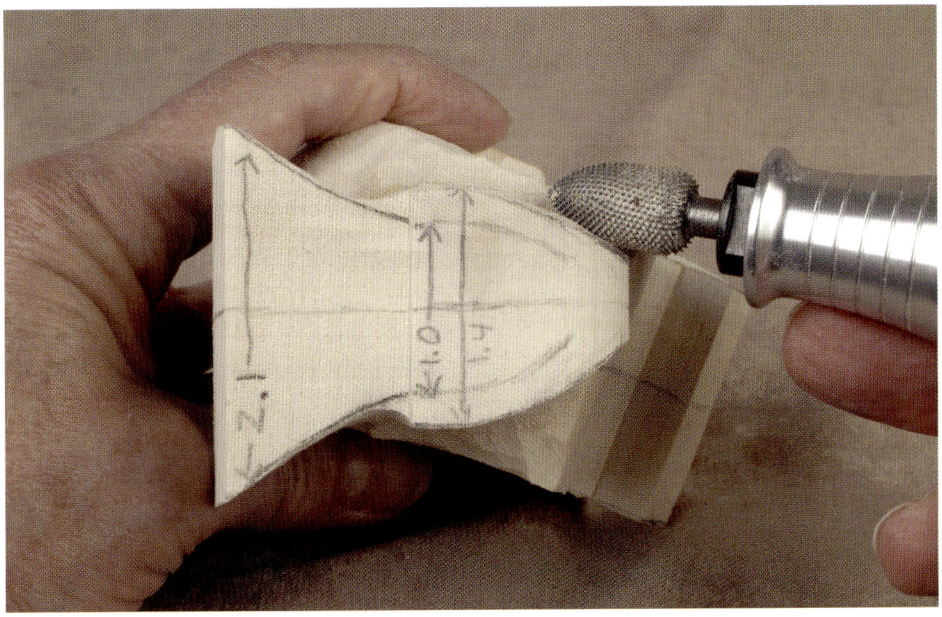

Figure 18. Cut away the excess wood outside of the drawn lines. Keep the sides of the ears and head straight up and down. Check the carving from every different view to make sure that the sides are vertical.

Figure 19. Using the calipers, check your width and keep taking off wood on the sides of the head until you can get the 1.4" measurement on the cheek area.

Figure 20. Now that we have the excess removed from the sides of the head and ears, let's get back to the front legs and paws. Hold the acetate up to the right side of the front leg area, and trace the dotted lines (as a solid line) for the right paw. On this carving, I'm putting the right paw a little bit ahead of the left one, but you can do whichever you want—both the same or different.

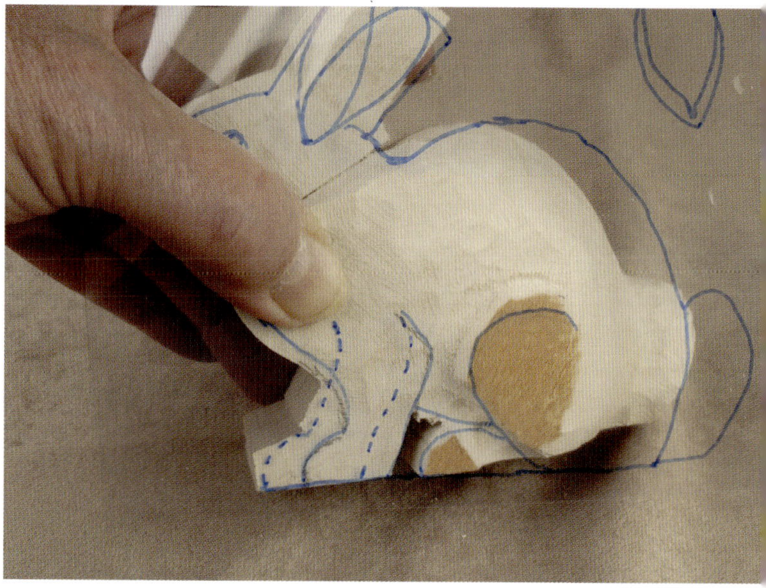

Figure 21. On the bunny's left leg, I will be sneaking my pencil under the acetate and drawing the solid line, placing the left leg and paw slightly closer to the hind foot than the right one.

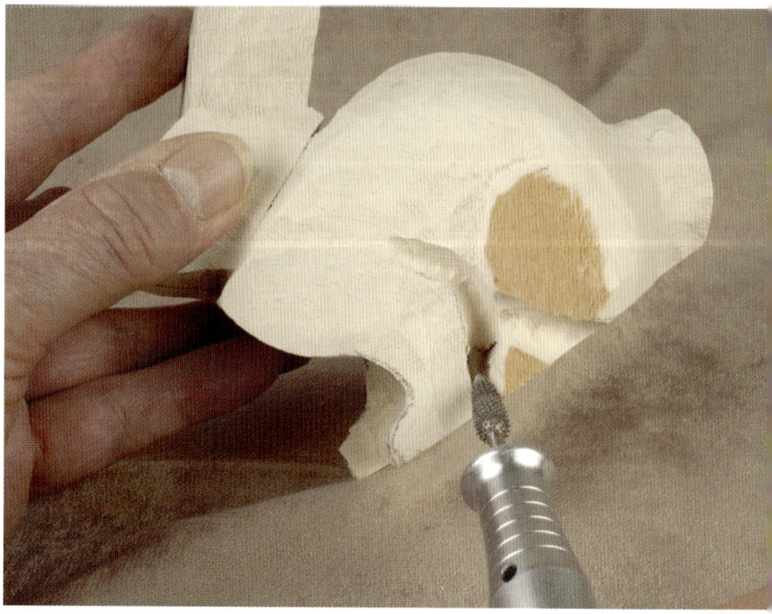

Figure 22. Using the bud Typhoon carbide cutter, rough out the front and back of the left front leg, being careful not to damage the left hind toe area. Cut this area out all the way to the centerline front and back of the leg.

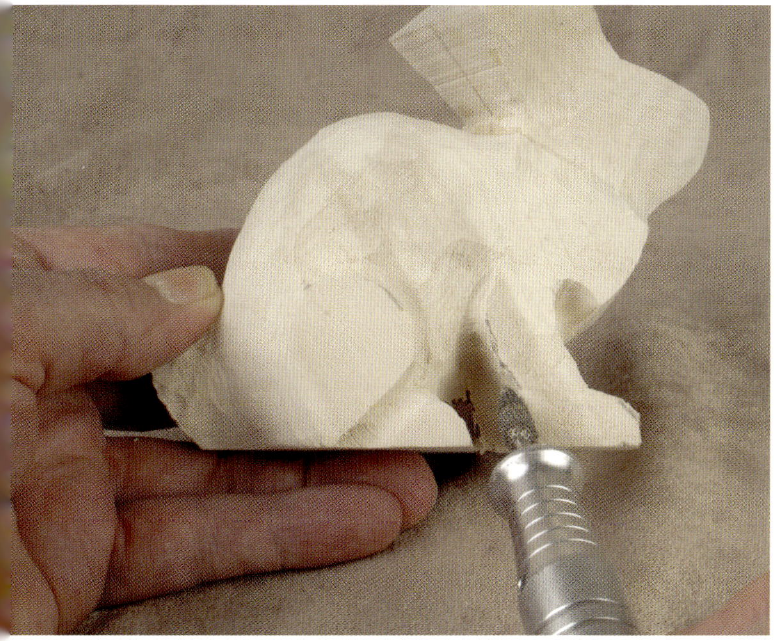

Figure 23. Cut out the excess wood in behind the right front leg and shape the toe area. There is a little more room here behind the right leg, so that there is less chance of dinging up the right hind toes, but still work carefully. Again, cut all the across the centerline front and back.

Figure 24. Measure and mark 0.6" from the outside of both paws for the roughing-out paw width. I always allow a little extra roughing out room, and then trim down to the true size with something less aggressive (usually ruby carvers). Draw the paws and legs straight up and across the lower chest.

Figure 25. Trim the excess wood from between the front legs and paws, keeping everything going straight back. The width between the inside edges is 0.55" and each paw is 0.6" across.

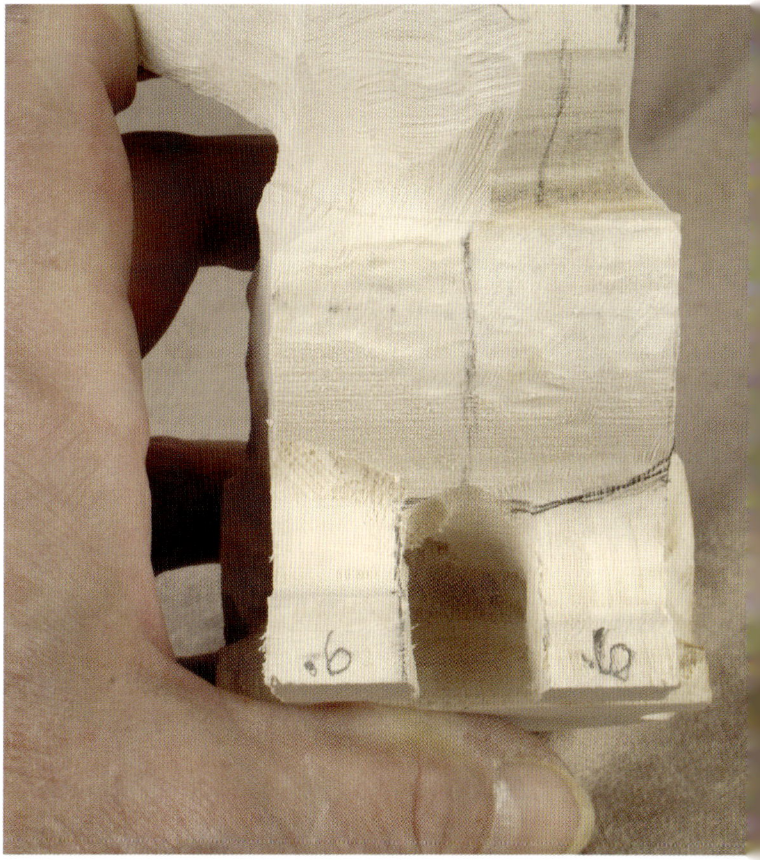

Figure 26. Draw in the separation between the chest and the left front paw, matching the level with the one on the right front paw.

Figure 27. Cut below the line on the left side of the chest at the front of the left upper leg, and match the other side's depth and shape.

Figure 28. Before doing the details, let's get back to work on the head. Using a #3 flame ruby carver (RC-25), narrow up the sides of the head, working about halfway down the sides. Make the narrowed portion slightly concave which fits the contour of the bit perfectly.

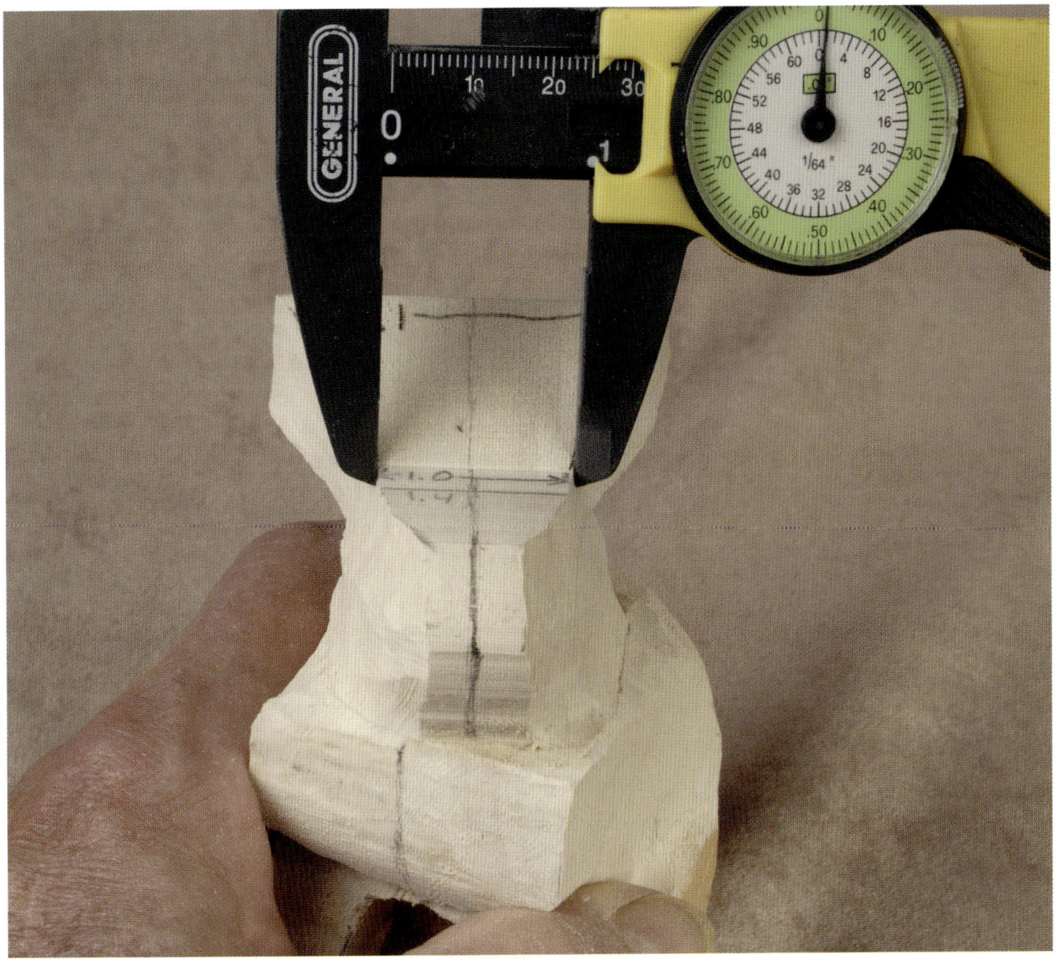

Figure 29. Keep narrowing, keeping the head balanced across the centerline, until you get a 1.0" measurement across the crown right in front of the ears.

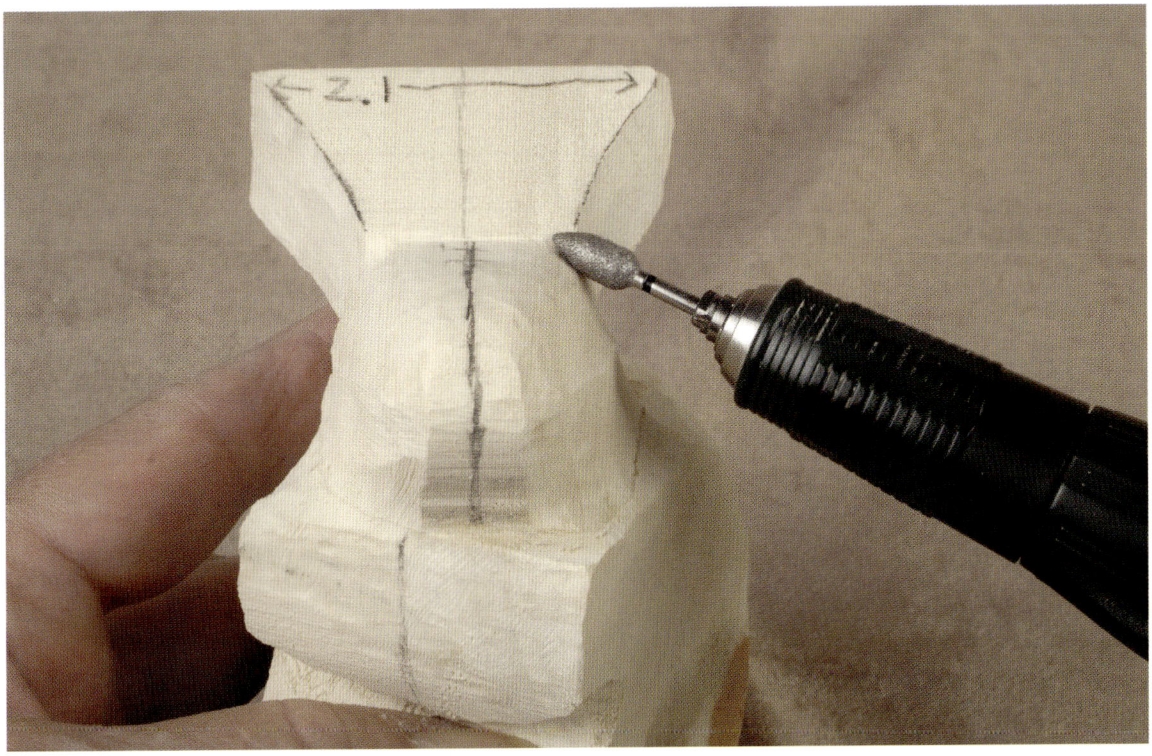

Figure 30. Round over the sharp edges of the crown from the fronts of the ears to the nose on both sides.

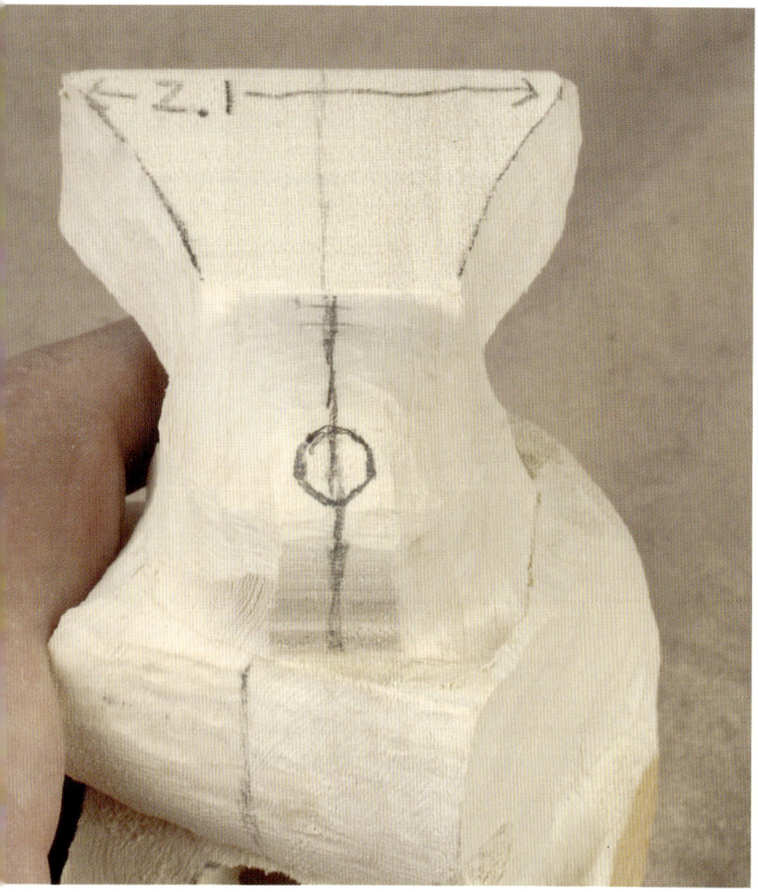

Figure 31. Draw in the nose. It measures 0.25" from side to side and the same from the rounded top to the "v" at the bottom. Measure and mark the dimensions first. Then draw the curved top, straight sides, and the "v" point at the bottom.

Figure 33. Flatten out the end of the muzzle so that the nose is protruding from the surface.

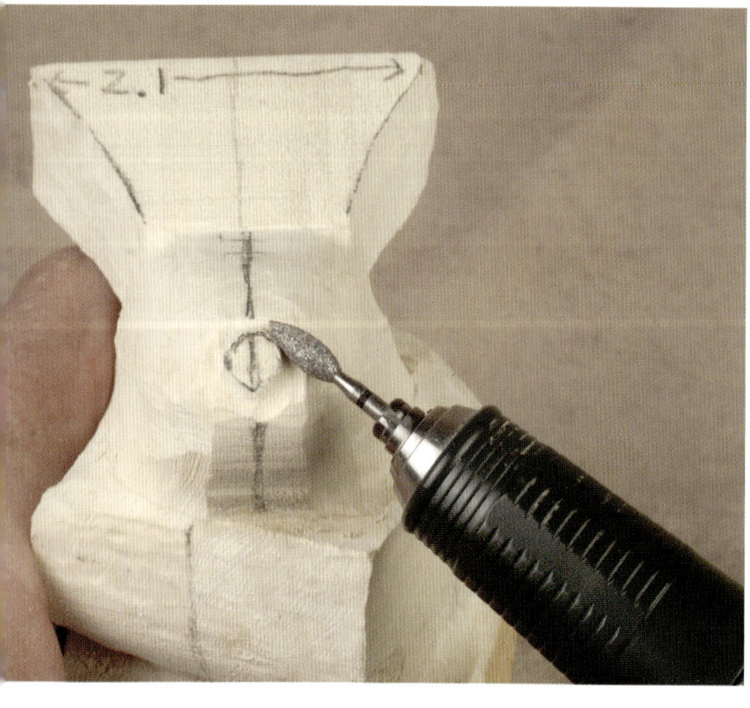

Figure 32. Laying the #2 flame ruby carver (RC-20) down, cut a channel around the nose drawing. The channel is shallower on the top than the sides and the "v." By laying the bit down, you will be carving with the circumference of the bit and not the tip.

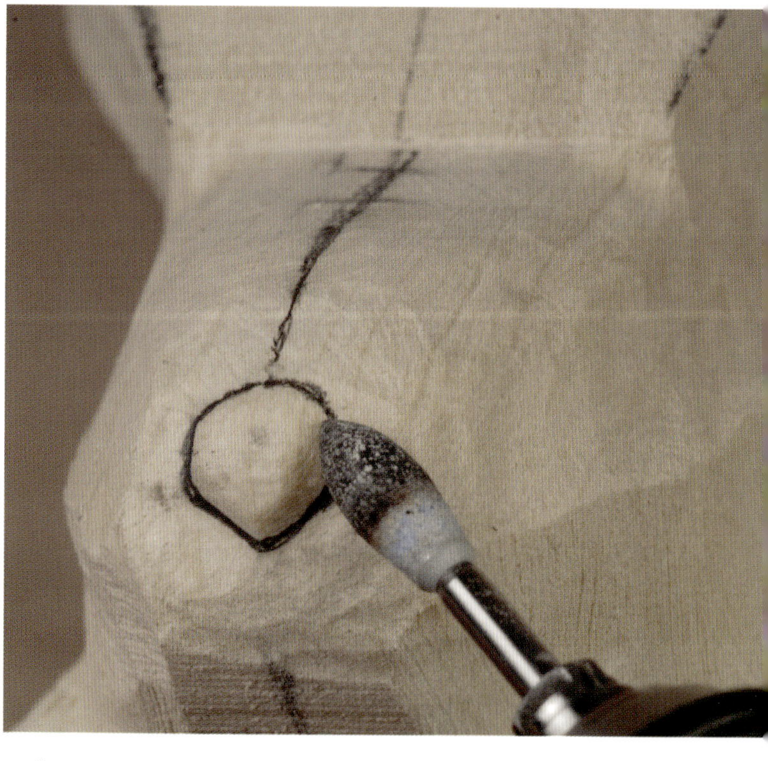

Figure 34. Using a small pointed stone, round over the sharp corners of the nose and smooth any scratches off of it.

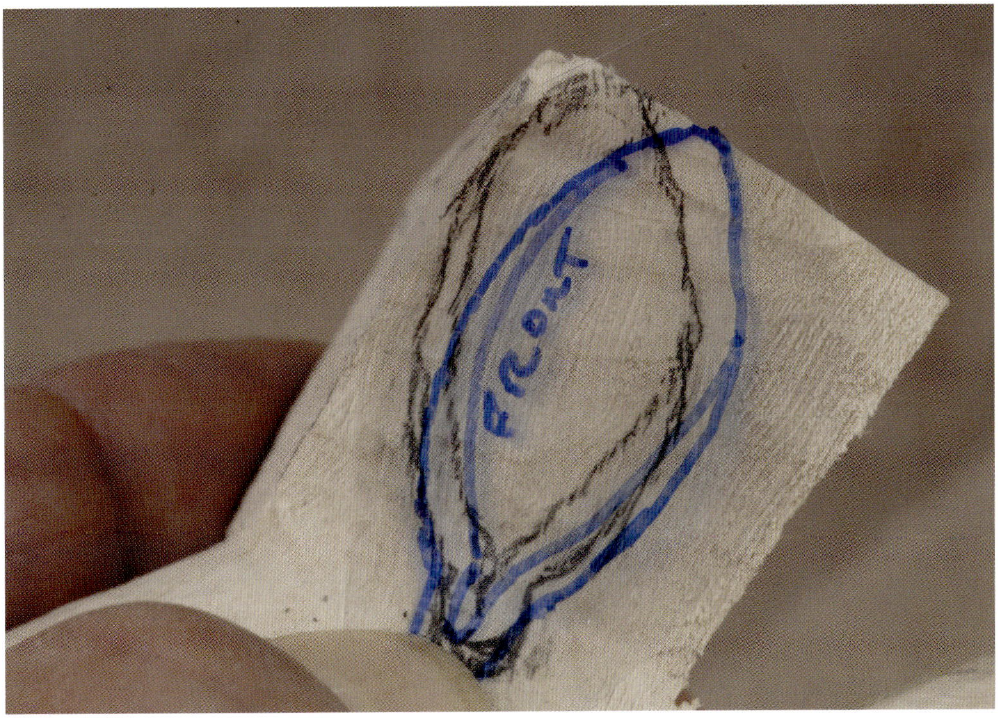

Figure 35. Trace the ear pattern on a small piece of acetate. Make sure you mark the front of the ear on the acetate. Note that the front flange is slightly longer than the back one. Hold the acetate up to the ear blank with the tip of the pattern at the top of the blank. You can pivot the ear backward or forward, depending on the attitude that you want the bunny to have. A bunny's ears can move independently.

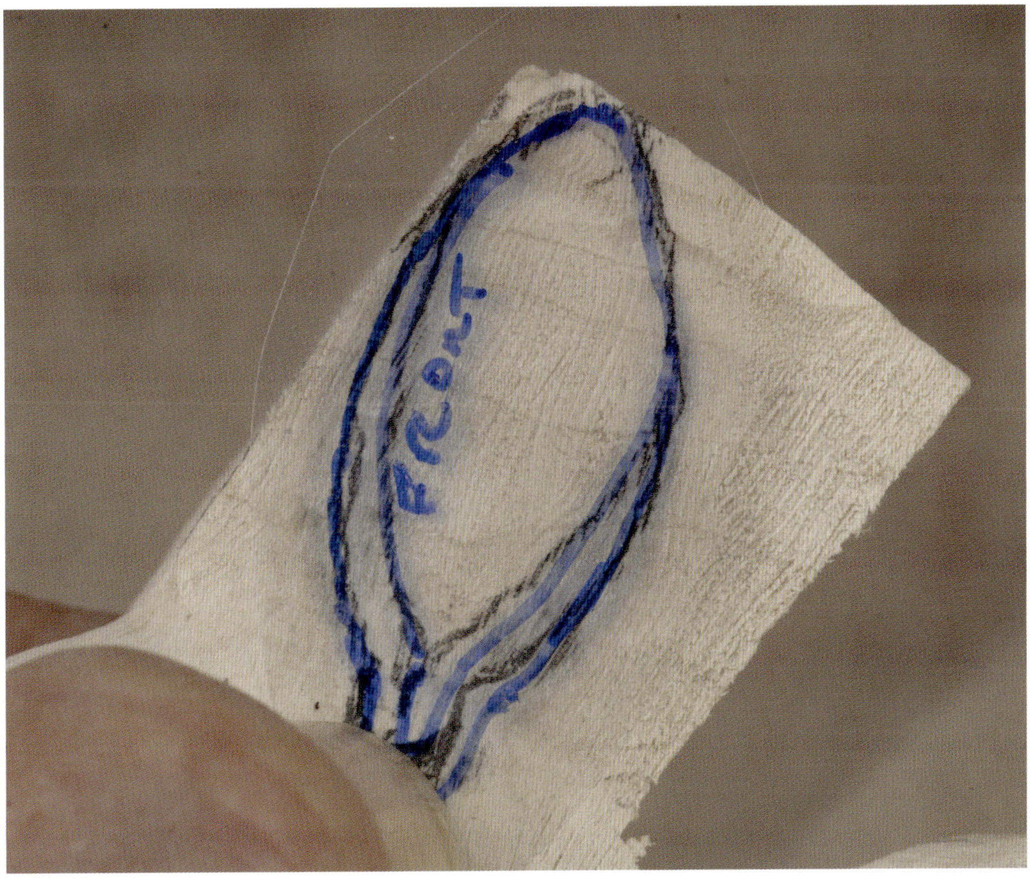

Figure 36. On the left ear, I put the ear forward as if he has heard something and is trying to pick up the direction of the sound. Position the acetate where you want the ear, sneak a pencil underneath the acetate, and sight-draw the ear.

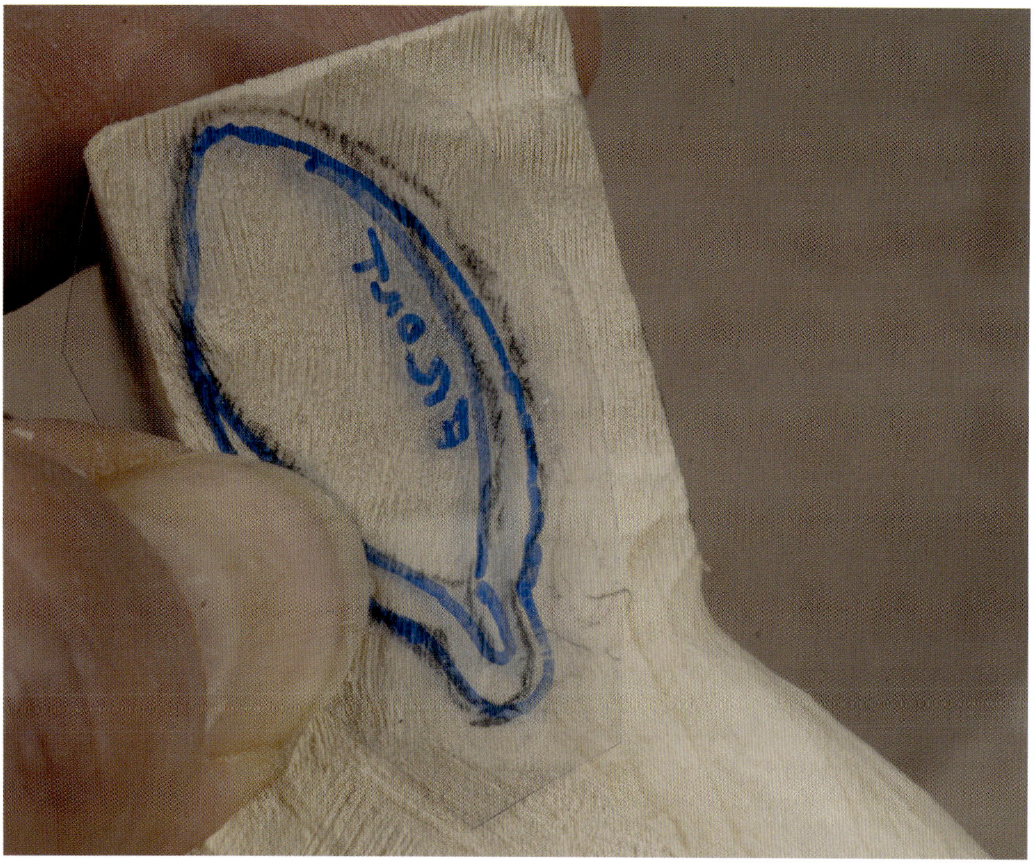

Figure 37. On the right ear, I flip-flopped the acetate and positioned the ear slanting backward.

Figure 38. Draw the front view of the ears. The widest part is 0.4" for roughing out purposes, since I will be using an aggressive bit, and the line tapers to the ear tip.

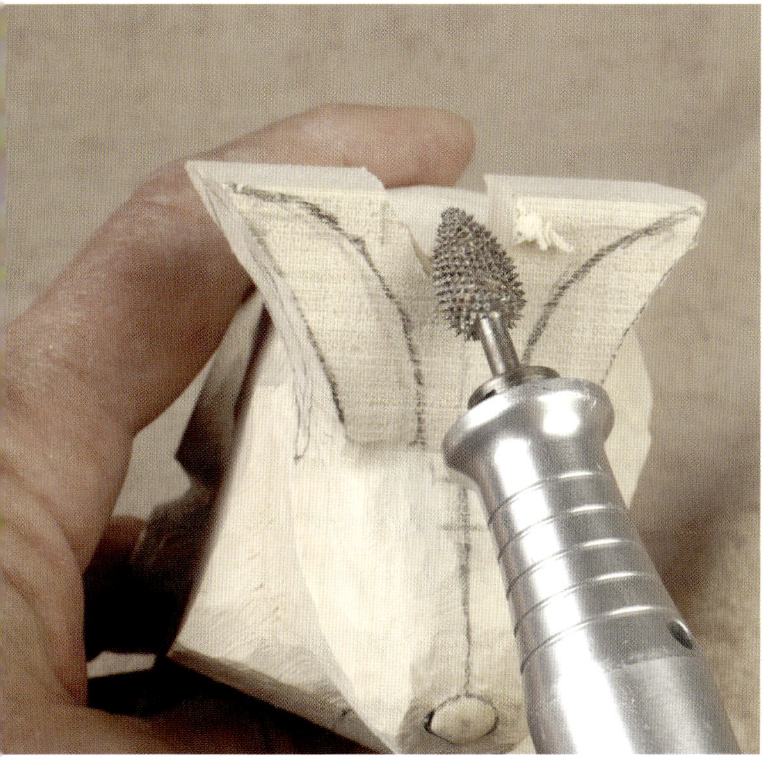

Figure 39. When working the wood out between the ears and cutting straight back, start in the middle and work towards each ear. Try not to start carving from a corner, since the bit can sometimes grab and run—either injuring your hand/fingers or dinging up the ear itself. I am starting out by using the small flame Typhoon carbide, but I will need to switch to the bud because of the tight space at the base of the ears.

Figure 40. Take this area almost down to the surface of the head. I did leave a little to finish up with the ruby carver.

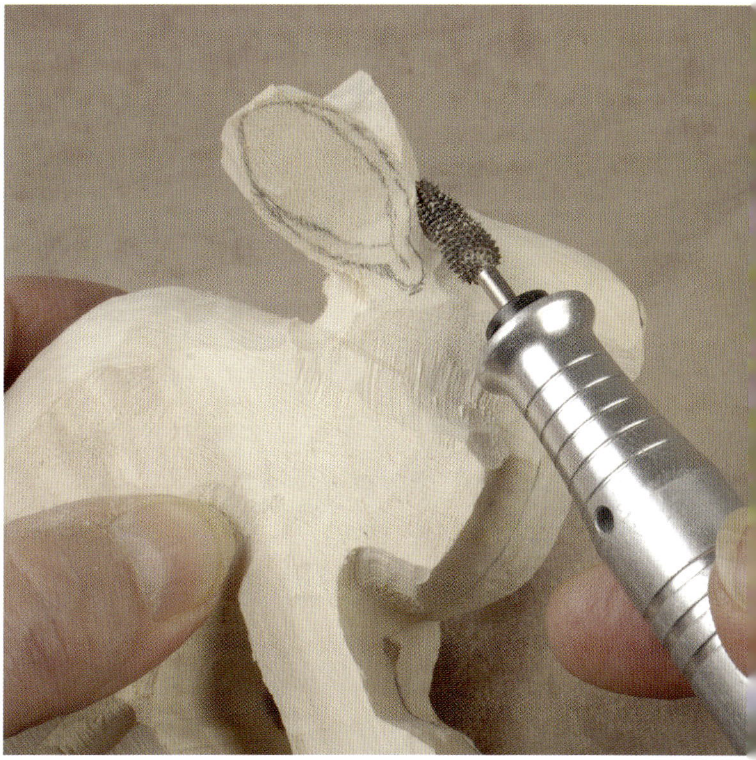

Figure 41. Start removing wood from in front of and behind the ears on the profile view and make the cuts straight in towards the middle of the head. Cut near the drawn line but not right to it. Leave a little bit for the final cuts with the ruby carver.

Figure 42. Using the pear-shaped ruby carver bit (RC-23), remove the rest of the wood right the ear line.

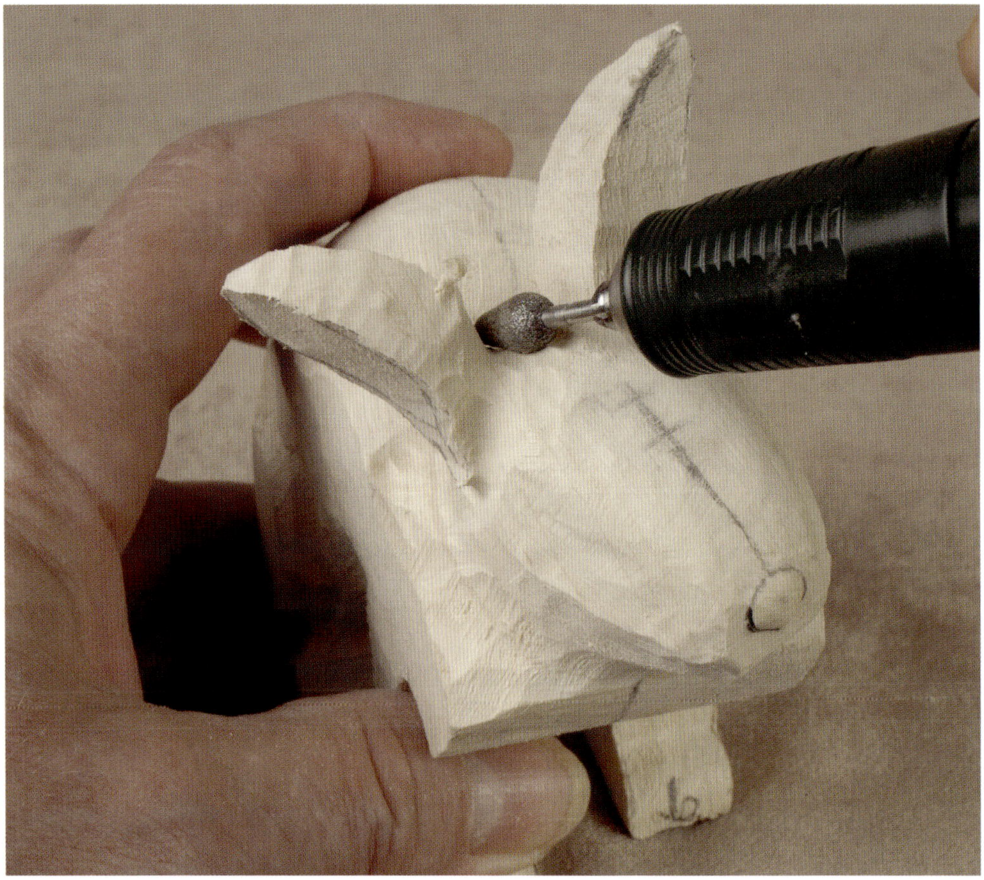

Figure 43. Channel around the base of the ear and blend the channel up the ear on that side and out onto the head of the other side.

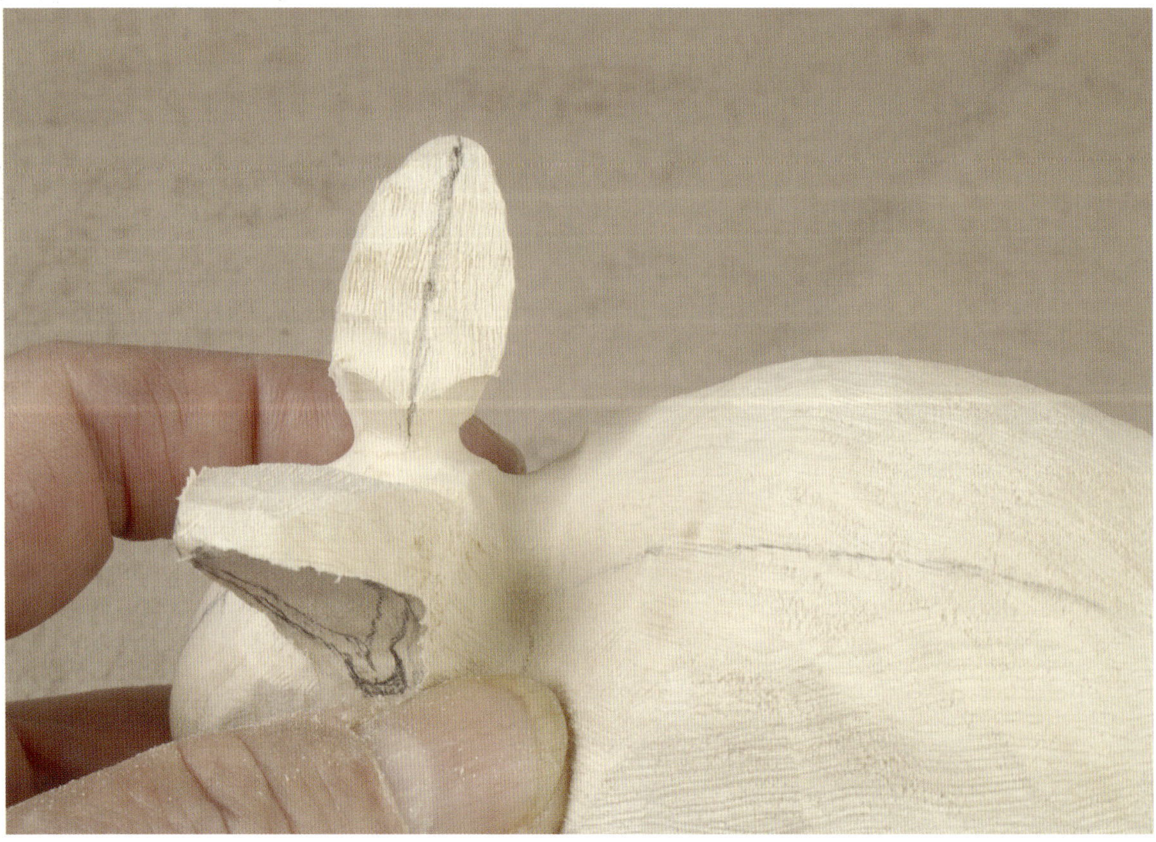

Figure 44. Draw a centerline on the backside of the ear.

Figure 45. Remove the excess wood off the backside of the ears. The area is rounded right at the centerline, and, every-so slightly, it rounds to the ear edges. It almost appears angular. We will be doing some more work inside of the ears but not just yet. Once you have the inside ear details done, it will make the ears significantly more fragile, and it is best to leave that until more of the shaping is done.

Figure 46. Make sure that the head rounds from the top and on around to the back of the neck.

Figure 47. Using the calipers, check the thickness of the ears at the base, middle, and tip to make sure both ears are the same. Adjust if necessary.

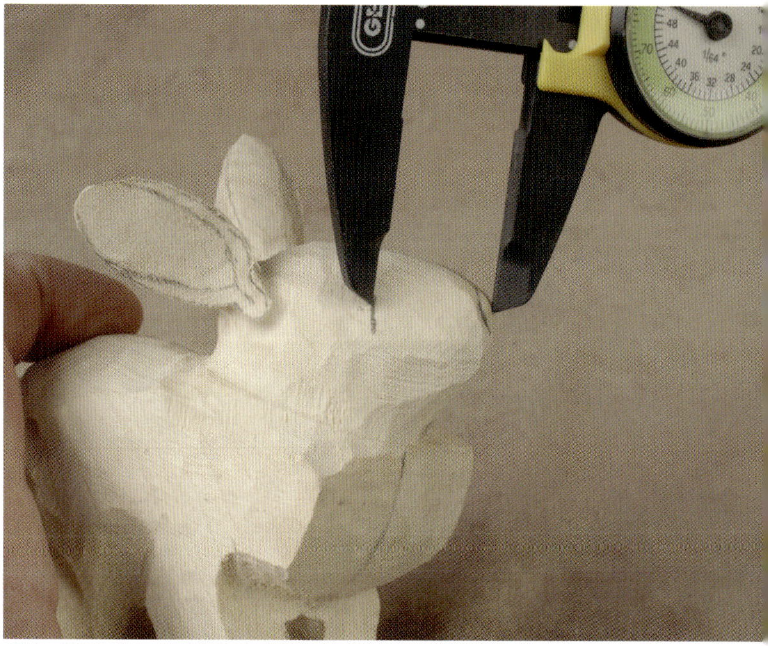

Figure 49. Measure and mark in with a vertical line 0.8" from the end of the nose. Do both sides and check from the top plan view to make sure the lines look even.

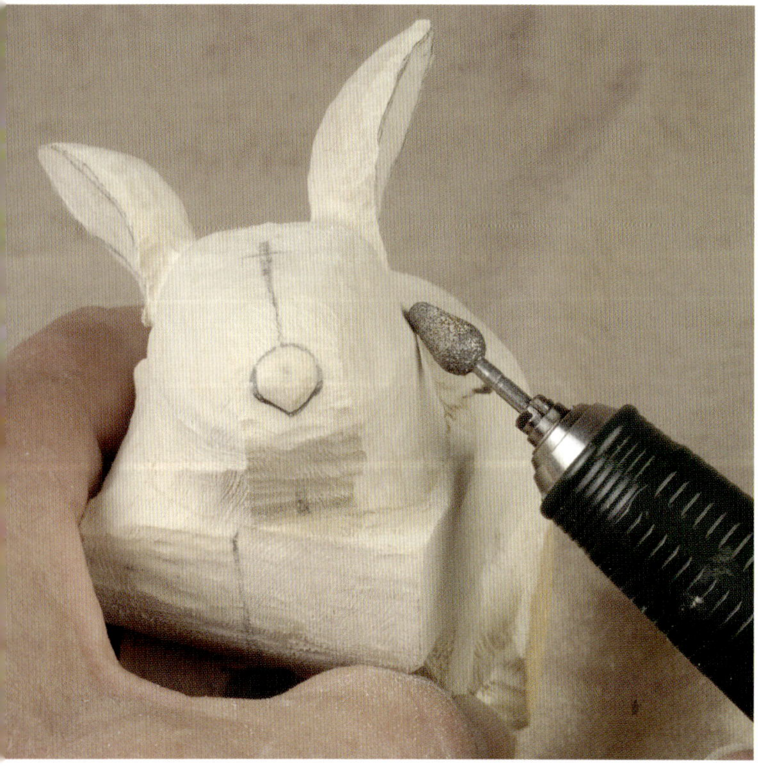

Figure 48. Blend the sharp angles along the sides of the face into the cheek and muzzle areas.

Figure 50. Draw in the cross mark as shown in the photograph. If you are right-handed, do the right side of the bunny first. Do the left first if you are left-handed.

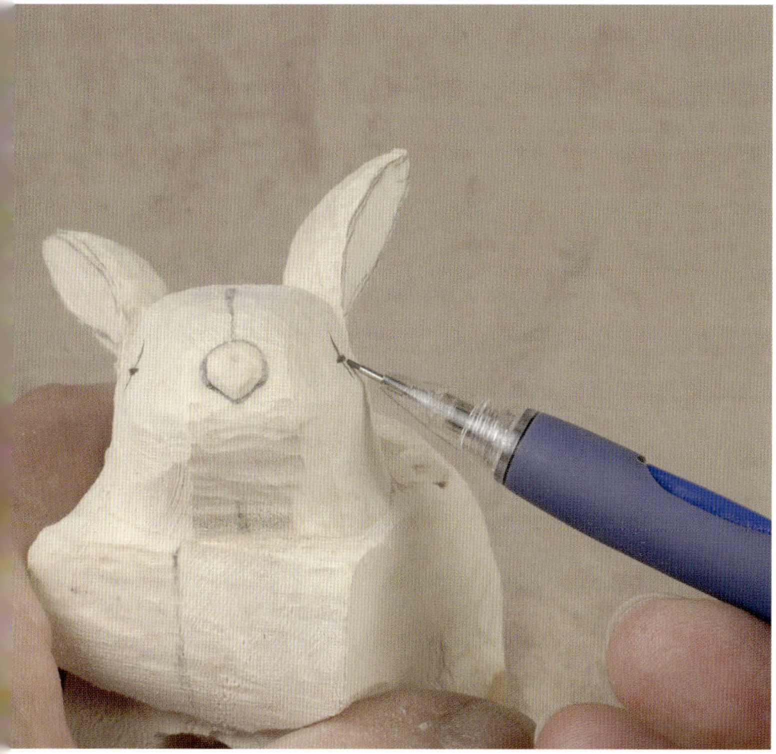

Figure 51. Holding the head of the bunny level, draw in the opposite side even with the first one. Draw a 6mm circle around both crosshairs and check from all views that the eyes are even.

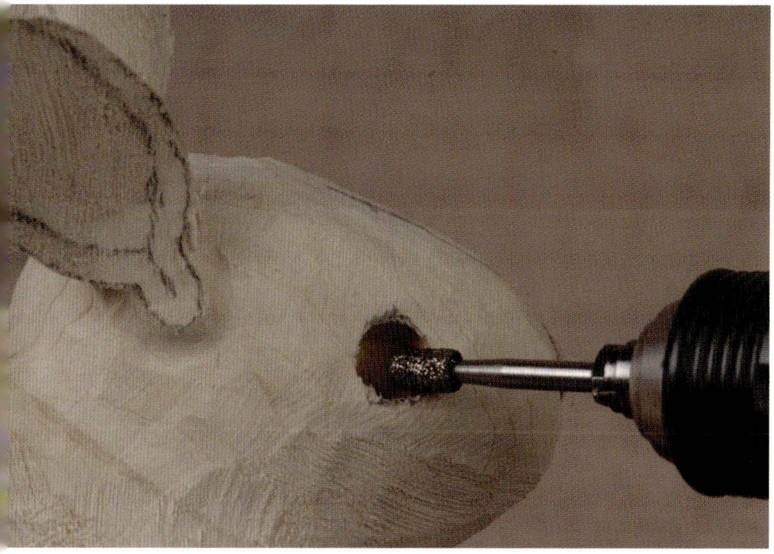

Figure 52. Using the slightly domed straight-sided ruby carver (RC-18), drill the eye holes at lease twice the depth of the thickness of the eyes.

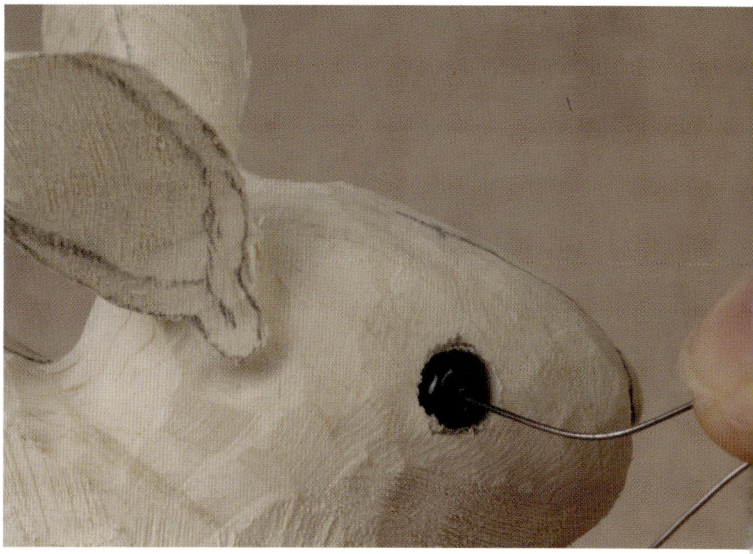

Figure 53. The extra depth is necessary since we will be cutting into the corners and lessening the length of the holes. Make sure both eyes fit in both holes. There is usually a small discrepancy in the size of most pairs of eyes.

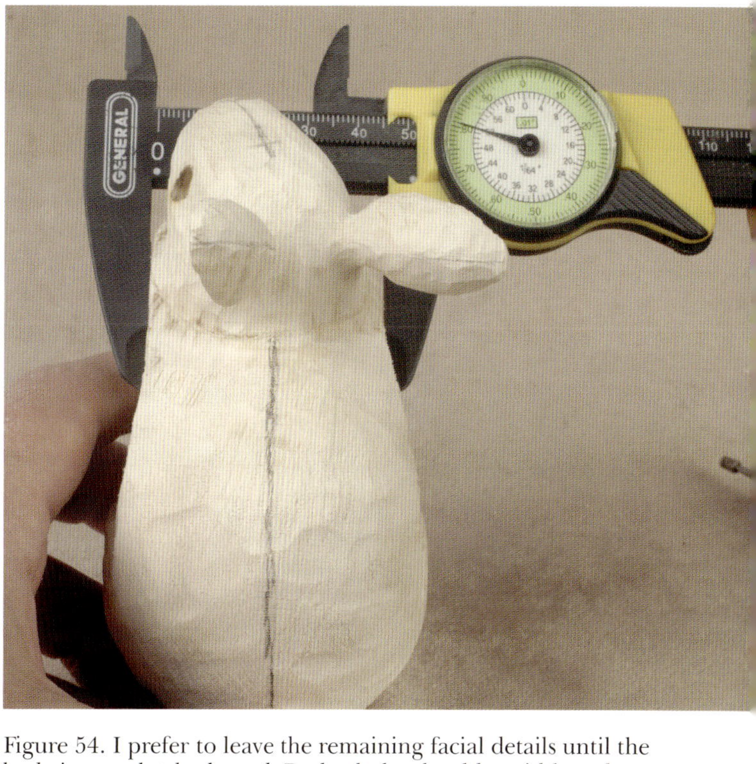

Figure 54. I prefer to leave the remaining facial details until the body is completely shaped. Recheck the shoulder width and make sure that it is 1.8" wide at this time. The shoulders will be slimmed up a little more as we work on the neck. My bunny's shoulders seemed to grow overnight. Note the tapering from the haunches to the shoulders along the back.

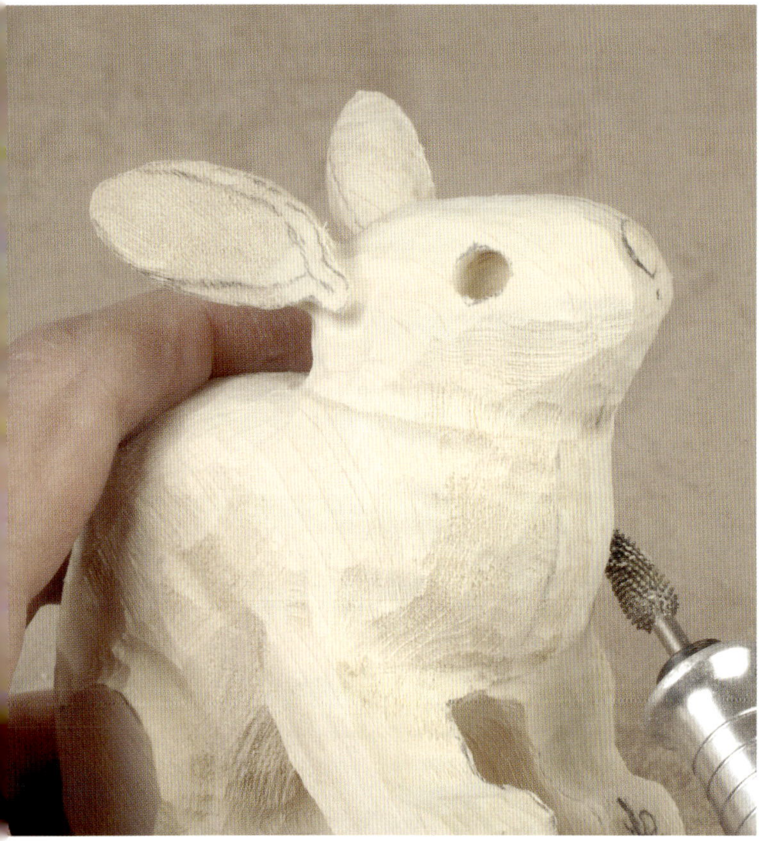

Figure 55. Using the bud Typhoon carbide bid, round over the chest area. More will likely need to come off the upper chest when we thin the neck.

Figure 56. To thin the neck, use the bud Typhoon bit and take the neck down to 1.3" from front to back. More will need to come off the front of the neck than the back. Make sure you blend the neck into surrounding upper chest, shoulders, and upper back.

Figure 57. Thin the neck to 1.2" from side to side. Blend the neck into the shoulders, upper chest, and upper back.

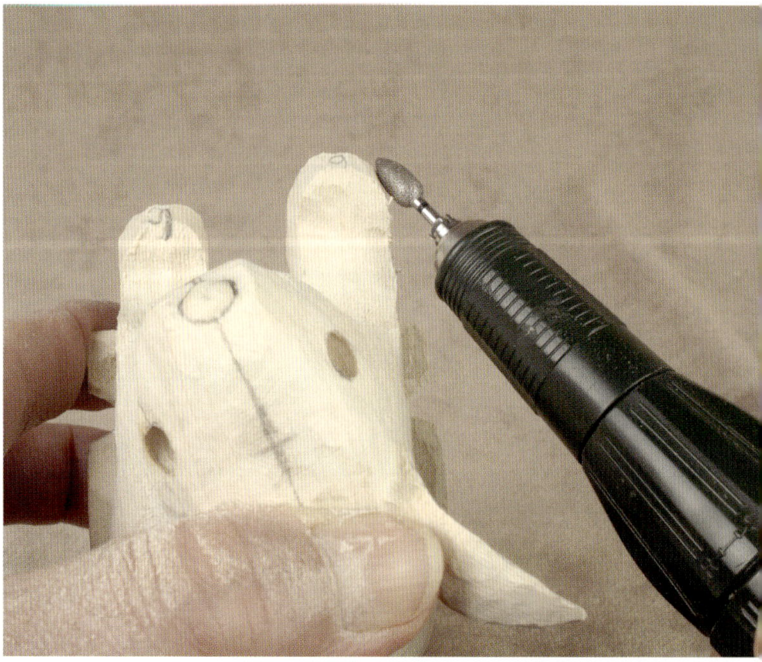

Figure 58. Using the #3 flame ruby carver (RC-25), round the ends of the front paws.

Figure 59. Using the pear-shaped ruby carver (RC-23), round over the paws from side to side and from the wrist to the toes. Round over all the sharp corners on the forelegs.

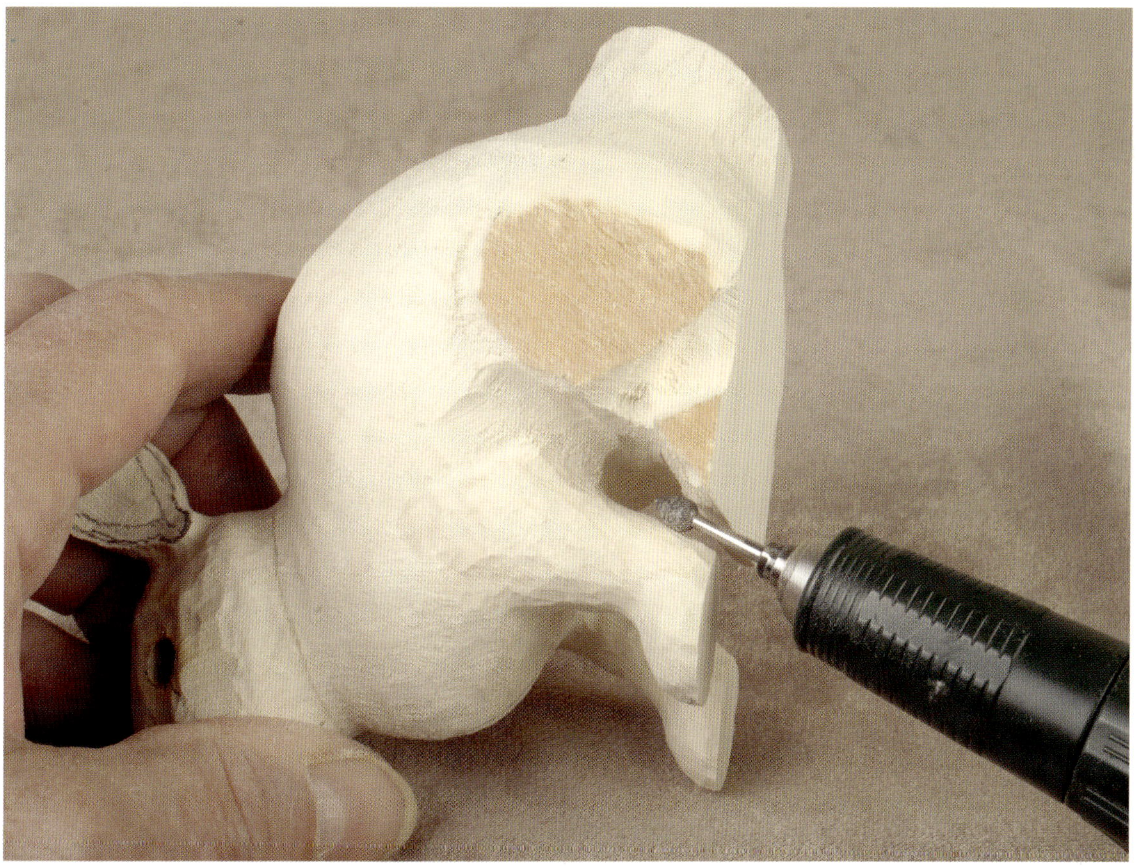

Figure 60. The larger pointed-ball ruby carver (RC-17) is a great bit to use in rounding behind the left foreleg where the hind paw is so close.

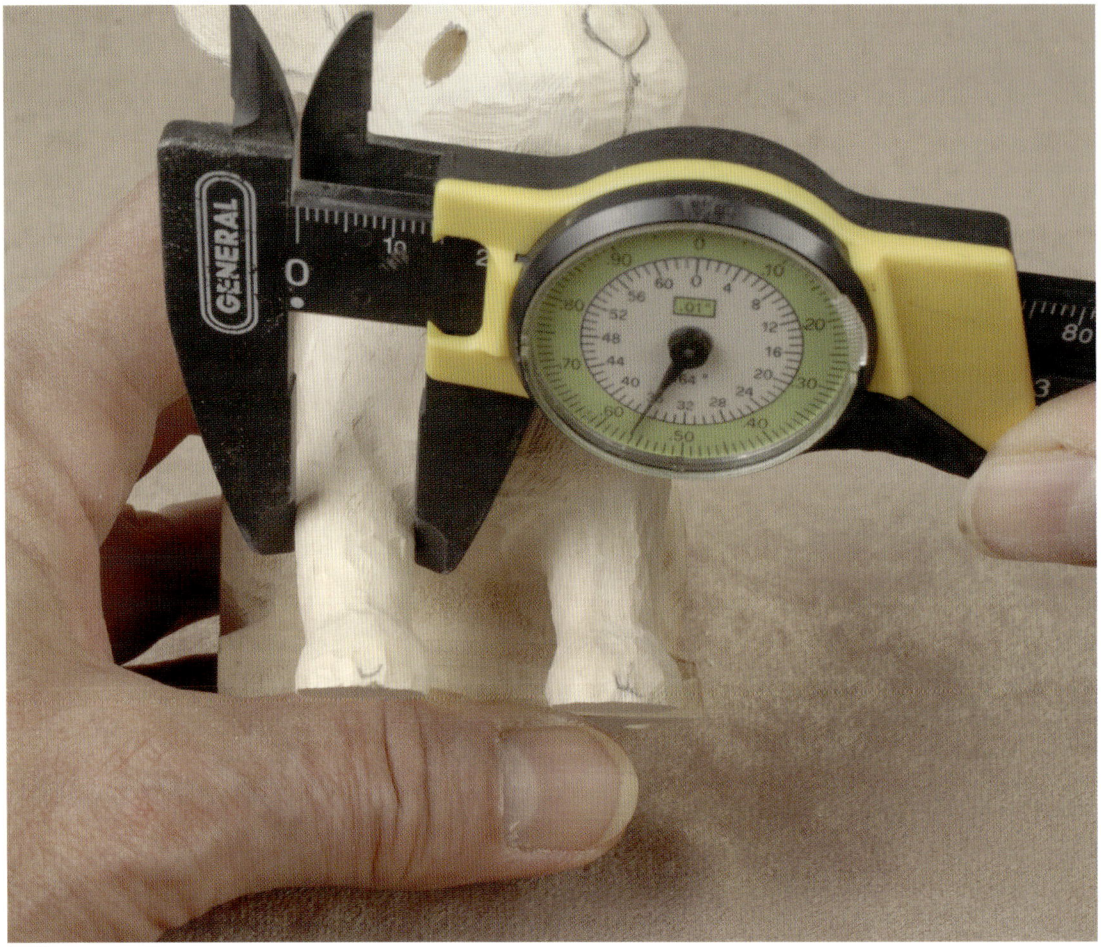

Figure 61. Make sure that both legs and paws are the same dimensions. The top of the foreleg is 0.56" to 0.58" wide.

Figure 62. There is a slight depression at the wrist (the juncture where the foreleg meets the paw). The width is 0.48".

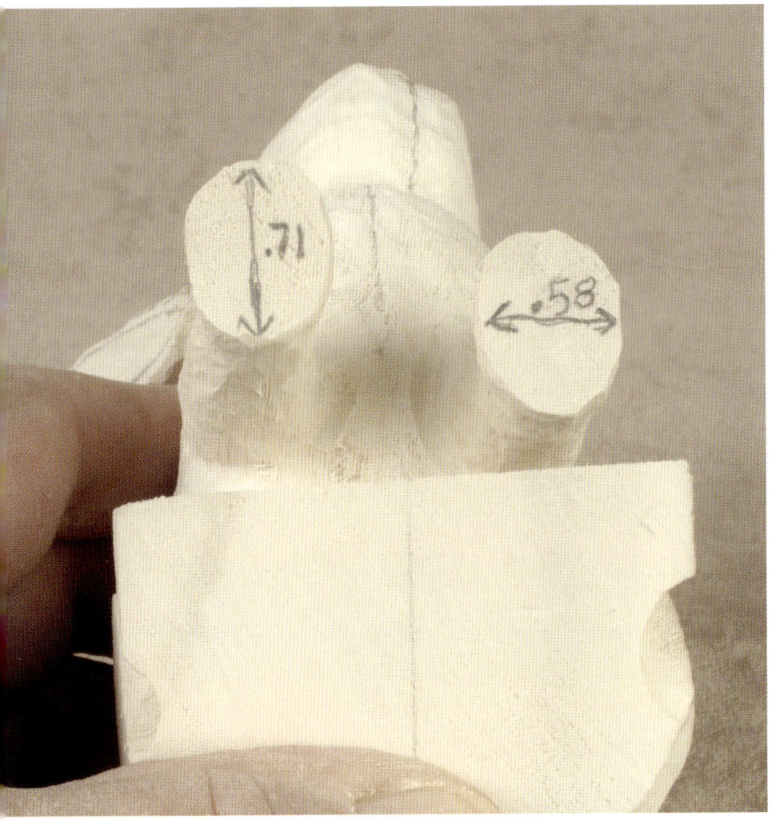

Figure 63. Make sure the bottoms of the front paws are the same size and shape. Each paw should be 0.71" from front to back and 0.58" from side to side.

Figure 64. Using the tip of the pear-shaped ruby carver (RC-23), carve a shallow channel around the sides of the breast and the inside of the upper front legs. Blend the edges of the channel in the breast sides and the upper belly.

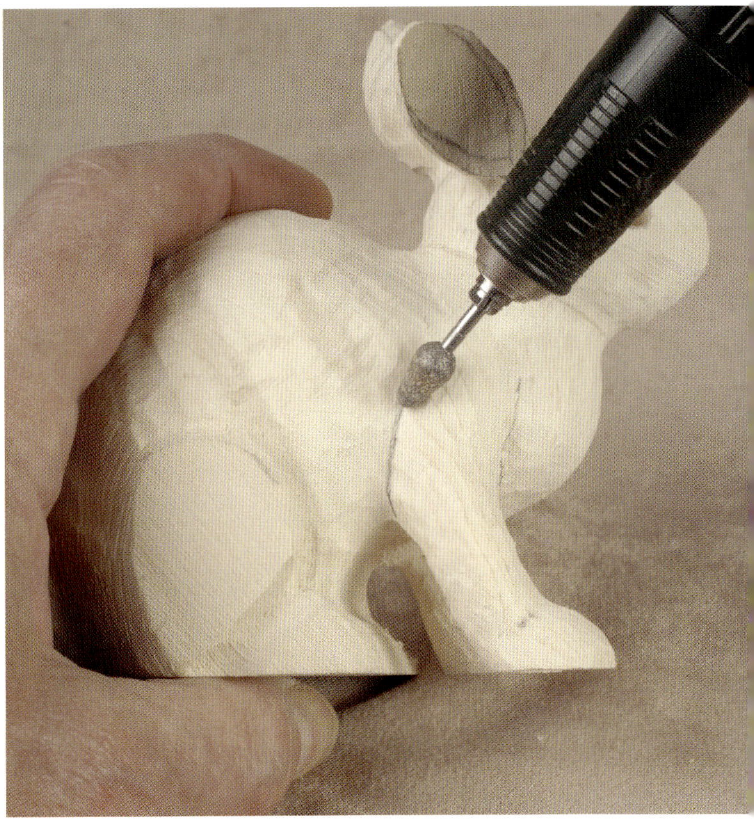

Figure 65. Because the right front paw is moved a little forward, you will see a little of the upper front leg on that side. Using the pear-shaped ruby carver (RC-23), carve a shallow channel and flow it out onto the top of the upper foreleg and out onto the bunny's side between the front and back legs.

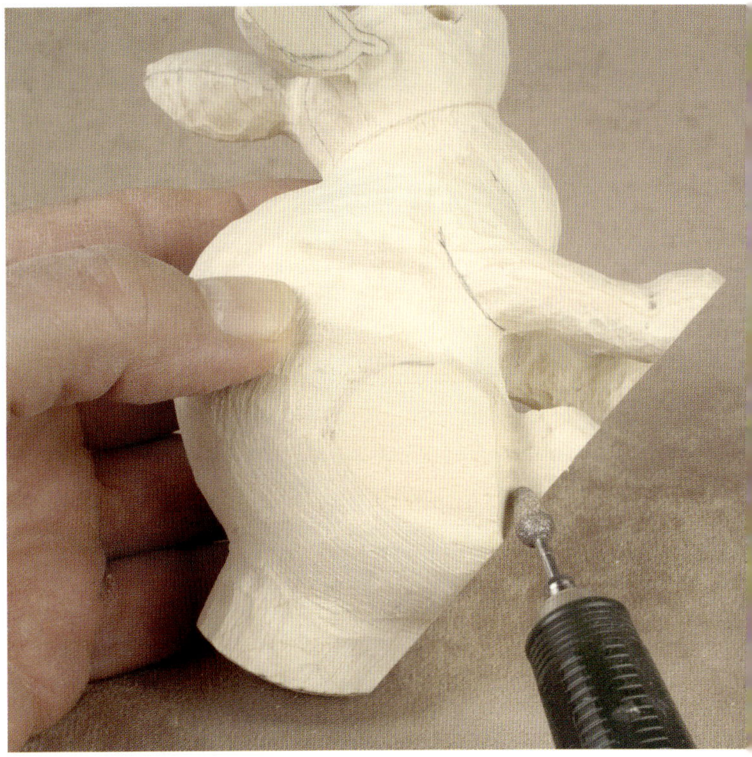

Figure 66. Deepen the channel between the haunch and hind paw. The side of the hind paw at the attachment point is 0.3" inside the outside of the haunch. Angle the outside of the toes back to the bottom of the channel.

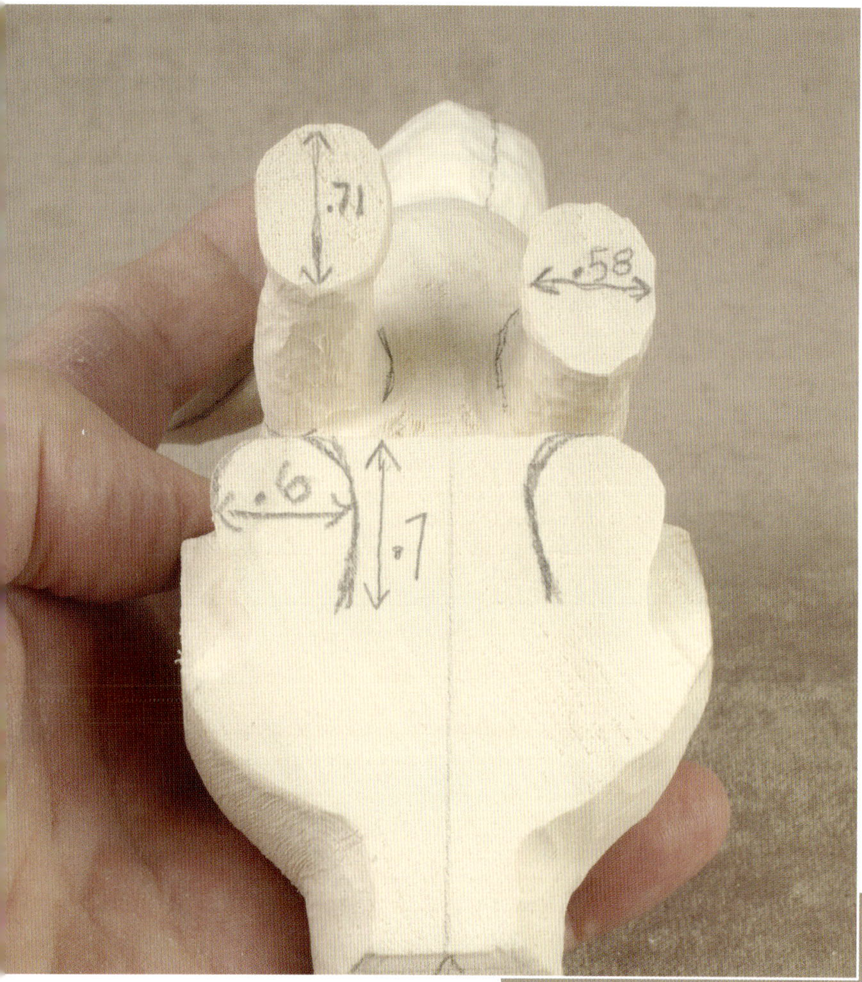

Figure 67. On the bottom of the blank, draw in the hind feet. The widest part of the toes is 0.6" and the length is 0.7".

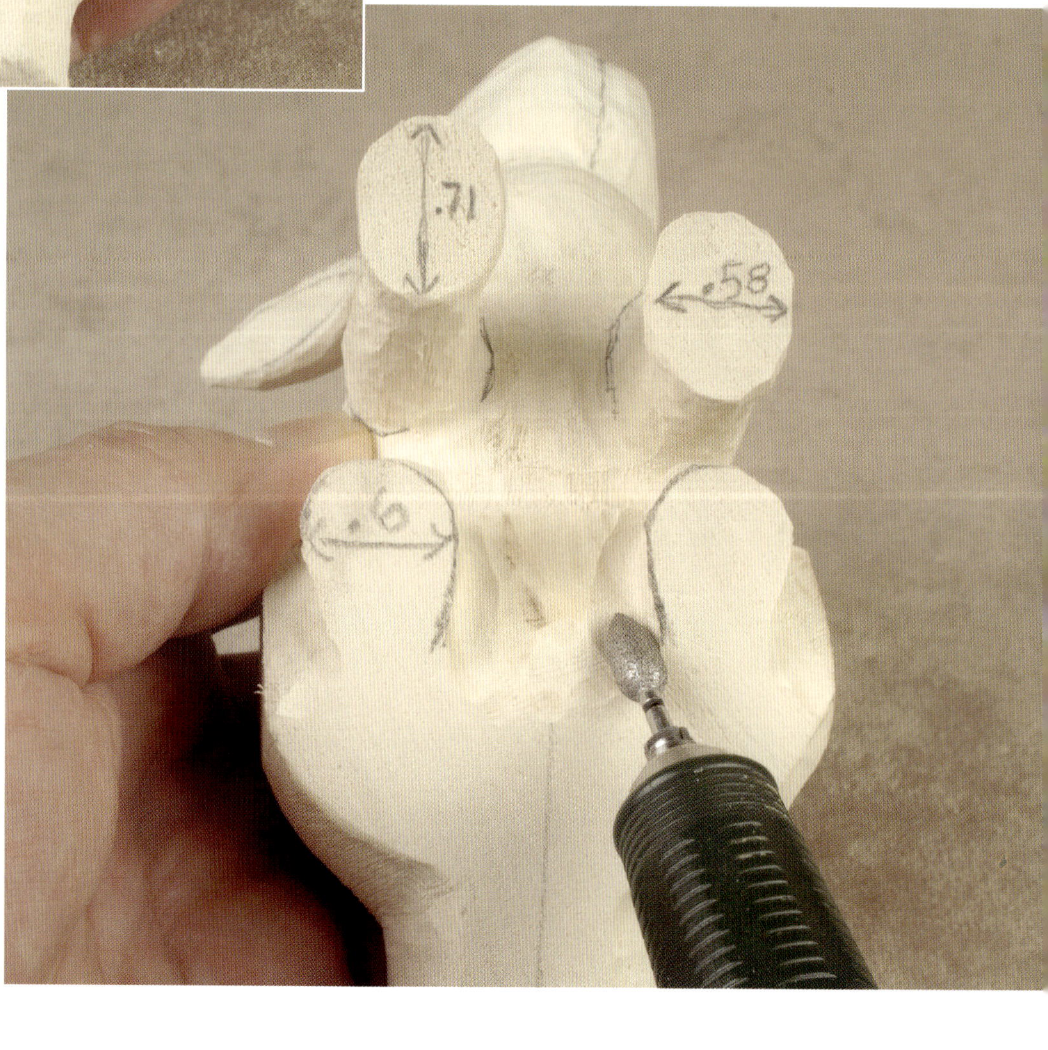

Figure 68. Cut away the waste wood in between the hind feet, and flare the hind belly slightly under the rump.

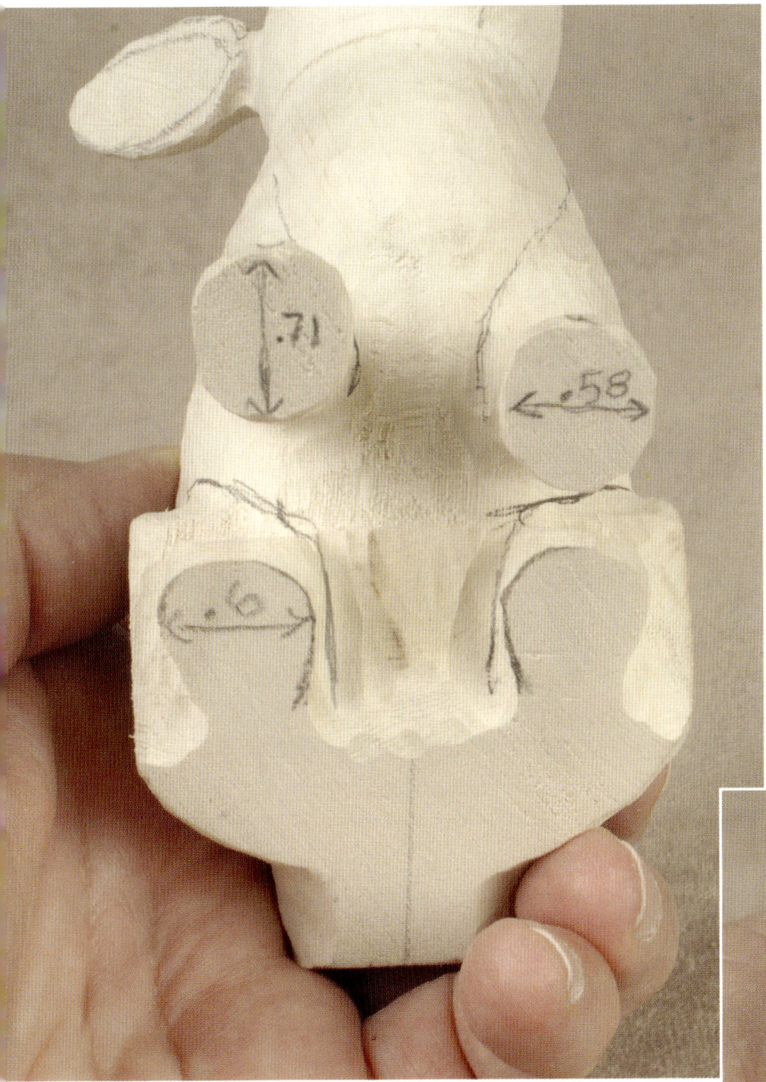

Figure 69. Draw a line from inside of the foot to continue in the haunch channel on both sides.

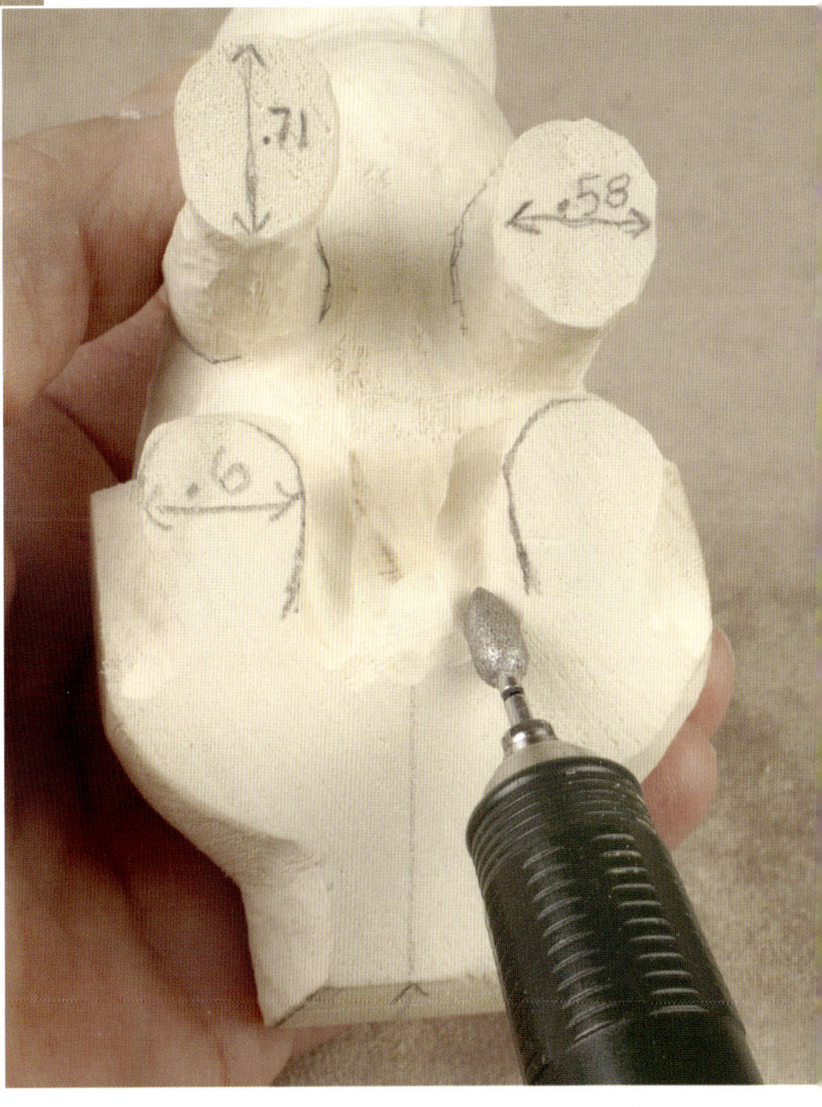

Figure 70. Start the channel at the inside of the hind paw, and push the #3 ruby carver (RC-25) forward around the arc as far as you can go.

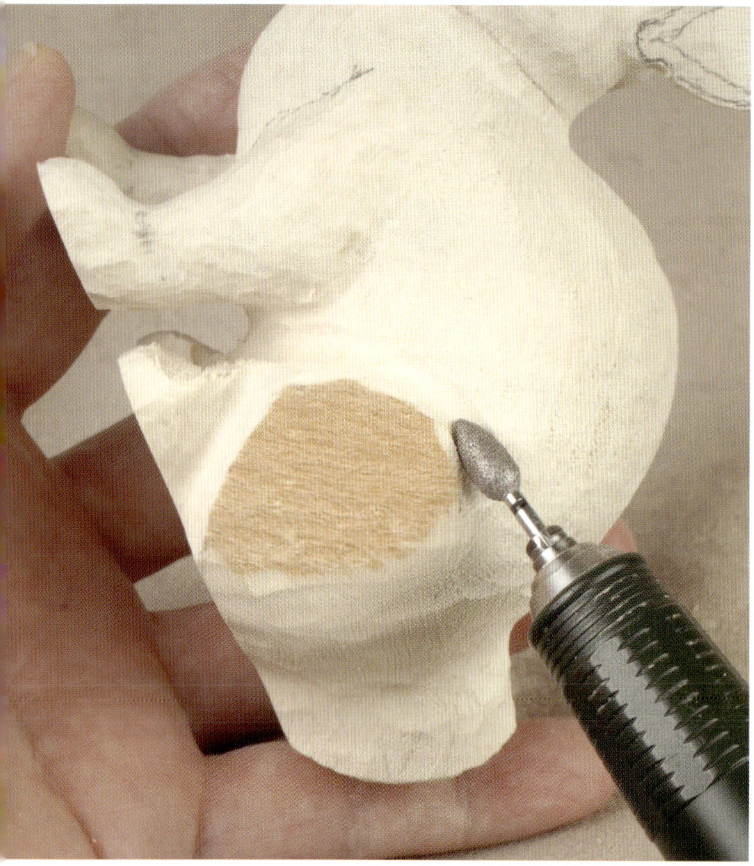

Figure 71. Then turn the bunny so that you can work on the side. From the stopping point you just cut, drag the #3 flame ruby carver (RC-25) around the rest of the curve and end on the top of the haunch. Do both sides.

Figure 72. Round over the entire haunch, making sure that there is NO flat area on the outside. Blend the back of the haunch into the back rump, and blend the area above the haunch toward the middle of the back.

Figure 73. No flats on the haunches! Each haunch rounds to the bottom of the blank.

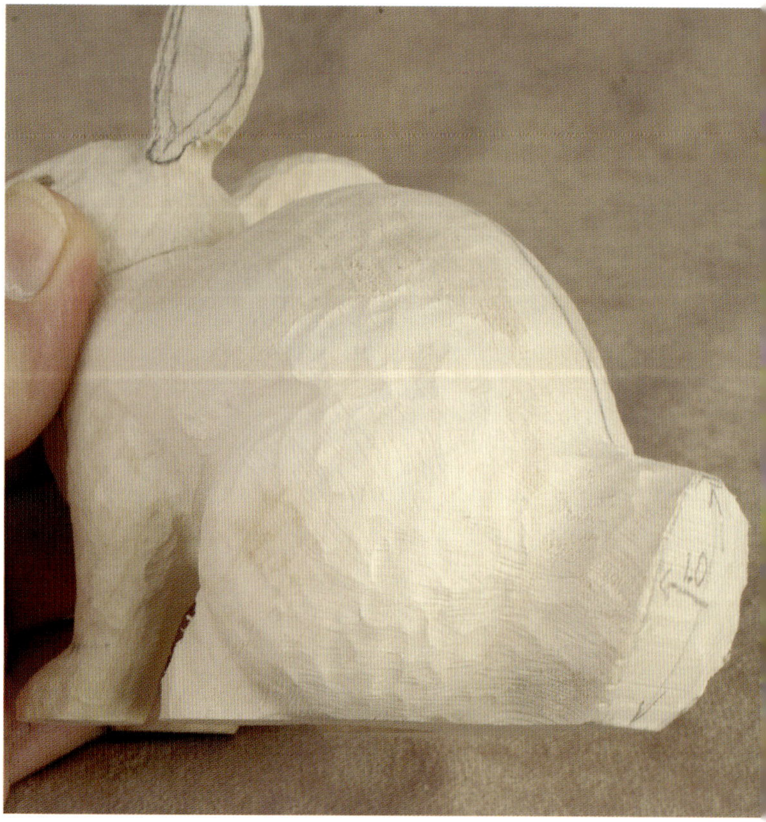

Figure 74. Here you can see the entire rounded haunch.

Figure 75. Flow the other side of the channel out toward the flank and the belly on both sides.

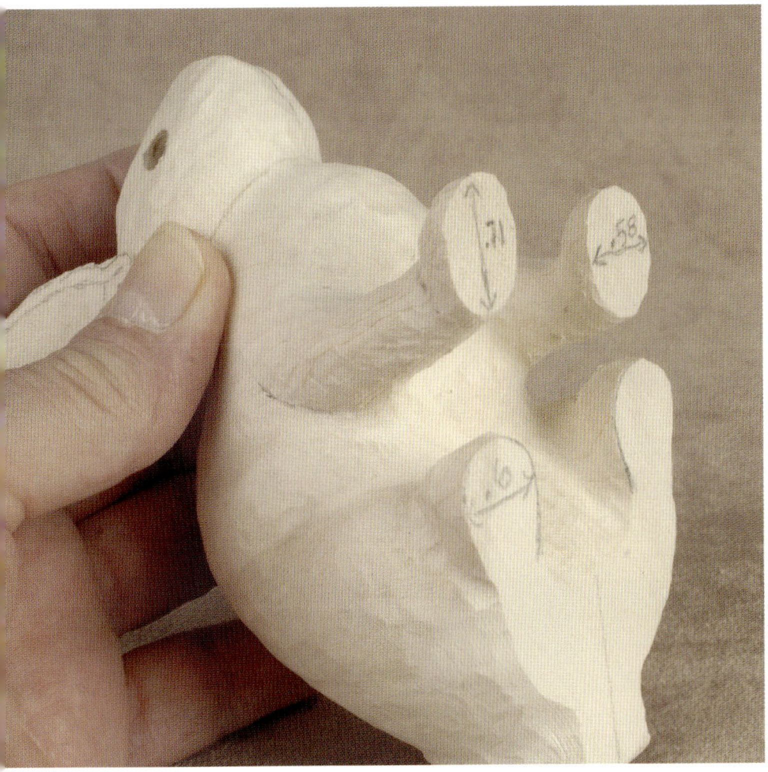

Figure 76. Make sure that the flanks round around to the middle of the belly. You may find it helpful to use the large pointed-ball ruby carver (RC-17), working from the chest and also working from the butt forward, to make sure there is some concavity to the belly itself.

Figure 77. Thin the thickness of the entire hind paws to 0.3".

Figure 78. The channel you made to thin the height of the hind paw needs to flow upward into the front of the haunch and out toward the tips of the toes. Round over the hind paws from back to front and side-to-side. Since there is not much clearance on the inside, it is easier to do that part with the small pointed-ball ruby carver (RC-16).

Figure 79. Draw in the front paw toes. You need 4 lines for 5 toes. The toes are approximately 0.1" wide. Draw the middle toe first. Then divide what is remaining on the left in half and put a line, and do the same on the right—this gives you 5 toes.

Figure 80. A bunny has 4 toes on the hind paws. You need 3 lines for 4 toes. Draw a line down the middle of each hind paw. To the right of that line, divide that space in half and do the same for the left side of the centerline.

Figure 81. Draw the #1 flame ruby carver (RC-19) down each toe line. On the hind toes, you will likely have to work from inside the front paws in order to reach the inside lines.

Figure 82. Using the #1 flame ruby carver (RC-19), round over each of the toes on the front and hind paws. The inside toes on the hind paws are difficult to get to. I used the small pointed-ball ruby carver (RC-16) to be able to round the inside hind toes.

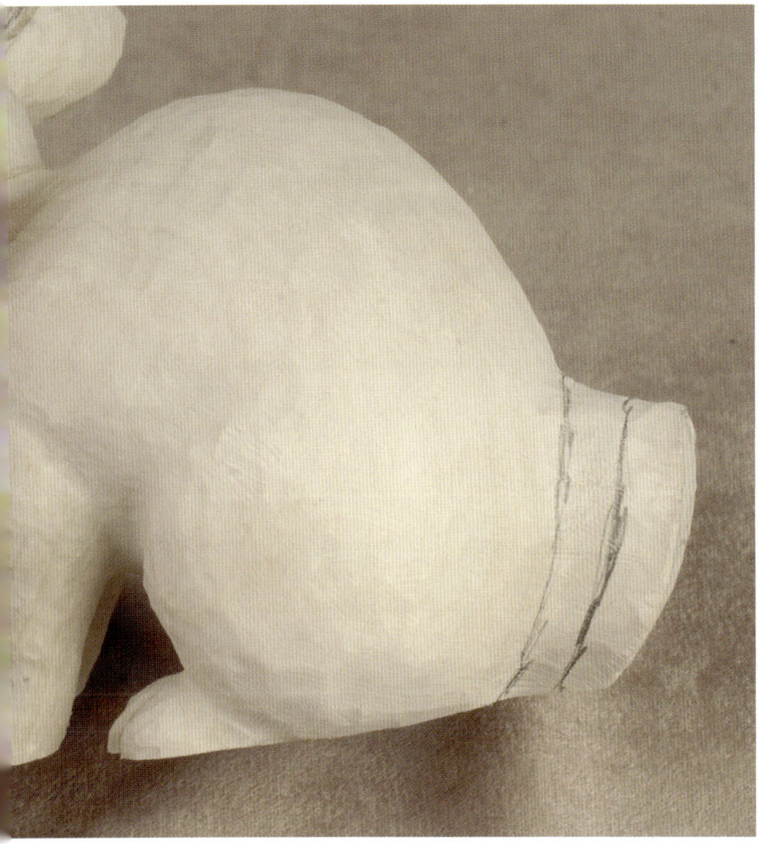

Figure 83. Now to work on the tail! Draw a line at the base of the tail, which is a continuation of the back rump. Optically divide this thickness in half, and draw a line around the tail. Before proceeding, check the tail measurements. The width should be approximately 1.0" and the height about 1.0" to 1.5". Adjust your bunny's tail if necessary.

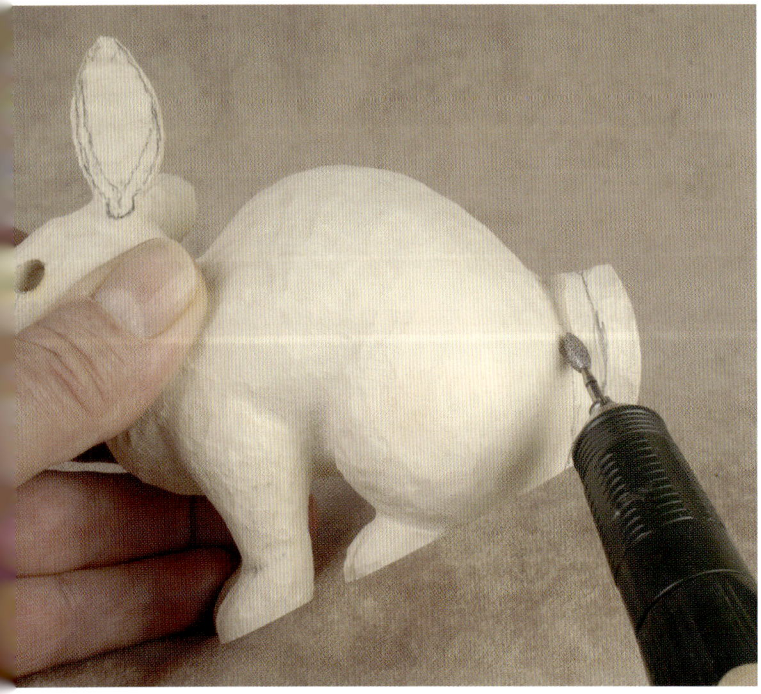

Figure 84. To separate the tail from the body, start cutting the line around the base of the tail with a #2 flame ruby carver (RC-20). Make sure that you don't cut into the body. The left side of the bit should just barely cut the line.

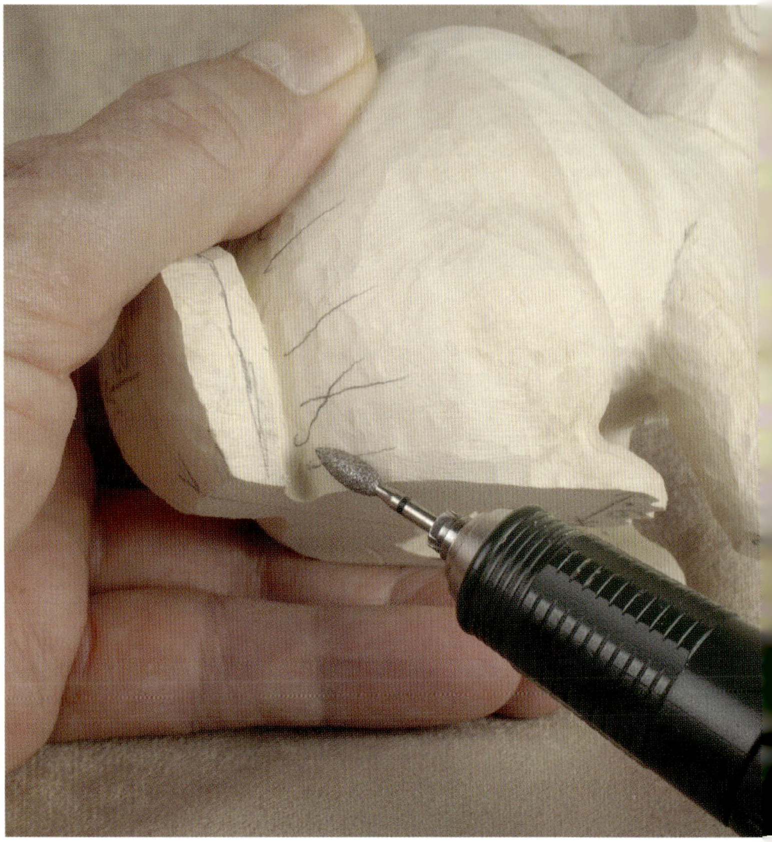

Figure 85. Finish cutting the channel all the way around. Drag the point of the #2 flame right along the crease, making a sharp-angled "v." Blend the body side of the "v" back towards the body and rump. If you can still see evidence of your original cut, you have not flowed the channel out enough.

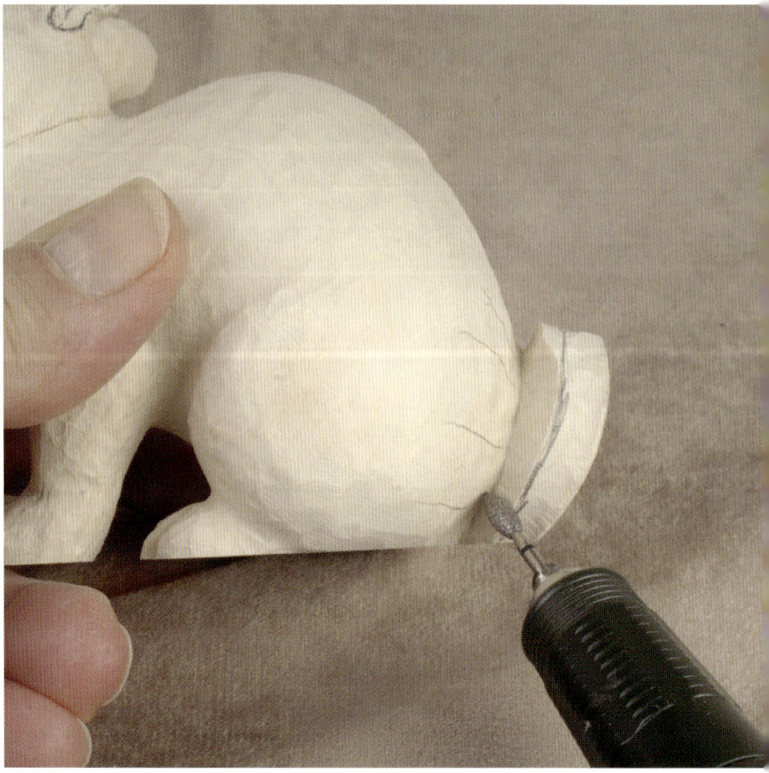

Figure 86. Next, the bottom of the channel should angle out to the centerline we put around the tail.

Figure 87. Round over the tail from a center-point to the outside edges. A # 3 flame ruby carver (RC-25) is useful for this procedure.

Figure 88. Before beginning the heavy contouring, check the outside of the tail to the outside of the breast area length. This measurement should be approximately 4.0". If your bunny's is longer than 4.0", adjust on the breast and/or on the tail. Drag a #2 ruby carver (RC-20) in curving and "S" curving strokes from the bottom and middle of the tail out towards its edges.

Figure 89. Also groove the underside of the tail. Actually, this is the top of the tail; when a bunny lays its tail down, this side is the top of the tail. Because this bunny has its tail raised up against the body, I am calling it the underside of the tail in this step.

Figure 90. Groove the breast in the same way as the tail. Work from the bottom and center of the breast and lower throat out towards the head and shoulders. Later, when we texture the bunny all over with the slightly domed, straight-sided cylinder ruby carver, we will knock most of the hard edges off that the #2 ruby carver left.

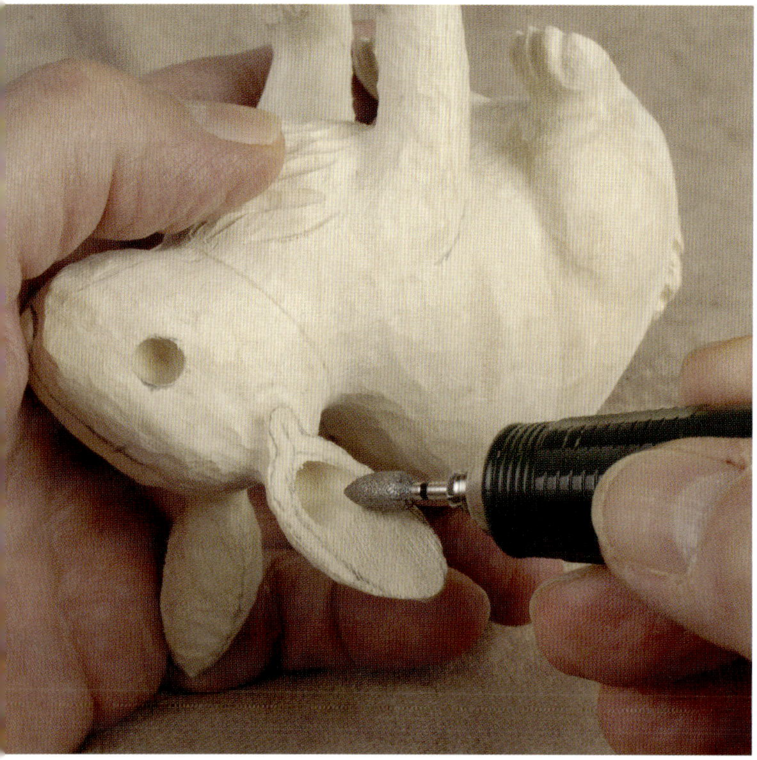

Figure 91. Using the #3 ruby carver (RC-25), begin to remove the excess wood from inside the ear. Make sure that you point the tip of the bit down towards the head.

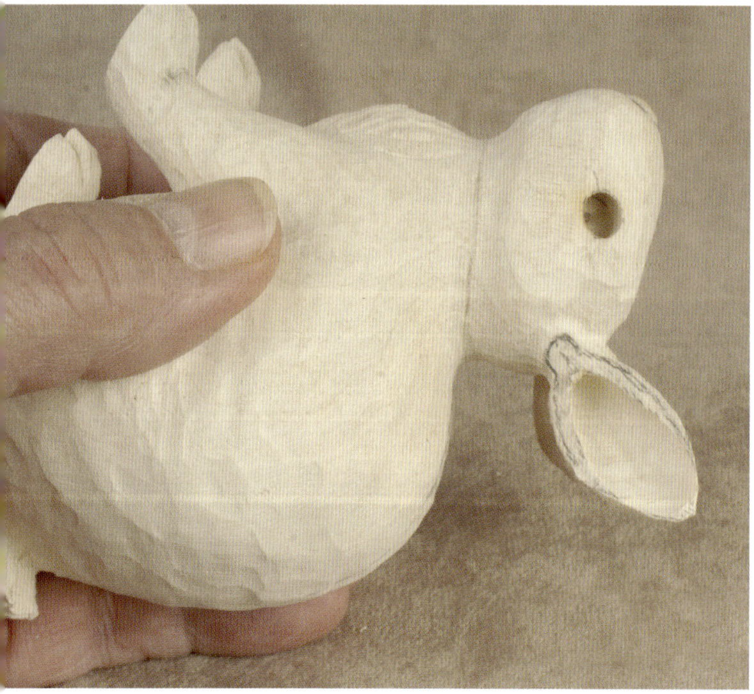

Figure 92. Work the excess wood from the entire inside of the ear leaving a concave contour. Hold the ear up to your adjustable light to make sure that you are not getting the ear too thin. It would be better to leave it a little thick than to make it too thin and go through to the other side. Work carefully here! Pull the concave surface lightly all the way to the top edge of the ear. Note that the front flange of the ear is higher than the back one. If you should get this area too thin, you can always patch the inside of the ear with some of the ribbon epoxy putty or some type of epoxy repair product.

Figure 93. Here you can see the pointed hole shape that the bit carved.

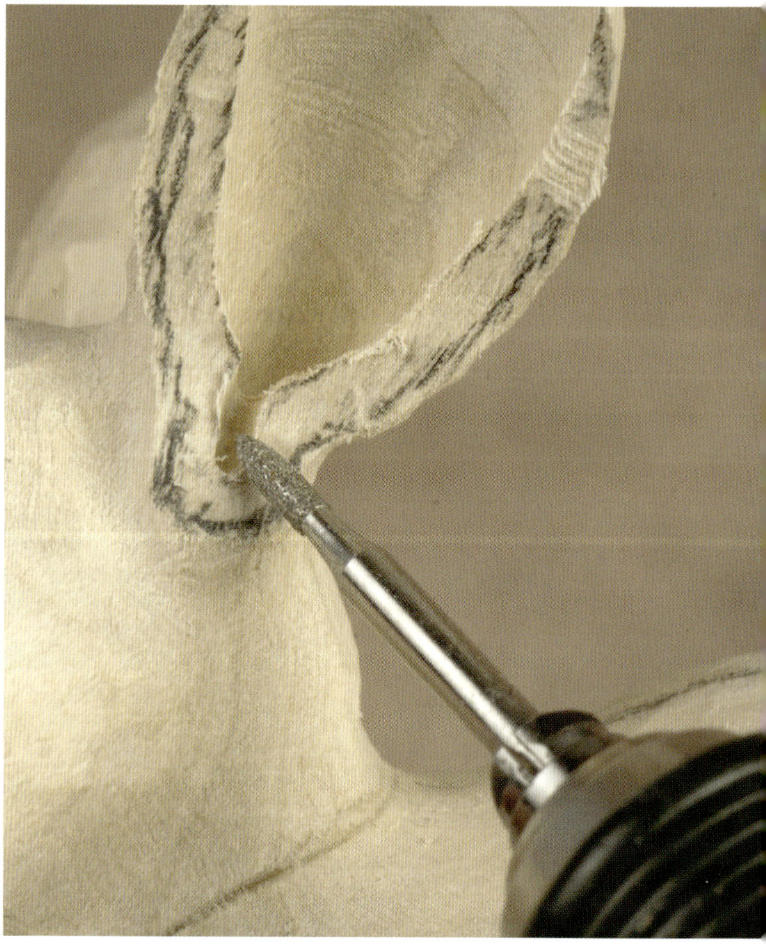

Figure 94. Use a very small detail diamond cutter to carve in the slit at the bottom of the ear.

Figure 95. The small pointed-ball ruby carver (RC-16) should be used to finish off the ear canal, which doesn't need to be very deep. Again, make sure that the point is pointed towards the bulk of the ear attachment into the head. The direction is down and in.

Figure 96. Using a large bullet-shaped stone, sand/smooth the inside of the ears. There are some fine hair lines inside the ear, but we will painting them in.

Figure 97. Roll over the outside edges of the bottom, front, and back edges of the ear.

Figure 98. Sand the outside of the ears smooth.

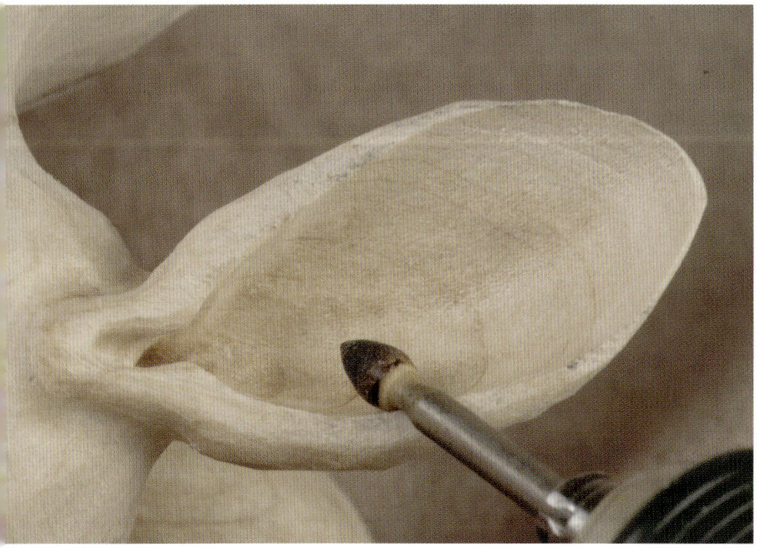

Figure 99. You can sand the deeper parts of the ear with a small pointed stone.

Figure 100. Blow the dust out of the bunny's ears and apply super-glue just to the inside of the ears. Loctite makes a brush-on super-glue that is very easily controlled for such gluing operations as this. Wait until the super-glue hardens before proceeding. You don't want sawdust to harden in the glue.

Figure 101. Round the muzzle and throat. Make sure the head/muzzle is balanced from all views.

Figure 102. Draw in dashes in the middle of the eye front and back. The front dash should be shorter than the back one. These are the lines that separate the upper eyelid from the lower one. The dashes should point from the ear to the nose. Do this on both sides.

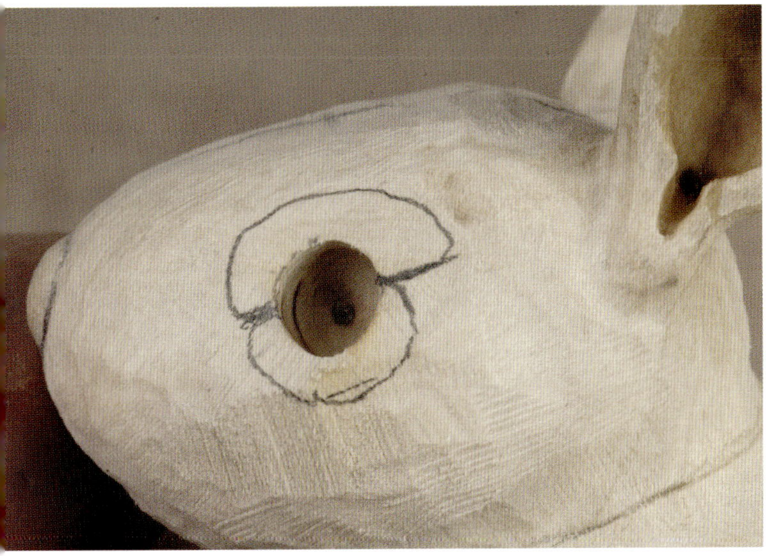

Figure 103. With the two eyelids meeting at the dashes, draw in the upper and lower eyelids. Note that the upper lid is longer and more full than the lower one.

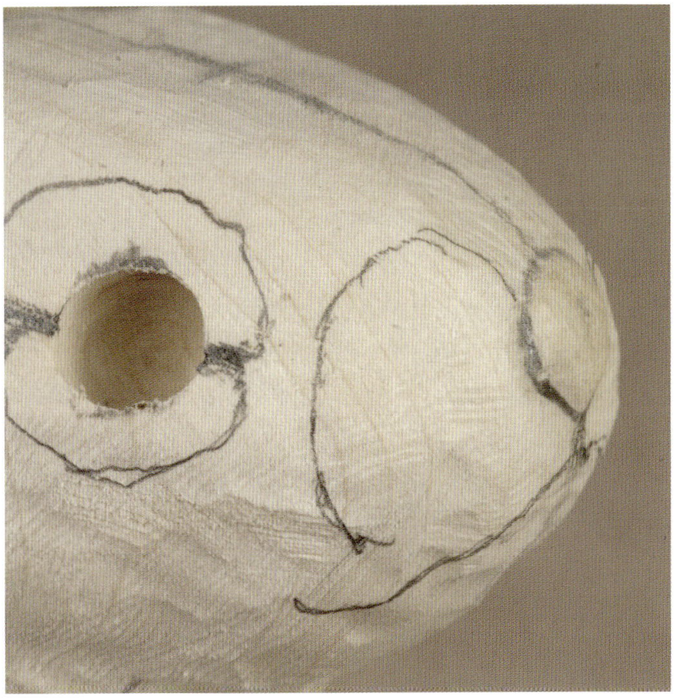

Figure 104. Draw in the whisker pads on both sides. The line starts from the back of the nose and curves around like a "C" on the right side and a backwards "C" on the left side. The lines do not reach the mouth line, which we are drawing next.

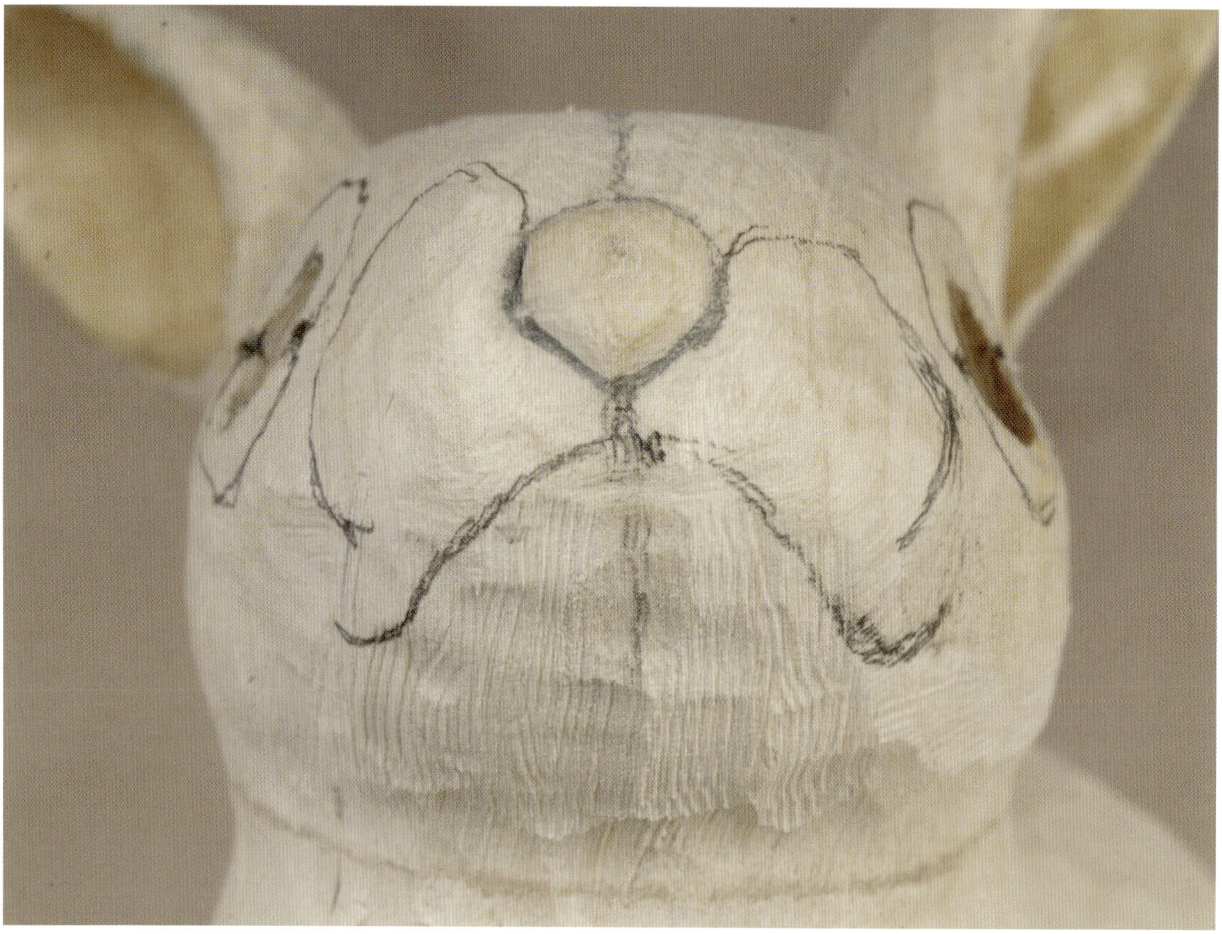

Figure 105. At the bottom of the nose, draw as short dash that delineates the little slit under the nose. Then draw the mouth symmetrically with a slight upturn at the backs of the line.

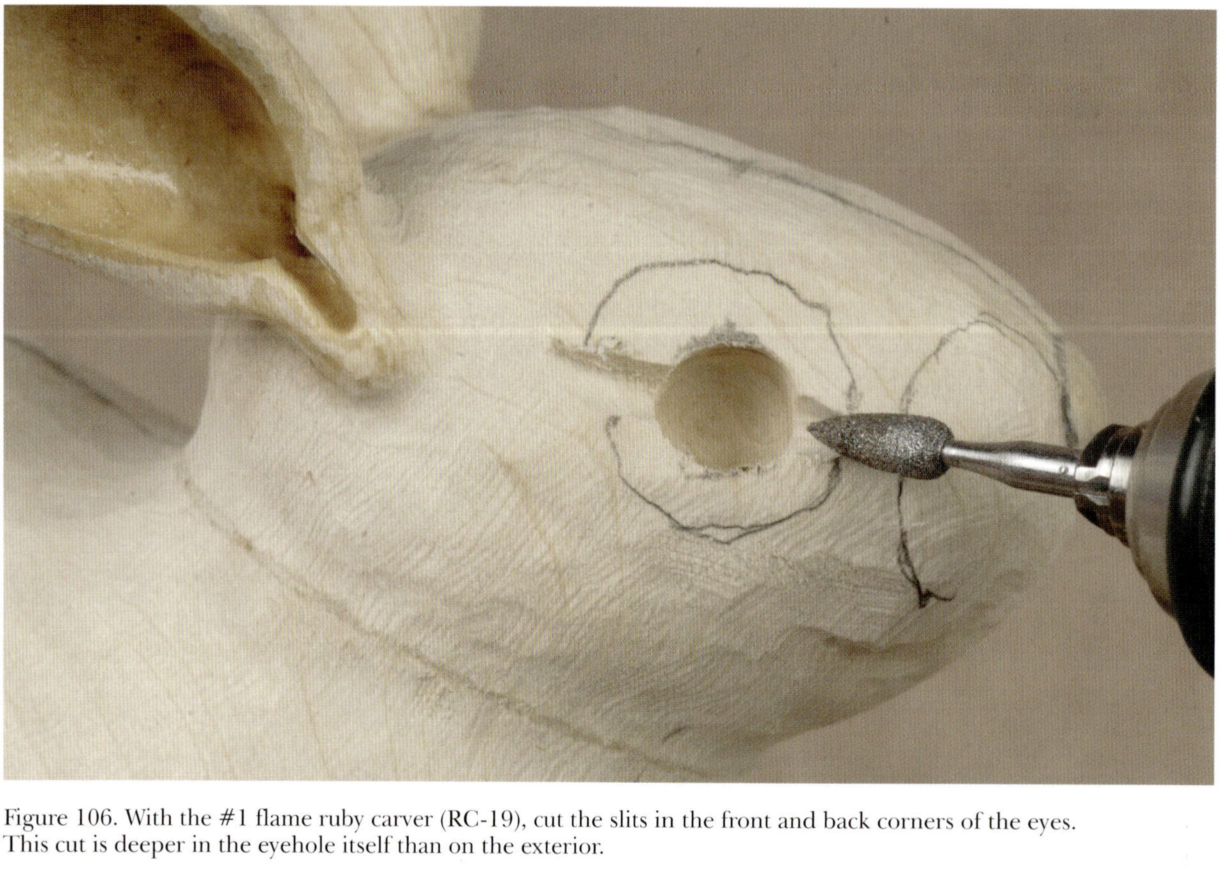

Figure 106. With the #1 flame ruby carver (RC-19), cut the slits in the front and back corners of the eyes. This cut is deeper in the eyehole itself than on the exterior.

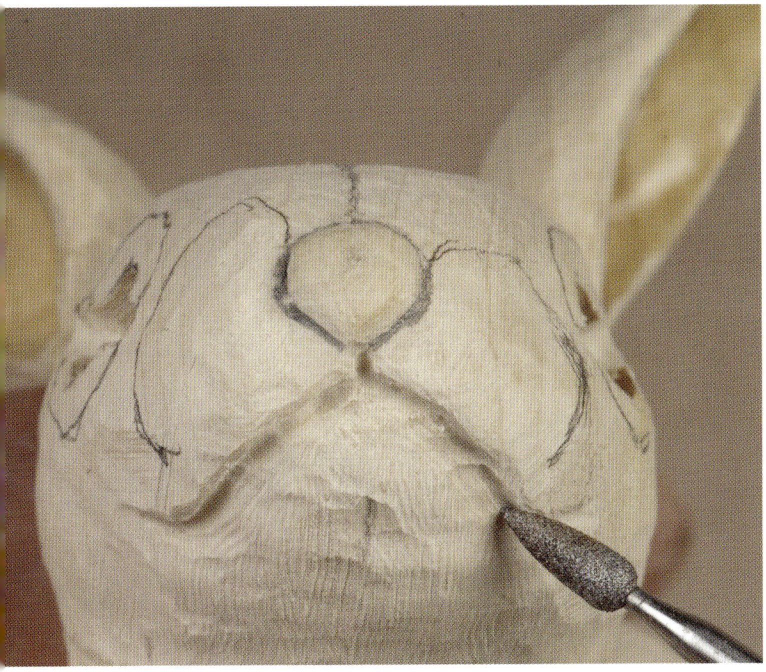

Figure 107. Because I'm right-handed, I start the mouth channel on the right side of the bunny's face, and then pull the bit around the mouth-line I've drawn. I drag the tip of the bit to create a sharp crevice. Flow the bottom/underneath part of the channel out on the chin, and lightly round over the sharp corner on the upper lip.

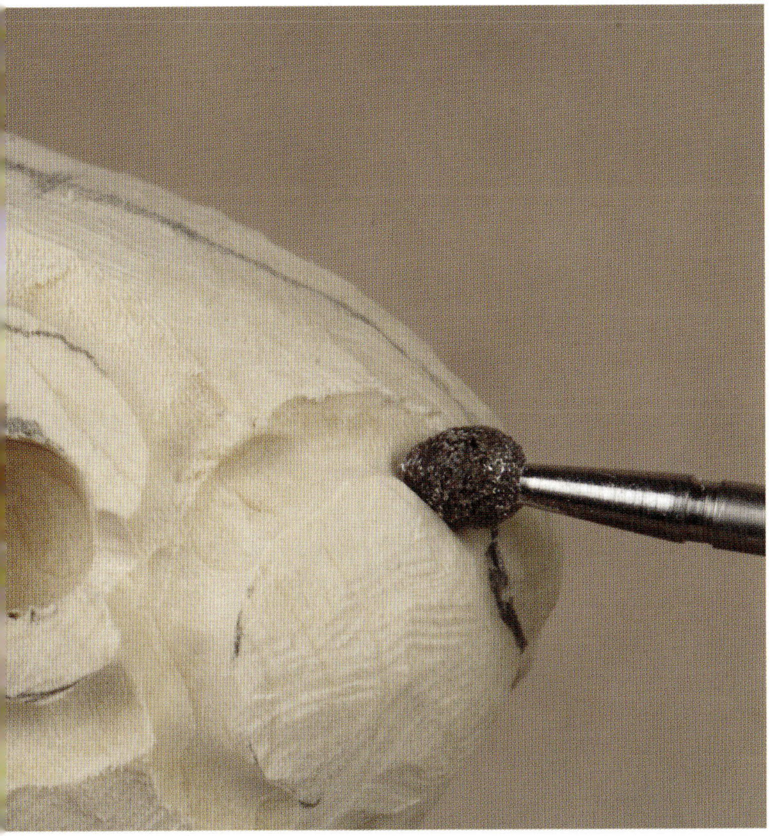

Figure 108. Use the small pointed-ball ruby carver (RC-16) to carve channels around the eyelids and the whisker pads. Lay the bit down so that you are using the diameter of the bit and not the tip. The channel for the whisker pad is the same part of the forward channels for the upper and lower eyelids.

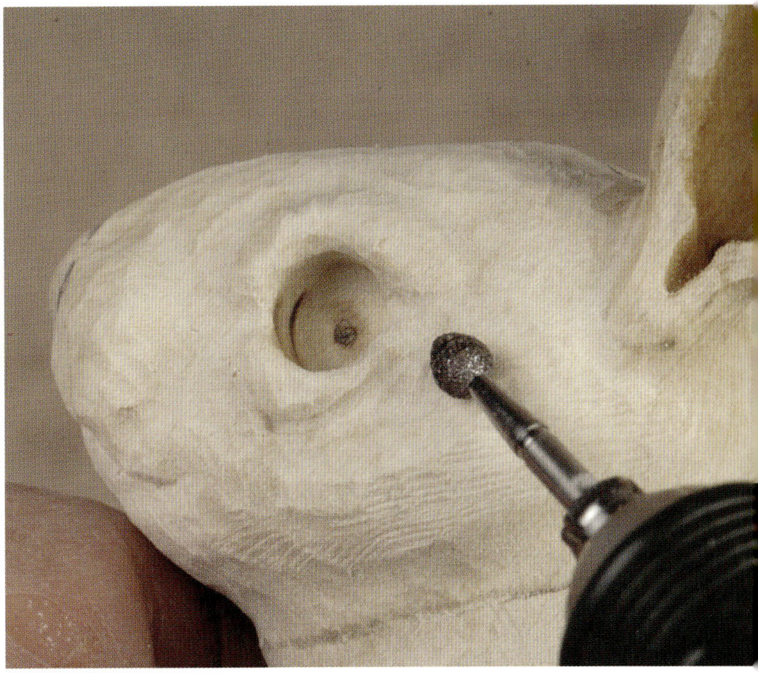

Figure 109. Round over both the upper and lower eyelids inside and out, and blend them into the surrounding area. Round over the whisker pads and blend them as well.

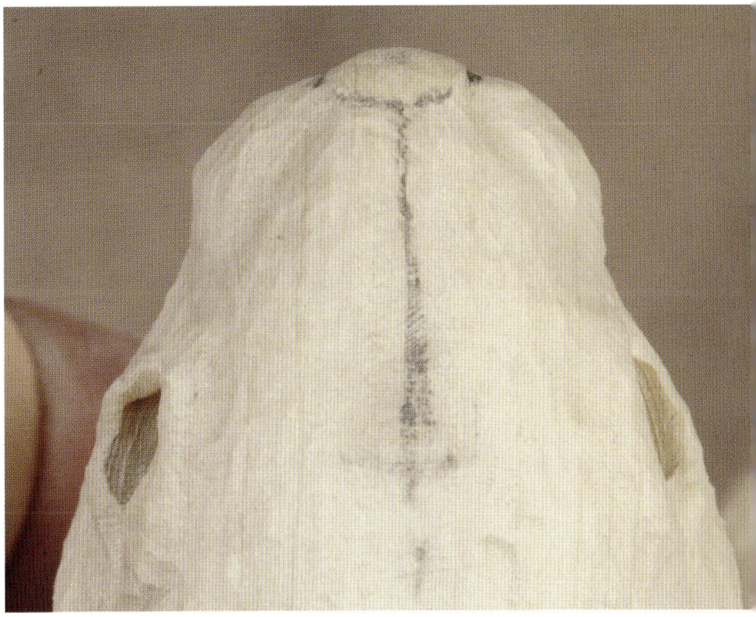

Figure 110. Check the head from all views to make sure the muzzle and the head are symmetrical and balanced.

Figure 111. Draw in the flow lines for the fur. Start at the nose where the flow radiates. Generally, the hair flows from the nose to the tail. Look at the way hair grows on your body. It grows the same on the bunny. You can also study bunny photographs. Gravity will affect longer hair/fur.

Figure 112. Here you see the flow lines on the back and rump.

Figure 113. Here you see the flow lines on the belly.

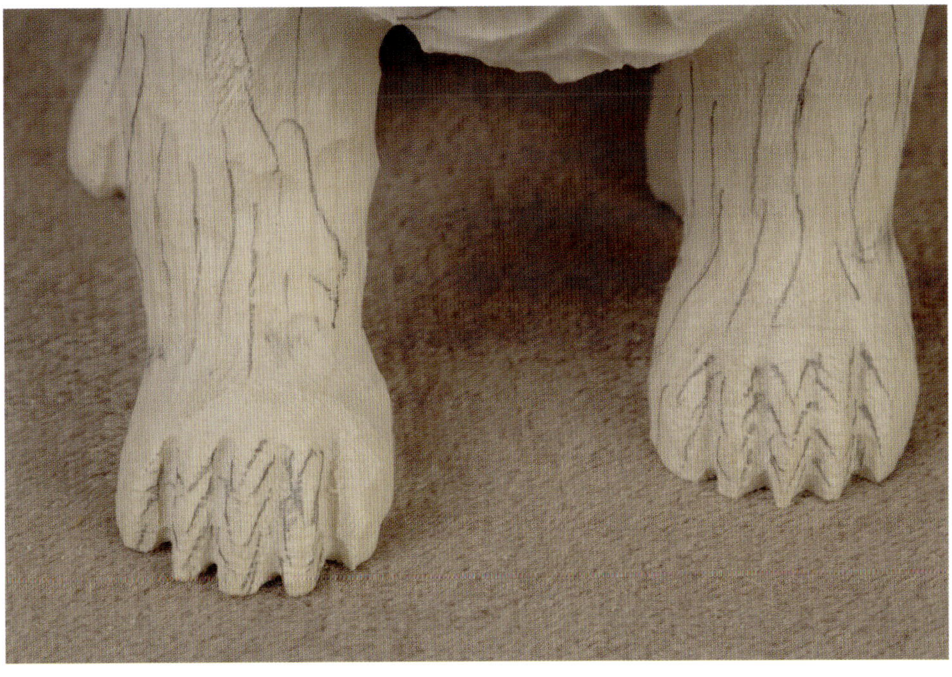

Figure 114. The hair flows down the front legs to the paws. We will not be texturing the paws or toes, but here you can see the direction that the burning strokes will take when we do get to the burning.

Figure 115.The hair flows at an angle from front to back on the front legs. Note the direction of the hair flow on the haunches and sides.

Figure 116. The hair flows from the nose back to the rear of the head. The ear hair flow starts at its base and goes up toward the tip.

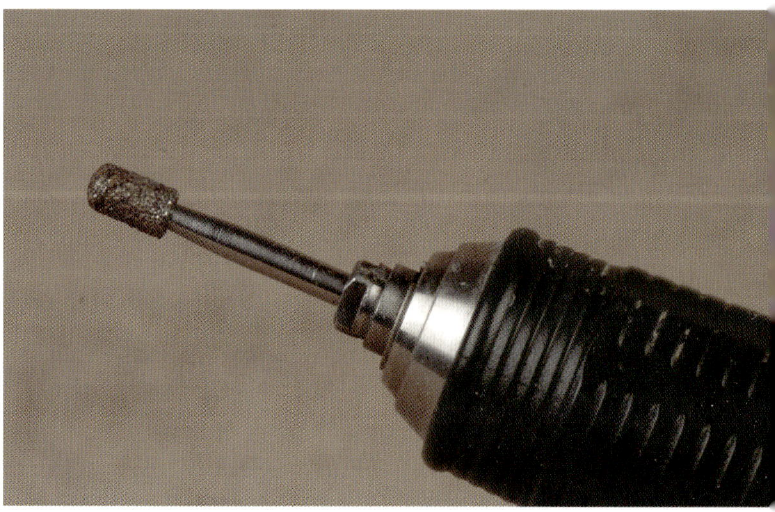

Figure 117. I use the slightly domed straight cylinder ruby carver (RC-18) to begin to get the multiple levels of fur. Hold the bit at an angle so that you are just using the corner.

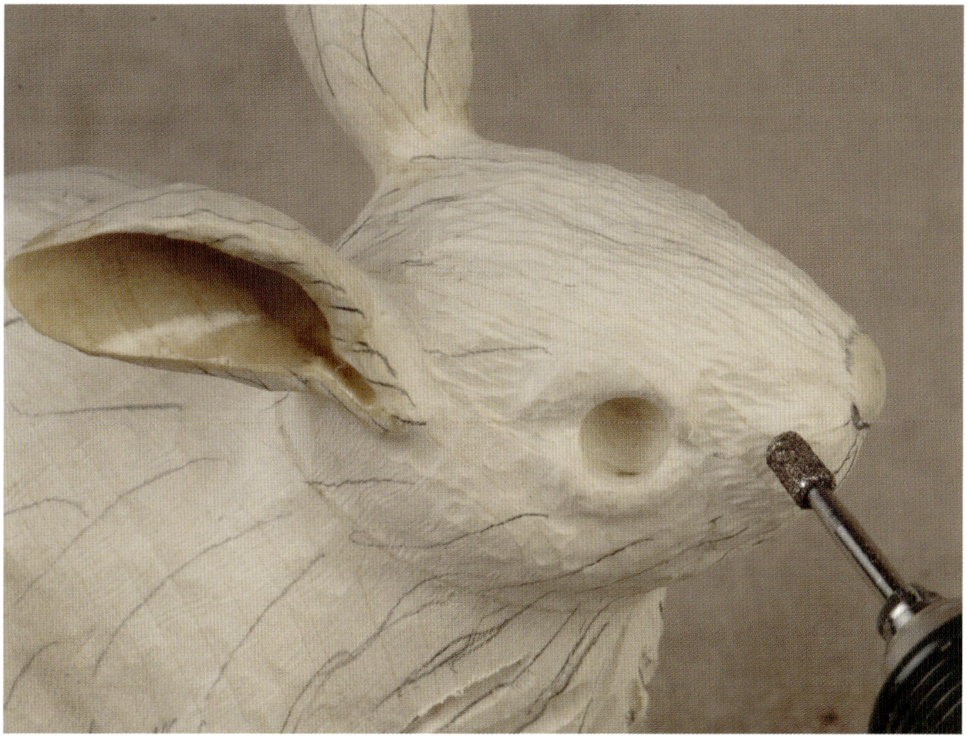

Figure 118. When doing fur or hair, you need multiple levels in the wood. Study up-close pictures of fur, and notice all the different levels and directions that the hair flows. To get that same effect on wood, we need to create the multiple levels first with a ruby carver, and then refine it with the burning pen. The texturing is the first step in creating fur. **Do not texture the nose, eyelids, paws, or ears**. We will be burning in the hair there, but the hair is not as long as on other parts. Starting out around the nose and following the flow lines, hold the burr at an angle so that you are just using the corner to create the texture, and do short strokes, leaving no flat areas in between. You want the entire surface textured. Texture lightly on the head, slightly deeper on the body, and deepest on the tail and breast. You can do one stroke at a time, or do as I do, let the burr ride across the surface with a scribbling stroke. Do the scribbling stroke as you used to color in a picture when you were a kid! Doing the scribbling or scrubbing stroke covers a large area more quickly since the bit is cutting in both directions. You need to do the texturing at different angles and not all straight inline strokes. You still need to follow the flow lines, but just not in a straight line.

Figure 119. When texturing the area where the glued line is, you will need to press harder. Note the deeper texturing lines on the breast area. When you do the breast area, you will need to knock off the sharp edges where you dragged the curvy lines with the #2 flame ruby carver. Continue working your way to the shoulders and front legs.

Figure 120. The texturing needs to be slightly deeper once you get below the neck joint.

Figure 121. Follow your flow lines down the front leg, on the sides, and over the haunch.

Figure 122. Leave no flat areas between the texturing strokes.

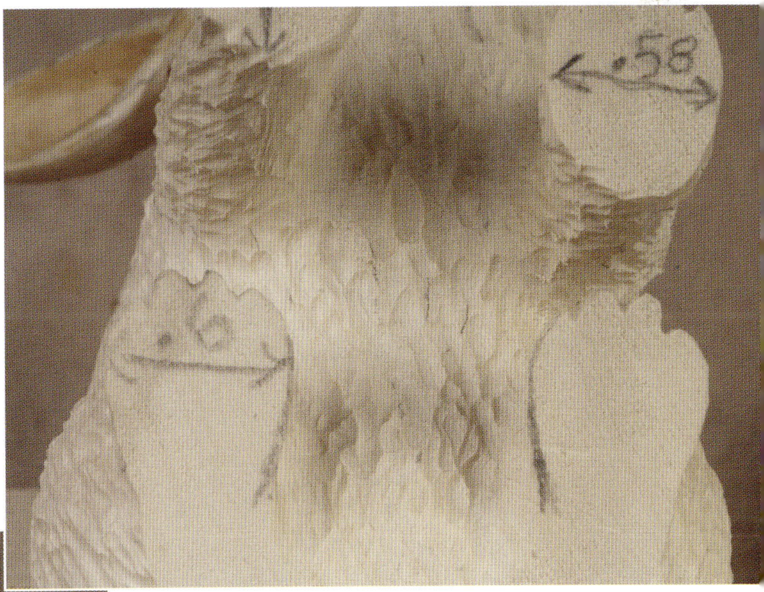

Figure 123. The most difficult areas to reach are on the belly, between the ears, and between the paws. You will need to attack these areas from different directions in order to texture there.

Figure 124. Like the breast, the tail requires deeper texturing. You will be knocking off the edges from the curvy channels that we put in earlier.

Figure 125. These are the three burning pens that I use for burning the fur on this bunny. The medium skew, on the left, is the one I use the most. You will need the rounded tip for getting in particular areas, as well as the small pointed one for tight or close areas.

Figure 126. Burning fur takes practice. You will want to burn at a much higher heat than when doing the feathers on birds. I change the angle of the burning pen with each stroke, putting them so close that there is little or no unburned wood in between lines. I try not to let the point dig in. Check the bunny pictures after it has gesso applied. And you can see the detail better. Start burning around the nose and follow your flow lines and texturing. The strokes on the head should be short. Make sure that you check the nose for symmetry after you have burned around it. You start lengthening the strokes when you get to the neck area. The strokes get longer on the body and are the longest on the fluffy breast and tail.

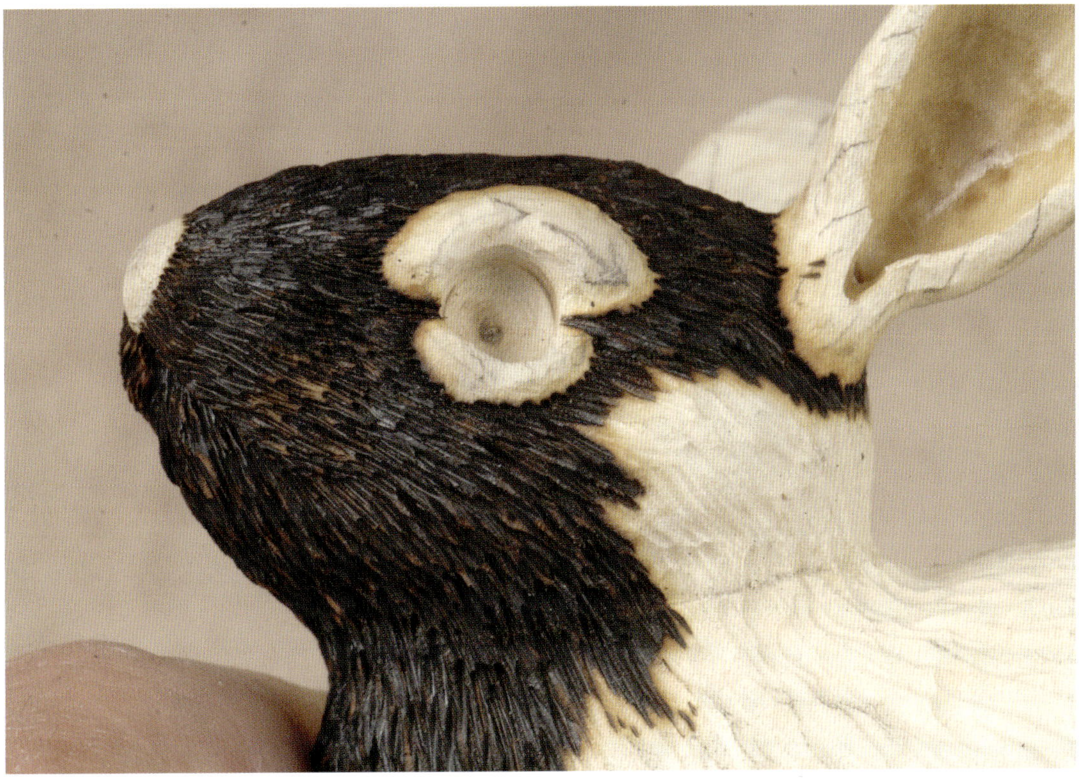

Figure 127. Burn the fur back and around the eyes and ears. I usually burn most of the head before I come back and do the eyelids. I save the ears until last since they are more fragile than the bulkier parts.

Figure 128. To burn the hair on the eyelids, start in the front corner and follow the contour back to the back corner. The strokes here are very short.

Figure 129. The neck area is one of the areas where I use the rounded tip burning pen.

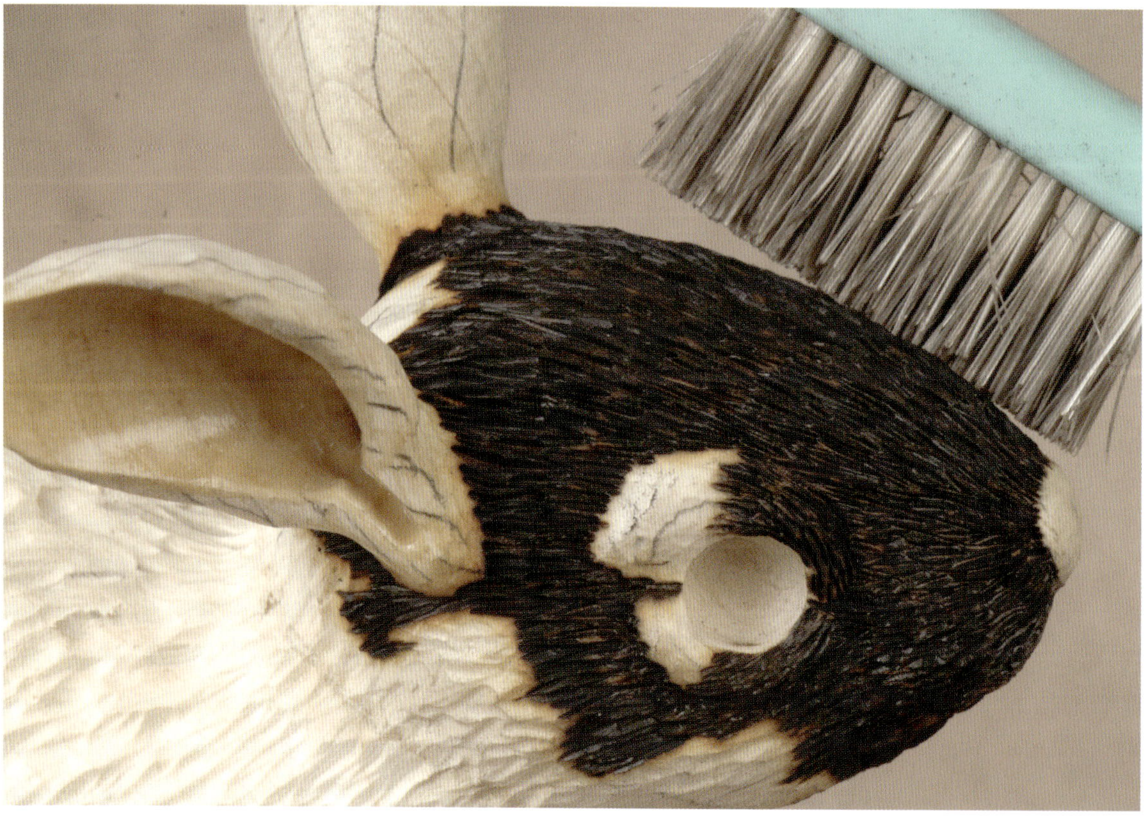

Figure 130. Clean any loose carbon off the burning with a natural bristle toothbrush.

Figure 131. Continue burning over the shoulder and on toward the front leg.

Figure 132. Work your way down the breast to the belly area.

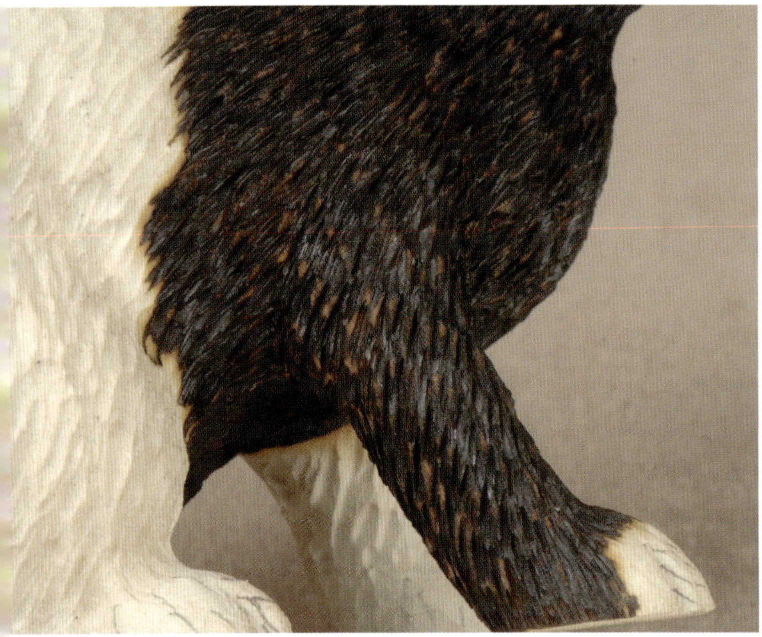

Figure 133. When burning the front legs, carry the burn lines down and angle them from front to back, just as in the texturing.

Figure 134. Work your way over the shoulder area and down the sides of the bunny. Here I use the medium skew burning pen.

Figure 135. To get over and onto the haunch, I switch to the rounded tip.

Figure 136. Burn your way down the back to the tail.

Figure 137. Finish burning the haunches back to the tail and all the way to the bottom of the blank. Start burning the tail from the bottom to the top and out to its edges. Do longer strokes with a curve to each line.

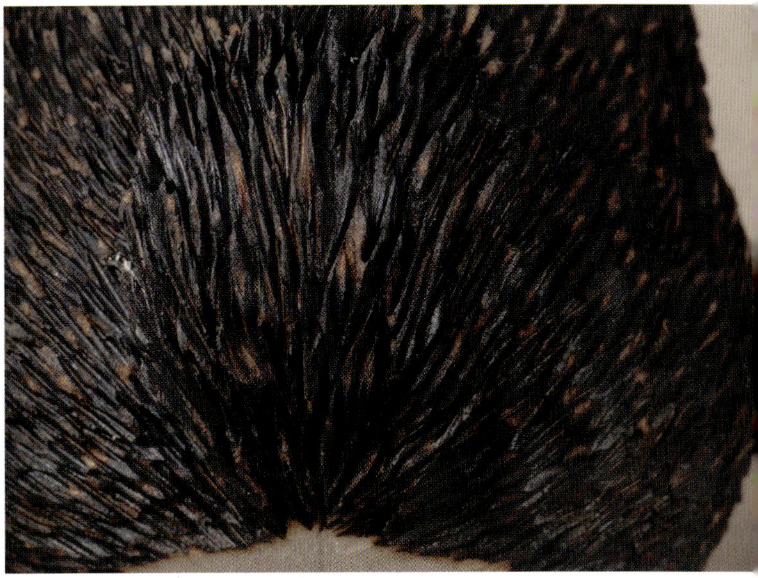

Figure 138. Finish burning the tail out to the edges.

Figure 139. Burn the body side of the tail, which is really the topside when the tail is laying down.

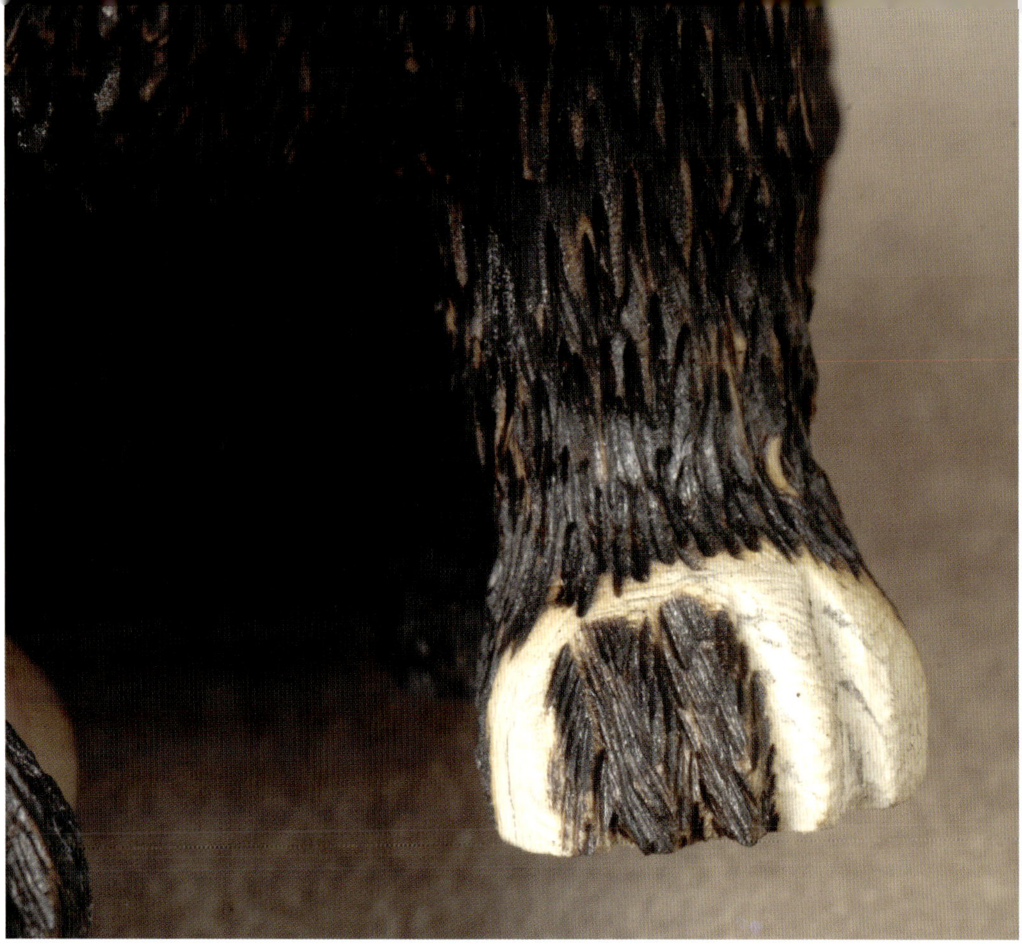

Figure 140. Burn in between the toes, starting in the angled "V" and burning out to each toe top.

Figure 141. Here is one of the front paws completely burned.

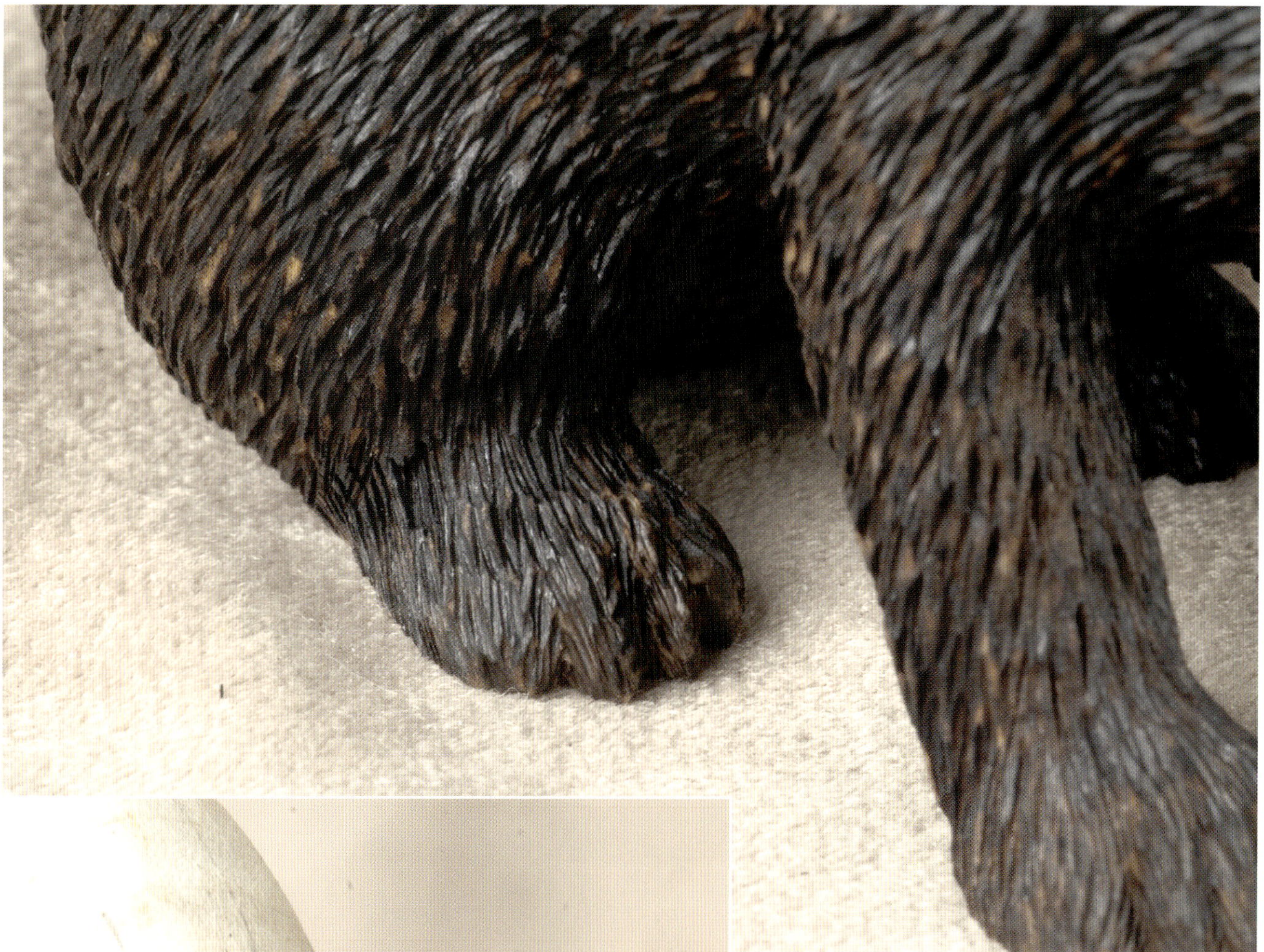

Figure 142. Burn the hair on the hind paws the same way.

Figure 143. Start burning the hair on the ears by beginning at its base and working upward toward the tip.

Figure 144. Burn the front and back flanges with the burn lines going toward the middle of the ear at an angle.

Figure 145. Finish burning the ears. Brush the entire surface with the natural bristle toothbrush.

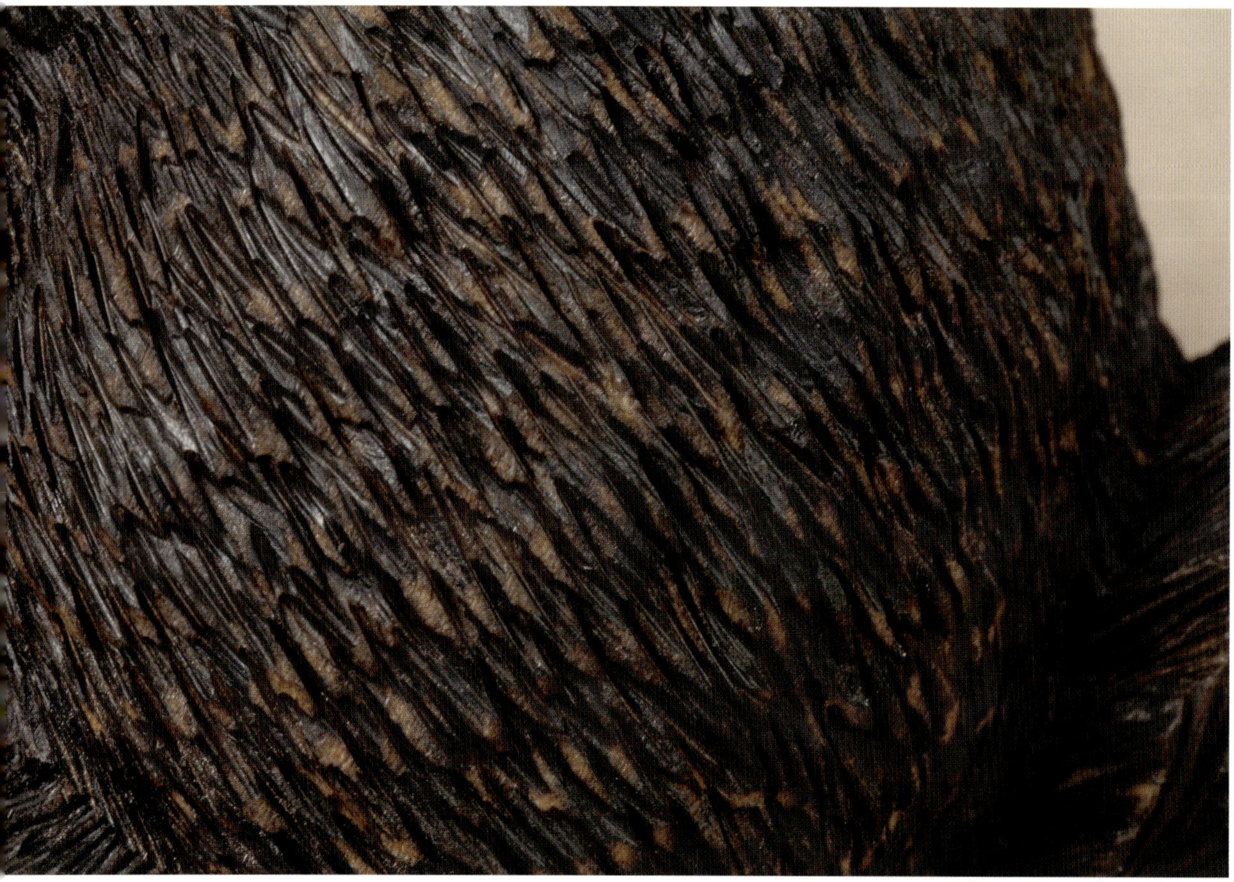

Figure 146. Check the entire fur and look for areas that may need enhancing. I found that the fur/hair on the haunches needed to be shaggier. So, I burned some lines deeper to make the surface appear fluffier and longer haired. Don't forget to re-brush if you change any of the burning.

Figure 147. It is now time to seal the bunny. If you use the Krylon Crystal Clear 1301, spray one coat, wait 5-10 minutes, and re-spray. Tupelo really sucks that spray in. If you want to dip the bunny, get a quantity of gloss brushing lacquer, dilute 50/50 with lacquer thinner, and then dip the bunny in the solution. I let it stay in there until most of the bubbles have stopped rising to the surface. I prefer dipping heavily textured animals in the 50/50 lacquer and lacquer thinner because I feel that there is probably better coverage in all of the deep nooks and crannies of the burning and texturing.

Figure 148. When the sealant is dry, it is time to set the eyes. Try the eyes in the eyeholes to make sure that nothing has changed and that there is the proper depth and diameter of the holes. Fill the eyeholes almost, but not quite, full of the oily, non-hardening clay. Use the "eye" tool that we made in the sleepy bunny eye-setting procedure.

Figure 149. Cut the eye wire right up close to the back of each eye, and place the eye in the clay on both sides. It is always easier to set both eyes at the same time to check for balance and symmetry.

Figure 150. Use the end of a dowel or pencil with an eraser to push the eyes to the proper depth.

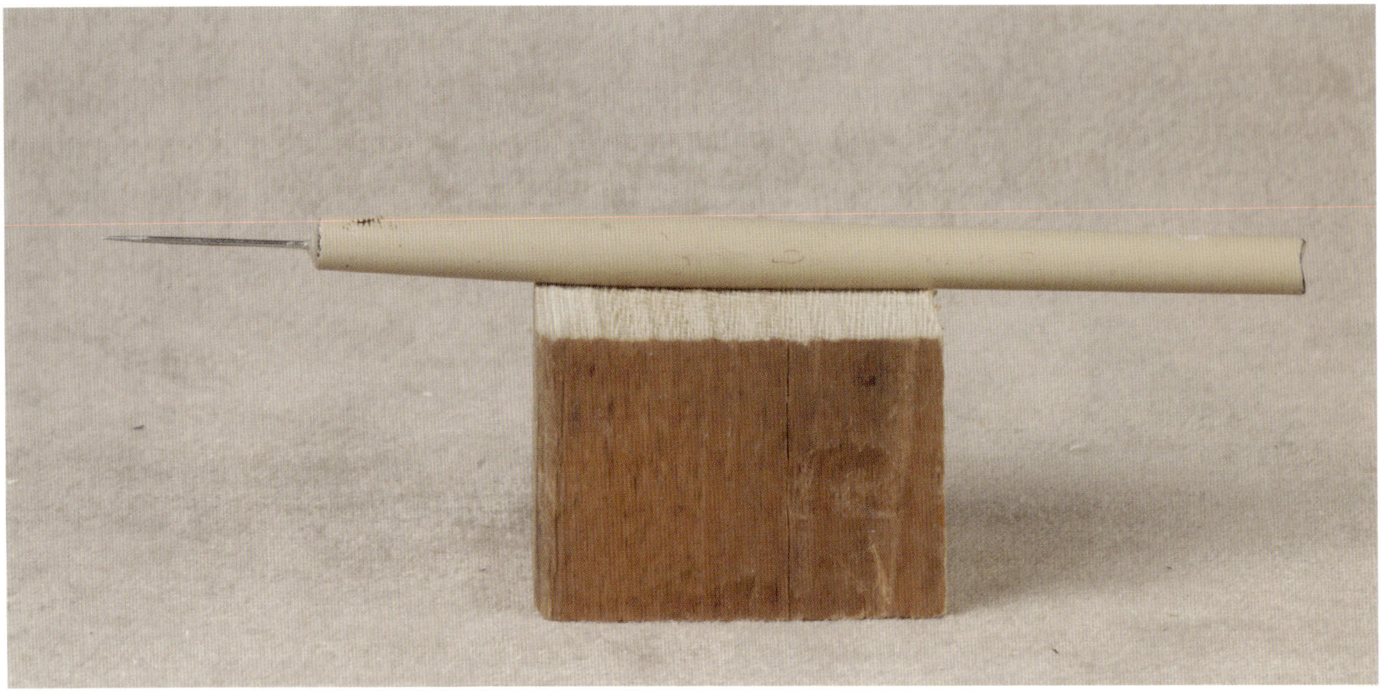

Figure 151. This is another handy tool you can make. I used part of a worn out paintbrush, but you could use a dowel as well. I super-glued a large needle into one end, and then I made the other end concave with a #2 flame. The tool is helpful in setting the eyes to the proper depth, as well as changing the eye angle with the concave part.

Figure 152. The needle end of the tool is useful for cleaning the excess clay in the crevice.

Figure 153. Use a natural bristle toothbrush to brush the eye areas to remove any clay in the texturing. The putty will not stick easily if any clay is left behind in the texturing.

Figure 154. The eyes should be balanced. They should not be protruding out too far or too deep in the holes either.

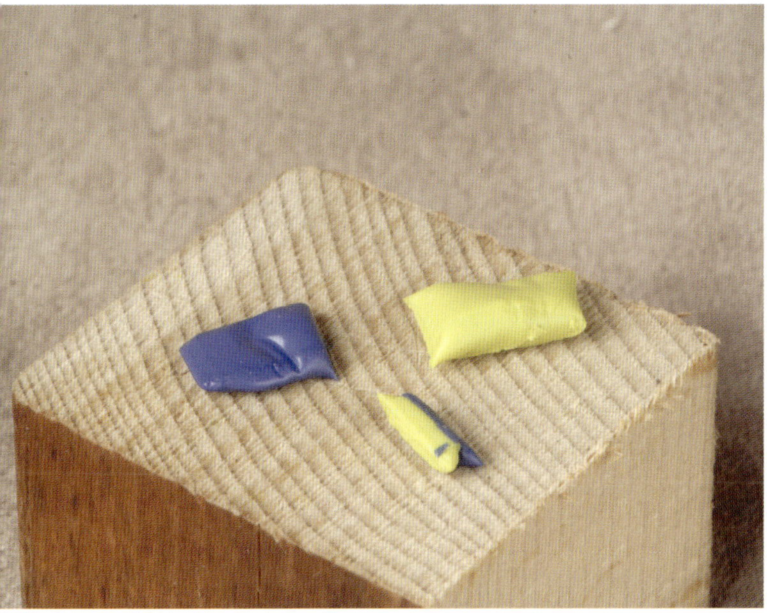

Figure 155. Cut a small piece of the ribbon epoxy putty straight across. Cut the center out where the two sides have already bonded where they were touching.

Figure 156. Knead the two colors together until they are an even green color. It should have NO streaks of either color in it.

Figure 156. Roll a small diameter worm. It is probably easier to handle if the worm is too small rather than too large. If it's too small, you can always bunch it up where needed. If it is too large, you will need to stretch it out. Don't worry about getting it exactly the right diameter, as the crevice around the eye is different dimensions in different areas. I think it is easier to bunch it up to fill up the crevice than it is to stretch it out. So, smaller is better in this instance.

Figure 158. Push the spatula end of your eye tool into the end of the worm. Lightly pinch the end of it down at one of the eye corners. You are sort of crimping it down and then pulling down and back. Once you get it stuck, just start working the putting in the crevice all the way around the eye. Note that there is a little ridge of putty that I've allowed to form between the end of the spatula and the glass of the eye. This little ridge is essential—it is the eye ring.

Figure 159. Don't put your clay away when you have filled the eyeholes. You will need to leave it out on your bench so that you can stick your eye tool ends in the clay to keep them from sticking to the putty. After manipulating the putty three or four times, you will begin to hear a smacking sound as you pull the eye tool away from the putty surface. This is the signal to dip the tool end into the clay. The clay provides a little oily coat to the tool's surface, and keeps it from sticking and pulling the putty off.

Figure 160. You don't need a quarter inch of putty around the eye—just enough to fill the eyehole crevice, to form the eye ring, and to blend into the surrounding texturing. With the pointy end of the eye tool, blend the outer edges of the putty into the texturing around the eye.

Figure 161. You can use a narrowly pointed knife blade or the pointed end of the eye tool to form the sharp corners in the front and back of the eye.

Figure 162. If the eye ring/putty comes down too far on the eye, you can use the spatula end of the end tool to push it back. When you have finished the putty eye rings on both eyes, be sure to check from the front end view that they are equal.

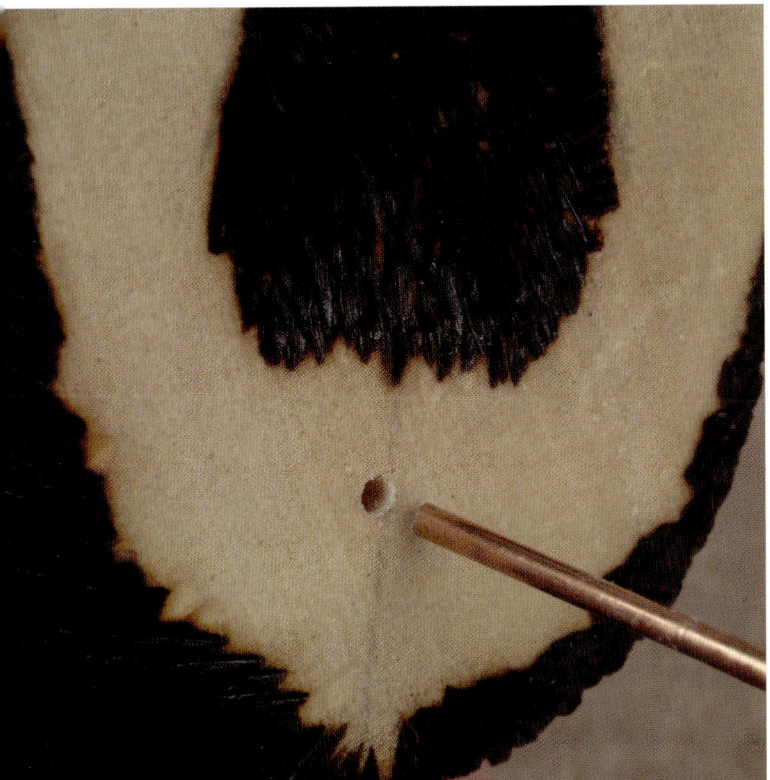

Figure 163. I don't like to hold any project to paint it. On this project I drilled a 1/16" diameter hole about ¼" deep into the flat area on the bottom. Super-glue a piece of 1/16" brazing rod or galvanized wire into the hole. The wire or rod should be about 1-1/2" long.

Figure 164. The contraption that you see holding the wire is called a pin vise. This is an old-fashioned tool that workmen carried in their toolboxes to hold drill bits or various things when out on a job. I use a pin vise to hold my bird or animal when I'm painting. You can, occasionally, still find pin vises, although it is getting more difficult all the time. In lieu of a pin vise, you could just super-glue the end of the wire in a hole in the end of a large diameter dowel or block of wood. The round piece of wood that the pin vise is in is just a piece of wood with a hole, slightly larger than the diameter of the pin vise.

Figure 165. After the putty around the eyes has hardened (about 4-6 hours), the sitting bunny is ready for painting! Whoopee!

Bunny Painting

Note: In color swatches * denotes a little bit

Figure 1. Using a stiff bristle brush, scrub gesso back and forth in the texturing and burning. Go right over the eyes–it is easier to scrape the gesso off the eyes than it is to paint around the eyelids and eye rings. Using the stiff brush will keep the gesso from pooling in the bottom of the texturing and filling it up. You will find that you use the gesso much more liberally on animals than on birds, as the texturing and burning are so much deeper.

The gesso you use should be very fluid and should slosh when the bottle is shaken. Avoid the pasty kind of gesso for this application!

Figure 2. Gesso the entire rabbit, making sure that you do not leave any globs of gesso anywhere. Brush it out well.

Figure 3. If you are doing the sleep bunny, apply the gesso all over the entire top surface. You do not need to do the bottom.

Figure 4. Here you can see a close-up of the deep texturing on the front and hind legs, the side, and the back.

Figure 6. Carefully scrape the gesso from the eyes. If you use a knife for this, make sure that it does not have any nicks or burrs on the blade, as they might scratch the glass. I keep an Exacto knife with a #16 blade in my paint box, and I only use that blade to scrape eyes of animal and bird carvings. As in birds, I scrape the eyes frequently during the painting process, as I like the glint of the glass looking back at me!

Figure 5. Note the deepest burning on the tail.

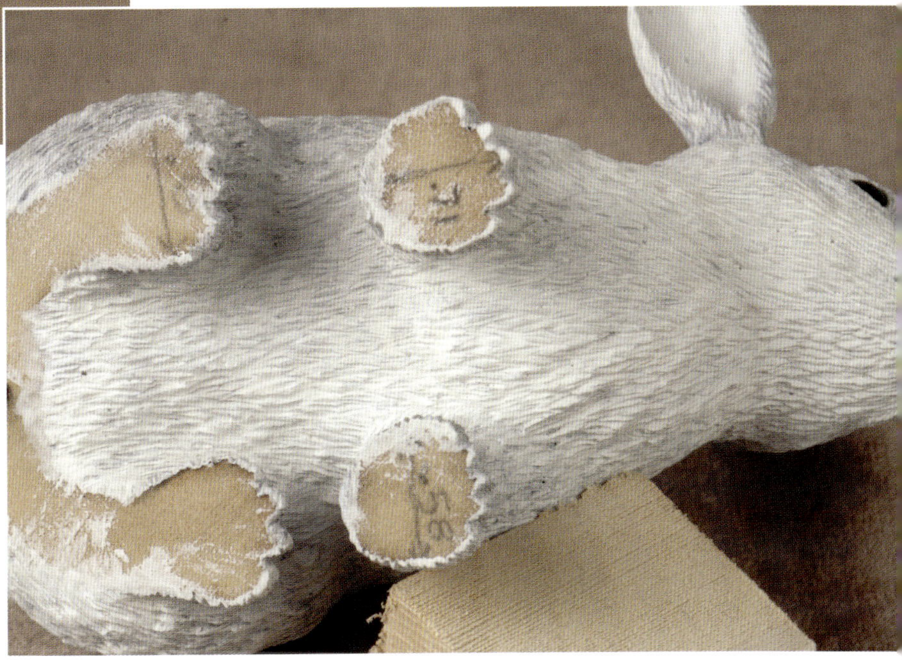

Figure 7. Do a second coat of gesso on the under parts, the back of the tail, and on the lower cheeks and muzzle—the parts that will be whitish when completed.

Figure 8. Mix raw umber, raw sienna, and white gesso together, and apply the basecoat to the head, ears, front legs, back, sides, haunches, hind paws, and the topside of the tail (not the backside, which is the underside). Do the nose and inside of the ears even though they will be different colors when finished. Keep your paint thin and apply multiple coats of the same basecoat color. If your paint is too thick, it will not go down into the texturing/burning where you need it to go. If you find that there are some white pinholes where the paint is not going down into, load a liner brush with a thinned basecoat mixture, and just use the tip to force paint down into the pinholes. Use a clean, dampened brush to blend the areas where the brownish color meets the white, such as the flanks, cheeks, and neck areas.

RU + RS + W

Figure 9. Make a wash of the basecoat color by adding lots of water to a separate puddle, and apply two washes to the front of the chest. Again, use the clean, dampened brush to soften the transition areas along the white edge.

Figure 10. Using a mixture of burnt umber, black, and a small amount of white gesso, darken the deeper texturing and tick all the brown areas except the eyelids. Use a liner brush to splotch and line the areas that need to appear as deeper fur.

BU + B + *W

Figure 11. Also darken the eye rings and the bottom of the ear canal.

Figure 12. Darken the area between all of the toes.

Figure 13. There is an irregular stripe of the dark color on the outer part of the ear, all the way around. It is just inside the edge approximately 0.1".

Figure 14. With a mixture of mostly white and small amounts of both raw sienna and raw umber, load an old almost worn out paintbrush with the mixture. Dry most of it on a dry paper towel, leaving very little paint on the brush. Lightly stroke and even rub the heel of the brush across and along the fur texture over all the base coated areas. The tops of the texturing will pick up the paint but the lower levels will not. Do this application once and then highlight the brown areas again.

W + *RS + *RU

Figure 15. This is the old worn out brush that I use for highlighting animal fur. It is or was a high priced red sable round. Over the years of using it, the tip and end wore off at least 0.1". It has been resurrected as a highlighting brush. Because the tip of a brush wears off from repeated use on the rough fur surface does not mean you need to toss it in the trash. Use a worn out brush for highlighting or washes.

Figure 16. Using the light highlight mixture, paint in the eyelids and front ear flanges more solidly.

Figure 17. Do a raw umber wash over all of the brownish base coated areas, including the chest. Many times I tell students in my classes that it is always better to have to do 2 washes to get the effect you want than it is to do 1 wash that is too heavy. If the wash you put on has too much pigment in it, you will have to go back and do all the previous steps again. When you load the paintbrush with your wash, always touch the tip of the brush to your dry paper towel to remove some of it. You do not want so much wash on your brush that it runs into areas you don't want washed. You want to be able to control the application.

RU Wash

Figure 18. Do another application of highlights over the brownish areas. This time use a mixture of white gesso and a very small amount of yellow oxide. Use the same dry-brush technique as you used before. And then, do another raw umber wash. You may need to do the highlights and washes several more times to make the fur look soft. If you have any blobs of highlights, take a liner brush loaded with either the dark mixture or the base coat mixture, and break up the blob, stroking in the darker colors.

W + *YO

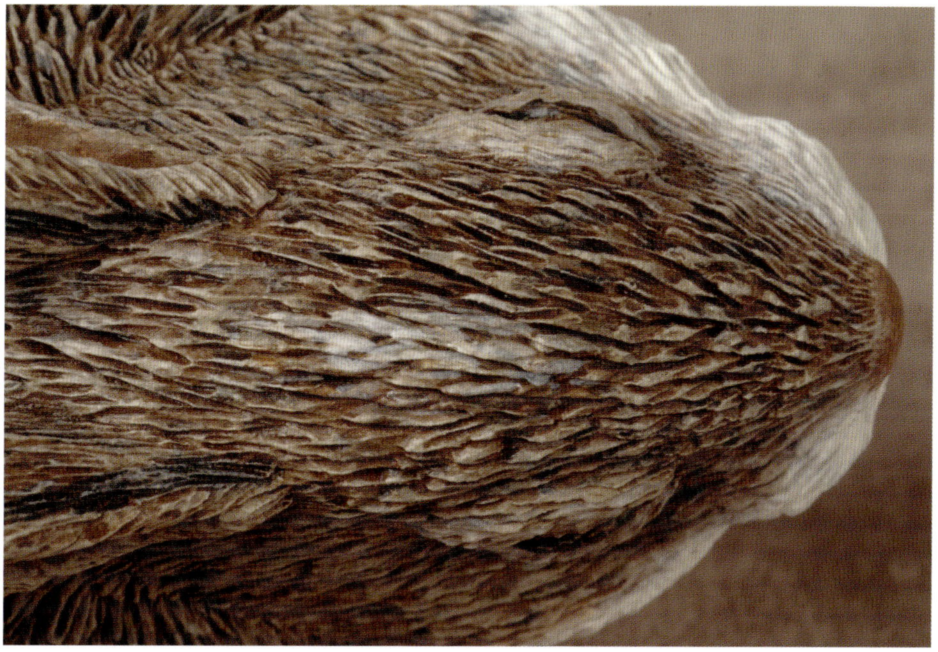

Figure 19. When doing the sleepy bunny, if you want to make the bunny a young one, paint in a narrow blaze on the top of the head. Many young bunnies have this blaze. Use a liner brush with the highlight mixture of white gesso and a very small amount of yellow oxide, stroking in fine lines. After it is dry, then wash with a very watery raw umber wash.

Figure 21. Drag the edges of the light color into the edges of the brownish color with a liner brush.

Figure 20. Make a mixture of white gesso and a very small amount of yellow oxide, and apply that to the lower part of the face/muzzle, throat, belly, and backside/underside of the tail.

W + *YO

Figure 22. Mix up a **super-thin** wash of a medium grey with black, burnt umber, and white gesso, and apply to the whitish areas on the lower part of the muzzle/face, throat, belly, and backside/underside of the tail. You want the thin wash to sink to the bottom of the texturing and provide some dimensionality to the fur.

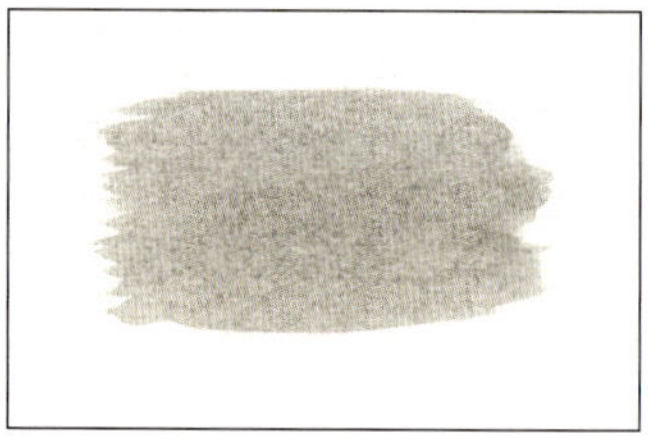

B + BU + W

Figure 23. For the basecoat for the nose and inside of the ears down to the ear hole/canal, mix burnt sienna, raw sienna, burnt umber, and white gesso to a dark flesh color and apply two coats.

BS + RS + BU + W

Figure 24. Paint a "V" shape on the bottom of the nose with straight burnt umber.

Figure 25. Using artistic license to increase the concave shape of the ear, paint four curving lines from the dark color of the ear canal out towards the tip. For the dark color, use a mixture of burnt umber and burnt sienna. Note that there are longer curving lines on the outside with shorter ones in the middle, but that all of them are differing lengths. When they are dry, paint lighter lines (using a mixture of white gesso with just a small amount of the ear basecoat color mixed in) on the insides of the dark lines.

BU + BS

W + Basecoat

Figure 26. Using a mixture of white gesso and a very small amount of yellow oxide, paint in light radiating lines on the inside of the earflaps and also lighten the ridge/flange around the base of the ear.

W + *YO

Figure 27. Do a **super-thin** raw umber wash on the inside of the ears and the front ridges/flanges.

Figure 28. Scrape the paint off the eyes. When I do an animal or bird without a base, I spray the piece with Testors Dull Cote to keep the paint from wearing off from the handling. Before spraying, cover the eyes with little pieces of masking tape. It is easier to not get the spray on the glass eyes than it is to scrape the sleepy eyes. Spray two light coats waiting a couple of hours in between. I do not spray a carving that is on a base, since the base will be handled and not the carving.

Figure 29. Poke 8 holes in the whisker pads (a row of 2 close to the nose, then 3 slightly further back, and the last row 3 slightly further back from the middle row) using a hat pin or a needle super-glued in the end of a brush handle or dowel. The angle on the top holes should be slightly upward, on the middle holes straight, and on the bottom holes slightly downward.

Figure 30. To insert the whiskers, cut any excess off the skin-side of the hair/bristle. This means that the tapered end is pointing out. Check out the "Whiskers" section of the "Helpful Hints" chapter. I am using hairs from a swatch of hide from the rump of a deer, on both bunnies. The two whiskers closest to the nose are approximately 0.65" long outside the wood and the others behind those two are approximately 1.1" long. Select a whisker, trim it to length, dip the blunt end into yellow carpenter glue, and insert in the hole. Of course, I am using magnifiers to find the hole.

Figure 31. If you have done the sleepy bunny, sign and date the bottom, and you are all finished.

Figure 32. If you have done the upright bunny, you will need to mount the bunny on a base. After mounting, sign and date the bottom of the base, and you are all finished.

Sitting Chipmunk

Tools & Supplies

- Band saw or coping saw
- Flexible shaft machine
- Micro motor machine helpful
- Variety of Kutzall/Typhoon carbide roughing out bits
- Variety of ruby carver bits and mounted stones
- Calipers and ruler, measuring in **tenths** of an inch
- Adjustable clamp for sitting bunny project
- Compass, pencil
- Knife
- Wire cutters, needle nose pliers, awl
- Drill and bits (1/16" and 5/64")
- Toothbrush (preferably natural bristle)
- Burning pen (rheostat type) and several burning pen styles
- Straight pin, hatpin, or fine dissecting needle
- Permanent ink marker (such as a fine point Sharpie)
- Dust mask, leather gloves, and safety glasses or goggles
- Optivisor or some type of magnification
- Clear acetate sheet (preferably .005 thickness)
- 2" piece of 16 gauge galvanized wire
- Super-glue and accelerator
- 50/50 lacquer/lacquer thinner mixture or Krylon Crystal Clear Spray
- Yellow carpenter glue
- Reference pictures

Materials

- 4.6"L x 1.8"W x 3.2"H tupelo block for sitting chipmunk
- 5mm black eyes
- Medium colored China bristle paintbrush (to use for whiskers)
- Ribbon epoxy putty (preferably blue/yellow) or Kulis Karvit
- Oily, non-hardening modeling clay
- Flat base or piece of driftwood for mount

Painting Supplies

- Hair dryer
- Freezer paper and masking tape
- Brushes
- Water container and paper towels
- Flow medium
- Paints: (preferably Liquitex jar acrylics) white gesso (W), mars black (B), burnt umber (BU), raw umber (RU), yellow oxide (YO), raw sienna (RS), and burnt sienna (BS).
- Note: In color swatches, *denotes little bit

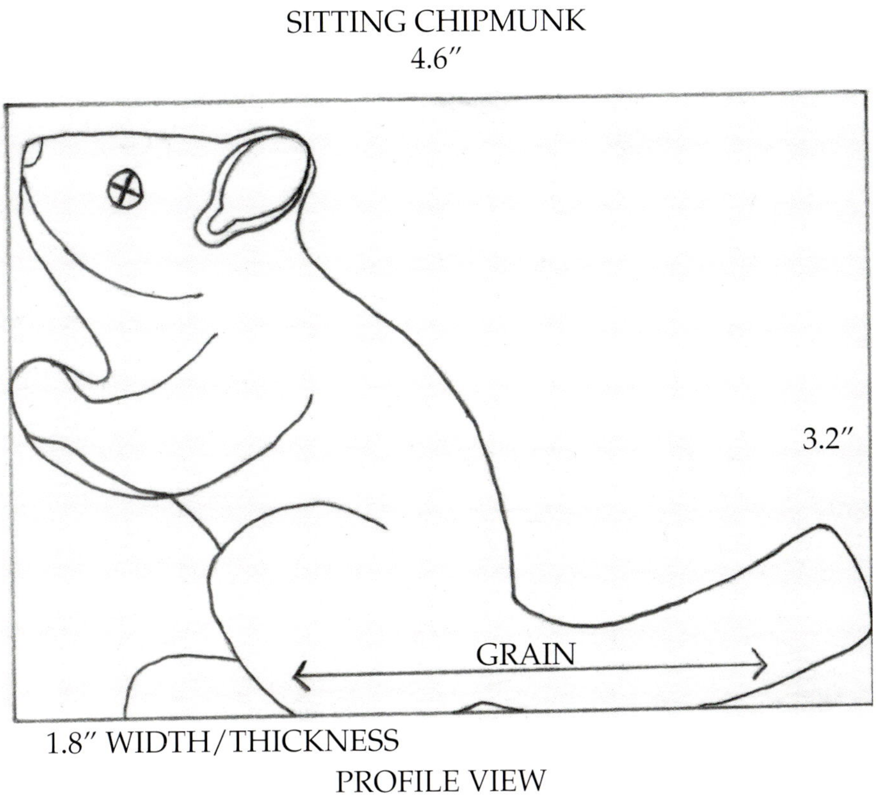

Figure 2. Draw in the tail shape and the centerline all the way around the body and head, including underneath the blank. The tail can curve to either side. The base of the tail is at least 0.65" wide and the remainder of the tail a little wider. For roughing out purposes, cut outside the line.

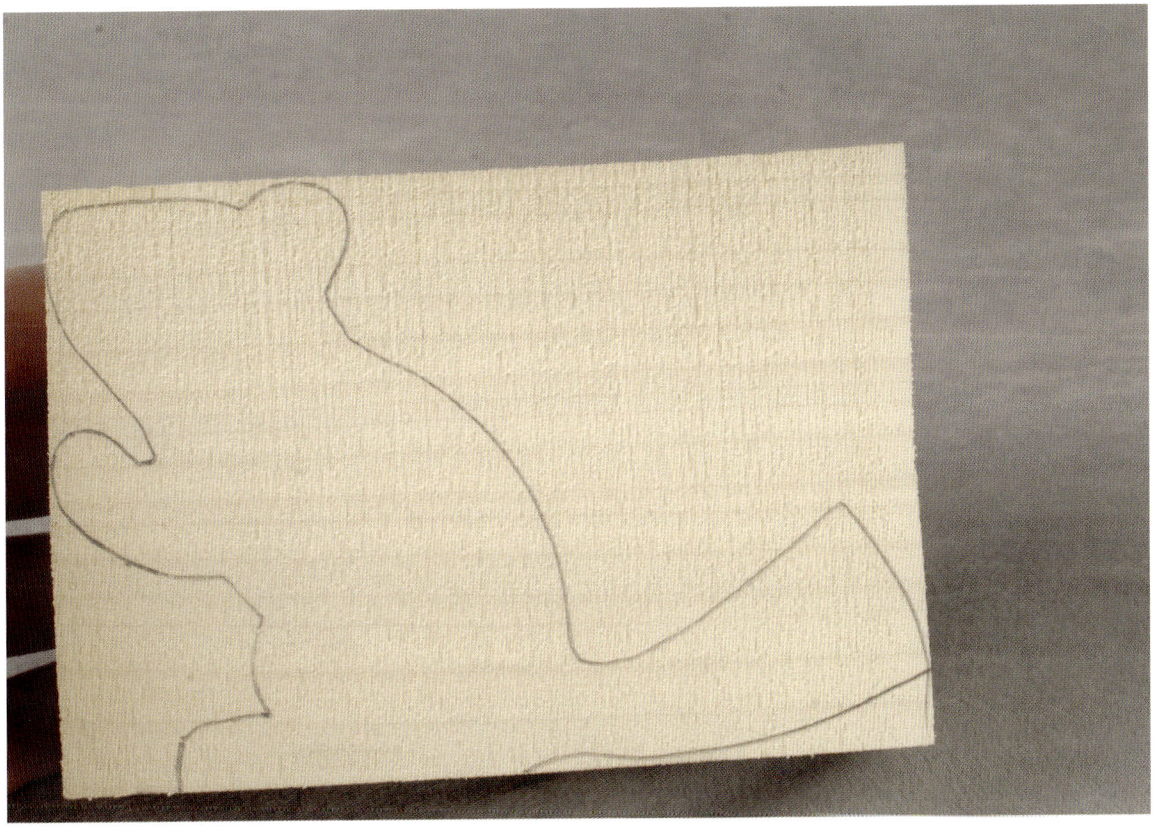

Figure 1. Draw the profile pattern on a block of tupelo wood that is 4.6"L x 1.8"W x 3.2"H. The grain needs to run from the hind paws towards the tail for strength in these areas.

Figure 3. If you are not experienced with the band saw, I suggest you grind the excess wood from around the tail. Keep the sides straight up and down at this point, just as if the band saw had cut it.

Figure 4. Round over the back from the bottom of the blank to the neck. Use a medium size taper Typhoon carbide cutter. Too small of a bit will cause the blank to be bumpy and follow the grain. With tupelo especially, use the largest bit possible to do the procedure. A bit that is small will go down in the softer wood and up on the harder grain, causing a "washboard" effect.

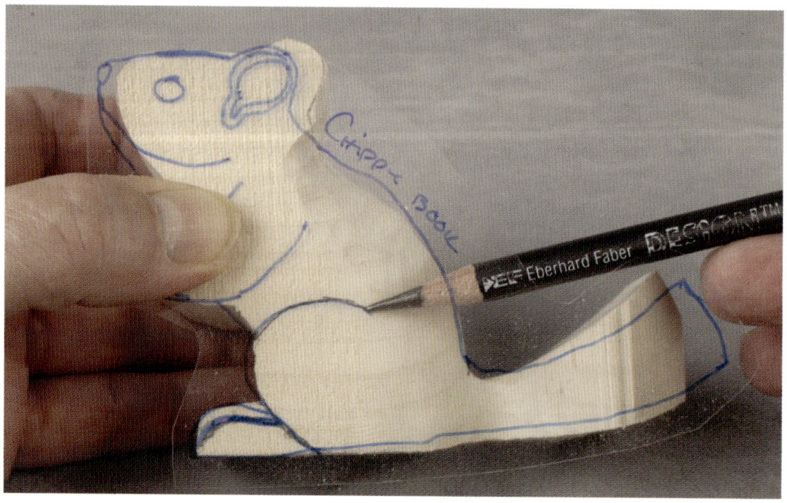

Figure 5. Trace the profile pattern on a piece of clear acetate (.005 is a little thicker and better than the .003 kind). Hold the acetate up to the side of the chipmunk, sneak a pencil under the acetate, and trace the haunch and hind paw on both sides.

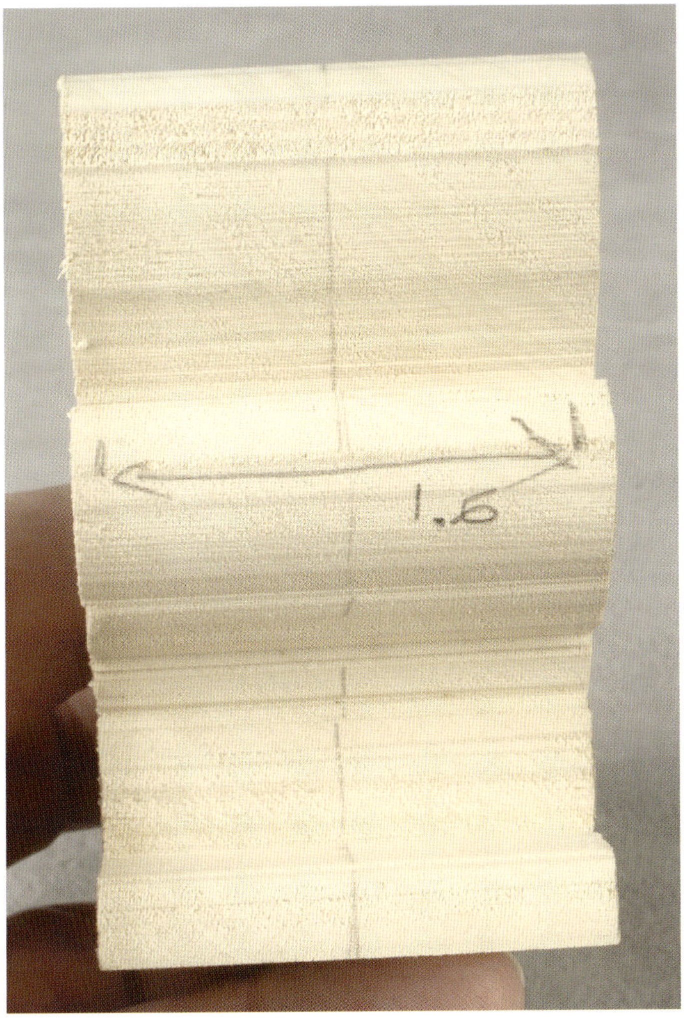

Figure 6. Across the front of the blank at the front paw level, divide 1.6" equally across the centerline (0.8" on each side).

Figure 7. A carpenter taught me this trick years ago. Take the pencil to the mark while holding your ring finger on the side. Don't change the configuration of your fingers, and slide along where you want to continue that dimension. Do that on both sides of the blank from just above the haunches all the way to the top of the blank.

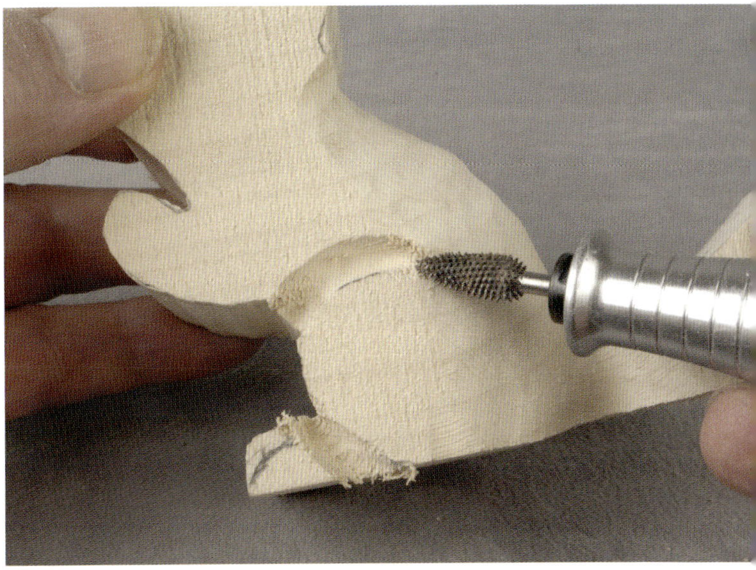

Figure 8. Starting in gradually, cut out the haunch, including the part at the base of the paw. The cut should be approximately 0.2" deep. This cut will be deepened slightly later with a ruby carver when we go to do the details.

Figure 9. On the underside of the blank, draw the outside edge line of the hind paws from the tip back to the depth of the cut around the haunch. Cut away this excess wood as on the left hind paw (which is on the right in the photo). Keep the cut straight up and down for right now.

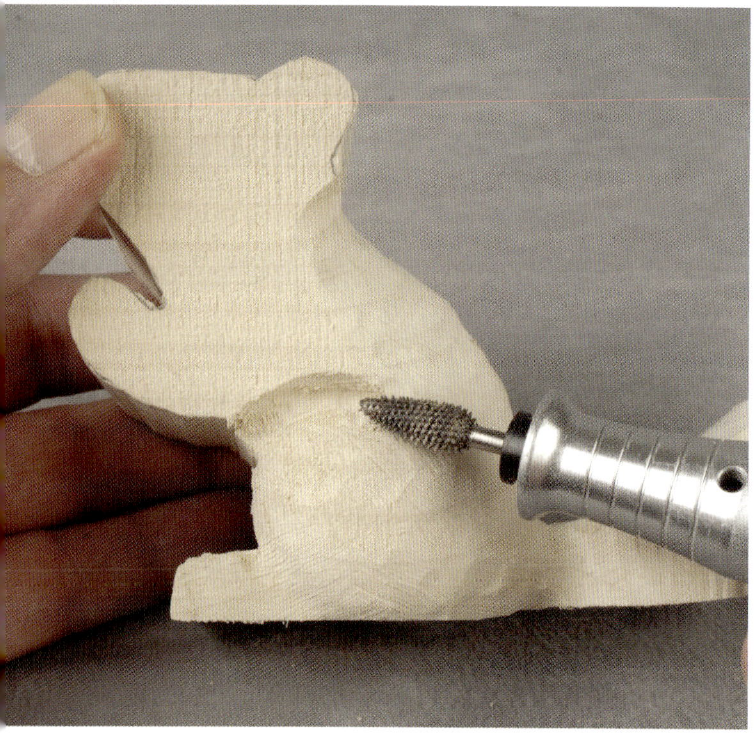

Figure 10. Using the bud Typhoon cutter, round over the top, front, and bottom of both haunches.

Figure 11. From the haunches up to the top of the blank, take off the excess wood. The 1.6" measurement is the roughing out shoulder measurement, but we might as well begin to thin him down now. The shoulders are usually slightly smaller than the width of the haunches.

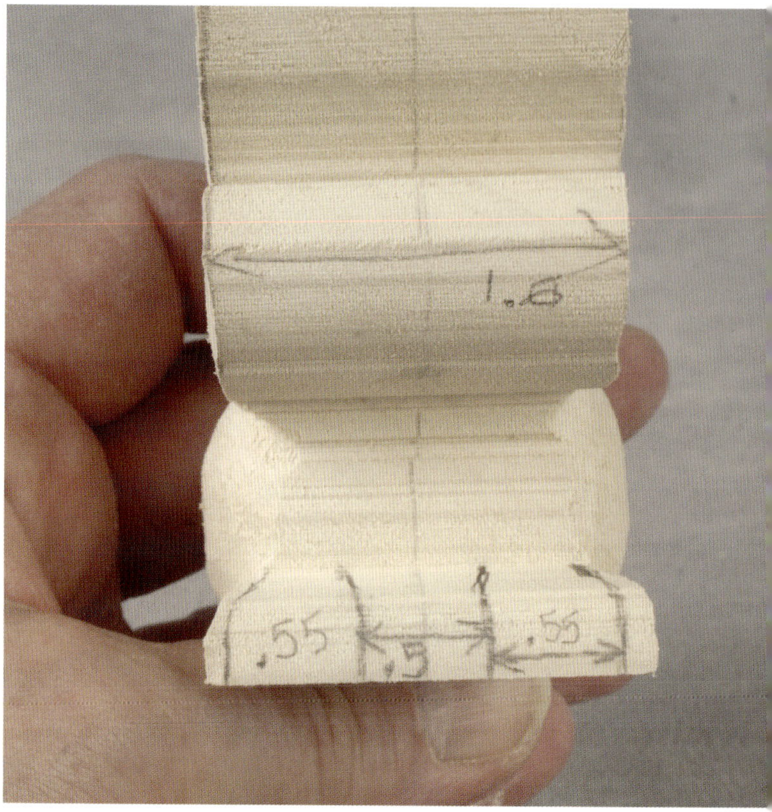

Figure 12. To draw in the paws, first measure 0.5" evenly centered across the centerline (0.25" on each side). That mark is the inside of each hind paw. The roughing out width of each paw is 0.55"—so measure and mark that on both paws.

Figure 13. Using a #3 flame ruby carver (RC-25), cut away the excess outside the paws and the excess wood in between the hind paws. Draw the inside haunch line continuing the haunches down inside the hind paws as shown.

Figure 14. Cut in the inside haunch channels with the #3 flame. You will need to get the upper part of the inside haunch from the top position and the lower part from the bottom. Roll over the haunches in all directions and round over the lower belly.

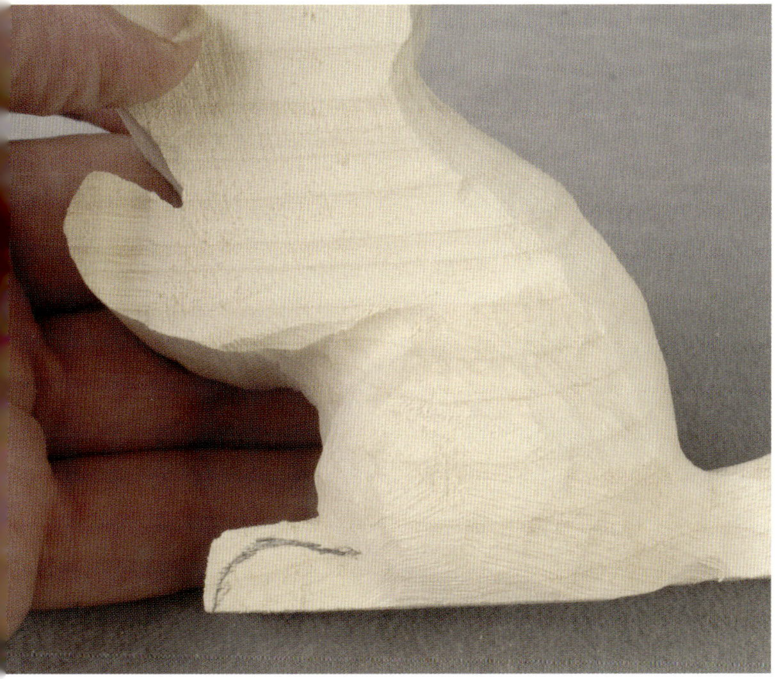

Figure 15. Use the profile acetate to check the shape and size of the haunches and to draw in the profile view of the hind paws.

Figure 16. Using the #2 flame ruby carver (RC-20), cut away the excess wood off the top of the hind paws, keeping the cuts straight across at this time.

Figure 17. Draw in and round the ends of the hind paws on the top plan view.

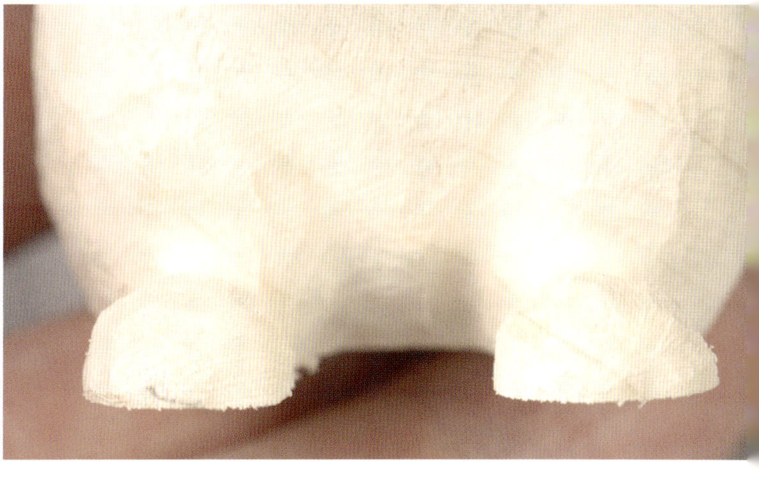

Figure 18. Round over the hind paws from back to front and from side to side. The final measurements should be 0.23" thickness at the back of the paw and 0.25" thickness at the toe area.

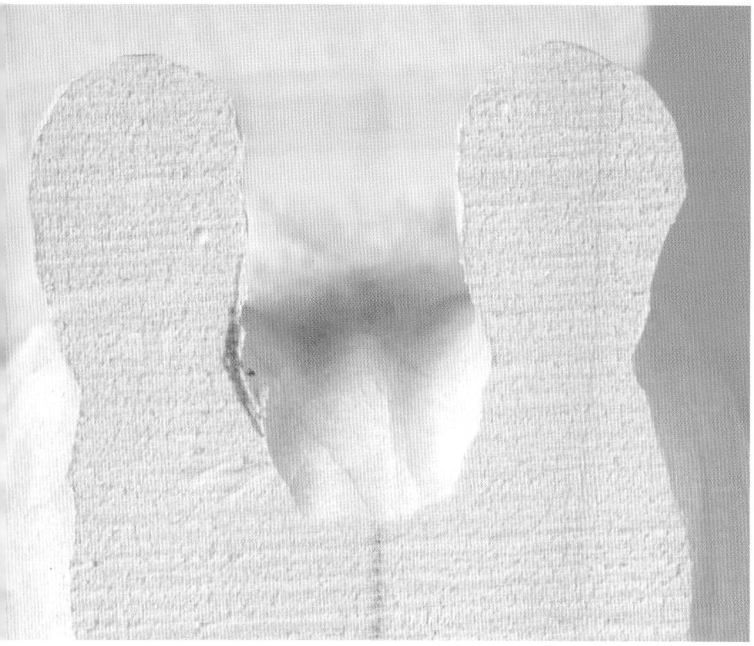

Figure 19. Check from the underneath view to make sure that the hind paws are the same length and the same shape. The pencil mark on the inside of the chippy's right hind paw indicates I need to take just a tad more off there! Yikes!

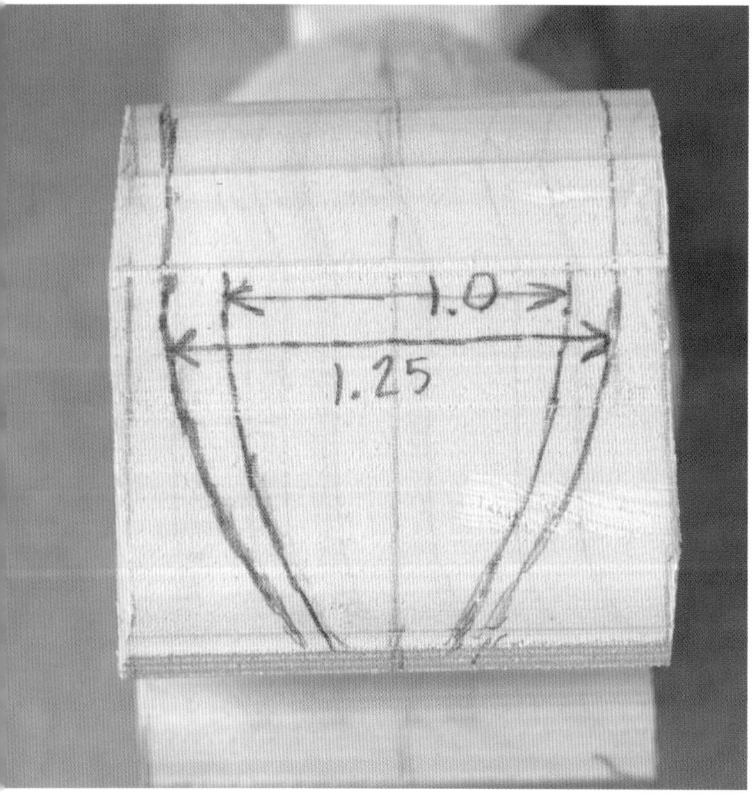

Figure 20. Okay, let's rough out the head. Just in front of the ears, equally divide 1.25" across the centerline—that is 0.625" on each side. Draw in the shape of the head leaving about 0.53" across the front end of the muzzle and carrying the lines to the back of the ears on the top plan view. Then, just in front of the ears, equally divide 1.0" across the centerline and draw that to the end of the muzzle, leaving 0.4" dimension across the end. These are roughing dimensions. The head will be slightly smaller than this when it is finished.

Figure 21. Using a medium taper Typhoon carbide bit, cut away the excess wood on the sides of the head until the width, back by the ears, measures 1.25", not just on the top but the full height of what you took off.

Figure 22. With the #3 flame ruby carver (RC-25), carve a depression on the sides of the head slightly longer than the length of the bit. Do not reduce the width of the back of the ears. The back of the ear sticks out slightly wider than the front of each ear.

Figure 23. Keep deepening the depression until the head width is 1.0" just in front of the ears.

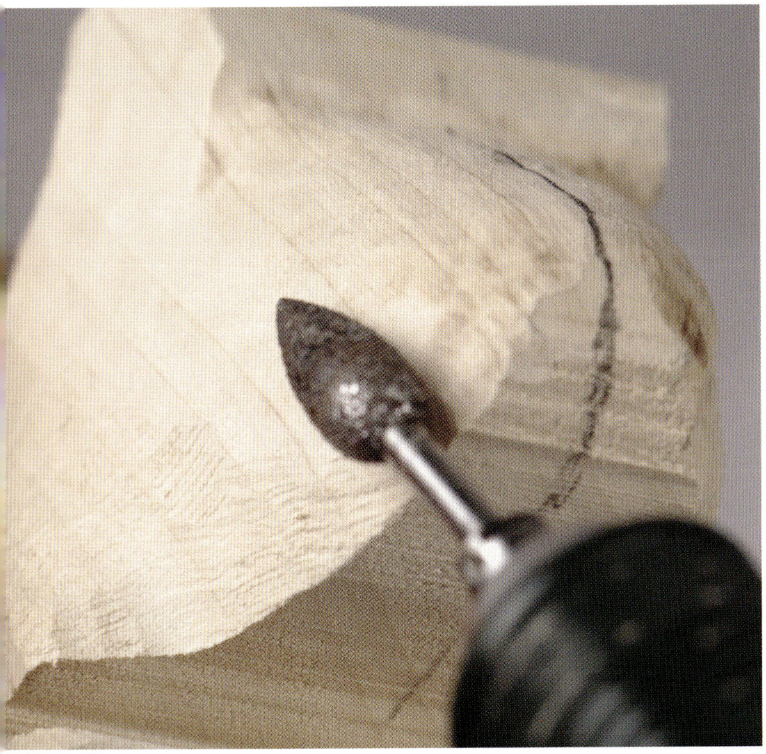

Figure 24. Taper the bottom of the depression onto the lower head on both sides.

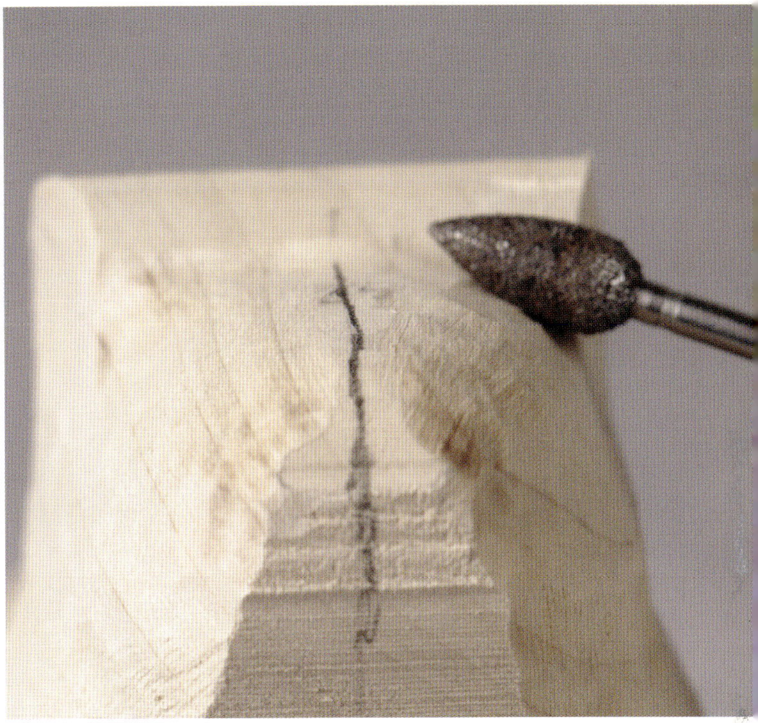

Figure 25. Round over the corners of the top of the head from just in front of the ears out to the end of the muzzle.

Figure 26. Who cut this blank out? A chipmunk's head doesn't have a bump like this! Shape the profile view of the head if necessary!

Figure 27. Okay, the bump is gone and the centerline redrawn. Round over the top of the muzzle so that we can draw in the nose.

Figure 28. Draw in the "U" shaped nose with the width 0.2" and the height 0.15".

Figure 29. Laying the #2 flame ruby carver (RC-20) down, channel around the nose line. Flow the channel out onto the front of the muzzle.

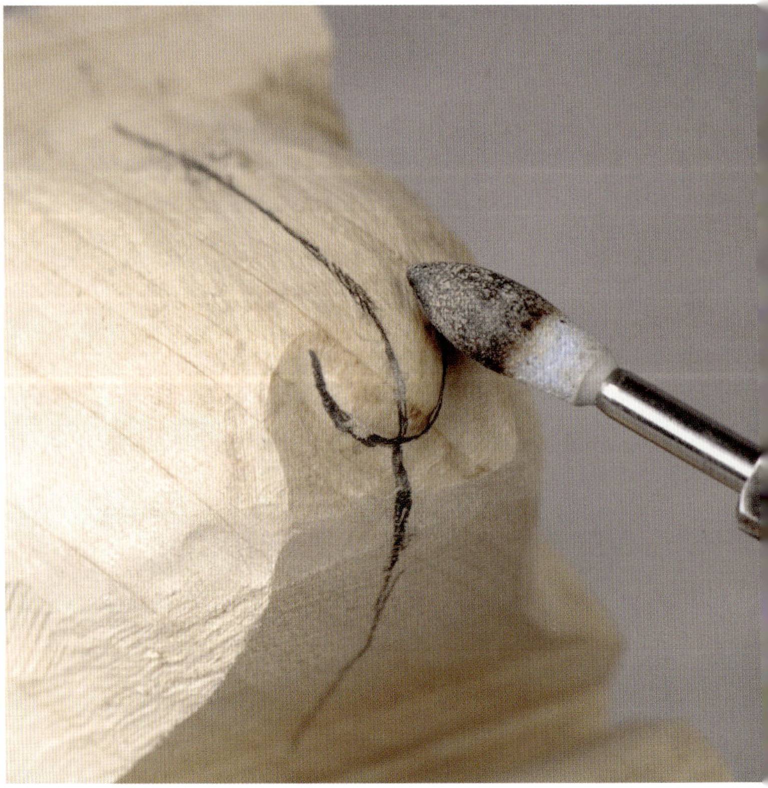

Figure 30. With a stone, round over and generally smooth all of the scratches off the nose. Redraw the nose line and centerline.

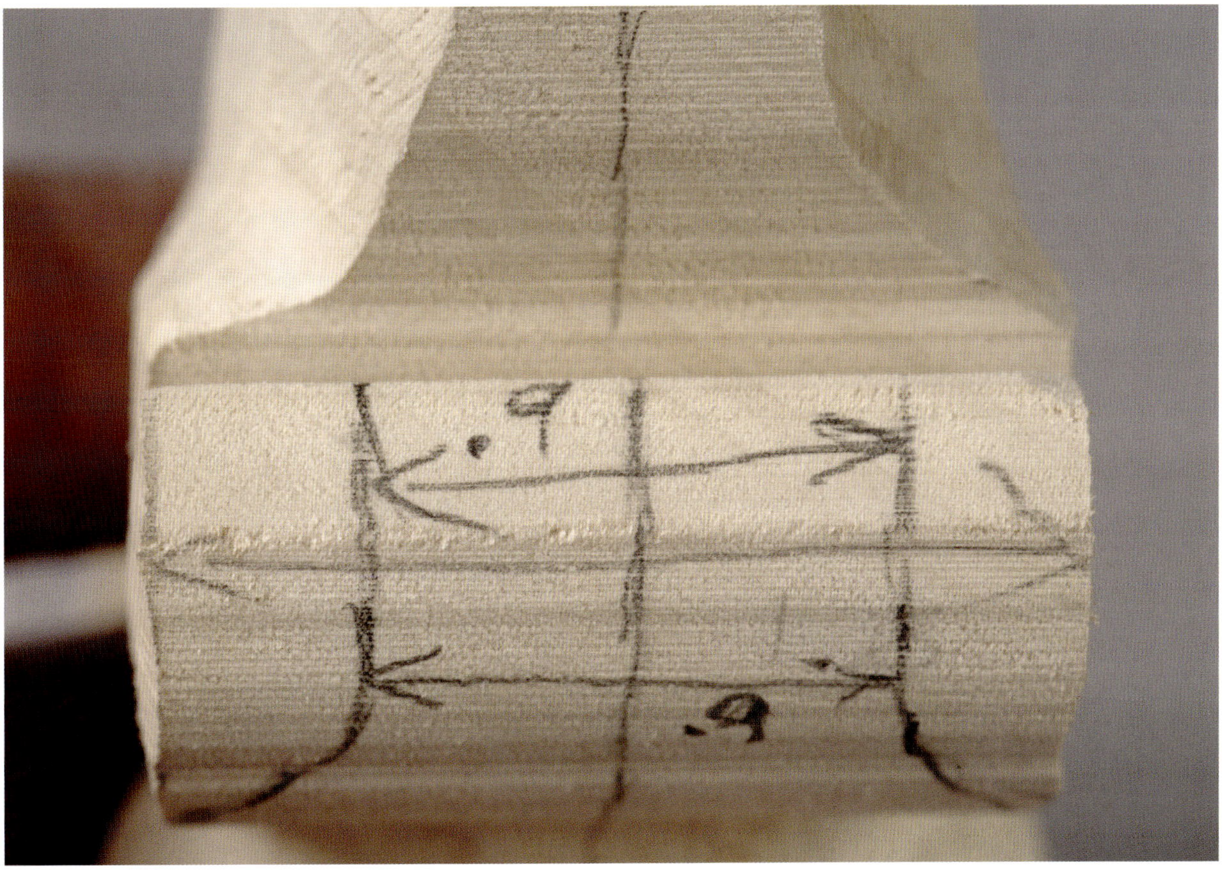

Figure 31. Divide 0.9" (0.45" on each side) across the centerline at the end of the paw block.

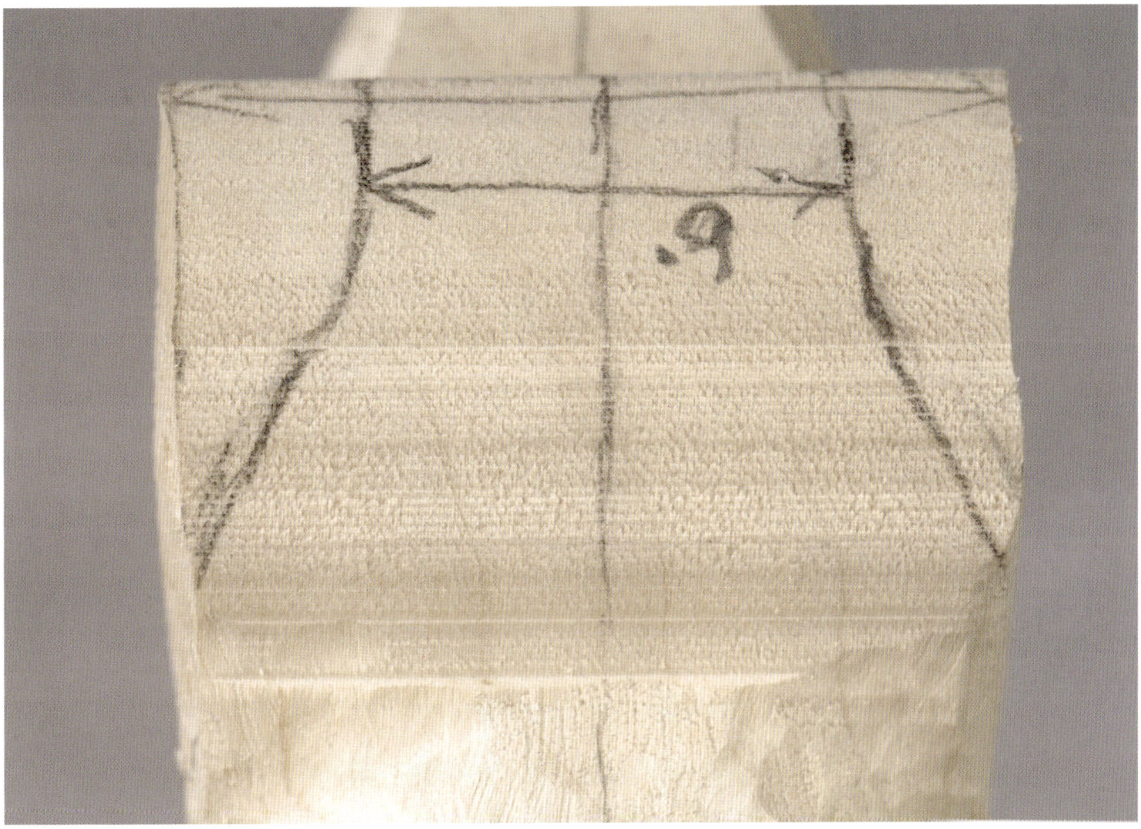

Figure 32. Draw the lines down around the end of the paws and then flare them out the sides.

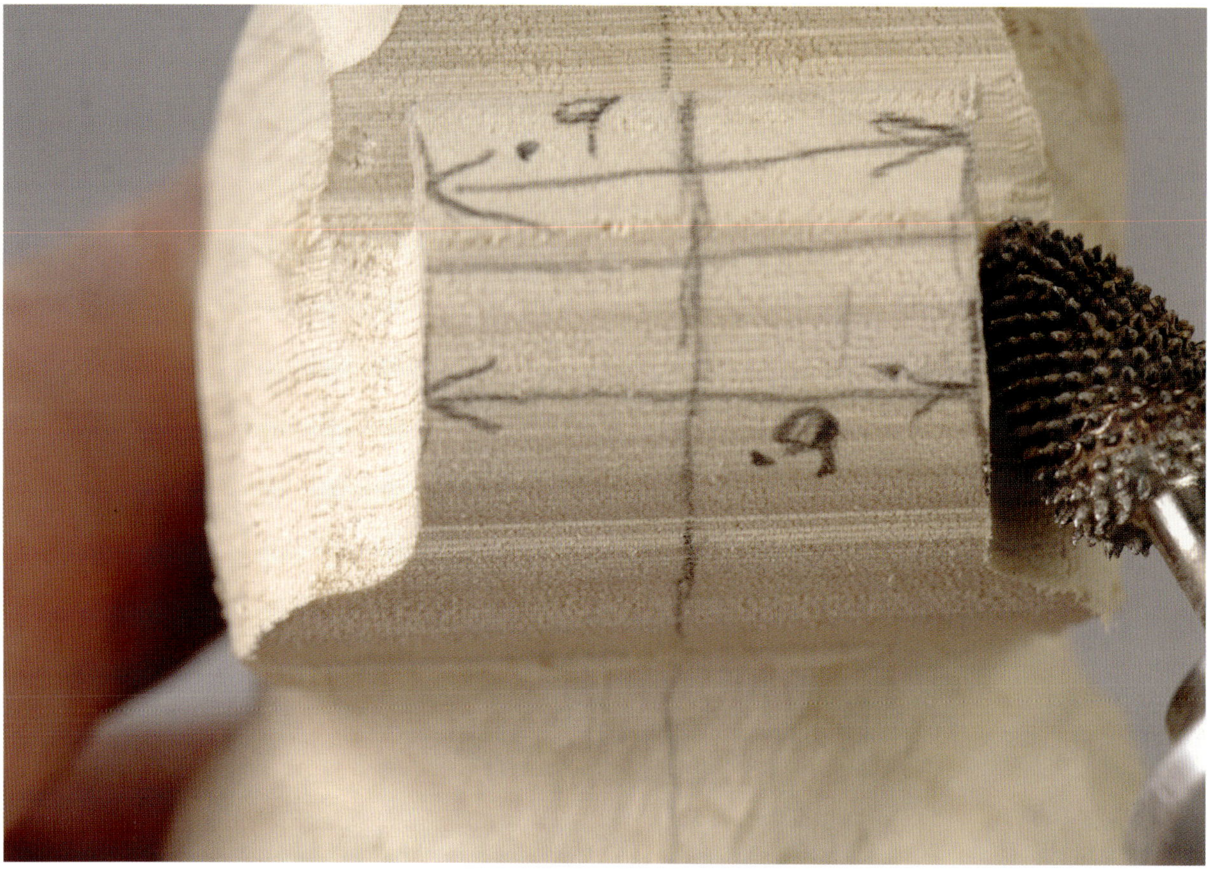

Figure 33. Trim the excess wood off the backs of the paws and arms with the bud Typhoon. Keep everything straight up and down for right now.

Figure 34. Keep removing the wood on the outsides of the paws until the width measures 0.9" with your calipers. This is just the roughing out dimension. The paws will be slightly narrower once the details are accomplished.

Figure 35. Round over the outside corners of the paw blank.

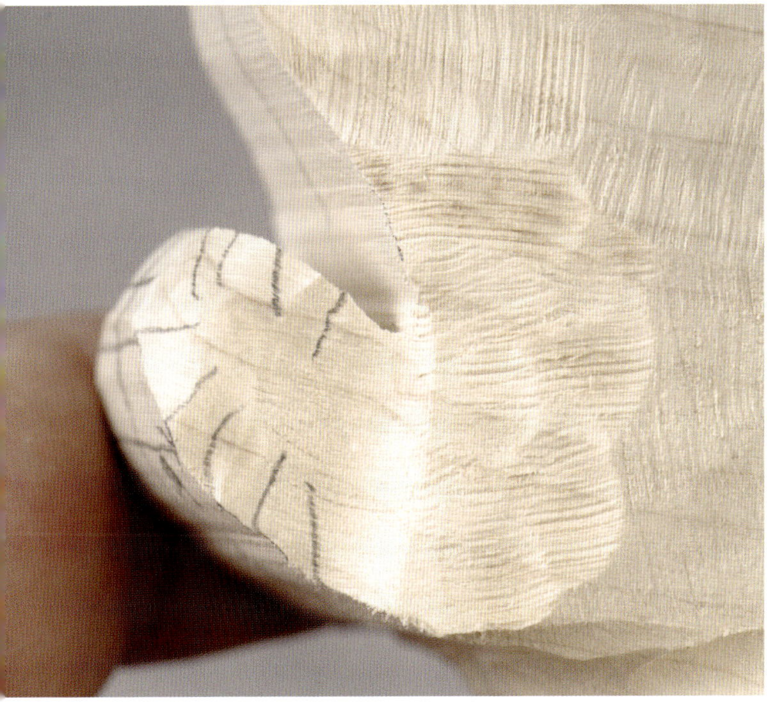

Figure 36. Mark in lines radiating from the middle of each paw to the outside edges.

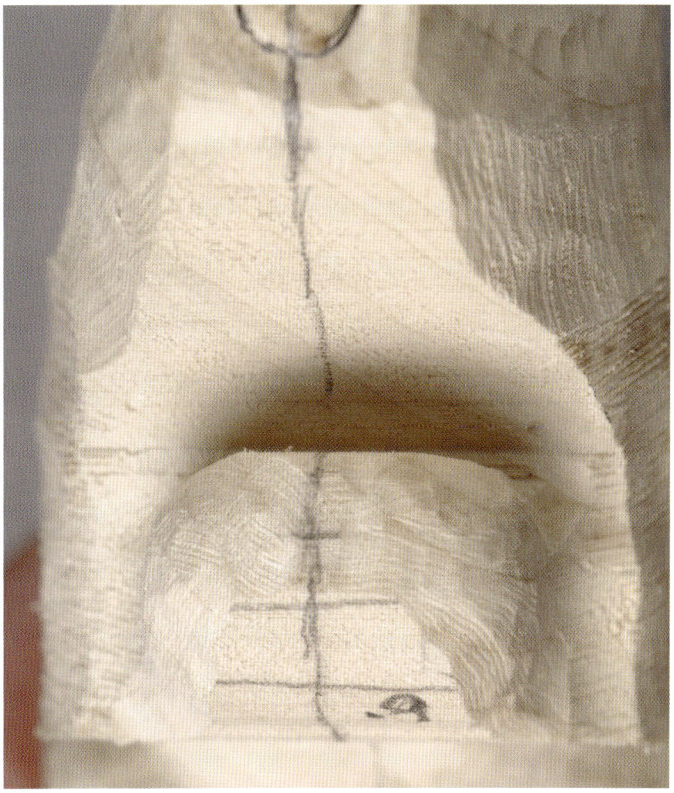

Figure 37. Round over the outside surface of both front paws.

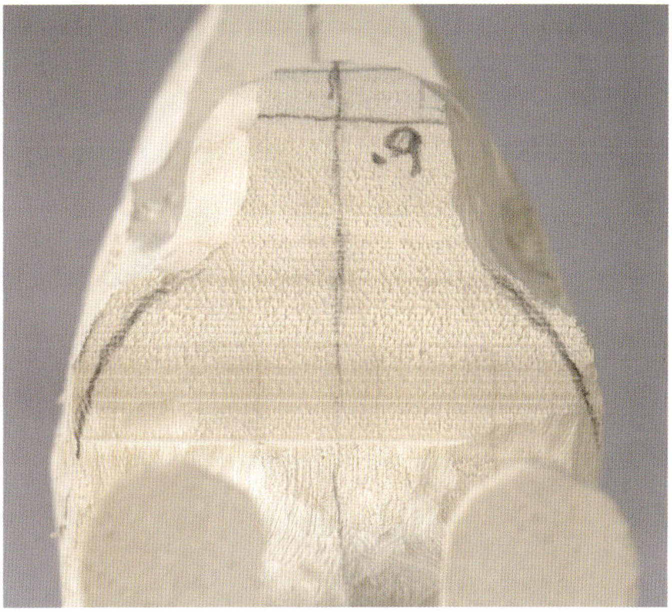

Figure 38. Draw in the transition of the wrists to the front legs/ arms. We need to remove a little more wood here.

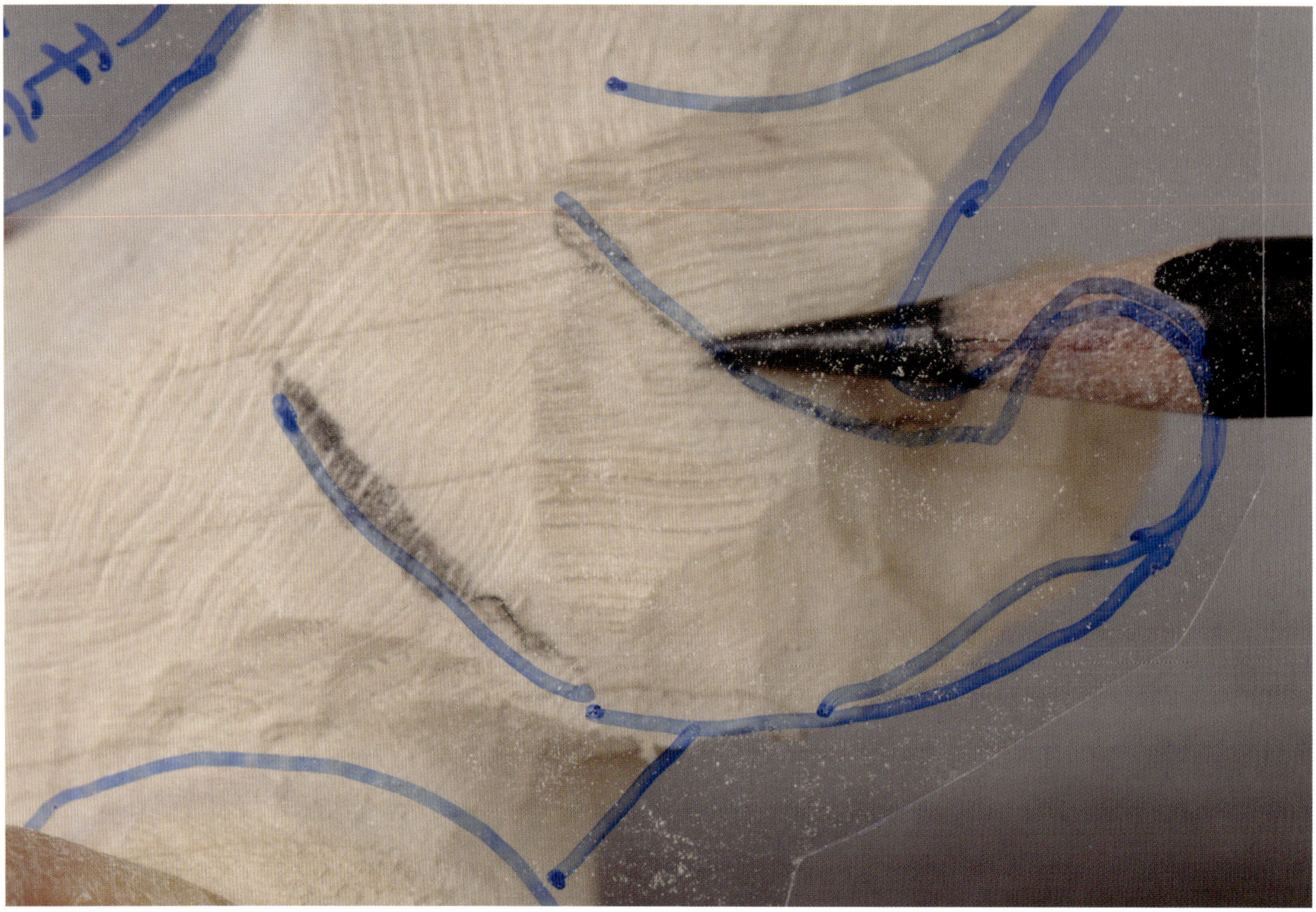

Figure 39. After removing the excess wood off the lower part of the front legs, hold the profile acetate on the outside of the haunch. Sneak a pencil underneath the acetate and trace/draw the rest of the front leg/arm.

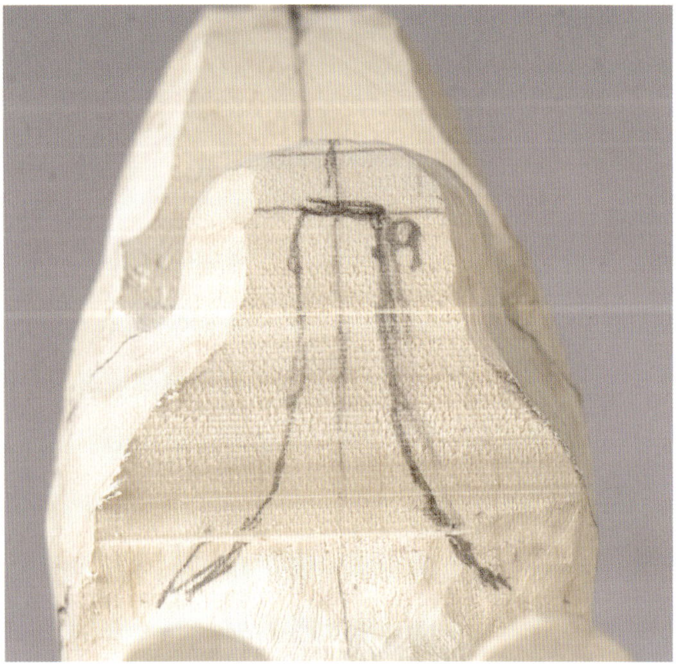

Figure 40. Draw in the rough out shape of the inside of the front legs/arms. For right now, leave at least 0.2" thickness between the inside and outside surfaces of the paws and at least 0.4" thickness on the widest part of the front legs/arms.

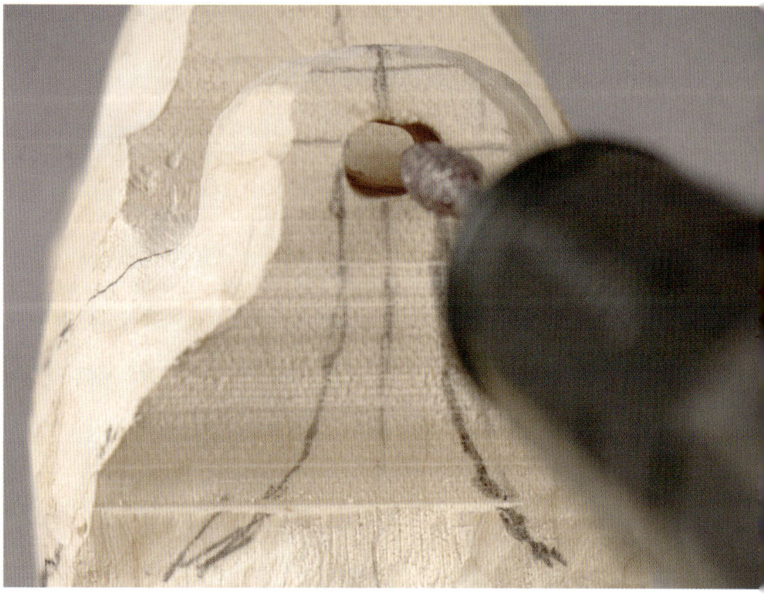

Figure 41. To start removing this excess wood from between the front legs, begin under the paws, using a #2 flame ruby carver (RC-20). Check the angle of the bit and make sure that it is parallel with the top plane of the outside of the paws. Keep watching the top part to determine when the bit comes through. You don't want to be so gung-ho here that you drill forcefully and go into the throat area.

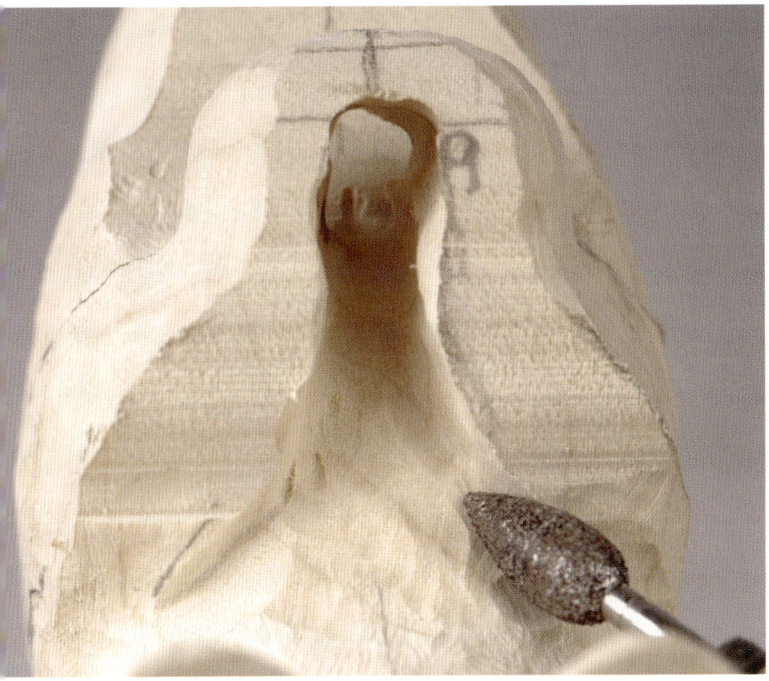

Figure 42. Switch to the #3 flame ruby carver (RC-25) to remove most of the wood between the front legs after the narrow part of the paws is accomplished.

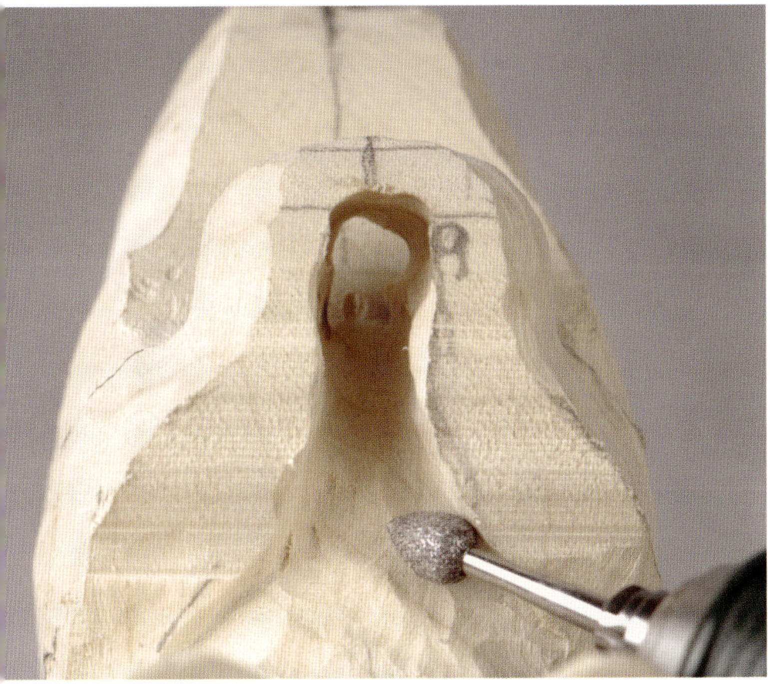

Figure 43. The larger pointed ball ruby carver (RC-17) is useful in clearing out some of the wood on the upper belly and chest.

Figure 44. The #2 flame ruby carver (RC-20) is the perfect bit to carve away the excess wood between the paws and front legs and the throat and neck. Work one side first and then the other, making sure that they connect in the middle of the upper chest/throat areas.

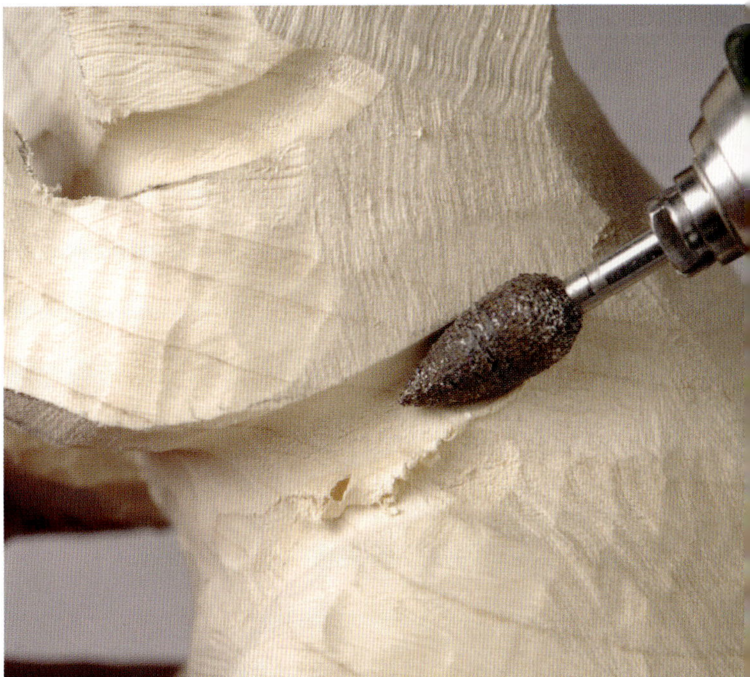

Figure 45. Channel the upper part of the front leg on both sides along the outside of the neck/throat, with the #3 flame ruby carver (RC-25).

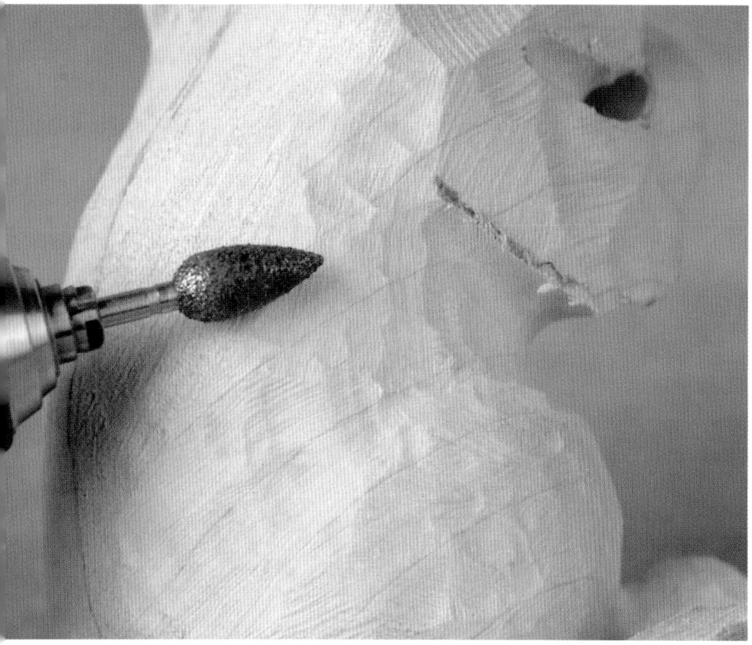

Figure 46. Flow out the channel, rounding towards the back and the flank toward the belly. Do both sides.

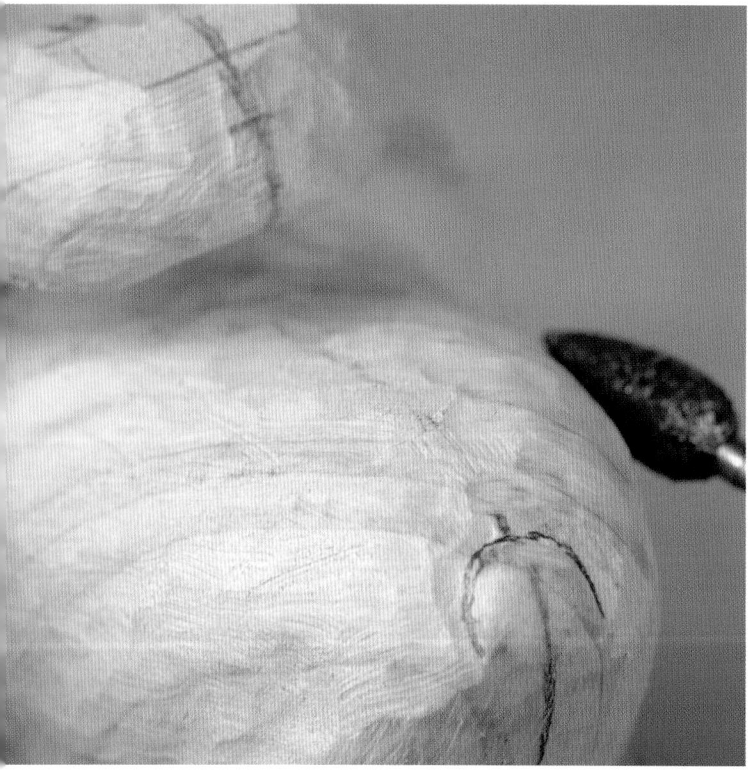

Figure 47. Continue using the #3 flame to round over the throat, chin, and muzzle. Be careful not to ding up the topside of the paws and front legs.

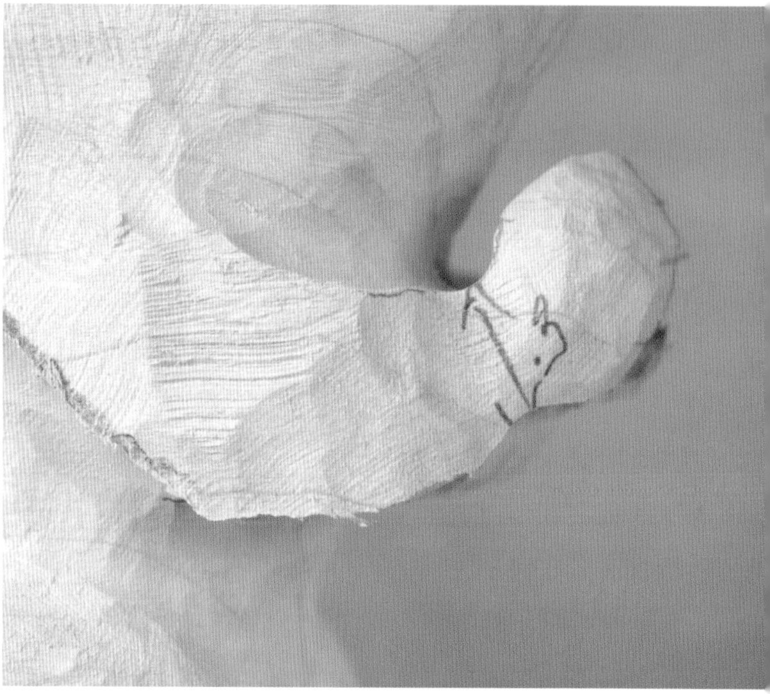

Figure 48. Using the #2 flame, carve in the top and bottom of the wrists on both front legs until each measures approximately 0.3".

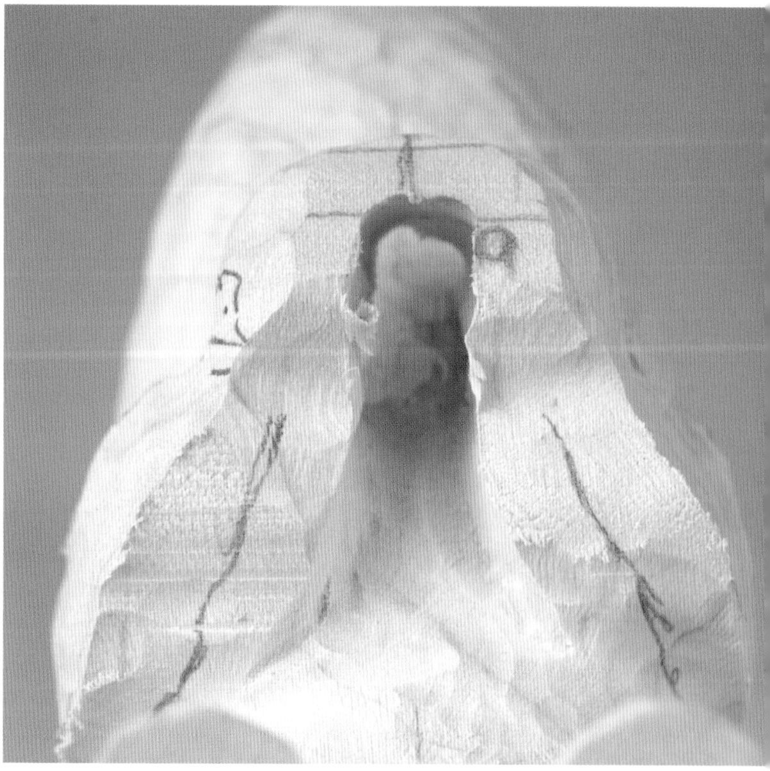

Figure 49. Draw in a centerline on the undersides of the front legs/arms.

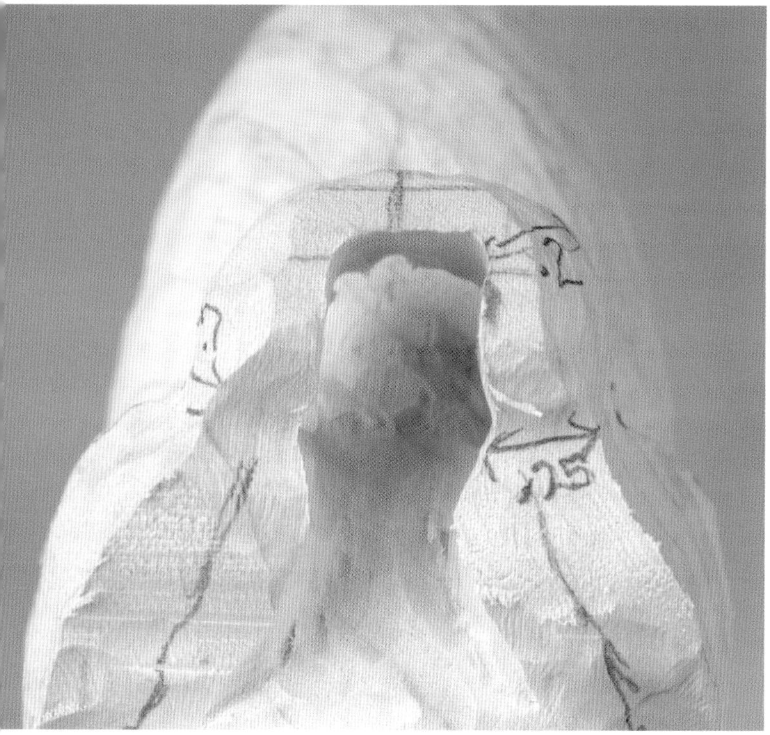

Figure 50. Thin the wrist on the inside until each measures 0.25" thick. Thin the palm of the each front paw on the inside until the thickness measures 0.2" right at the paw bend.

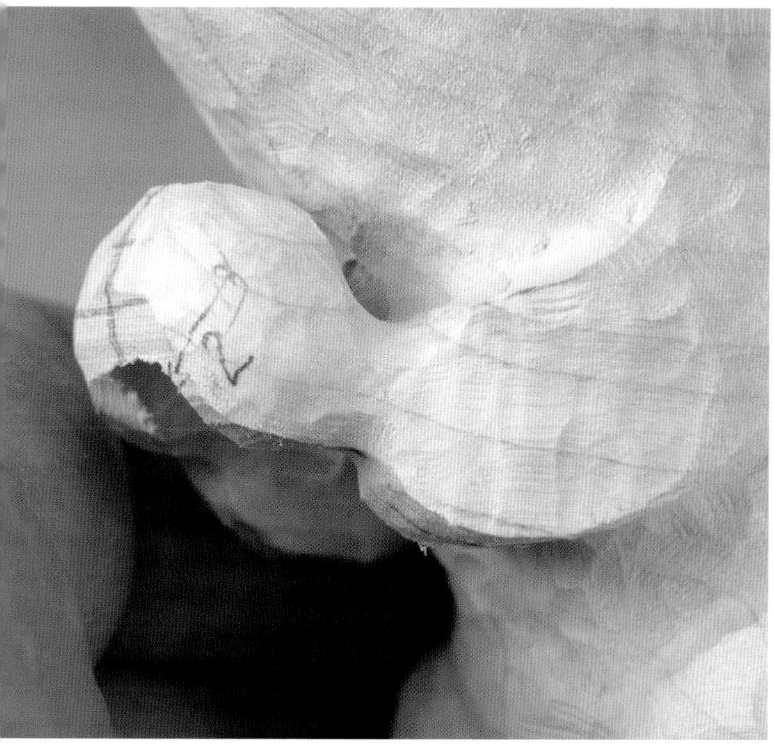

Figure 51. Round over the wrists all the way around.

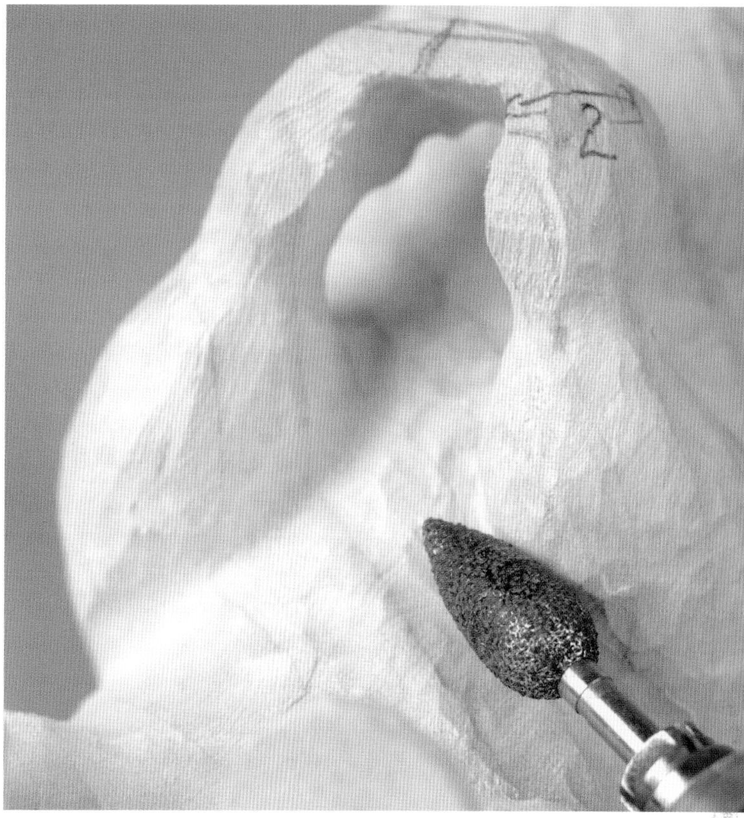

Figure 52. Now, round over the front legs. The underside of the front legs needs to be shaped like a blunt "V". Keep checking for balance to make sure that both front legs are similar in shape and size.

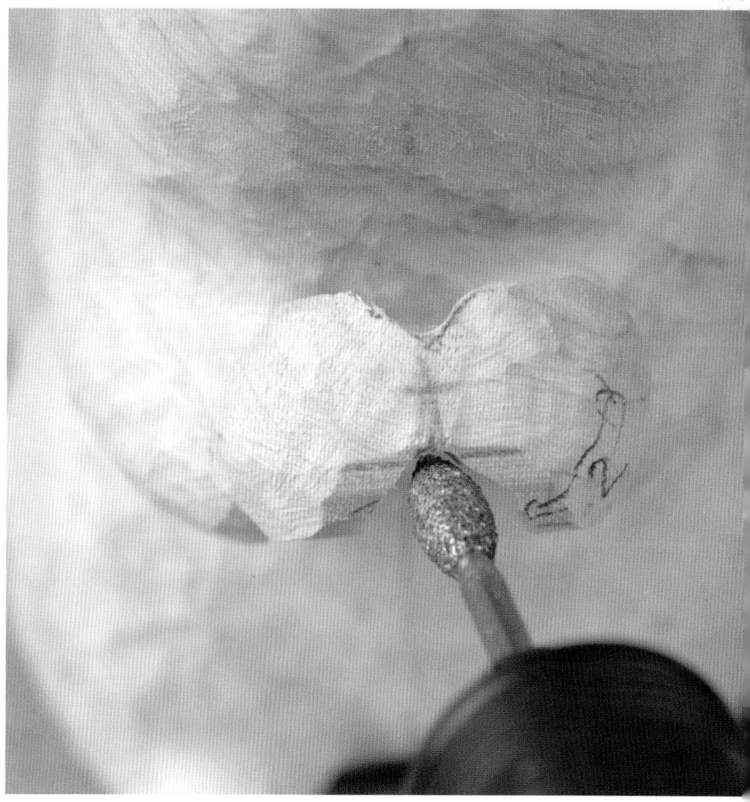

Figure 53. With the #2 flame ruby carver (RC-20), cut in a little "V" on top and on the bottom of the ends of the paws. Flow the channels out so that they blend into the natural rounded shape.

Figure 54. Continue using the #2 flame to cut a "V" groove into the front/top of the paws along the centerline.

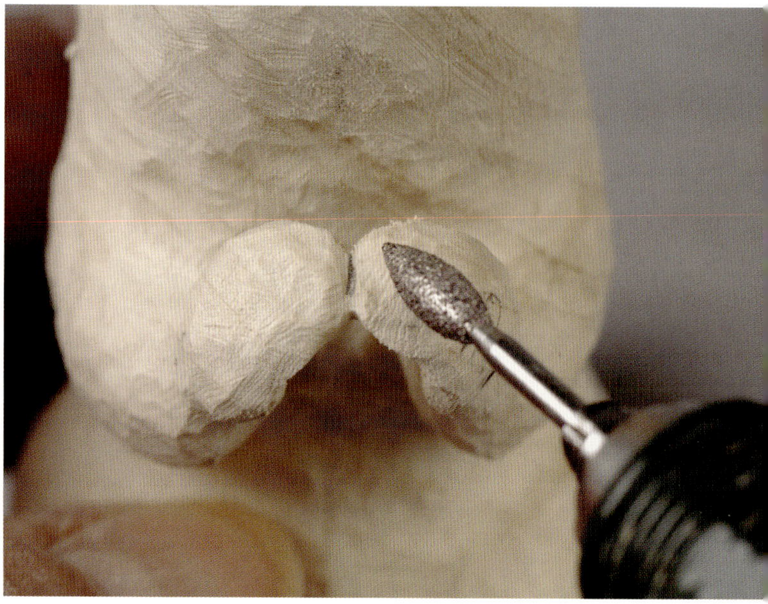

Figure 55. Flow the top surface of the paws down to the bottom of the "V" groove. Round all the corners of the paws with the #2 flame. Check all dimensions of the paws and front legs with the calipers to make sure that there is no large discrepancy between them.

Figure 56. Holding the profile acetate pattern flat on the side of the chipmunk's cheek, trace the ear and eye on both sides. Bending the acetate down to the concave area of the head or to the nose will foreshorten the eyes and the ears.

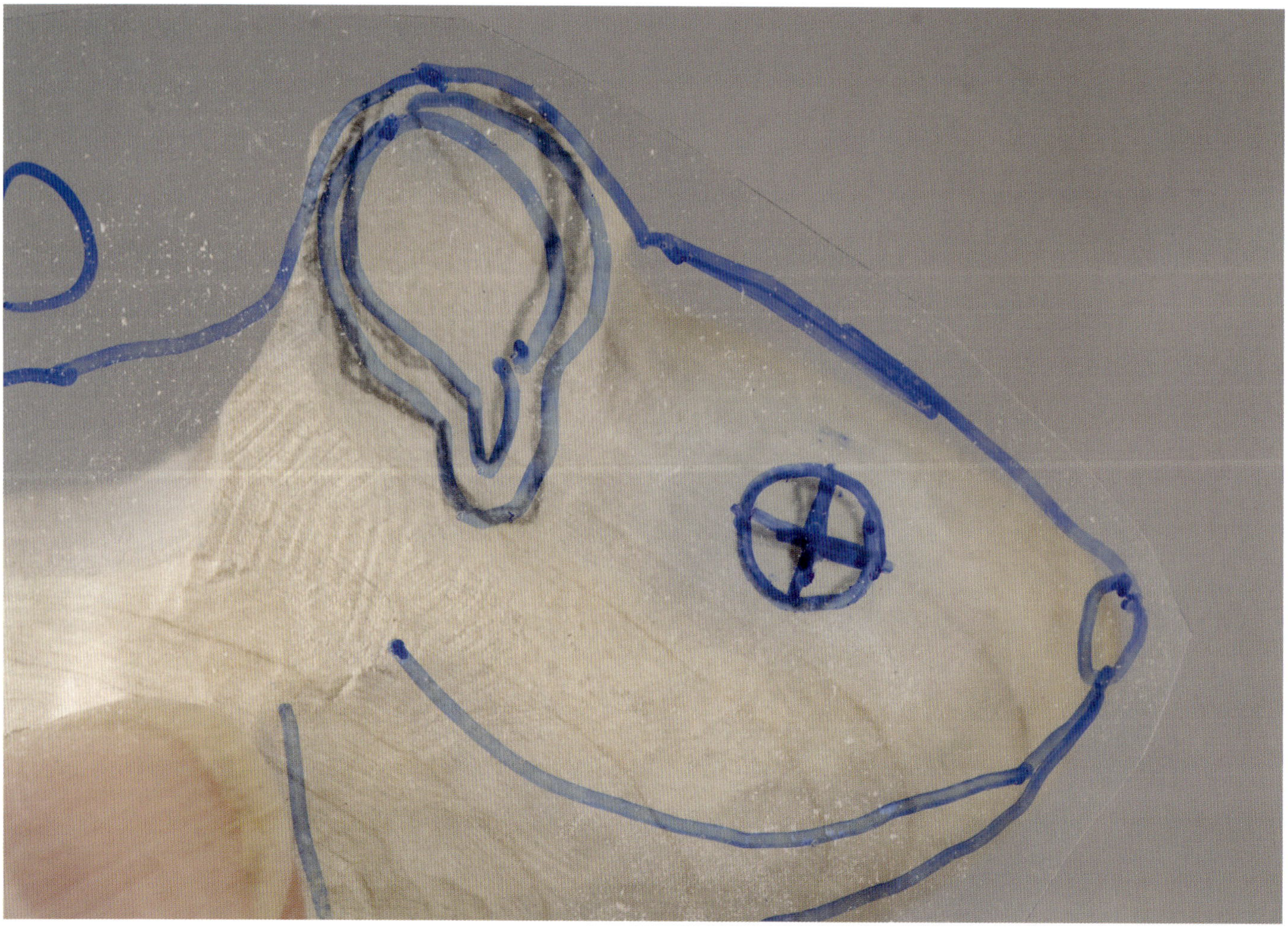

Figure 57. To check to see that you did not foreshorten the eyes, measure from the front of the ear to the eye center. This measurement should be 0.45".

Figure 58. You can use pushpins in the eye centers to check for balance and symmetry from the top and from the front view. If the positions are not equal, adjust as necessary.

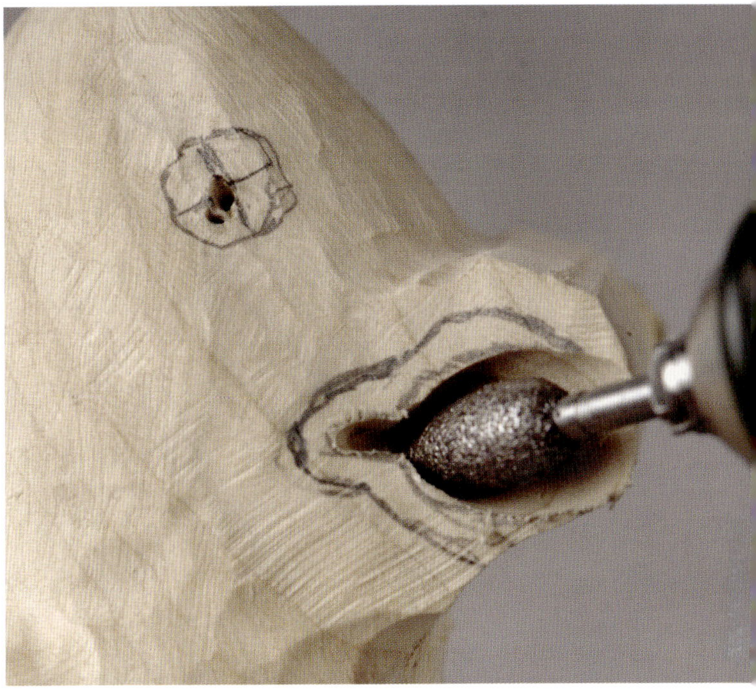

Figure 59. Carve out the interior of the earflap with the #3 flame ruby carver (RC-25). Make sure that the inside of the earflap is concave and that the point of the bit is angled into the head. Do both ears.

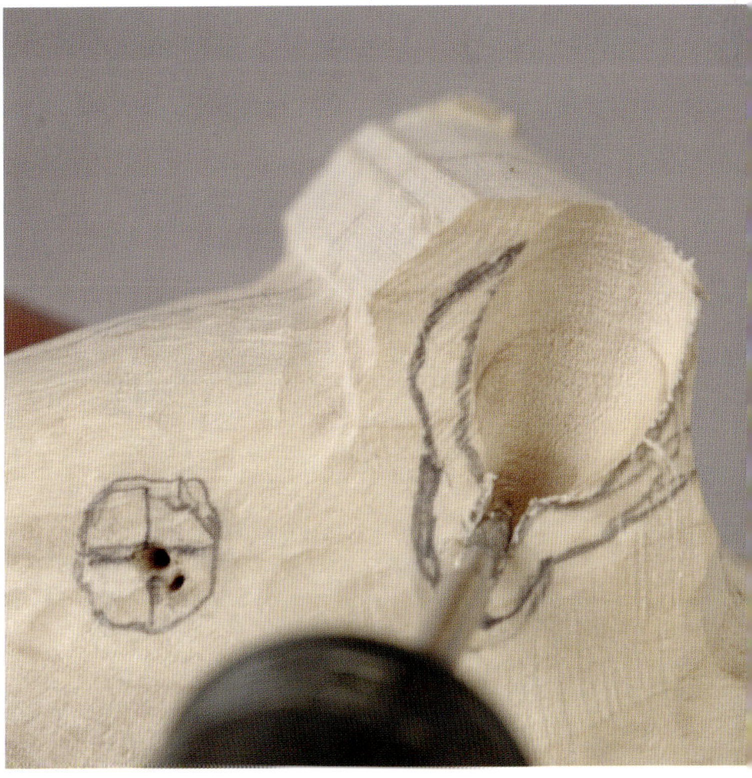

Figure 60. Carve in the little slit on each ear with a detail diamond or a very narrow diameter bit.

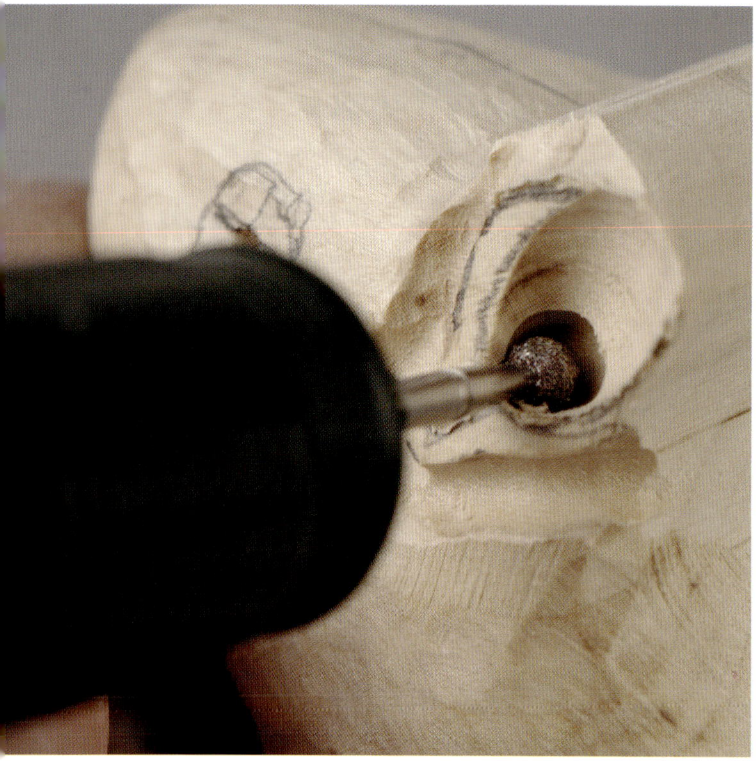

Figure 61. With the small pointed ball (RC-16), widen the ear canal down in the bottom of the earflap on each ear.

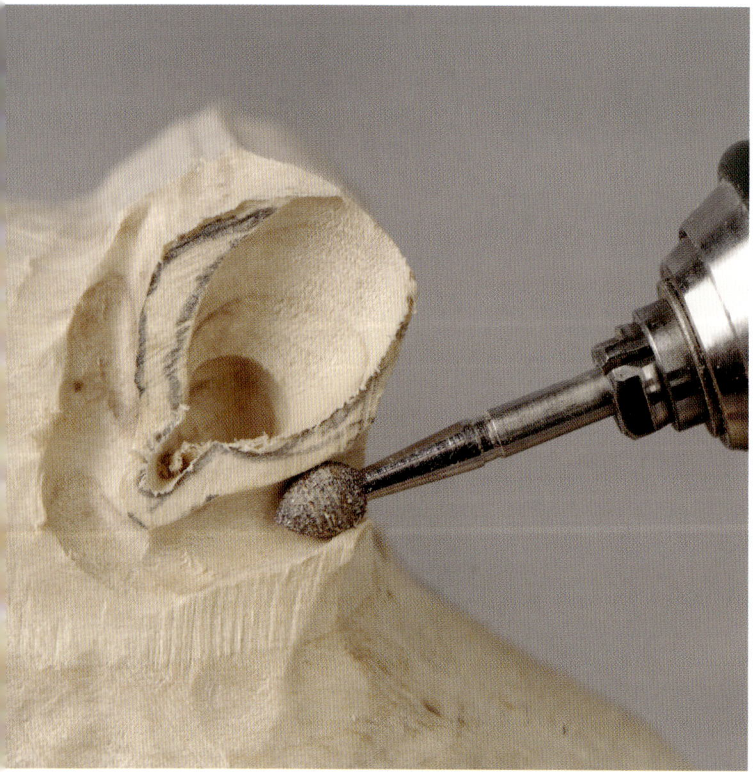

Figure 62. Continuing with the small pointed ball, carve a channel around the outside of the ear flange.

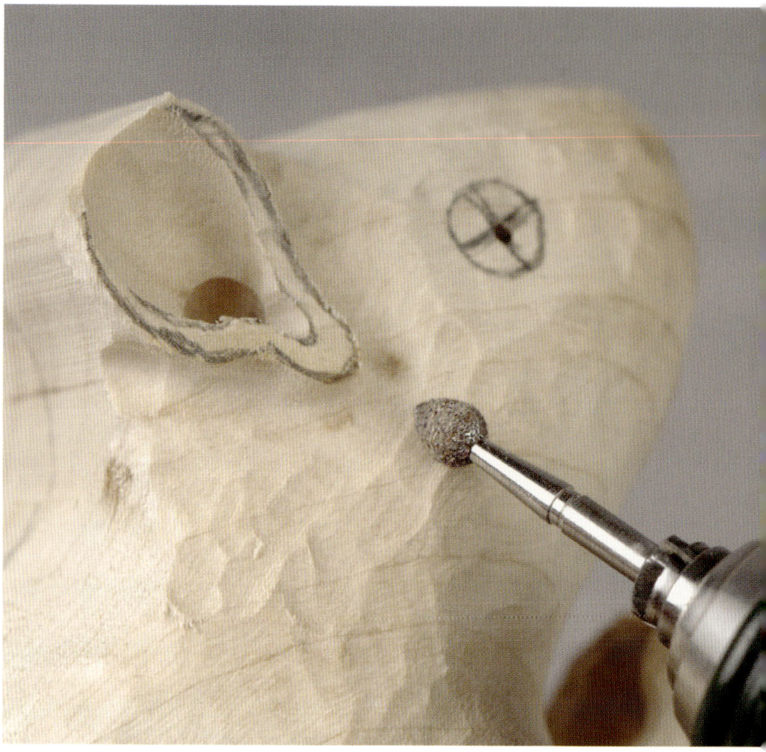

Figure 63. Flow this channel out and blend it into the sides of the head. Do both sides. Lightly round over the sharp outside edge of the flange itself.

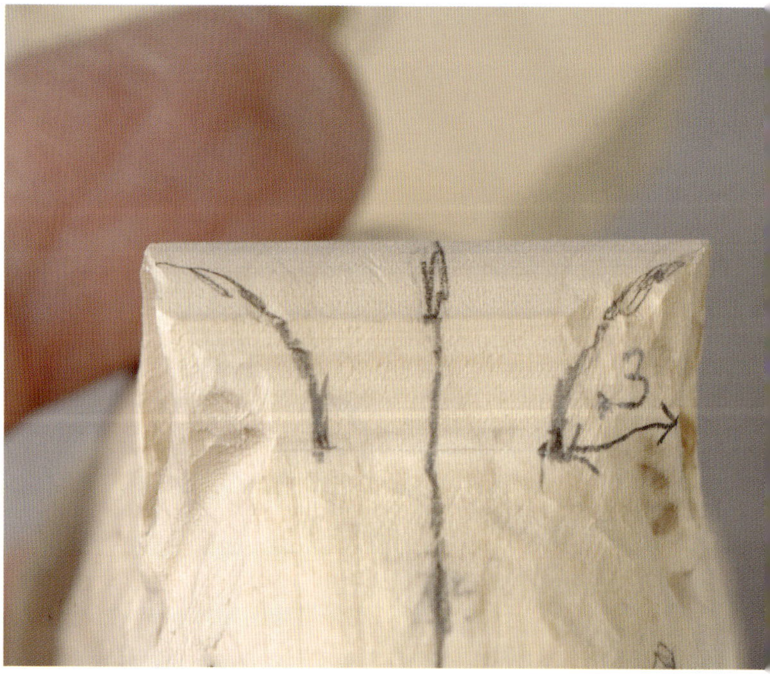

Figure 64. Before drawing in the inside portions of the ears, make sure that the outside is slightly concave from the front view. You also need the back outer surface stickling out slightly further than the front. If yours doesn't look this way, fix it now. Once the chippy ears are the correct shape, measure 0.3" near the head for the width of the base of the ear. Draw curving lines from the measurement marks to the tips of the ears. The wood in between the ears is waste wood.

Figure 65. Start taking this waste wood out along the centerline. Take it down to the level of the top of the head, but be careful about cutting too deep here. The cut should follow the shape of the crown and back of the head.

Figure 66. Keep removing the waste wood, working from the mid-channel out towards the inside surface line of both ears.

Figure 67. Continuing with the #3 flame, round the outside surface of the earflap.

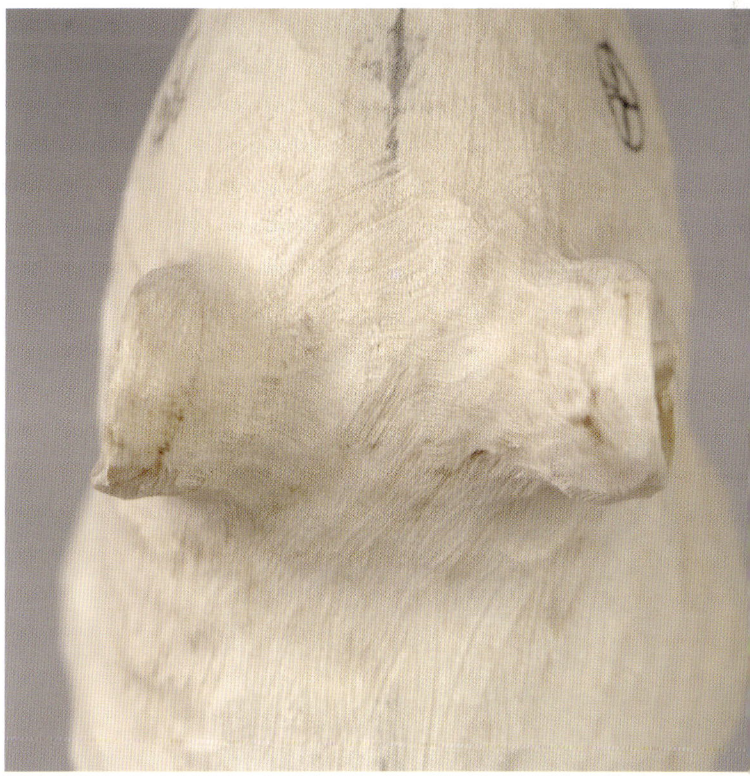

Figure 68. Here is what both round earflaps should look like.

Figure 69. Sand and smooth the inside of thc carflaps with a stone until there are no scratches left from the ruby carver.

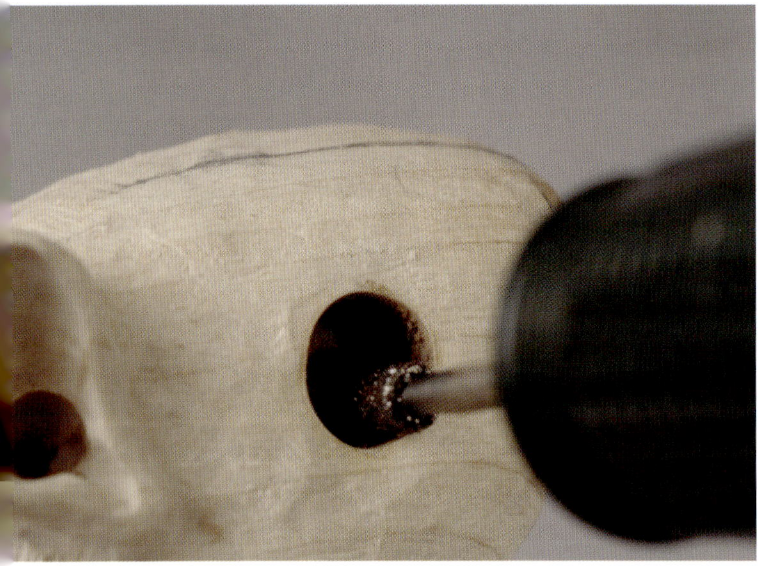

Figure 70. Using the slightly domed, straight-sided ruby carver (RC-18), drill the eyeholes. Because I am right-handed, I drill the right eye first, and then, looking straight on to make sure that the eyeholes are balanced, drill the left one. If you are left-handed, I recommend that you do the opposite. Drill the depth of the bit. In shaping the eyelids, some of the wood around the eyes will be removed, thus reducing the depth of the eyeholes.

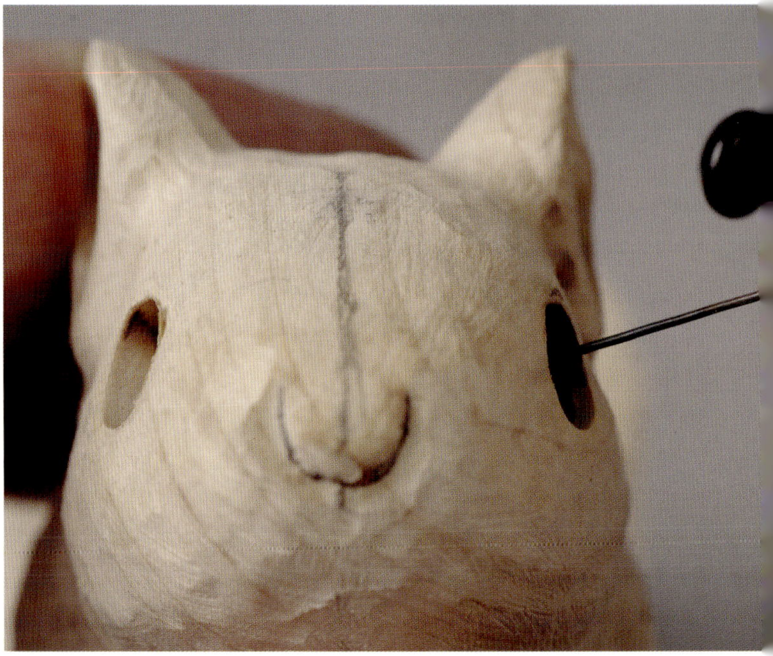

Figure 71. Make sure both eyes fit and will go to the bottom of both holes.

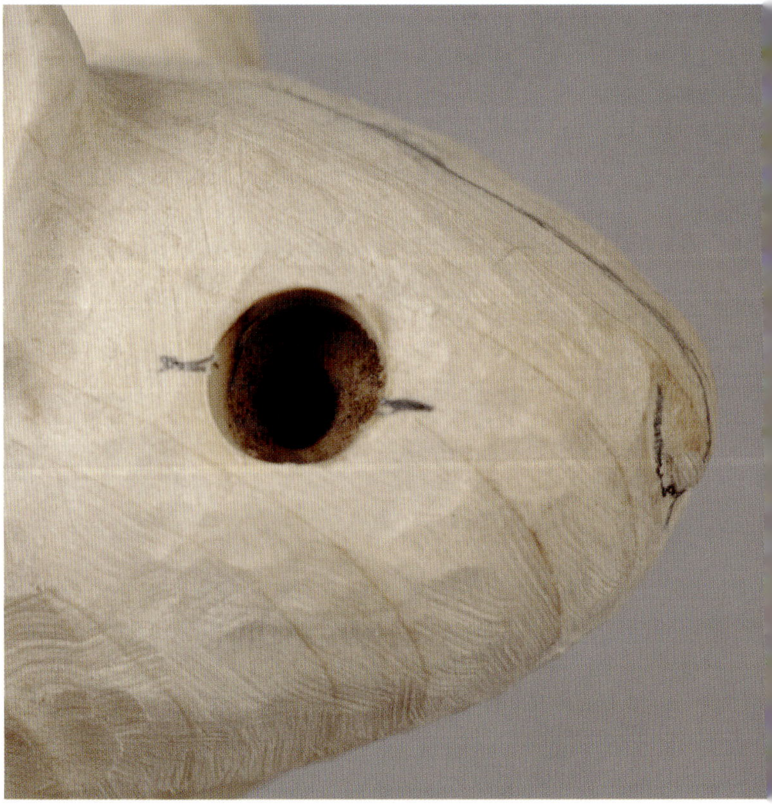

Figure 72. After the eyeholes are accomplished, draw two dashes (one in front and one behind the eye) with the level pointing from the base of the ear to the nose. Check both eyes to make sure that the dashes are even and balanced. The dashes represent the point at which the upper and lower eyelids meet.

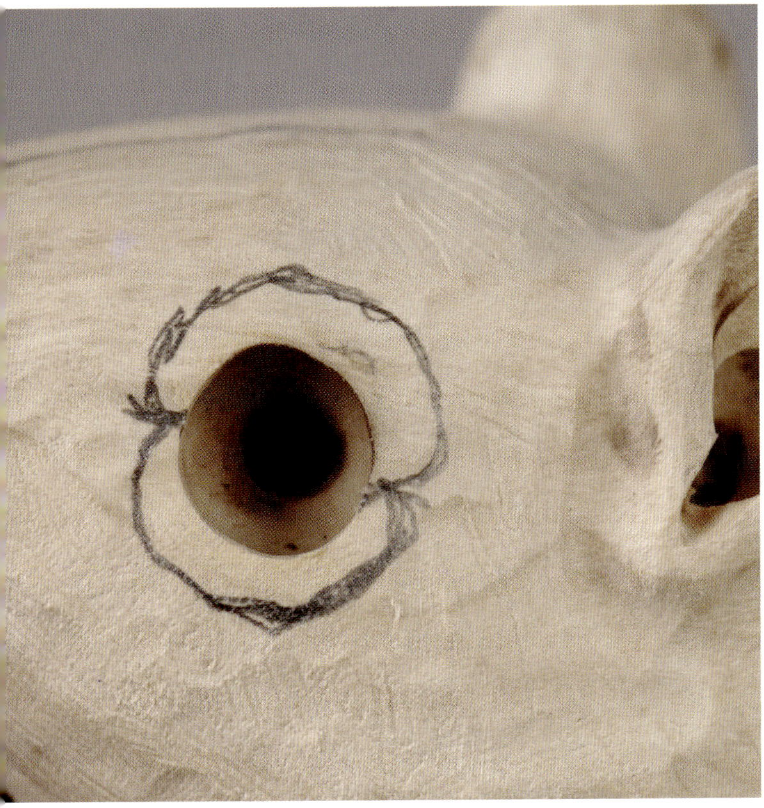

Figure 73. Draw in the eyelids, meeting at the dashes.

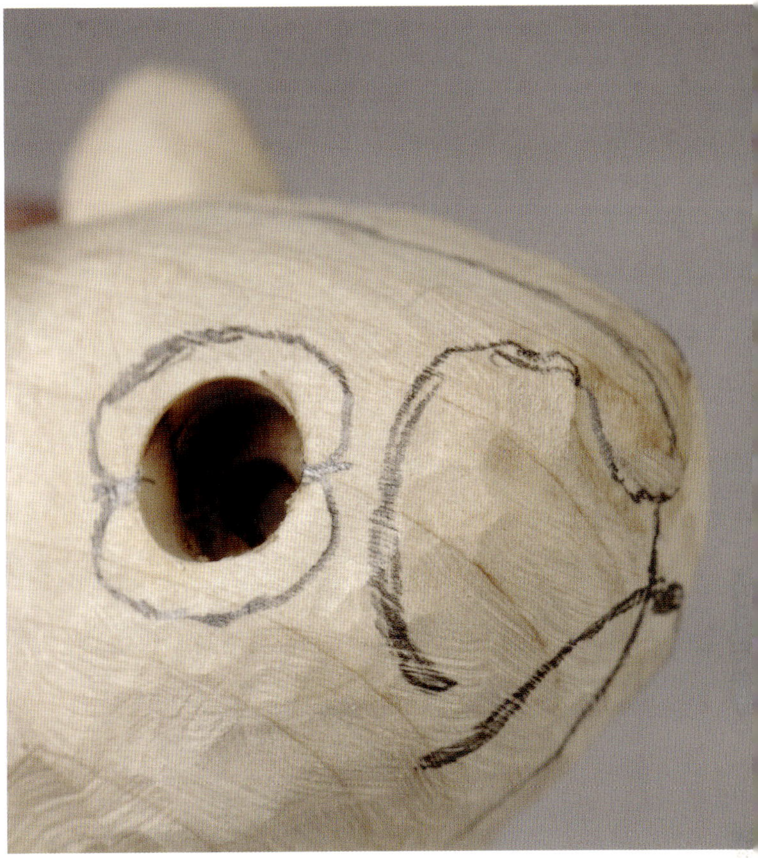

Figure 75. Draw in the whisker pads. On the chippy's right side, the shape is that of a "C" with the beginning of the line starting at the back of the nose and then curving around toward the mouth line. On the left side, it is a backward "C" shape.

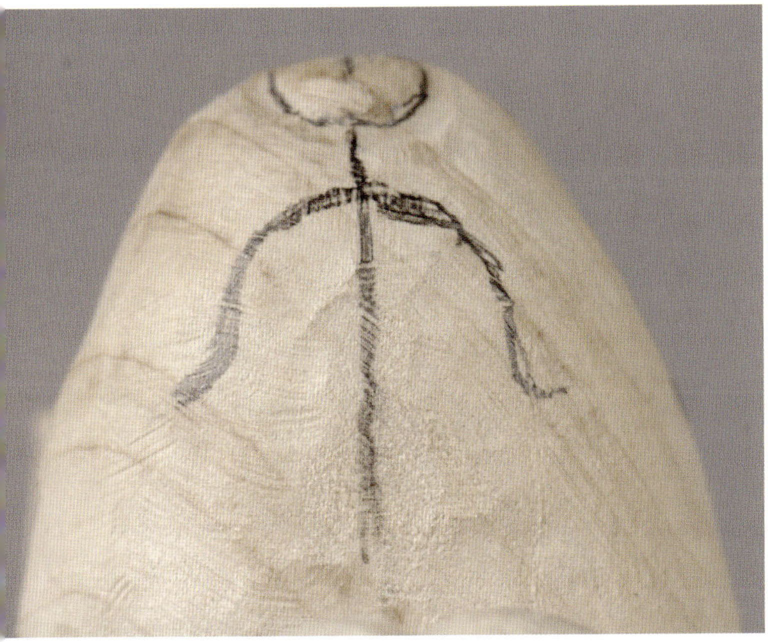

Figure 74. Draw a short mark underneath the nose on the centerline that is 0.1" long and then draw the mouth with slight upturns on both ends. The little slit underneath the nose is the dividing point for the growth of fur, which comes into play later.

Figure 76. Note that the whisker pad lines do not come to the mouth line.

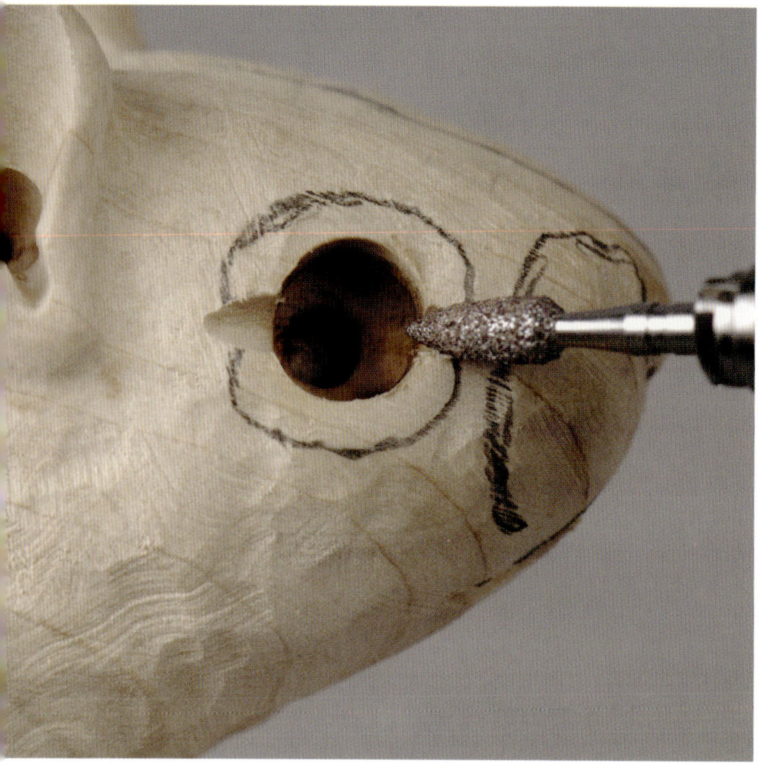

Figure 77. Using the point of the #1 flame ruby carver (RC-19), push the point of the bit down into the eyehole at the little dashes separating the eyelids.

Figure 79. Still using the #1 flame, roll the lower lip down to the bottom of the "V" groove of the mouth line cut. Take the sharp corner off the upper lip.

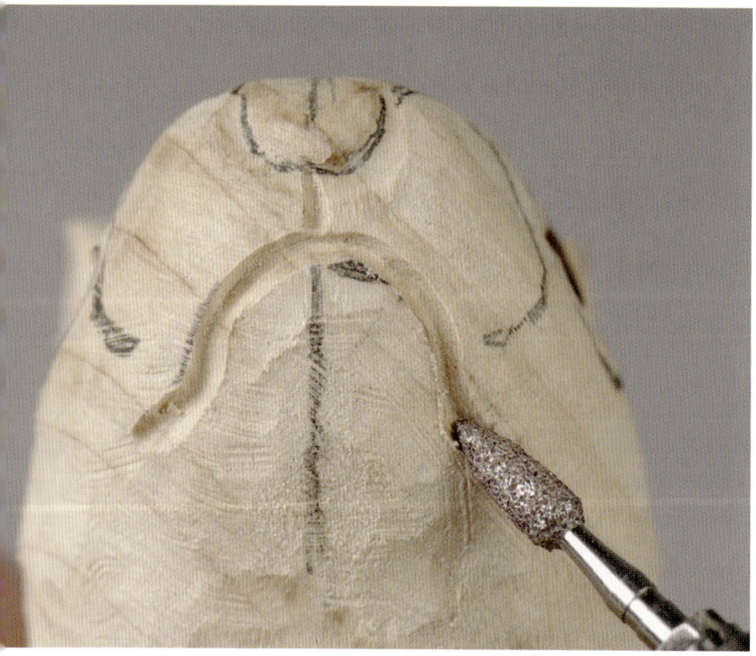

Figure 78. While we have that bit in the micro motor machine, cut the little slit under the nose on the centerline, and drag the point of the #1 along the mouth line.

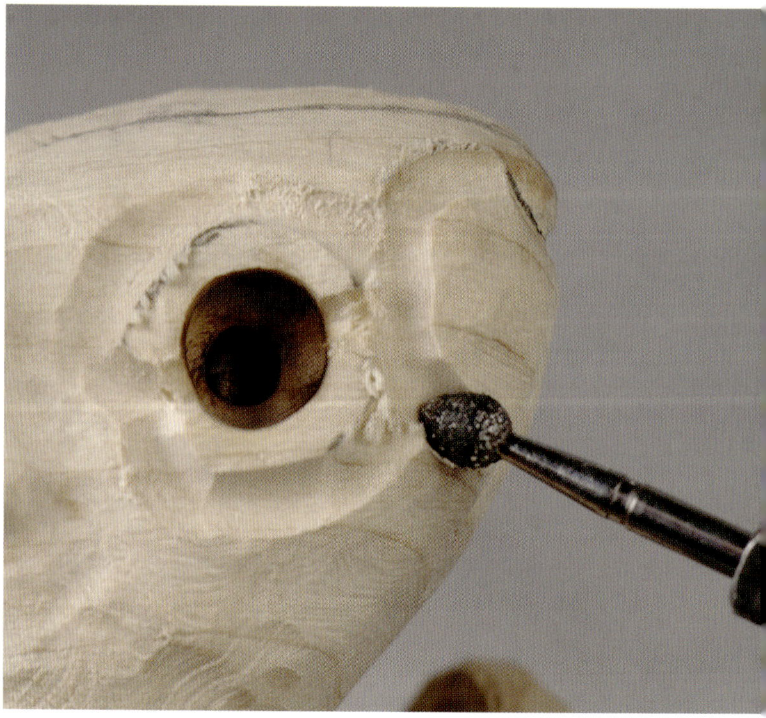

Figure 80. Using the small pointed ball ruby carver (RC-16), channel around the eyelids and the whisker pads. The channel in front of the eyelids becomes the channel around the whisker pads. Lay the bit down to do the channels and do not use the point except near the dashes/slits where the upper and lower eyelids meet. Do both sides.

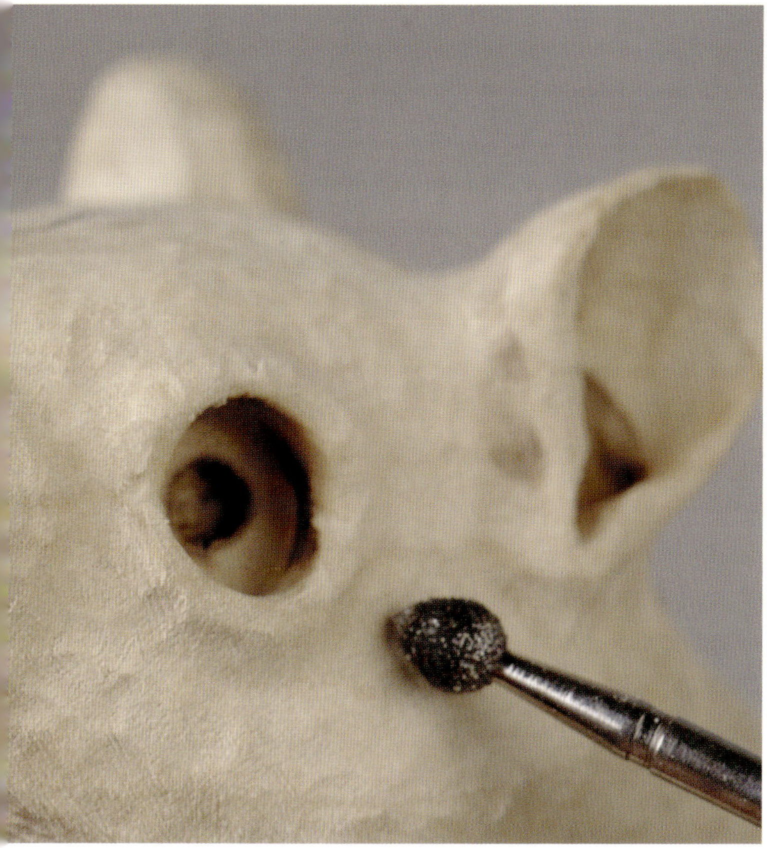

Figure 81. Flow all the channels out onto the surface on the side of the head. Round over the whisker pads. Round over the inside and outside of the eyelids and taper them down to the dashes/ slits. Check from the top plan view that you have the chippy's eyelids, cheeks, and whisker pads balanced and symmetrical.

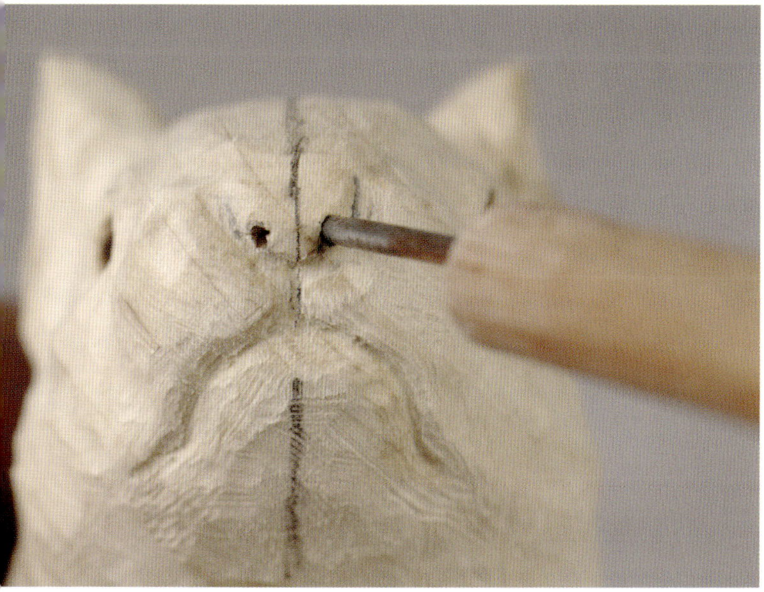

Figure 82. Mark in the nostril holes on the bottom of the nose. Use the poker end of the eye tool to make the nostrils.

Figure 83. To do the digits on the front paws, you need 3 lines for 4 digits. There is a little remnant thumb nubbin on the top of each paw—draw that in on both paws. Then, draw a line down the middle of the paw. Divide what is remaining to the left of that centerline and draw a line, and do the same on the right.

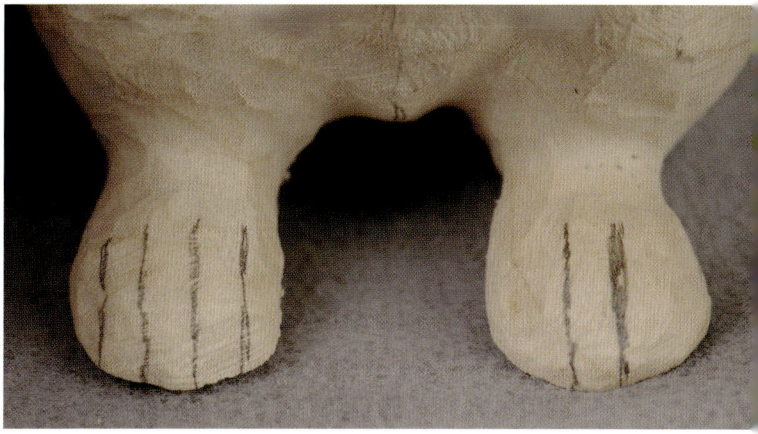

Figure 84. To do the toes on the hind feet, draw two parallel lines about 0.1" apart in the middle of the paw. Then, divide what's remaining on the left in half and put a line, and do the same on the right. Four lines will give the paws 5 toes. Do the paws this way.

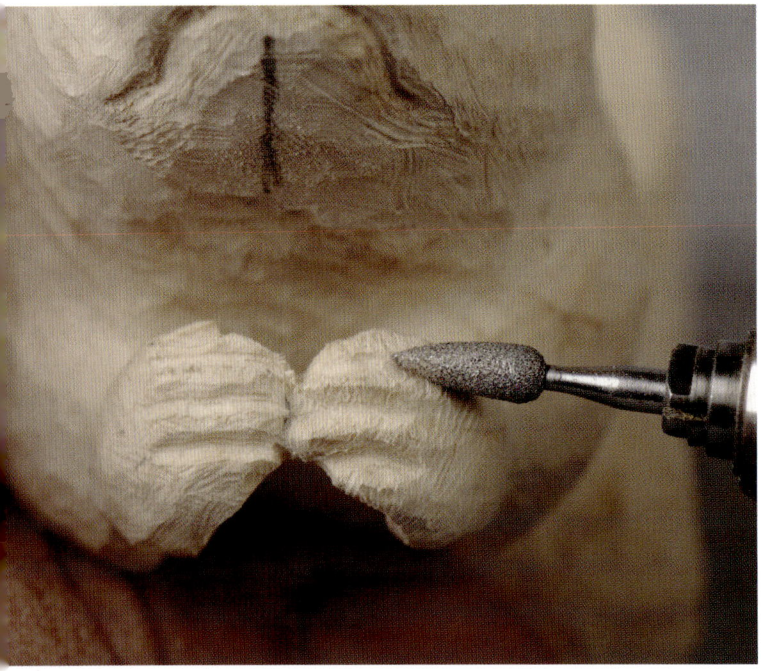

Figure 85. On the front paws, drag the #1 flame ruby carver (RC-19) down each line, letting the tip carve a "V" shape to separate each digit. Carve around the little nubbin thumb. Then round over all the digits/fingers.

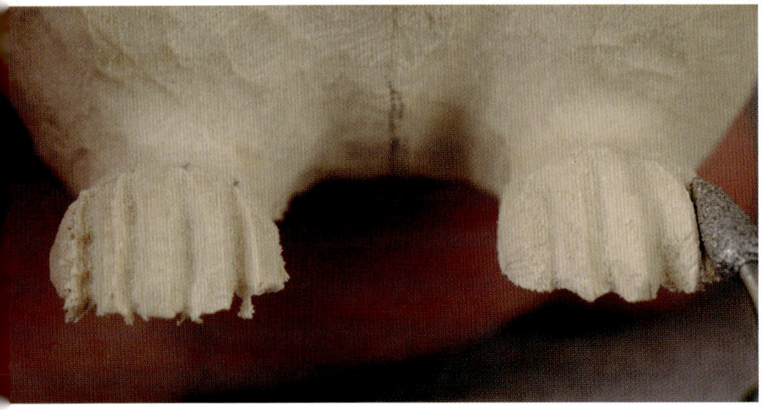

Figure 86. On the hind paws, drag the #1 flame down each line separating each toe with a "V" trough. Then round over each of the toes.

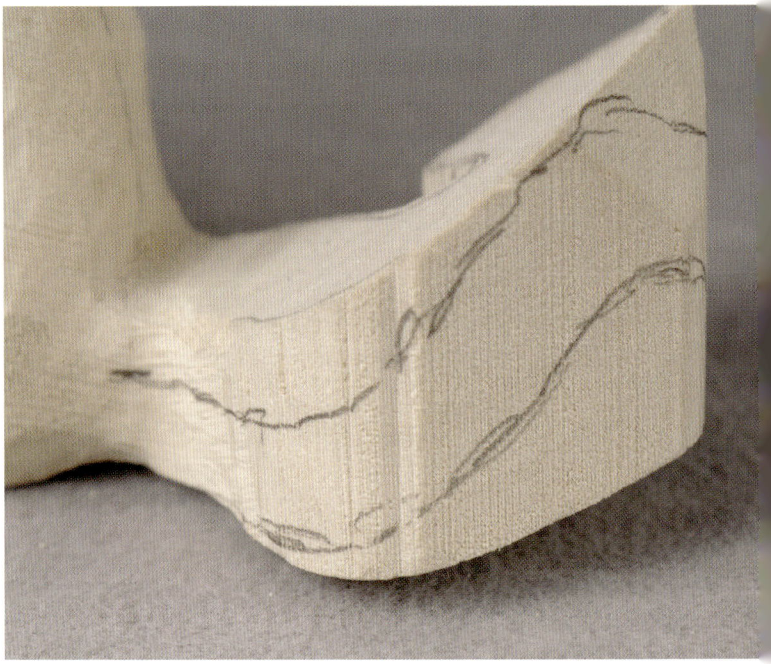

Figure 87. Draw in the tail allowing approximately 0.3" thickness height the entire length. There is sufficient wood allowed in the blank to undulate the tail, creating more motion in the piece.

Figure 88. The middle of the tail is high in the blank and drops down just before the upturned tip. There is a lot of wood here for you to create some undulations!

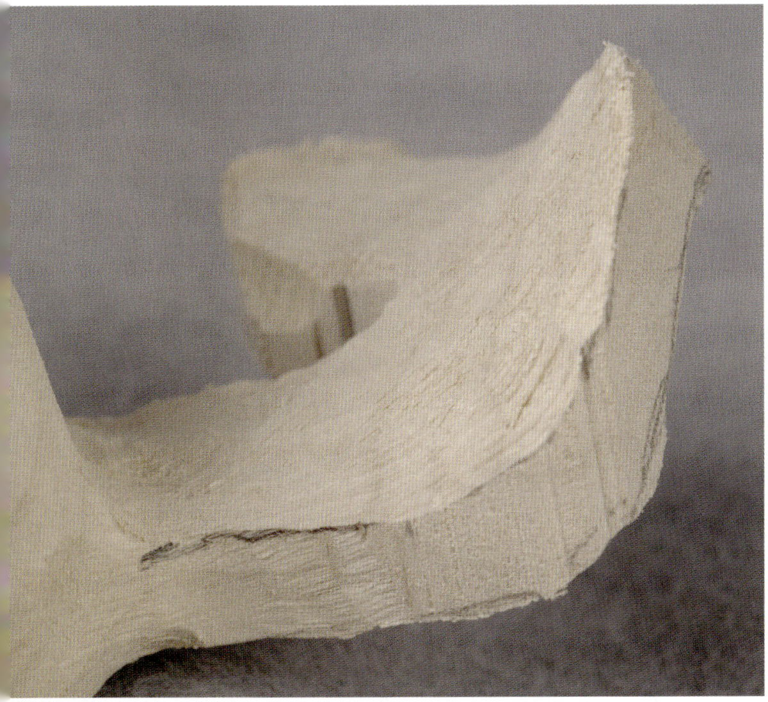

Figure 89. Rough out the tail thickness with the flame Typhoon carbide bit. The tail can be straight across from side to side but it can angle as well, as shown in the picture. Just maintain the 0.3" thickness and keep the top and bottom parallel at this point. Support the tail throughout the roughing out and the detailing work to keep it from breaking, since part of it is cross-grain.

Figure 90. Draw a centerline on the tail. Round it over to within 0.1" from the bottom edge. Also round the very tip over.

Figure 91. Lightly concave the tail underside with the flame Typhoon.

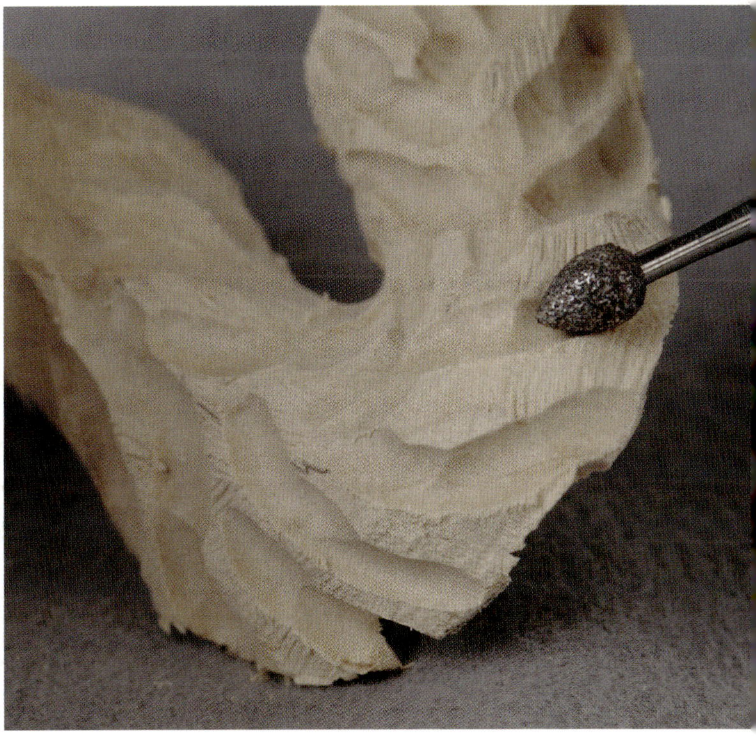

Figure 92. To make the tail surface more irregular, drag the #2 flame (RC-20) or the large pointed ball ruby carver (RC-17) in curving strokes from the center out to the edge.

Figure 93. Do the tail underside as well. Have the underneath cuts come in between the top strokes near the edge to make it more irregular.

Figure 94. Make sure that you have a smooth transition from the body to the tail. The tail width at the base should be 0.6".

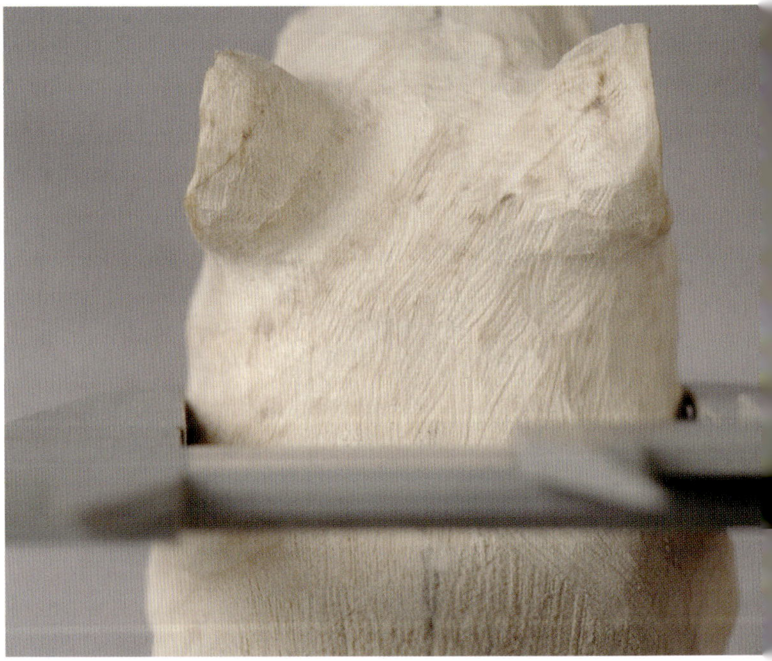

Figure 95. Okay, before we start texturing, let's check some measurements. Your chippy does not have to be exactly these measurements—close is good, just as in horseshoes! The neck width is 1.25". From front to back, the neck thickness is 1.1".

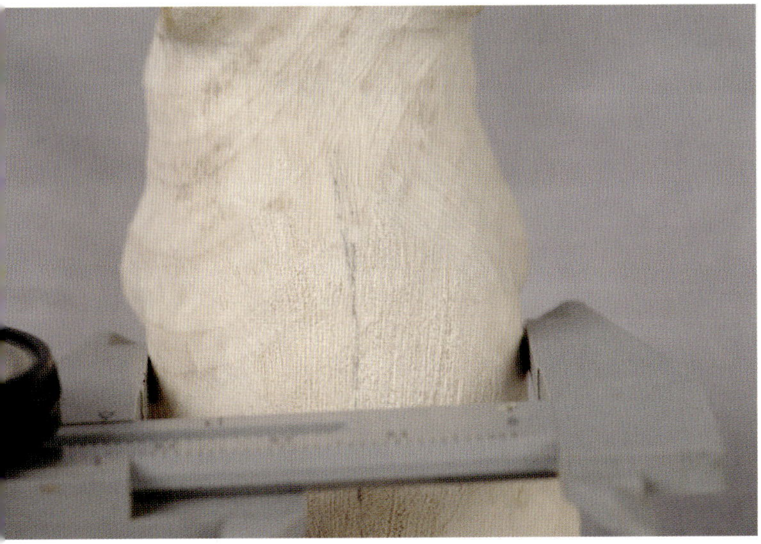

Figure 96. Just under the front legs/arms, the width should be 1.39". From the middle of the back to the middle of the belly, the thickness should be approximately 1.52".

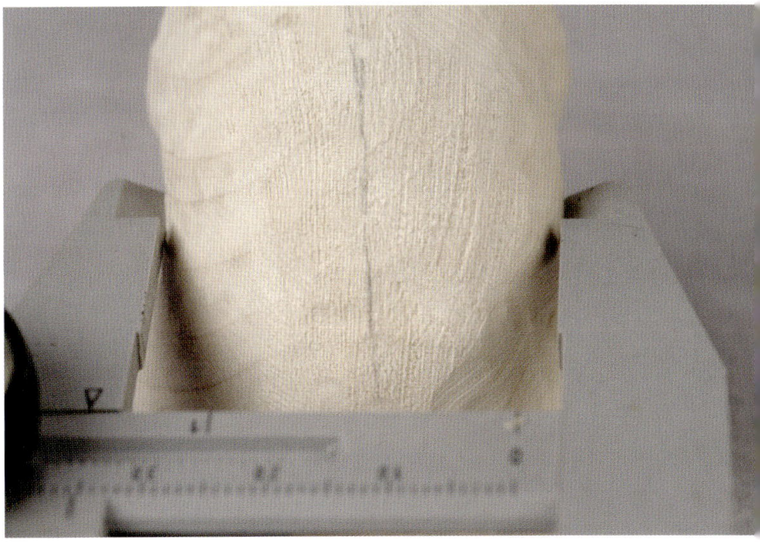

Figure 97. Just above the haunches, the width should be approximately 1.45".

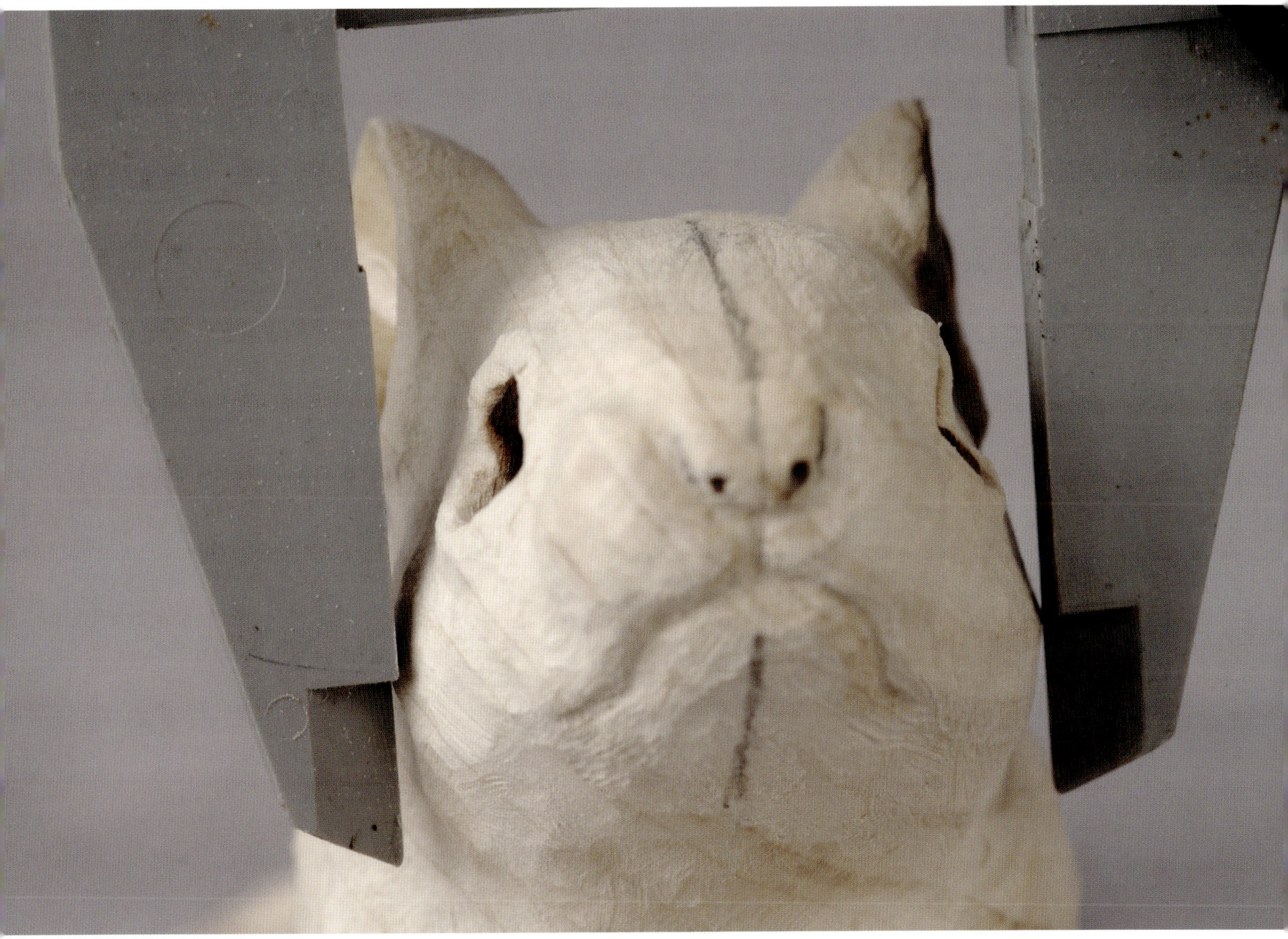

Figure 98. The head width at the cheeks should be approximately 1.2".

Figure 99. Before you start texturing, draw in the flow lines for the fur. Basically, fur flows from the nose back toward the tail and down each leg.

Figure 100. The fur flow lines come straight down the back toward the tail.

Figure 101. Here you see the flow lines coming down the belly and down the inside of the haunches to the hind paws.

Figure 102. Note that the flow lines droop on the whisker pads in a downward motion. On the inside of the front legs/arms, the flow lines come down the inside of the arm and then angle off the back edge.

Figure 103. This slightly domed, straight-sided cylinder ruby carver (RC-18) is the bit to use to texture.

Figure 104. **Do not texture the nose, eyelids, ears, or paws**! The eyelids, ears, and paws will be burned but not textured. Hold the texturing bit at an angle so that just the corner of the bit's tip is contacting the wood. Move it back and forth, changing angles frequently. Since the bit is cutting in both directions, the texturing goes quickly. Start behind the nose and follow the flow lines. The texturing on the head is very light since the fur is short.

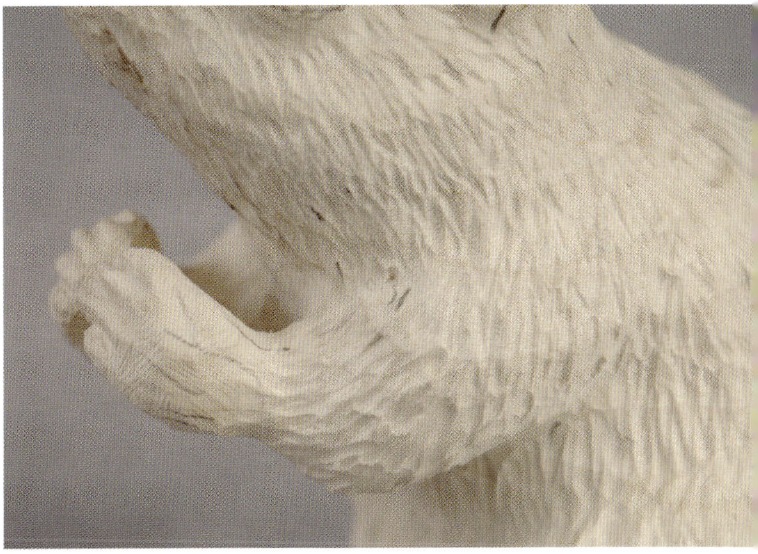

Figure 105. As you work your way down the head and to the neck, the texturing gets a little deeper.

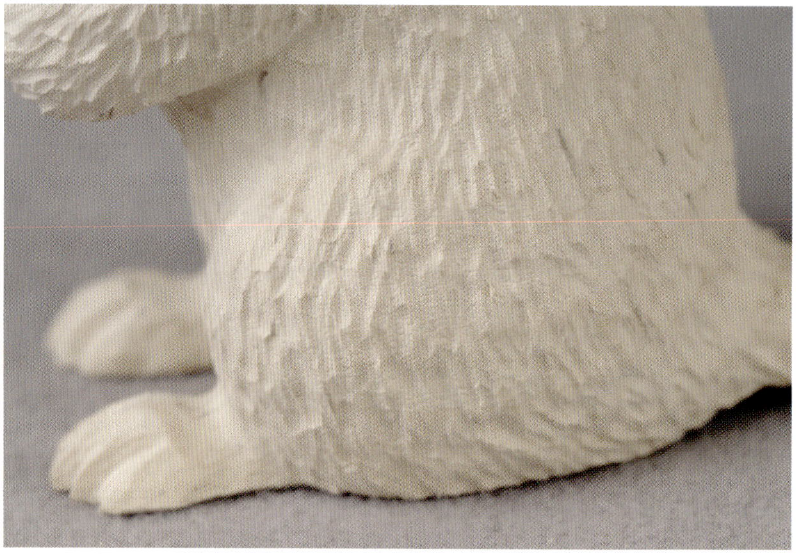

Figure 106. Follow the flow lines on down over the haunches to the tail.

Figure 107. Leave no flat spots by keeping the strokes close together.

Figure 108. When you do the tail, support the opposite surface so that the tail does not snap off. The texturing is deepest on the tail and the bit should be knocking off the corners of the grooves put in earlier. Do the underside of the tail as well. I usually do the center of the tail first and then come back and flare the texturing out to the edges.

Figure 109. Start burning with the medium size skew burning tip around the nose. Each stroke should be at a different angle to create the effect of fur. Try not to dig the point in the wood. The angle of the skew should be the same angle, whenever possible, as the plane/level of the wood.

Figure 110. The strokes are the shortest on the head because the fur is the shortest there. As you work your way to the back of the head and down the neck, the strokes get a little longer. Burn around the eyelids and ears at this point.

Figure 111. Use the natural bristle toothbrush to clean off any loose carbon on the burning.

Figure 112. To burn the eyelids, start in the front corner on each lid and follow the contour on around to the back.

Figure 113. Burn the fur on the ears by starting at the base and working toward the tip.

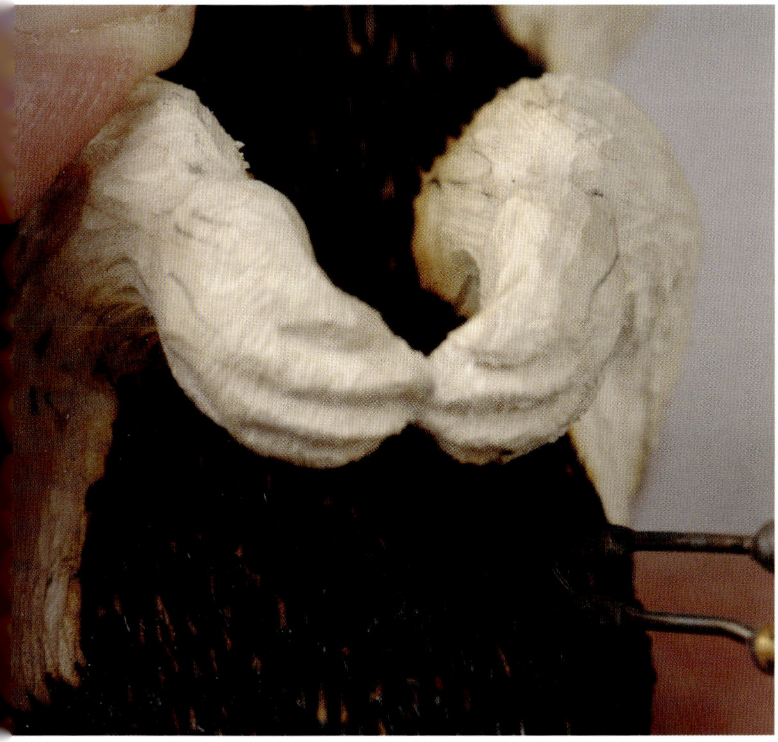

Figure 114. A rounded tip burning pen is useful for working on concave areas. To burn the throat, you will have to turn the chippy upside down because of the front legs and paws inhibit the strokes. Burn down the throat as far as you can.

Figure 115. Once you are down far enough on the throat, you will be able to right the chippy and get to the remaining part of the exposed chest from underneath.

Figure 116. Continue the burning down the side of the neck and onto the front legs/arms, following the flow lines and texturing.

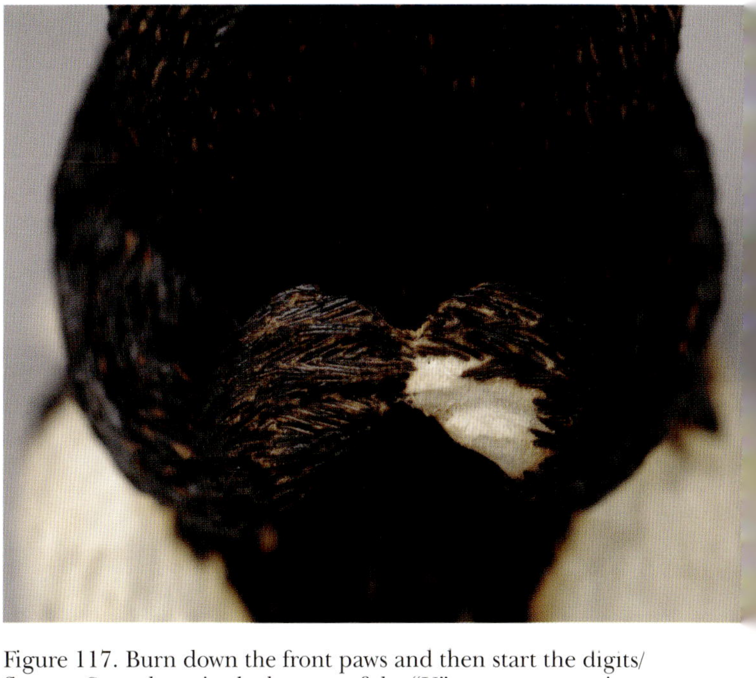

Figure 117. Burn down the front paws and then start the digits/fingers. Start down in the bottom of the "V" groove separating each finger and burn out at an angle to the top.

Figure 118. To burn the inside of the front legs/arms, start at the base and burn out at an angle toward the edge.

Figure 119. Following the texture and flow lines, burn the fur down the back to the tail.

Figure 120. Burn the fur on the haunches and down toward the tail.

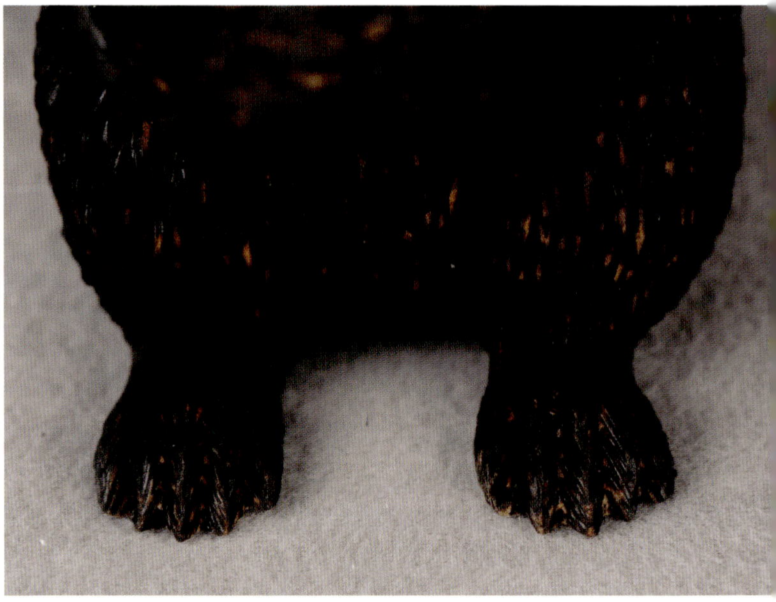

Figure 121. Burn in the fur on the hind paws just as on the front paws.

Figure 122. The strokes on the tail are longer and more curved. Burn the fur on the top and on the bottom of the tail.

Figure 123. Go back over the fur to look for places that need deepening. Then brush all of the burned surface well with the natural bristle toothbrush.

Figure 124. It is time to seal the chipmunk. You can use either the 50/50 lacquer/lacquer thinner mixture or Krylon Crystal Clear Acrylic Coating 1301. If you dip the carving, let it remain in the lacquer solution until most of the little bubbles have stopped rising to the surface. I feel that this soaking in effect actually strengthens the more fragile parts. If you choose to spray, do two coats. Wait about 10 minutes in between each spraying.

Figure 125. Allow the sealer to dry. To set the eyes, first fill the eyeholes almost full of oily, non-hardening clay.

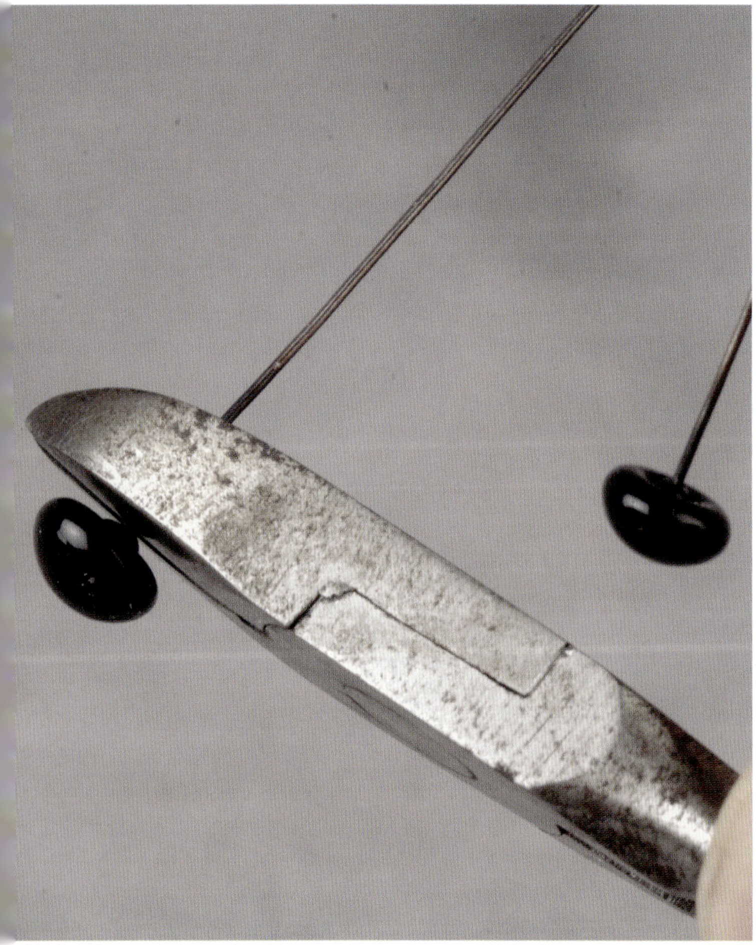

Figure 126. Cut the wire right up close to the back of the eye. Put this eye into the clay, and then cut and put the other eye in place.

Figure 127. Use the end of a pencil eraser, a dowel, or something made of wood to push the eyes into place. Do not use anything that might scratch the glass of the eye. The tool that I am using is one I made out of a worn-out paintbrush handle that I made concave at one end to use to set the eyes. I super-glued the end of a needle in the other end.

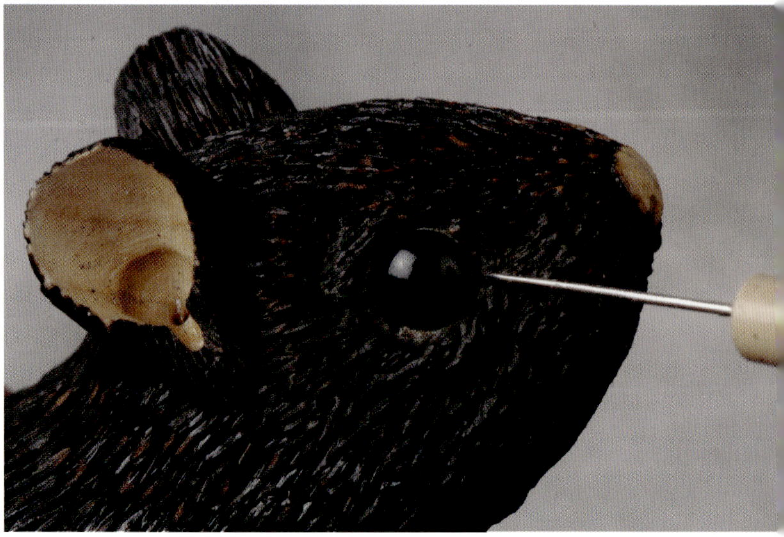

Figure 128. Using a dissecting needle or a regular pin or needle, clean the excess clay out of the crevice around the eye.

Figure 129. Brush around the eye with a toothbrush to remove any excess clay that may have gotten into the texturing/burning. Any clay residue may keep the ribbon epoxy putty from sticking.

Figure 130. From the top and front views, you should just be able to see some of the curvature of the glass eyes. There is no measurement for how deep or shallow to set the eyes. You do not want them too bug-eyed nor too deep—it is just a certain look!

Figure 131. Cut the ribbon epoxy straight across. Cut out the middle where the two have already chemically bonded and discard that little piece. Leave your clay handy as you will need to periodically dip the eye tool in it to keep the putty from sticking hard to it.

Figure 132. Knead the epoxy putty thoroughly until the two colors have mixed completely. Roll a small diameter worm about the size of the end of the eye tool (1/16" diameter).

Figure 133. Cut the worm in half and pick up half of it with the spatula end of the eye tool. Crimp the end of the putty down into the crevice around the eye. This motion is one of pressing down and pulling back at the same time. Note the small amount of the putty between the end of the tool and the glass of the eye. This little bead of putty is the beginning of the eye ring. The purpose of the putty is to fill and camouflage the hole and to form the little eye ring around the eye.

Figure 134. Work the putty into the crevice around the eye, making sure that you create the little ridge of putty, which is the eye ring. Pull off any excess. You do not need a quarter inch of putty around the eye—just enough to fill the crevice, create the eye ring, and blend into the surrounding burning. Use the sharp end of the eye tool to blend the putty into the texturing. Laying the tool down and pulling the putty is ideal for the blending procedure.

Figure 135. Use the sharp end of the eye tool or a knife blade to form the corners where the upper and lower eyelids meet.

Figure 136. Allow the putty to harden 4-6 hours before beginning painting.

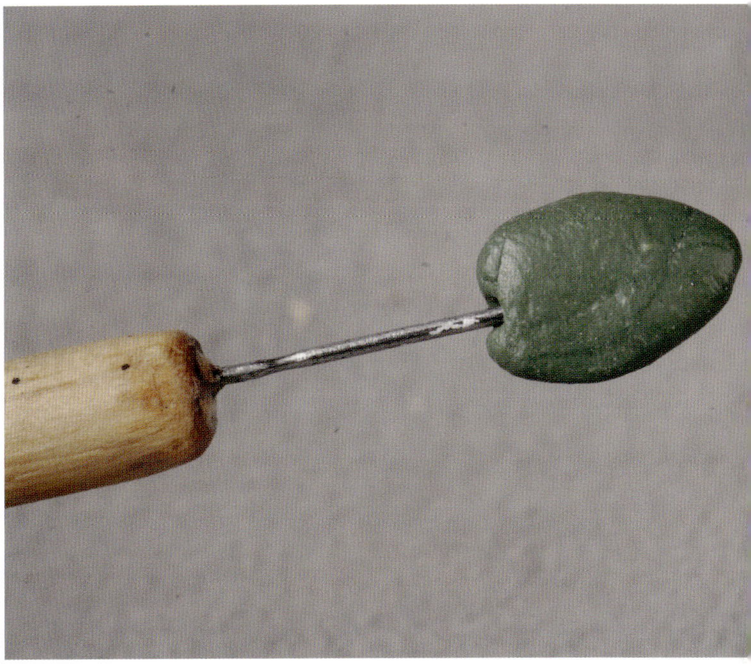

Figure 137. Now, we need to form a sunflower seed to fit in the chippy's paws. After setting the eyes, you can use your leftover putty to form a seed. Work the putty in your fingers and put the putty on the end of a needle or pin in the end of a dowel or paintbrush handle. Lightly pinch the perimeter and push toward the middle.

Figure 138. Try the seed in the paws. The sunflower seed should not be too tight. You will need to allow a little room for layers of gesso and paint. Allow the seed to harden before painting.

Scratching Chipmunk

Tools & Supplies

- Band saw or coping saw
- Flexible shaft machine
- Micro motor machine helpful
- Variety of Kutzall/Typhoon carbide roughing out bits
- Variety of ruby carver bits and mounted stones
- Calipers and ruler, measuring in **tenths** of an inch
- Compass, pencil
- Knife
- Wire cutters, needle nose pliers, awl
- Drill and bits (1/16" and 5/64")
- Toothbrush (preferably natural bristle)
- Burning pen (rheostat type) and several burning pen styles
- Straight pin, hatpin, or fine dissecting needle
- Permanent ink marker (such as a fine point Sharpie)
- Dust mask, leather gloves, and safety glasses or goggles
- Optivisor or some type of magnification
- Clear acetate sheet (preferably .005 thickness)
- 2" piece of 16 gauge galvanized wire
- Super-glue and accelerator
- 50/50 lacquer/lacquer thinner mixture or Krylon Crystal Clear Spray
- Yellow carpenter glue
- Reference pictures

Materials

- 5.5"L x 3"W x 3"H tupelo block for scratching chipmunk
- 5mm black eyes
- Medium colored China bristle paintbrush (to use for whiskers)
- Ribbon epoxy putty (preferably blue/yellow) or Kulis Karvit
- Oily, non-hardening modeling clay
- Flat base or piece of driftwood for mount

Painting Supplies

- Hair dryer
- Freezer paper and masking tape
- Brushes
- Water container and paper towels
- Flow medium
- Paints: (preferably Liquitex jar acrylics) white gesso (W), mars black (B), burnt umber (BU), raw umber (RU), yellow oxide (YO), raw sienna (RS), and burnt sienna (BS).
- Note: In color swatches, *denotes little bit

SCRATCHING CHIPMUNK PROFILE VIEW
5.5″

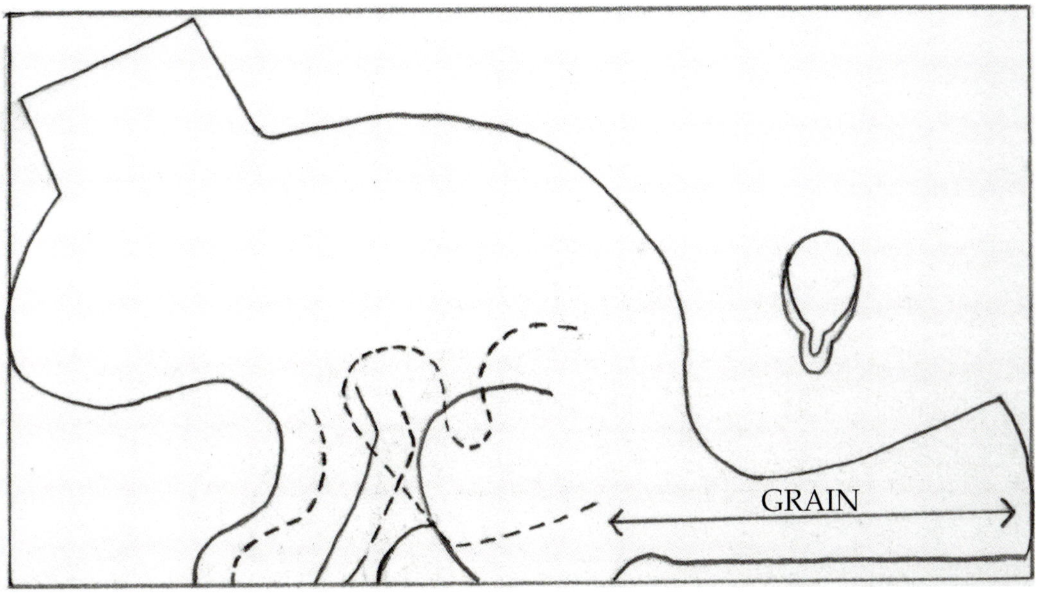

3.0″

3.0″ WIDTH/THICKNESS

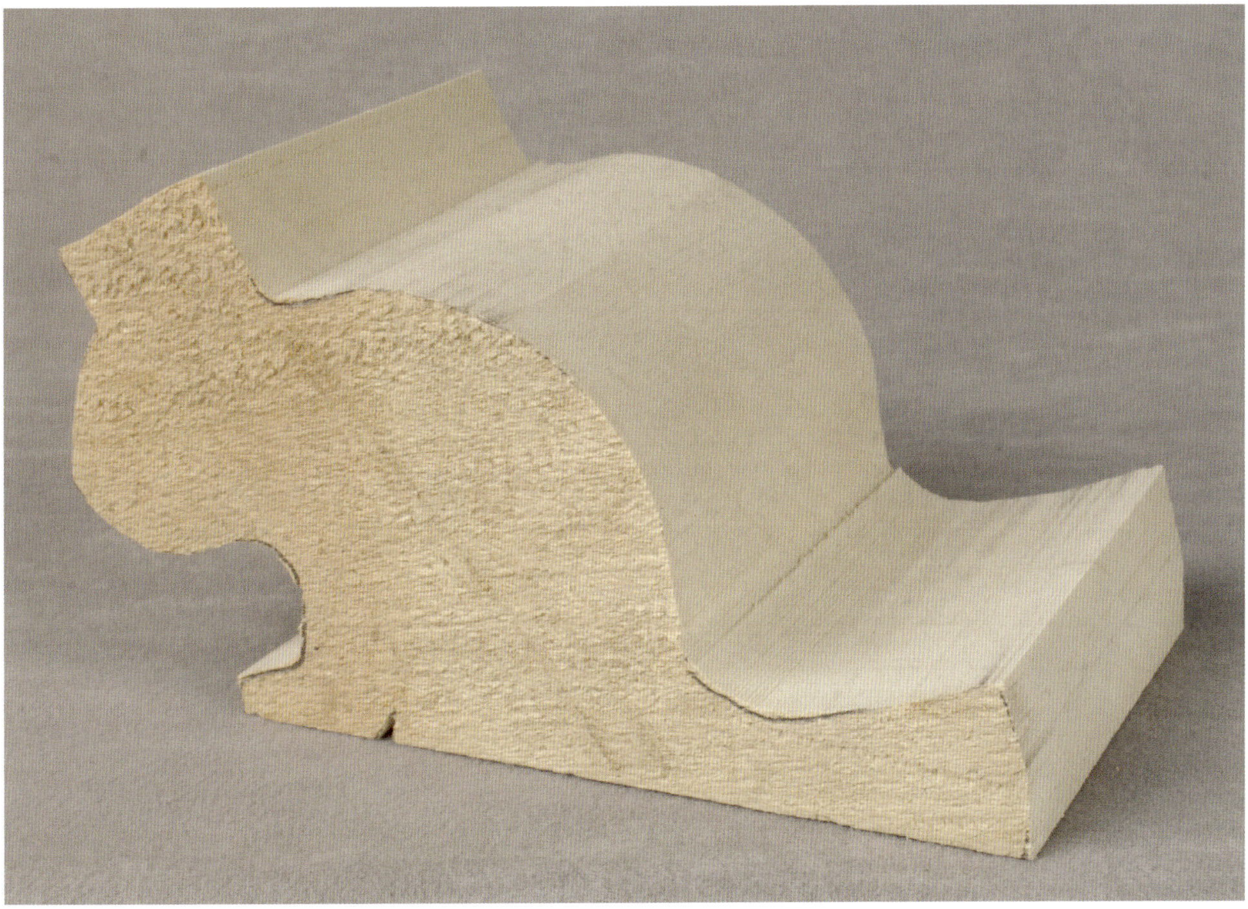

Figure 1. You will need a block of tupelo that is 5.5"L x 3"W x 3"H. It is critical that the wood for this project be tupelo because of its cross-grain strength. With this particular pose, there are significant parts that are at angles to the grain. Even though tupelo is very strong and stable cross-grain, you will still need to take care not to break parts off as the carving progresses. Transfer the profile pattern to a piece of card stock or cardboard. Trace the pattern on the block and cut it out with the band saw.

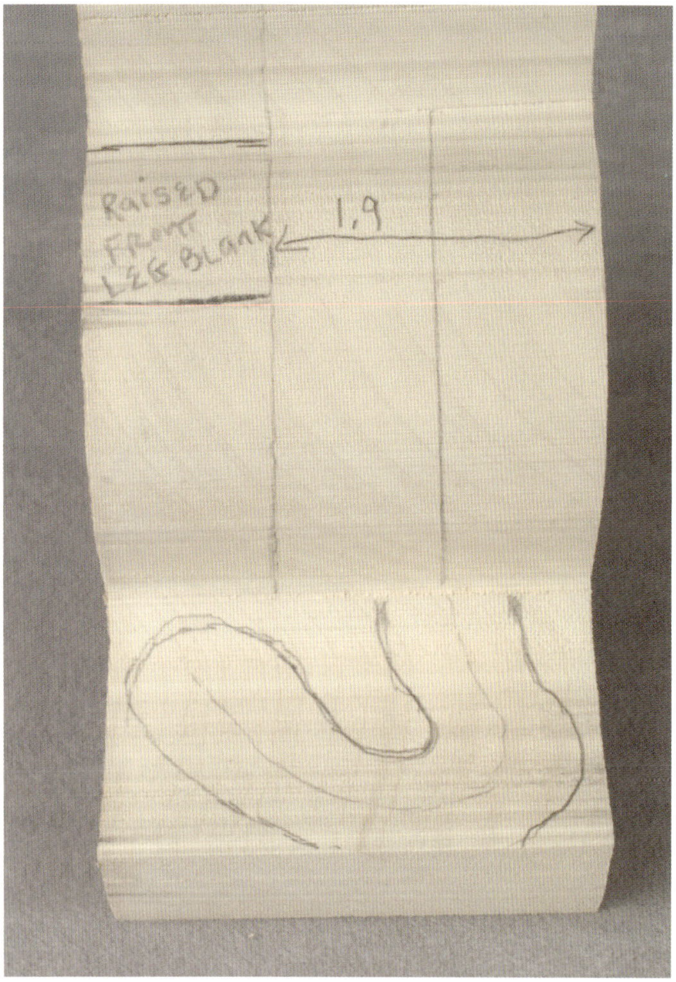

Figure 2. On the right side of the blank, measure, mark, and draw a line 1.9" from the right edge. This is the rough-out body width of the chipmunk. Divide this width in half and draw a body centerline. Draw the curved tail with the rough-out width of 0.85". At 0.2" back from the back of the ear blank, draw the rough-out block for the left raised front leg. This rough-out block section should be 1.0" wide. We are leaving plenty of extra room here for various front leg positions.

Figure 3. Continue down the front of the chipmunk with the body width of 1.9". You will only need the centerline on the bottom part of the blank since the head will be turned slightly.

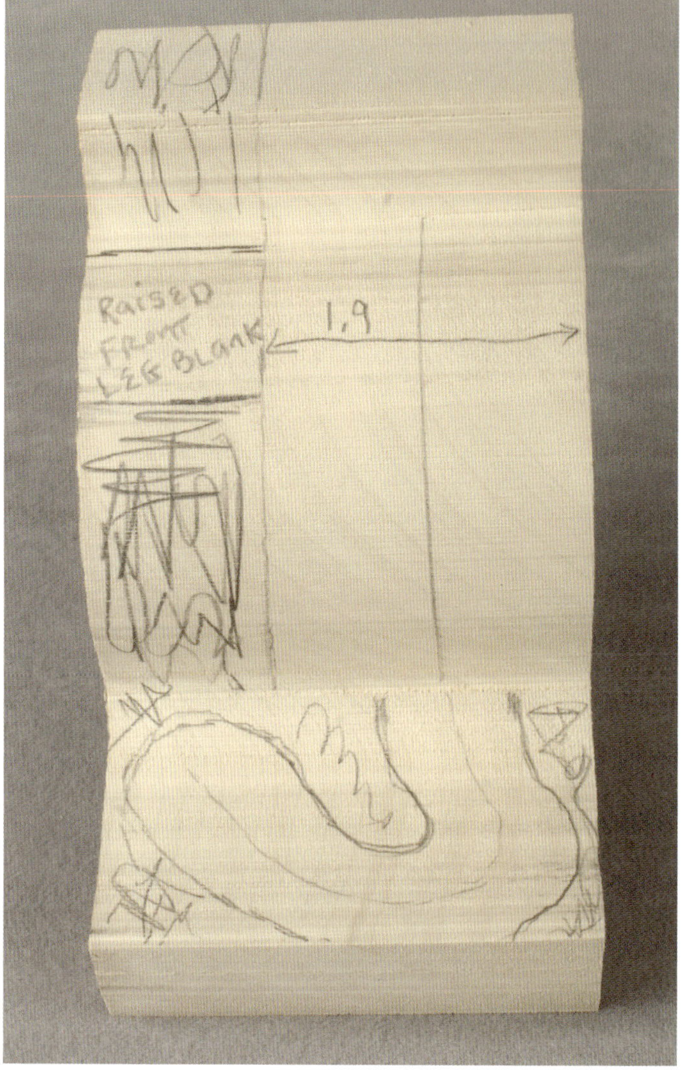

Figure 4. The scribbled parts are the ones needing to be band sawed off. Leave the left raised front paw block and the tail. If you prefer, these areas could be cut away with the flexible shaft machine, but be sure to keep the sides of all cuts straight up and down.

Figure 5. Here is what the blank looks like after the excess parts are removed. If you are not experienced with the band saw, I would highly recommend that you grind these parts away. There are several very tricky cuts to get to this point.

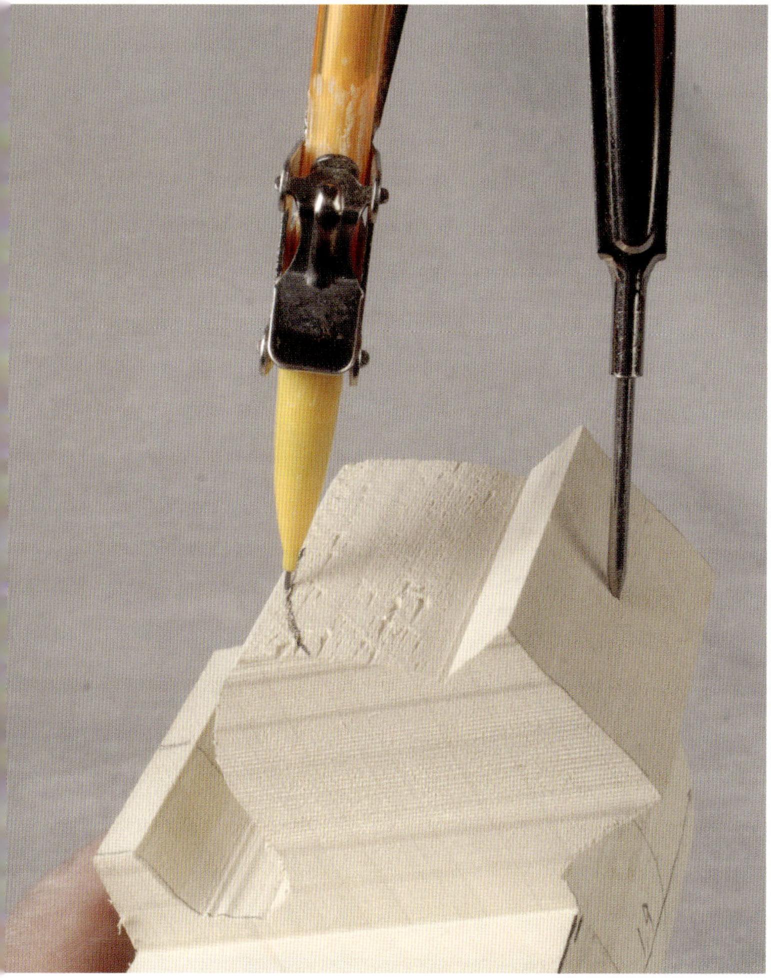

Figure 6. Find the center point of the ear block. Place the point of the compass there and extend the pencil to the tip of the nose. Swing this arc to the left.

Figure 7. Looking straight down onto the top of the head, draw a new center line less than 0.5" from the nose blank center. If you turn the head more than this, you will not have sufficient wood for the ears.

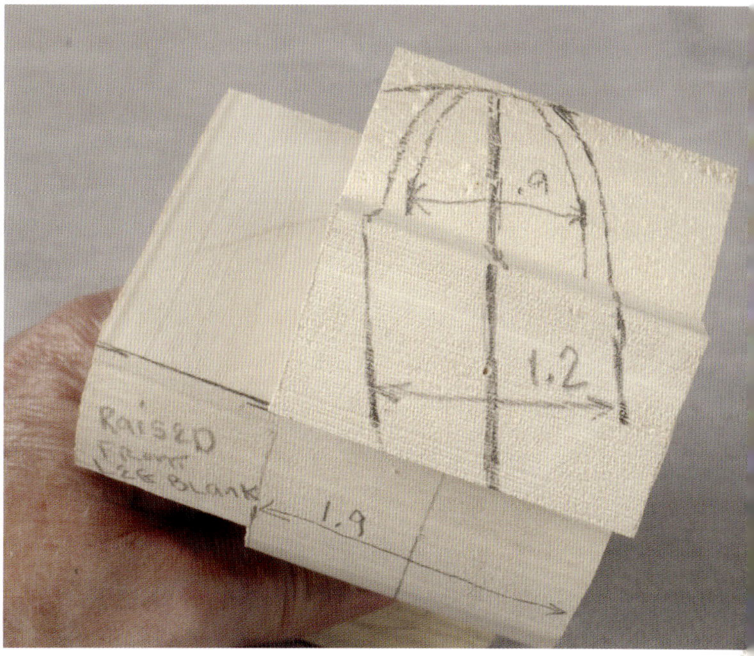

Figure 8. On the top of the ear blank, center 1.2" (0.6" on both sides). Just ahead of the ear blank, center 0.9" (.45" on both sides) on both sides. Allowing 0.6" (0.3" on both sides) across the front of the muzzle, draw slightly rounded lines back to the side back measurement marks on both sides. This is the roughing out drawing for the width of the head. Just inside these lines, draw the top of the head width roughing out lines going through the 0.9" marks.

Figure 9. Draw two parallel lines across the ear block. Start from the right forward corner and go **perpendicular** to the new centerline, and then go from the left back corner and **perpendicular** to the centerline and parallel to the forward line.

Figure 10. Cut away the excess behind the ears down to the hind neck

Figure 11. Cut the excess out behind the front of the muzzle.

Figure 12. Cut away the excess on both sides, keeping them straight up and down. Keep taking away the wood and keep things balanced across the centerline until it measures 1.2" just in front of the ear block. Draw the centerline down the front of the muzzle.

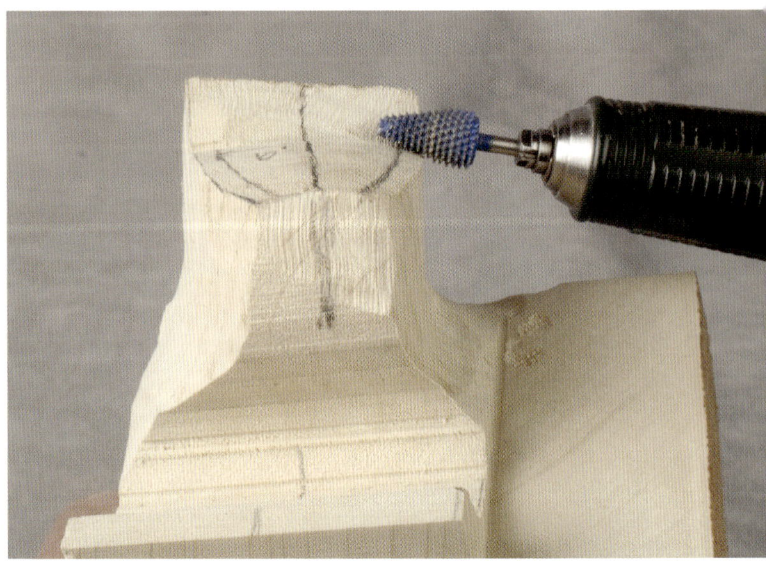

Figure 13. Take the excess wood off the top plane on the chipmunk's left side of the head. Make it match the chipmunk's right side. Do not round the head at this point. Redraw the line that marks the top of the head by measuring 0.9" from the one on the right side.

Figure 14. Round the back of the haunches and back from just behind the neck area all the way to the bottom of the blank.

Figure 15. When rounding the middle and upper back, the right side gets rounded down further than the left. Round the left down until the shelf for the extended front leg measures 0.3" high.

Figure 16. On the backside of the extended front leg blank, draw in the front leg with the upper part of the leg measuring 0.6" and the paw measuring 0.25" in height.

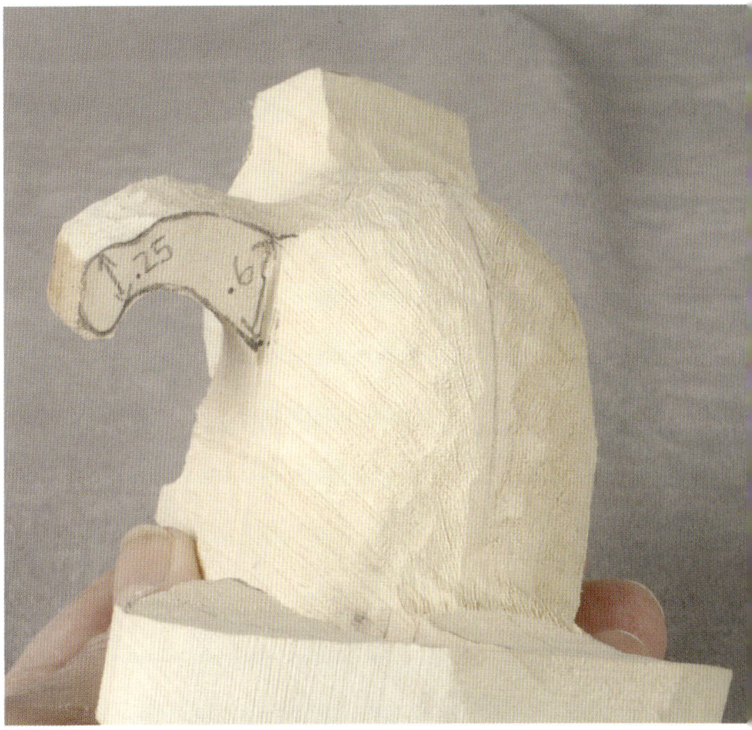

Figure 17. Okay, let's get rid of these big chunks! Cut away the excess on top of the extended left front leg and underneath as well. Keep the top and under surface of the front paw straight through and keep the left side flat for right now.

Figure 18. Measure and mark the height of the right haunch at 1.0" and the height of the right hind paw at 0.3. Draw in the backwards "C" shape for the haunch and the shape of the hind paw.

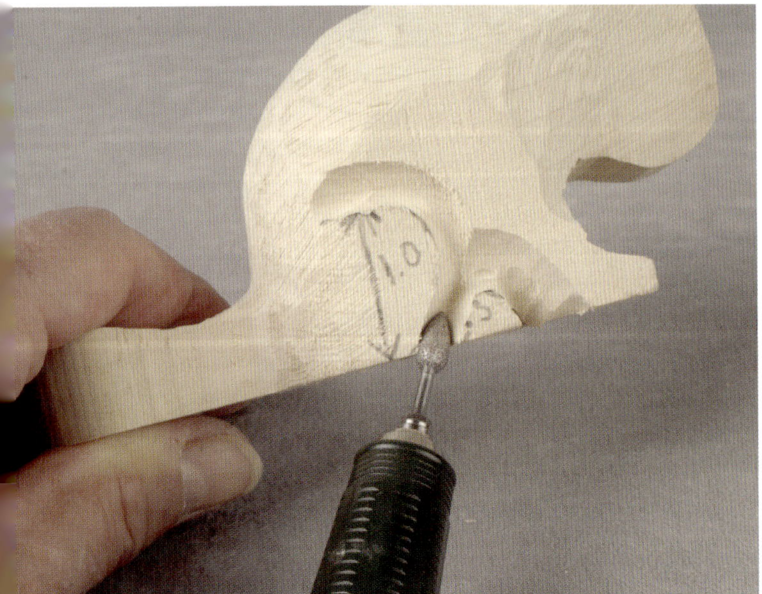

Figure 19. Drag the #3 flame ruby carver (RC-25) around the haunch and around the line for the hind paw.

Figure 20. Flow the channel out from the haunch and remove 0.3" from the entire right front side of the chipmunk.

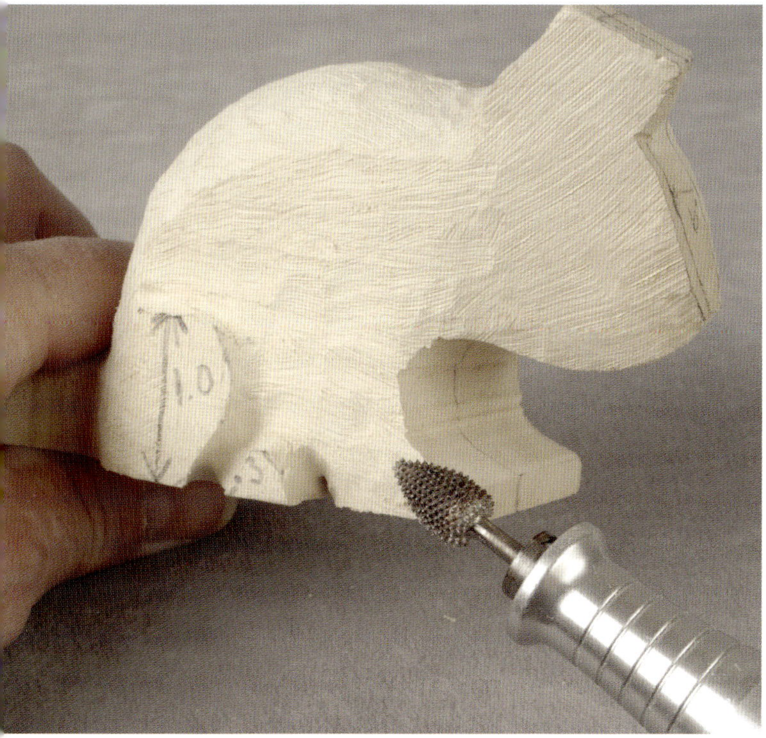

Figure 21. Remove that excess wood in front of the haunch toward the edge of the blank where the right front paw is.

Figure 22. Round over the right haunch and angle the outside of the hind paw back to the haunch.

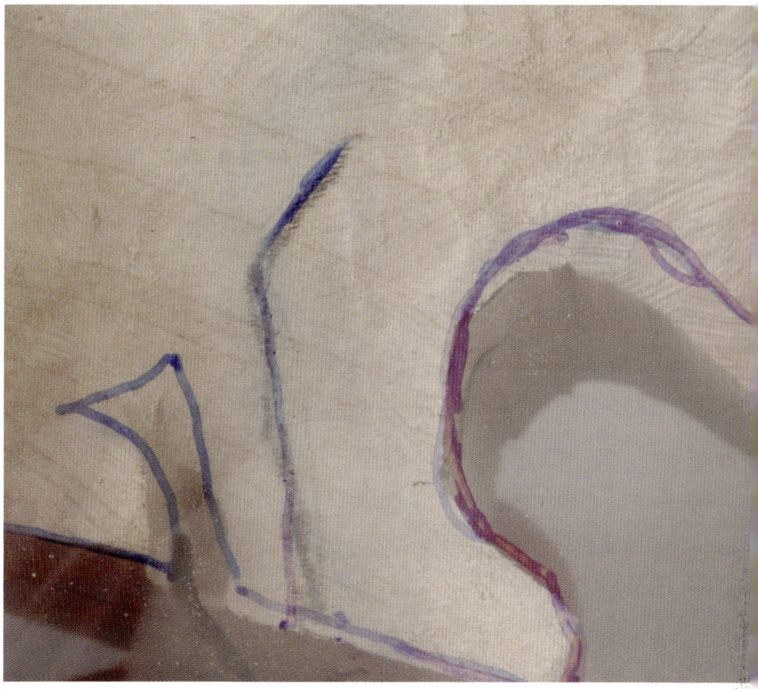

Figure 23. Trace the profile plan view pattern (right side) on a piece of clear acetate, hold it flat against the side of the right haunch, sneak a pencil underneath, and trace the right front paw.

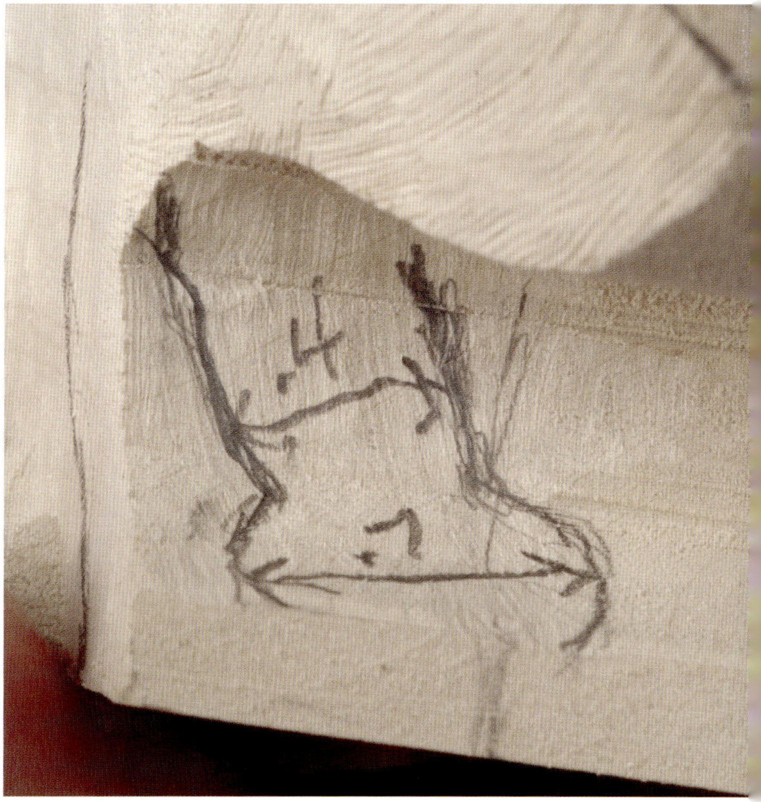

Figure 24. Draw the front view of the right front paw. The roughing out width of the lower portion of the leg is 0.4". Draw a circle 0.7" in diameter for the spread toes.

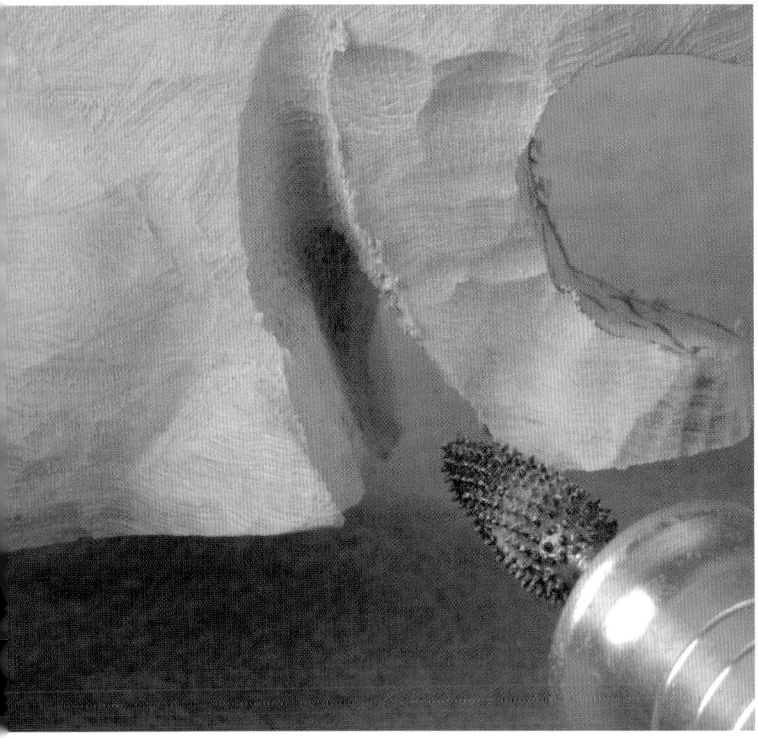

Figure 25. Using the bud Typhoon carbide cutter, remove the excess wood from behind the right front leg and paw, being careful not to damage the end of the hind toe area.

Figure 26. Carve away all of the excess in front of the left hind foot and haunch.

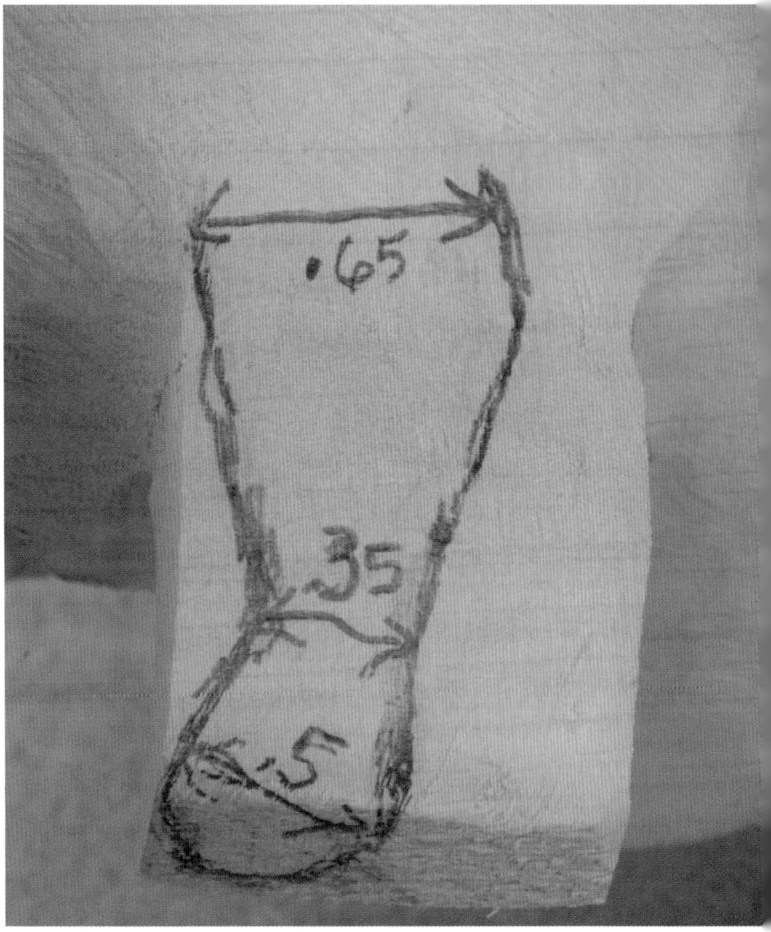

Figure 27. Draw in the shape of the raised left front leg with the widest part nearest the body being 0.65", the wrist 0.35", and the paw 0.5".

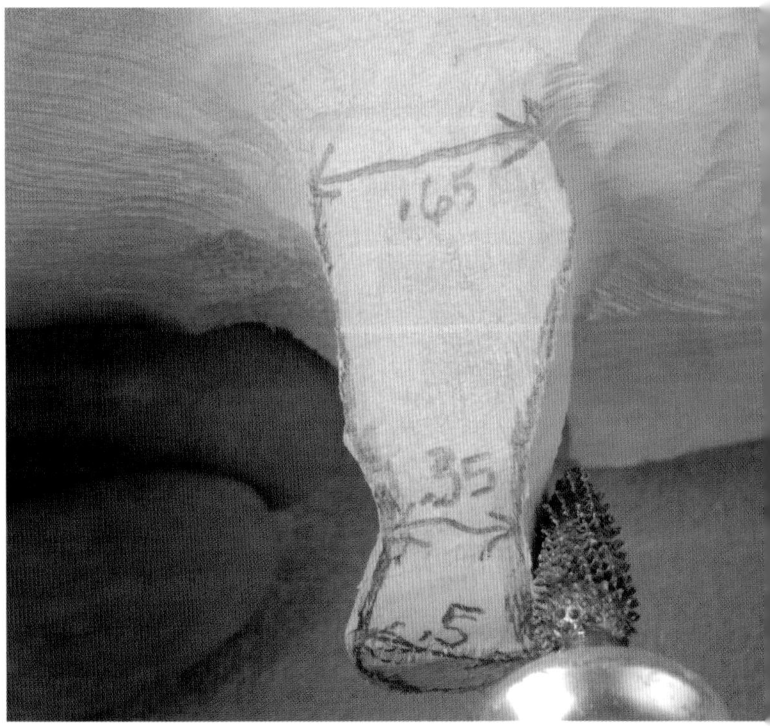

Figure 28. With the bud Typhoon carbide, cut away the excess wood from the front and back of the raised left foreleg. Keep the sides straight up and down for right now.

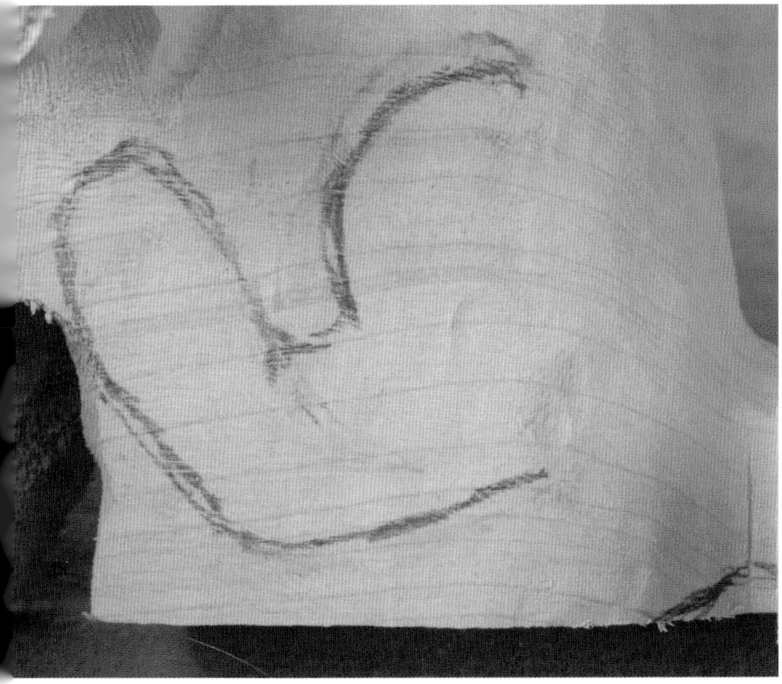

Figure 29. Trace the left side profile plan view on a piece of acetate, and hold that up to the chipmunk's left side. Sneak your pencil underneath the acetate, and draw in the left haunch and hind paw.

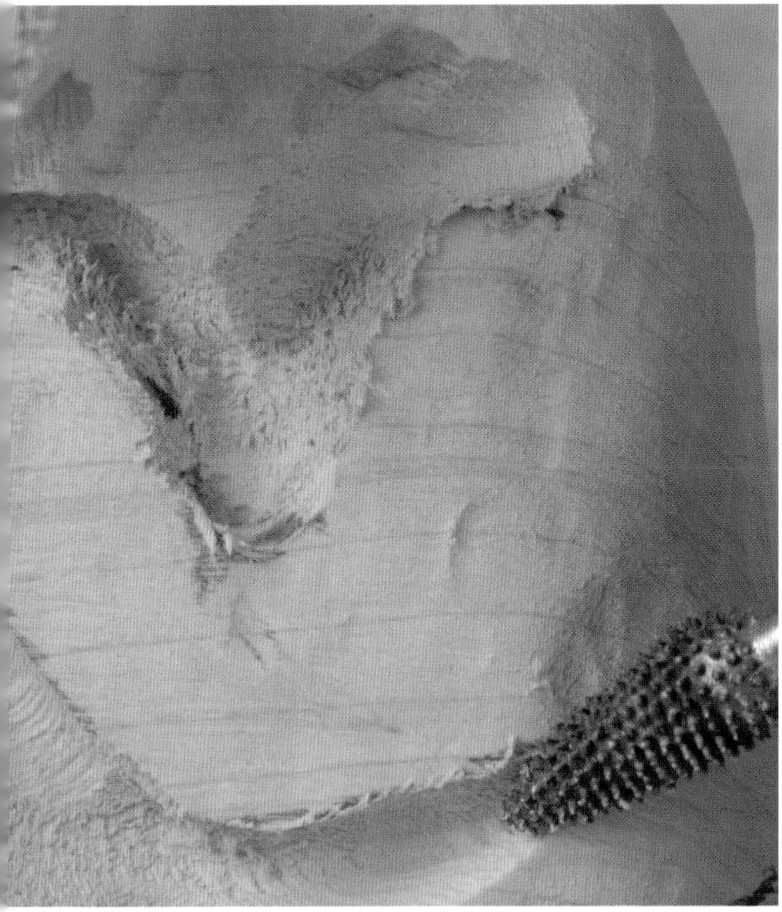

Figure 30. With the bud Typhoon carbide cutter, channel around the haunch and paw, coming out gradually at the top and bottom of the haunch. The channel depth around the paw should be approximately 0.3".

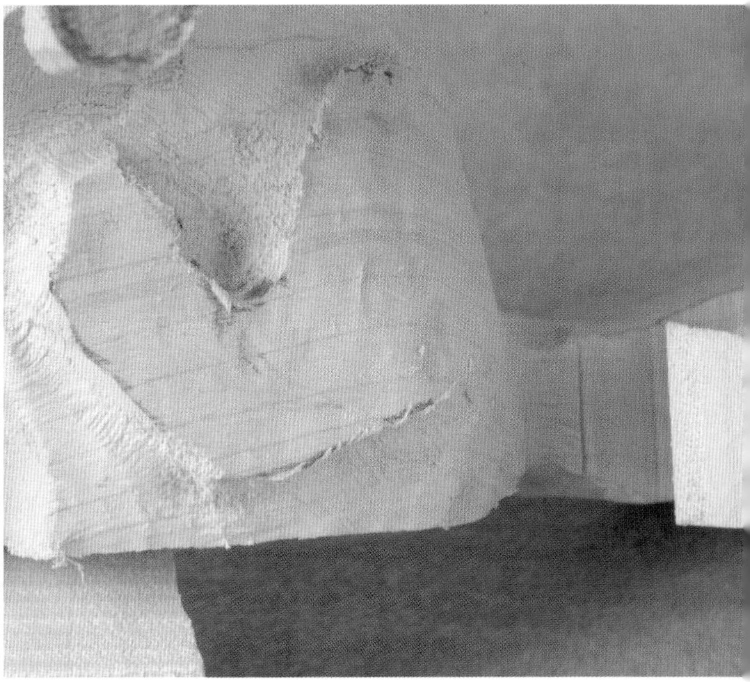

Figure 31. Flow the channel out onto the surrounding areas. Cut the depression on the underside of the bottom of the tail. Keep the channel straight across and do not round the tail at this point.

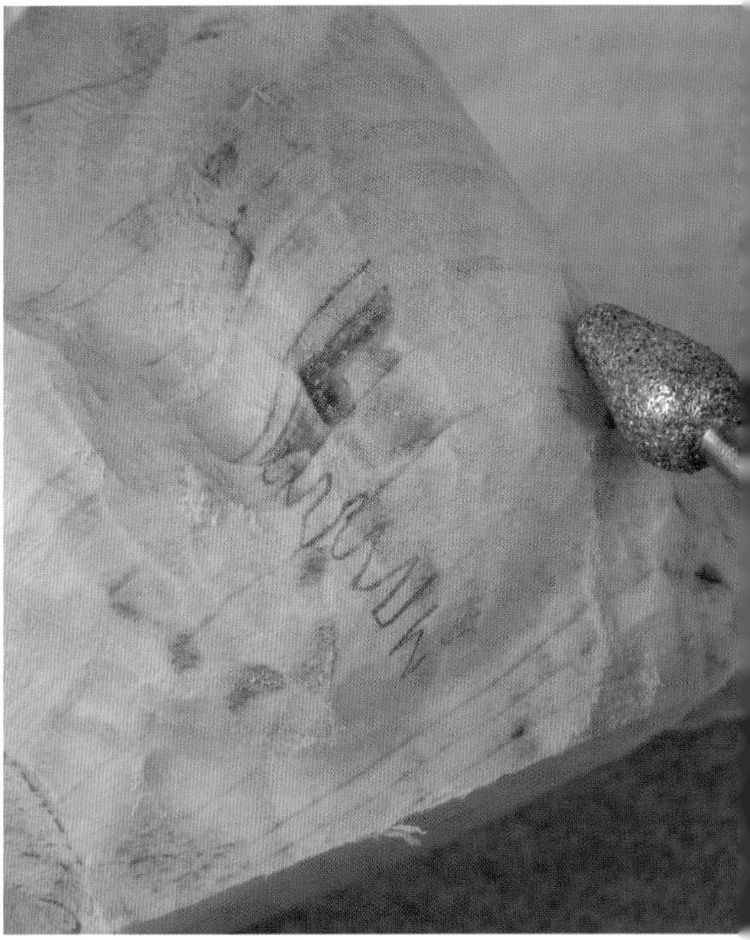

Figure 32. Round over the haunch and foot using the pear-shaped ruby carver (RC-23). There is a depression that needs to be made between the ankle and the lower part of the haunch.

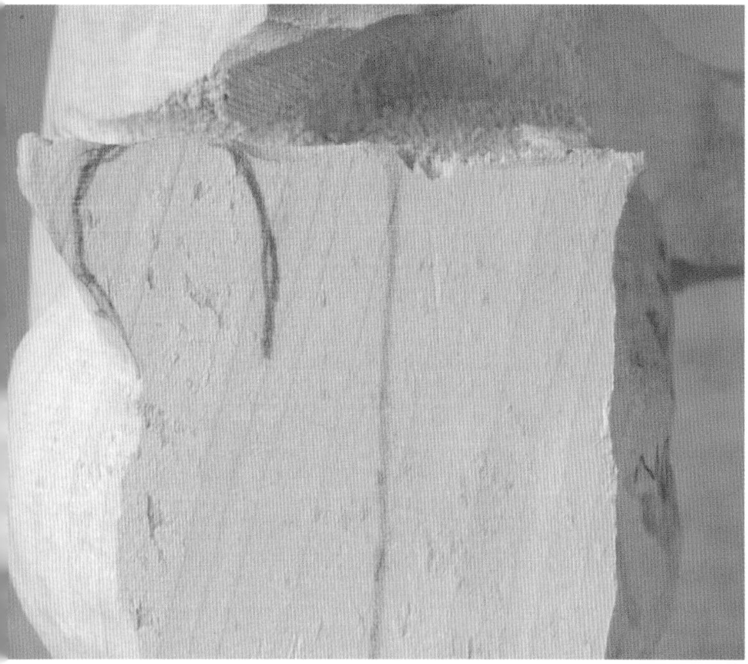

Figure 33. On the underside of the blank, draw in the right hind paw, which should measure 0.5" wide at the widest part and approximately 0.6" long.

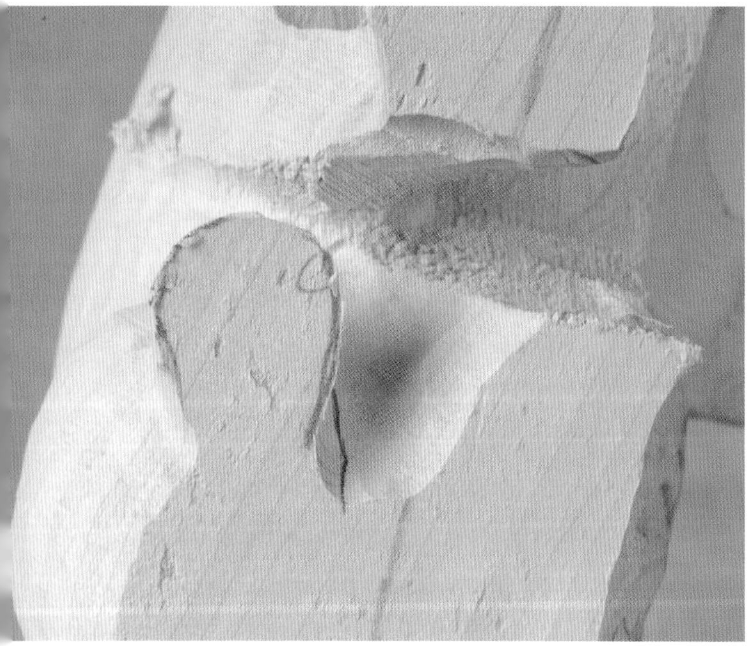

Figure 34. Cut the excess wood from around the right hind paw.

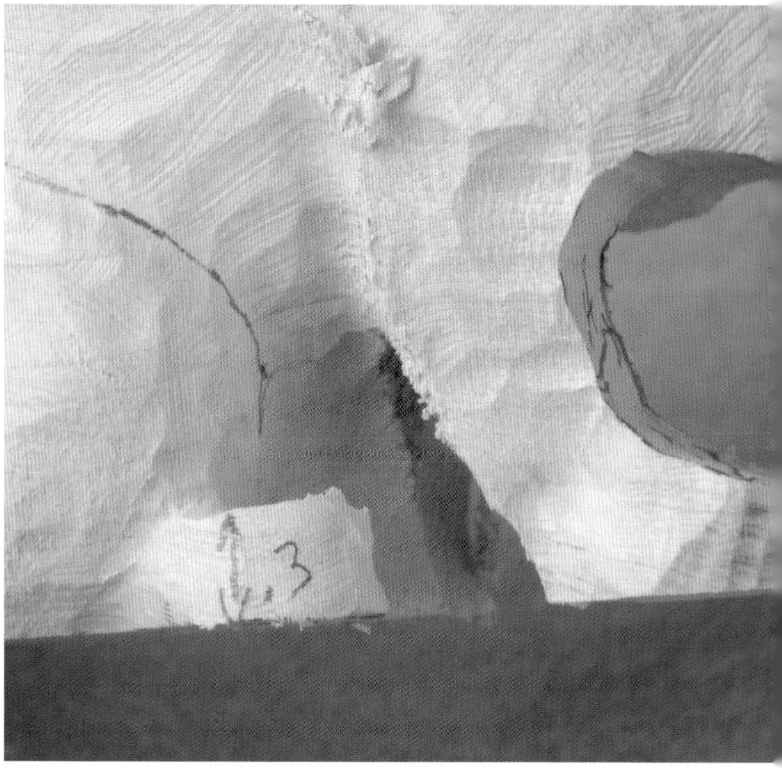

Figure 35. Lay the #3 flame ruby carver (RC-25) down to continue the haunch channel down inside the hind paw. Flow the channels out onto the haunch and out toward the belly area.

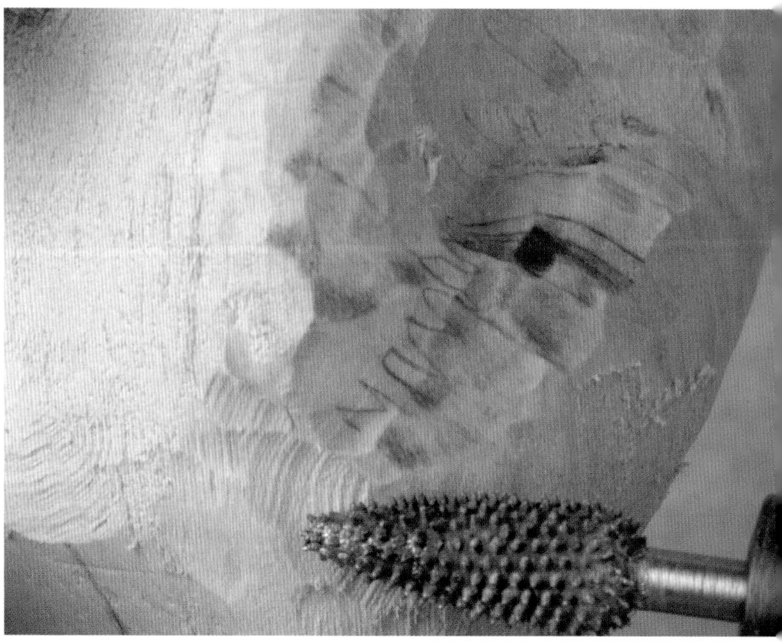

Figure 36. With the bud Typhoon carbide cutter, roll the left haunch underneath the butt and remove the excess belly wood to the outside of the left hind paw outer edge.

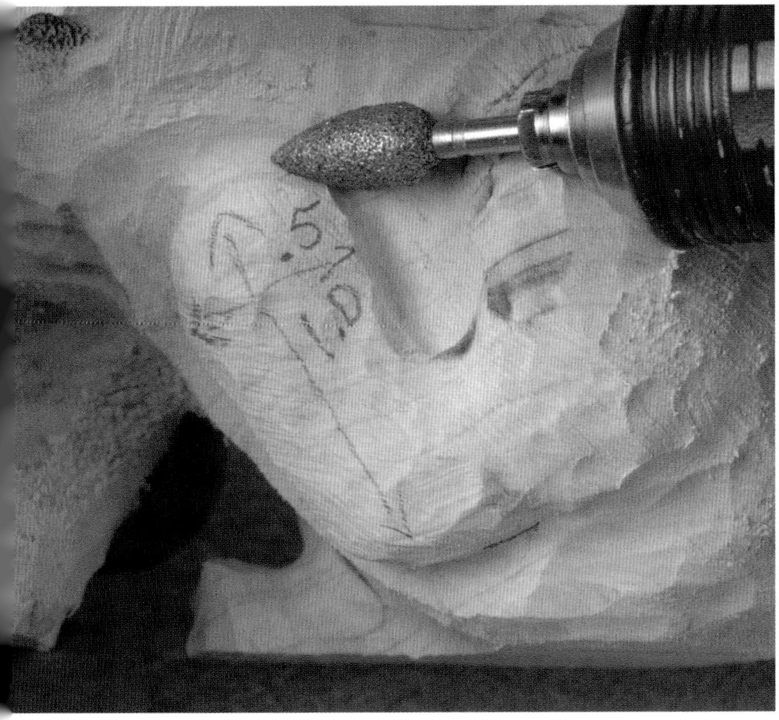

Figure 37. Now, to get the left hind paw down to its actual size, use the #3 flame ruby carver (RC-25) to shorten it to 1.0" from the tip of the paw to the back of the ankle and make it the correct width of 0.5" from side to side. It is much safer to rough out to a slightly larger size with the roughing out bits and to get the actual size with safer bits such as ruby carvers.

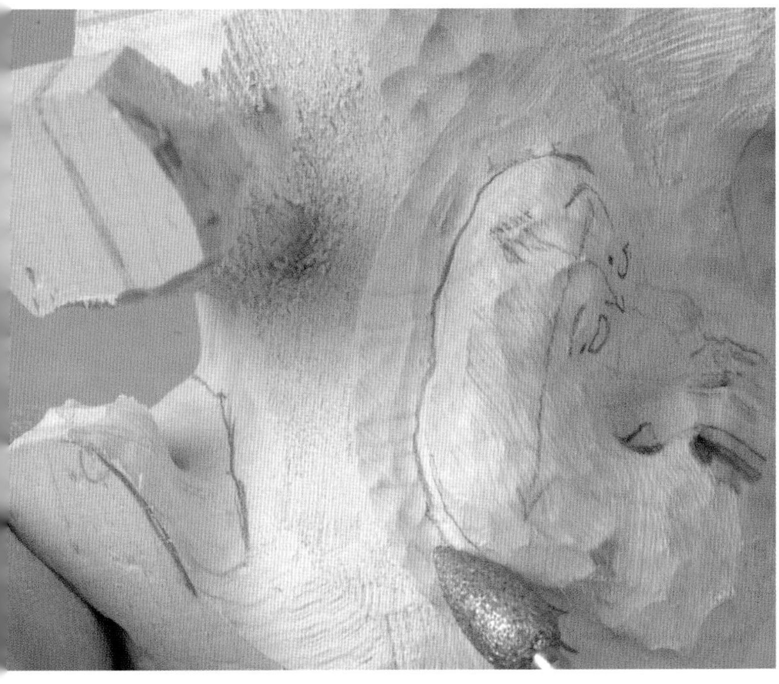

Figure 38. Drag the #3 flame ruby carver (RC-25) down the outside of the hind paw to narrow the thickness to 0.3".

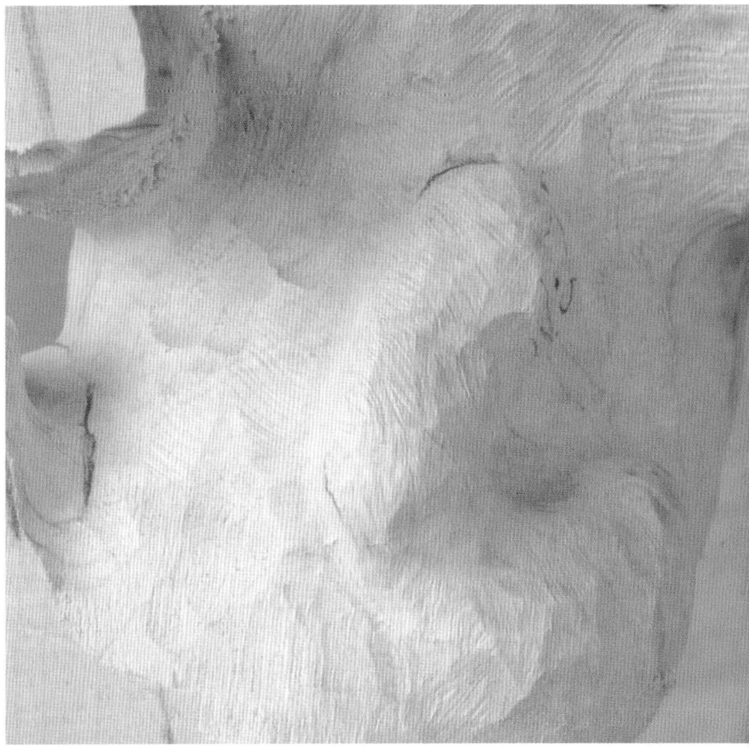

Figure 39. Flow the inside part of this channel toward the belly.

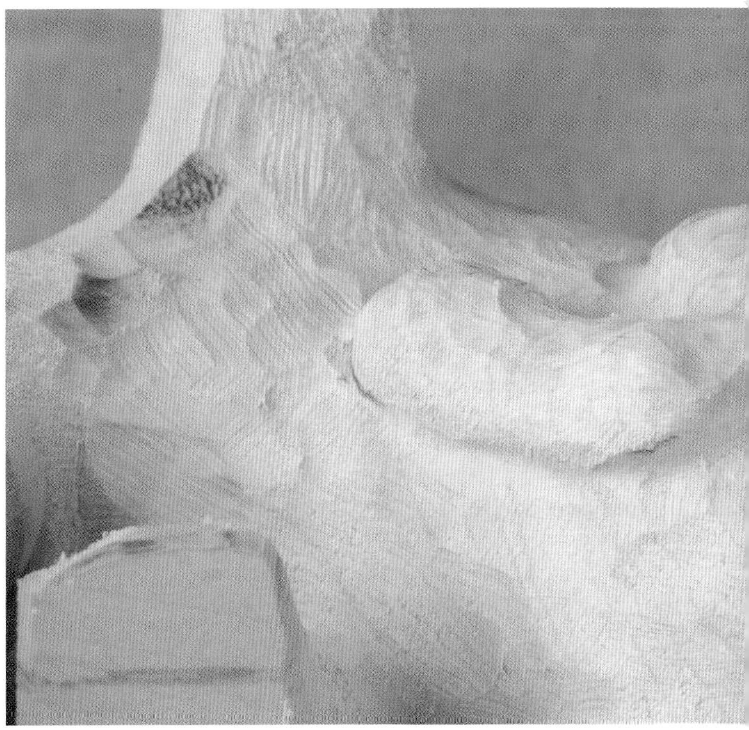

Figure 40. Concave the top part of the base of the hind paw between the ankle and the bulge of the toes.

Figure 41. Before we finalize the front legs and paws, let's get the head down to its actual size and shape. Concave the upper sides of the head with the #3 flame ruby carver (RC-25) about the length of the bit.

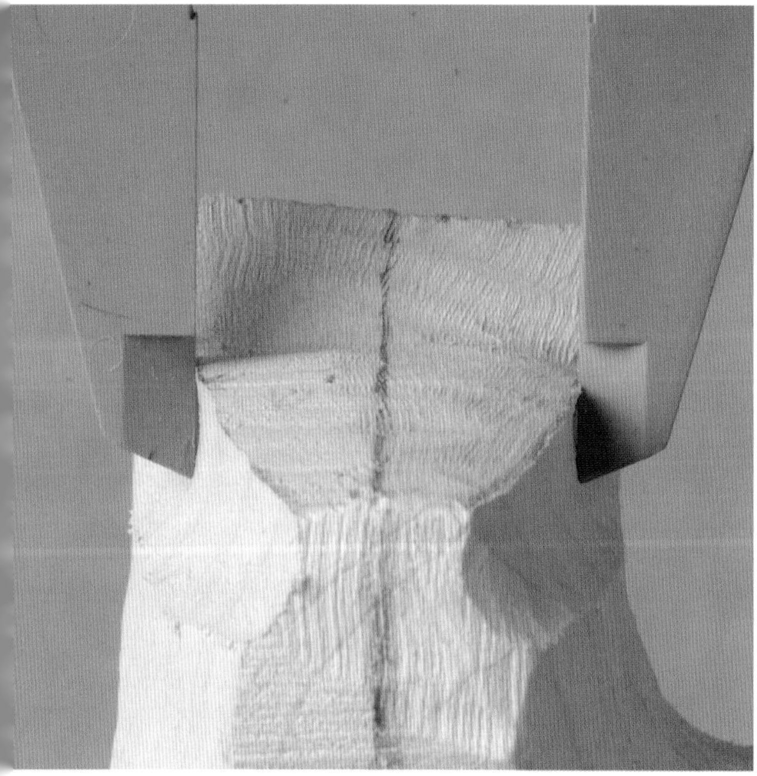

Figure 42. Keep taking wood away, keeping both sides balanced across the centerline, until the middle of the concavity measures 0.9".

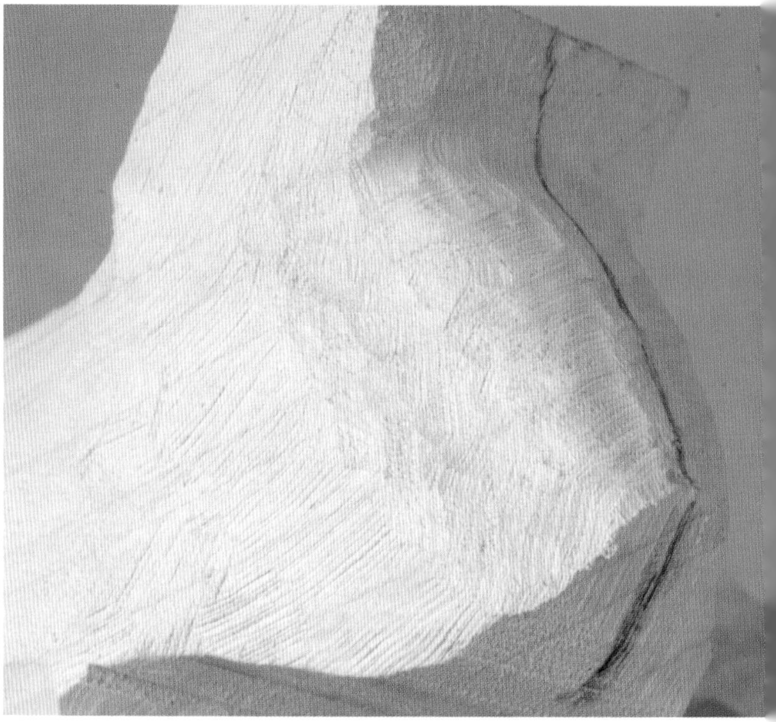

Figure 43. Take the sharp edge off the bottom of this channel and flow it into the cheek area. Do this on both sides. Begin to round the sharp corner on the top of the head.

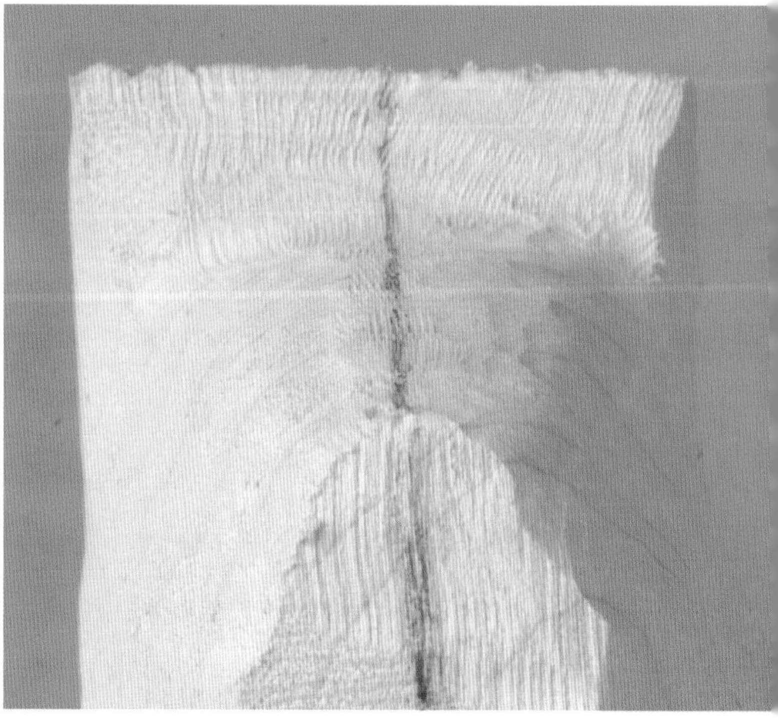

Figure 44. Round the head on both sides until there is no flat area around the centerline.

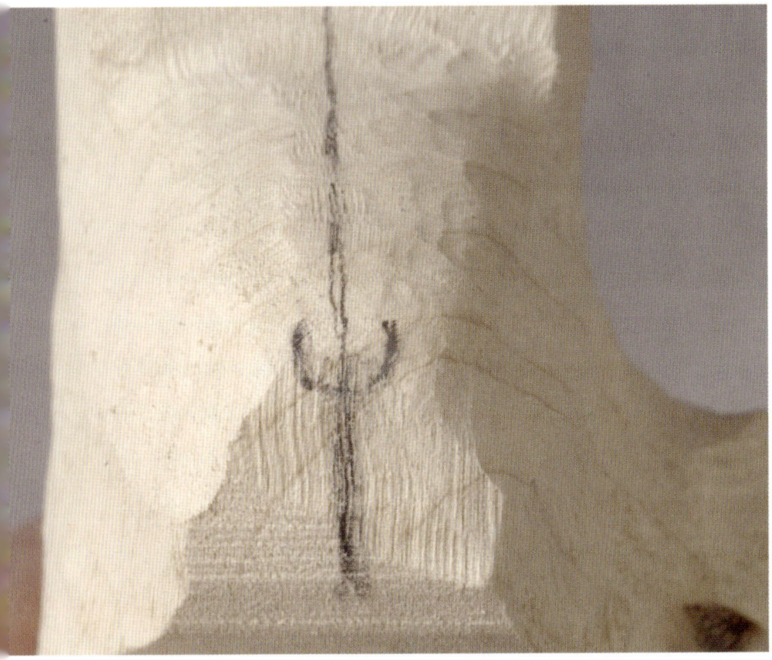

Figure 45. Round over the sharp corner on the top end of the nose area. Draw in the actual "U" shaped nose, which needs to be 0.2" wide.

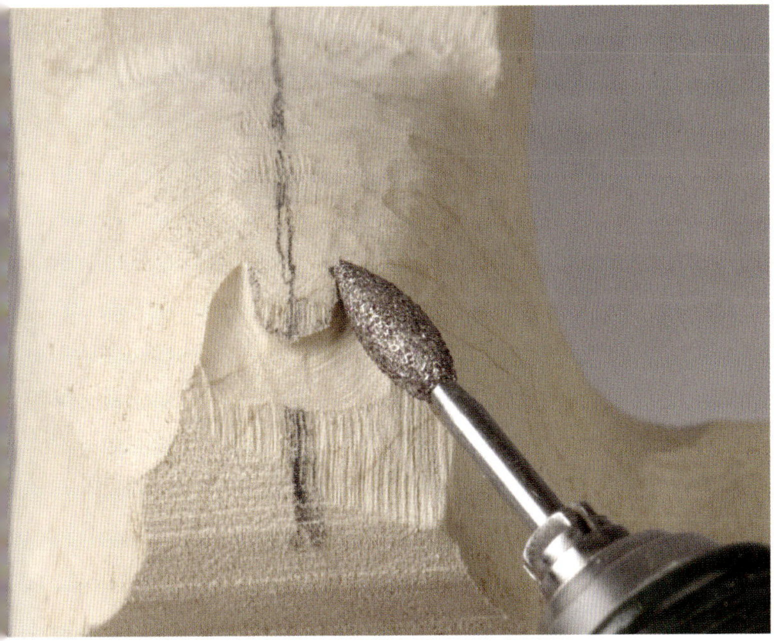

Figure 46. Lay the #2 flame ruby carver (RC-20) down and use the diameter of the bit to remove the excess wood from around the bottom and sides of the nose.

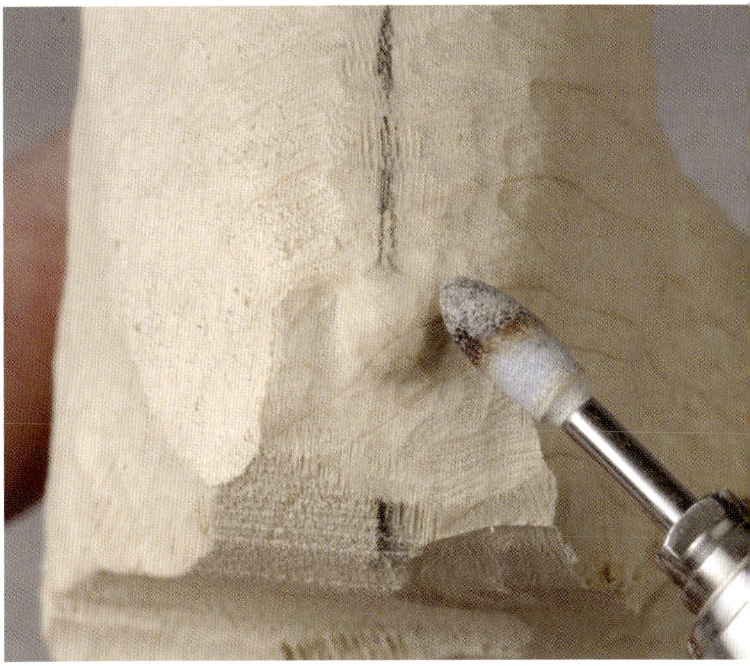

Figure 47. Flow this channel out and flatten out the end of the muzzle with the #2 flame. Round over the edges of the nose and smooth out the scratches with a stone.

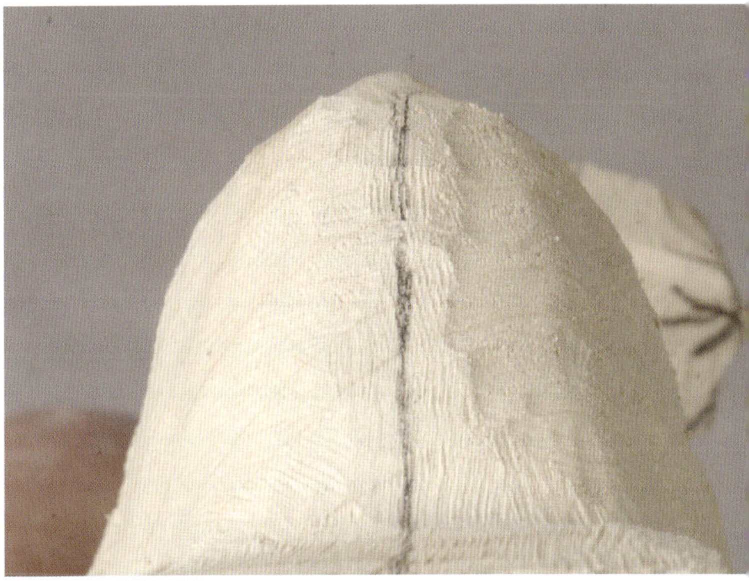

Figure 48. Round over the outside corners on the end of the muzzle.

Figure 49. On the profile of the head, angle the end of the muzzle back from underneath the nose to back toward the throat. Redraw the centerline.

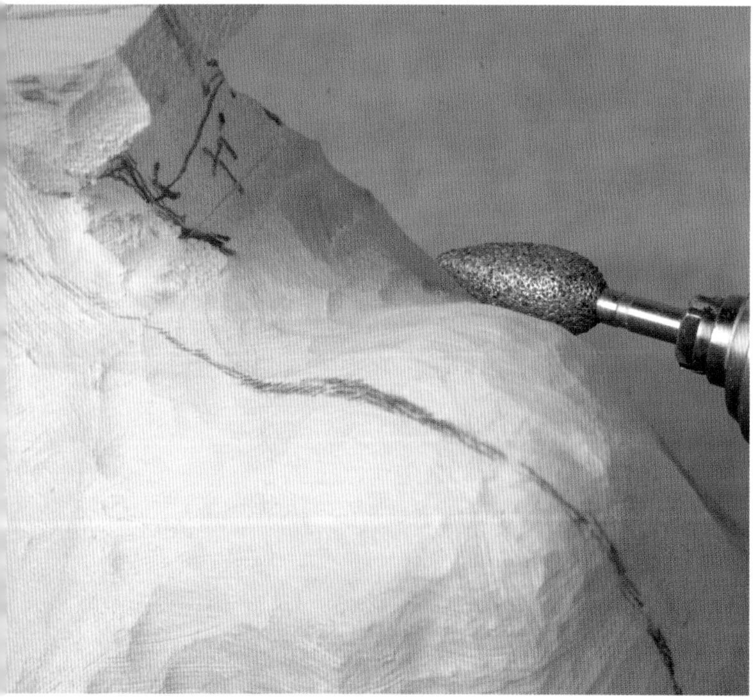

Figure 50. Round over the underside of the head, muzzle, and neck.

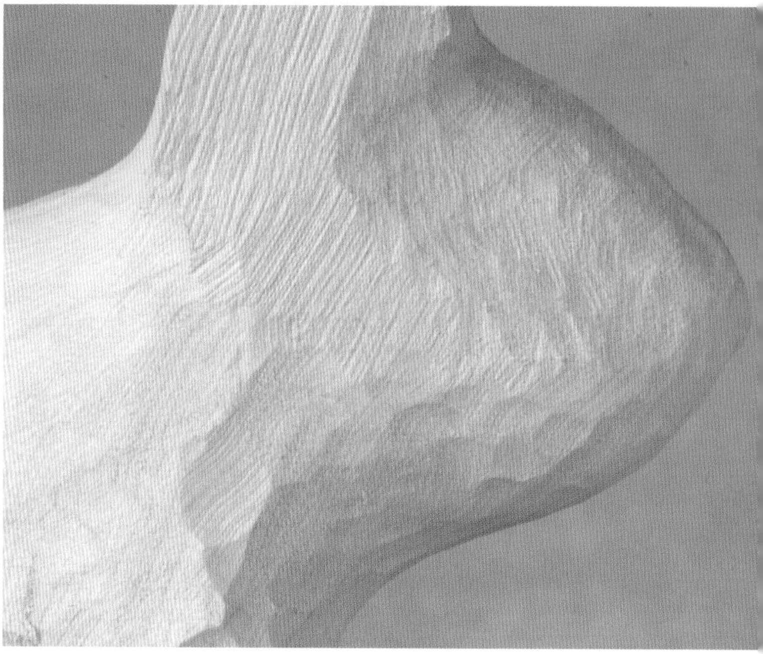

Figure 51. This is the shape of the head and the muzzle at this point.

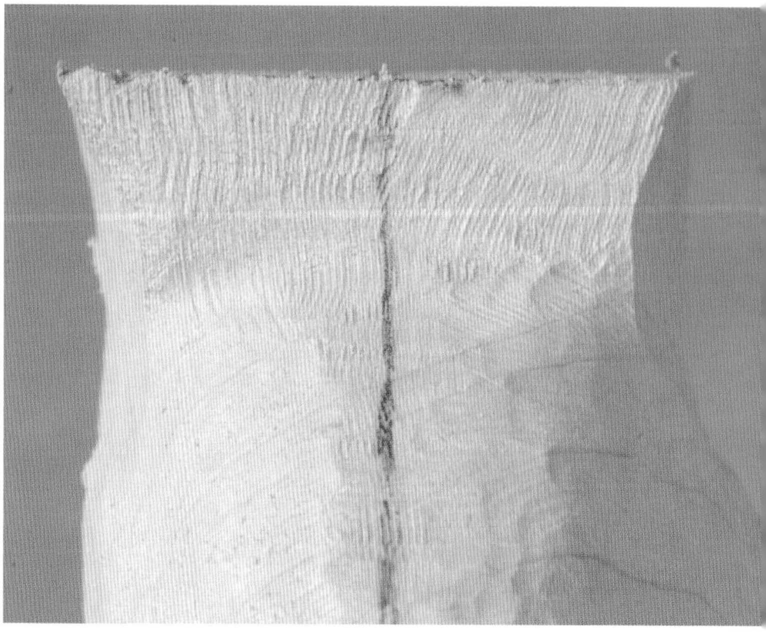

Figure 52. Concave the ear blank surface on both sides with the #3 flame ruby carver (RC-25).

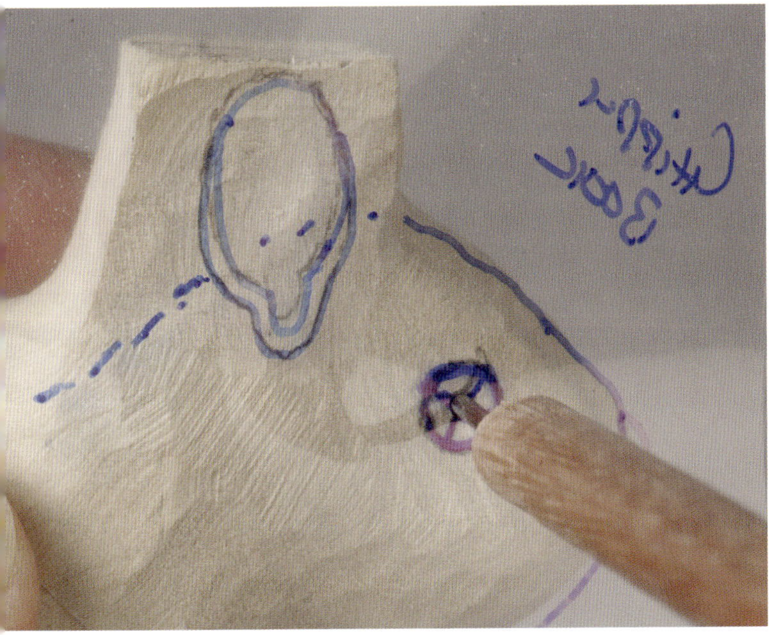

Figure 53. Trace the head, ears, and eyes on a small piece of clear acetate. Hold the acetate to the side of the head, sneak a pencil underneath, and trace the ears. To mark the eyes, you can pinprick right through the acetate to make the center on each side.

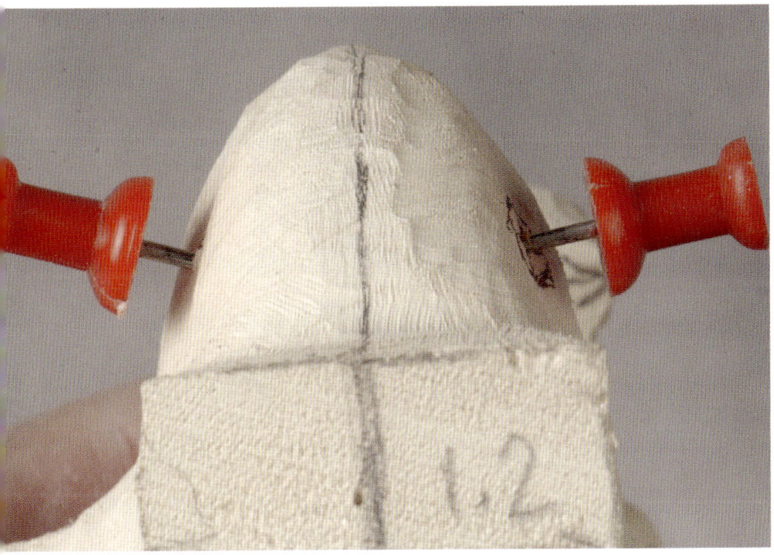

Figure 54. From the front and top plan views, check the evenness of the positioning of the eyes and ears. Use pushpins to check for evenness as well. You will need 6mm circles around both centers.

Figure 55. With the #3 flame ruby carver (RC-25), hollow out the inside of the ear. Angle the bottom of the hole slightly toward the inside of the head, and concave the actual inside of the earflap.

Figure 56. Slightly widen out the bottom of the ear with the small pointed ball ruby carver (RC-16) to create the top of the ear canal.

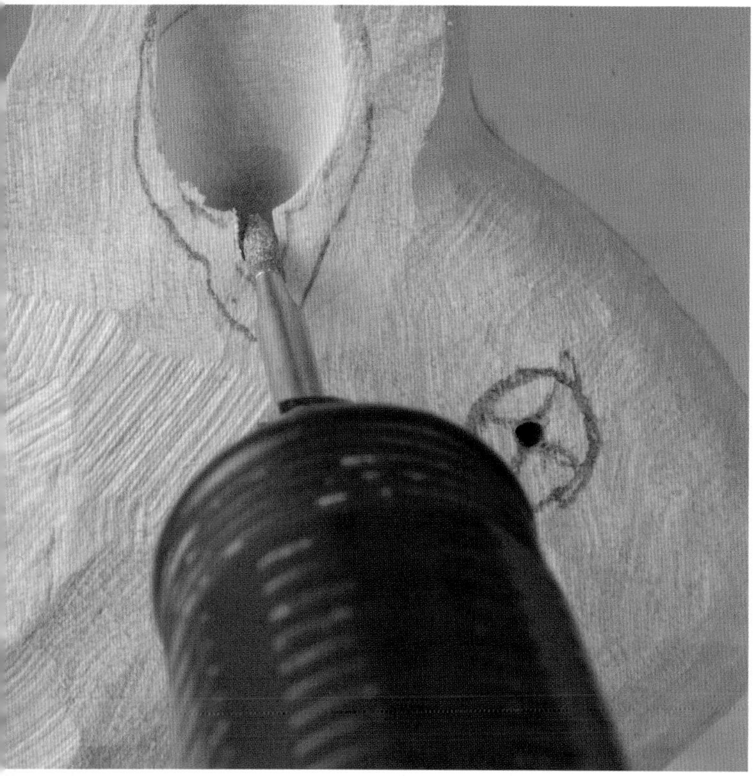

Figure 57. With a small diameter detail diamond, carve the little slit at the bottom of the ear.

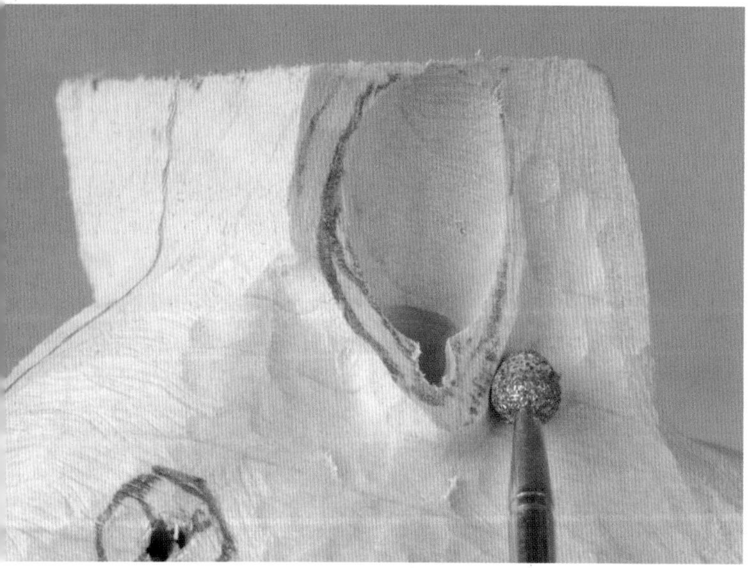

Figure 58. Carve the little flange around the bottom of the ear with the small pointed ball ruby carver (RC-16). Lay the bit down and use the diameter of the bit and not the point. Flow the channel out onto the sides of the head.

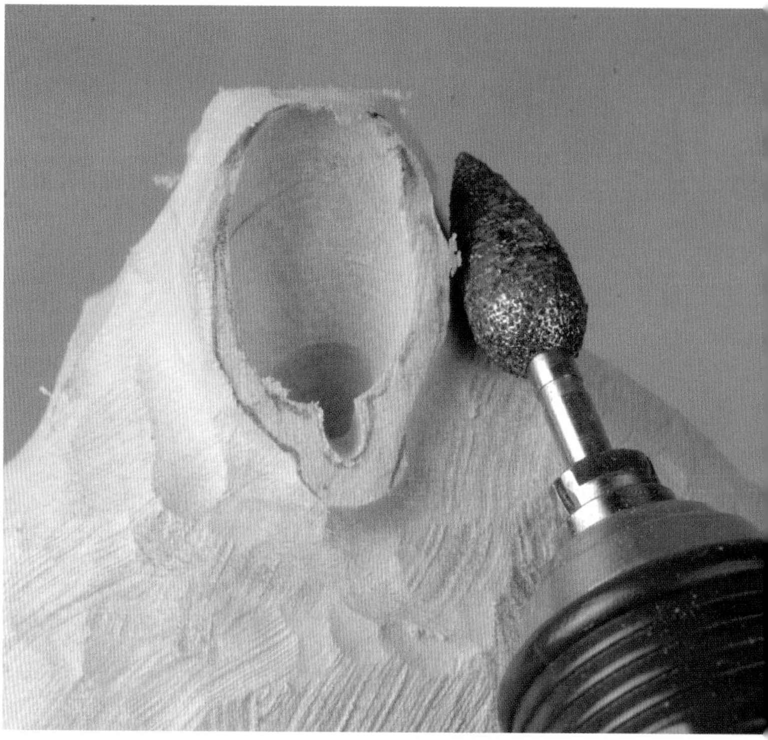

Figure 59. Cut away the excess wood around the middle and upper part of the ears using a #3 flame ruby carver (RC-25).

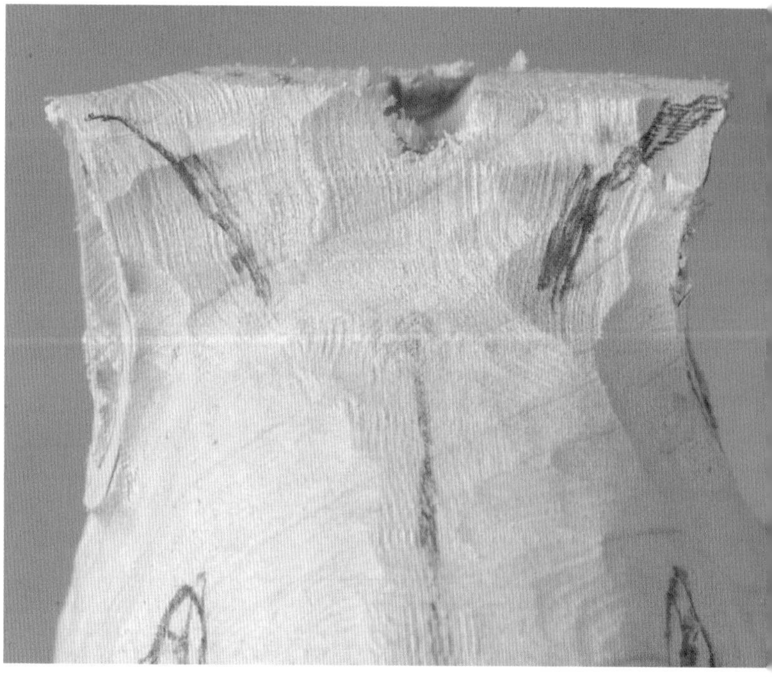

Figure 60. Draw in the back surface of the ear with the base being 0.24" wide and then tapering to the tip. Start cutting the excess wood from in between the ears by working the middle area first and then progressing to the drawn lines. Cut straight back at this point.

Figure 61. Here the wood is taken out in between the ears.

Figure 62. Round the back of the ears with the #3 flame ruby carver (RC-25). Round the back of the head and flow it down to the hind neck.

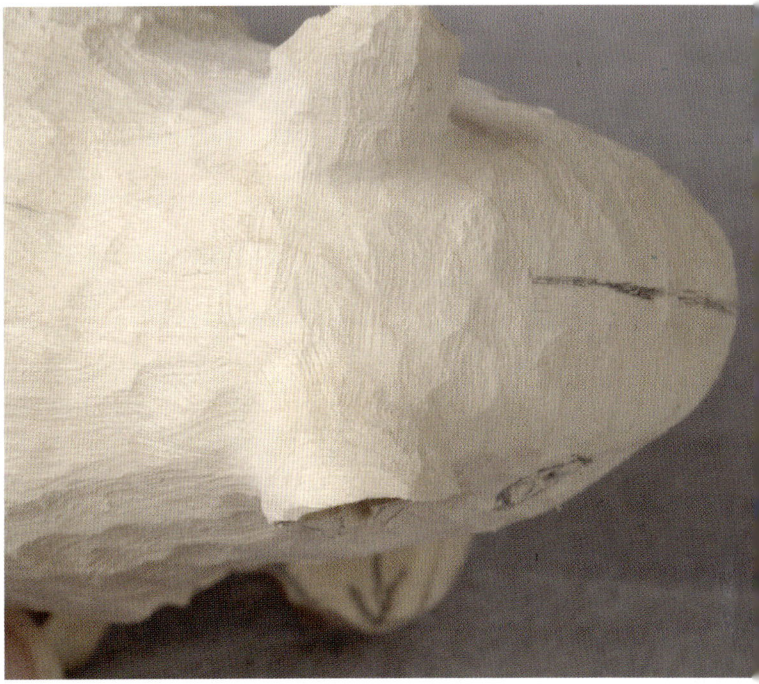

Figure 63. Here you see the rounded ears. To make sure that you do not get the ears too thin in spots, hold the ears up to a light and see just how thin you are getting. If you can see much light, quit cutting!

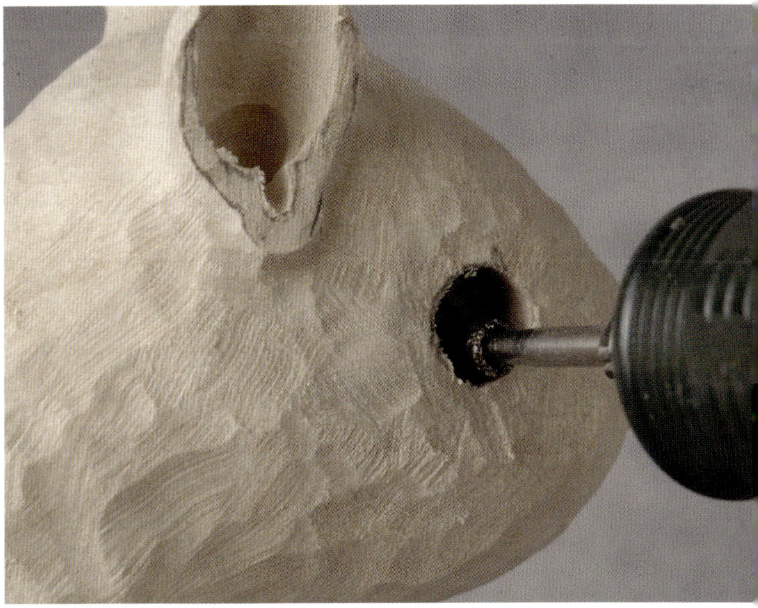

Figure 64. With the slightly domed straight-sided cylinder (RC-18), drill the eyeholes. Since I am right-handed, I do the chippy's right eye first. Then turn him and look straight on, and drill the left eye to match. If you are left-handed, reverse this process. Drill the hole the length of the bit since we will be removing some of the surface wood when we do the details around the eyes.

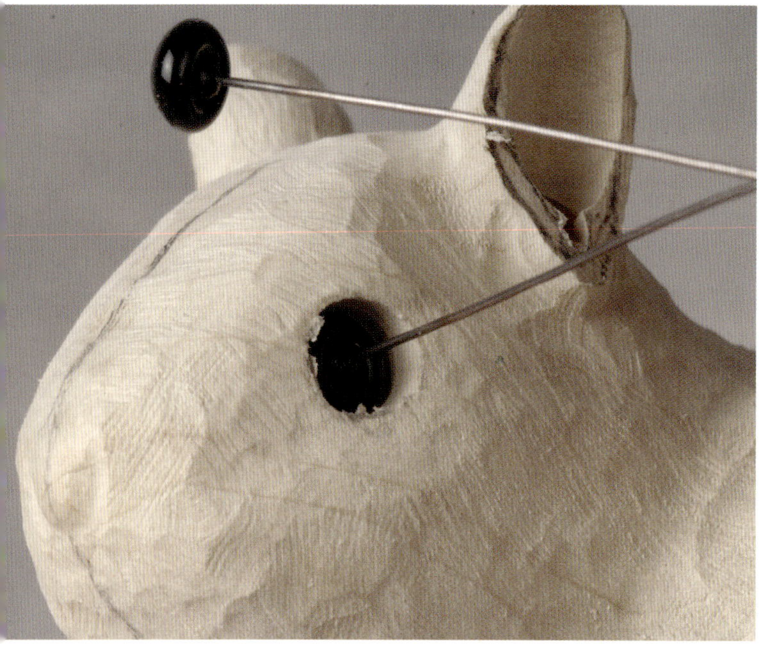

Figure 65. Drill the diameter of the holes ever so slightly larger than the 6mm black eyes. Make sure that both eyes fit into both holes.

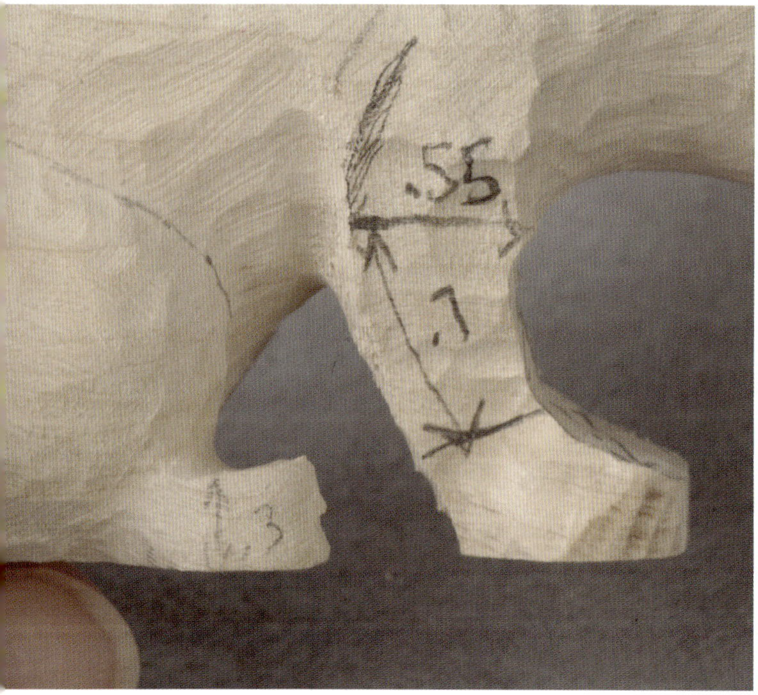

Figure 66. Okay, we are coming along nicely with this project. Let's do the details on the front legs and paws. On the right leg, measure from the middle of the wrist 0.7" and mark the elbow. The width of the elbow is 0.55". Draw in the little part of the upper arm as it blends into the shoulder area.

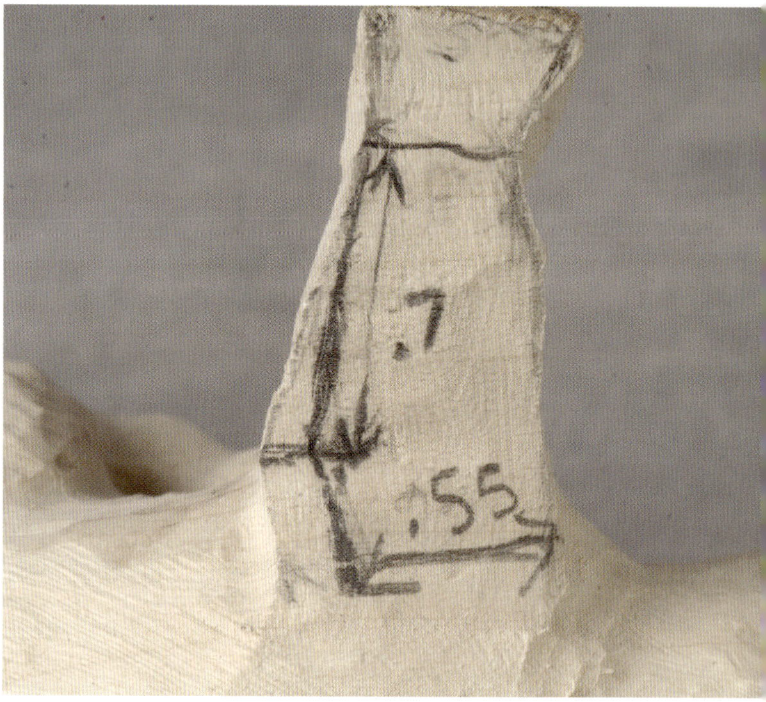

Figure 67. Do the same thing on the raised left front leg.

Figure 68. From the top plan view, check to see that the upper arm areas come into the shoulder area at the same level.

Figure 69. Cut in the short section of the upper arm and round the entire right front leg.

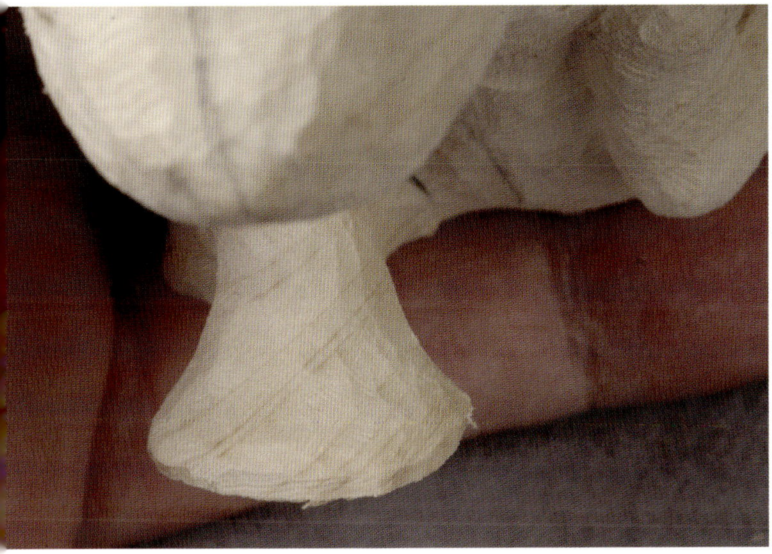

Figure 70. Shape the rounded contour of the right front paw and taper from the angle down to the front edge that should be 0.1" thick. The toes will be spread out in this pose so that he can balance himself while scratching.

Figure 71. Trim the excess wood off the backside of the raised front paw. With the #3 flame ruby carver (RC-25), cut in the wrist until it measures 0.35" from top to bottom and from side to side. Once you have the correct dimensions, round over the corners.

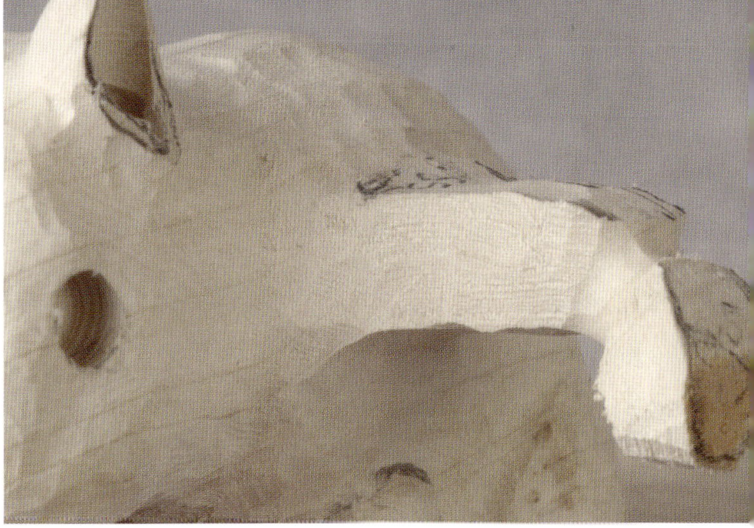

Figure 72. Thin the underside of the upper part of the front leg until it measures 0.5" and taper the underside to the wrist.

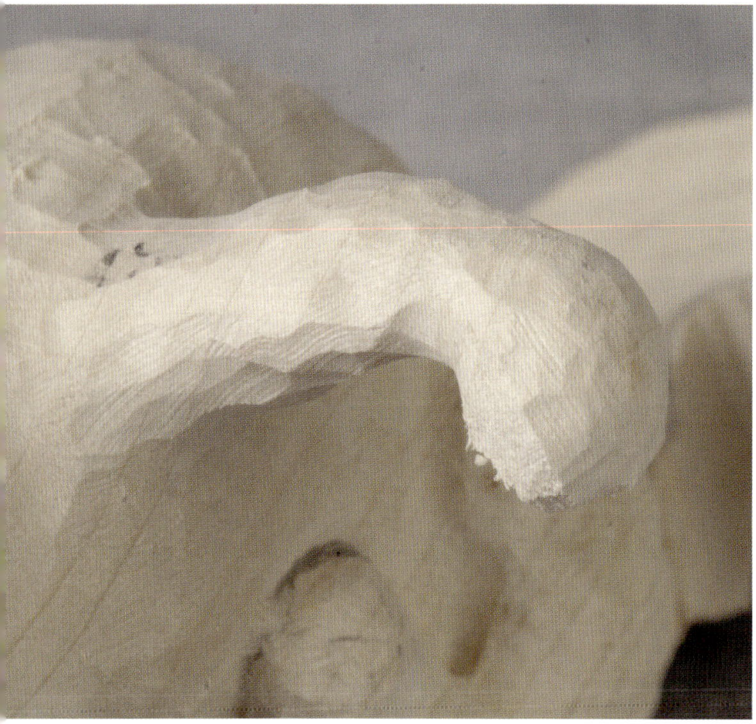

Figure 73. Round over the raised front leg from the shoulder to the wrist. Make sure that you blend the base of the front leg into the shoulder, flank, chest, and neck. Round the paw from side to side and from the wrist downward. Be very careful to support the raised leg and paw with your other hand while working in this area, which is all cross-grained.

Figure 74. While supporting the paw with your holding hand, thin the underside of the raised paw until it measures 0.25" thick.

Figure 75. Round over the right hind paw from side to side and from front to back, using the #2 flame ruby carver (RC-20).

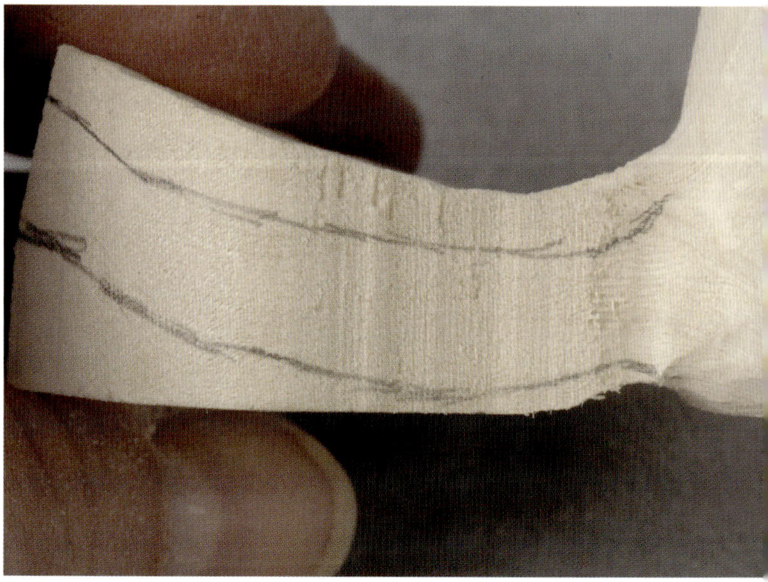

Figure 76. Draw in the tail. For roughing out purposes, make the thickness 0.3" at the base and throughout the length.

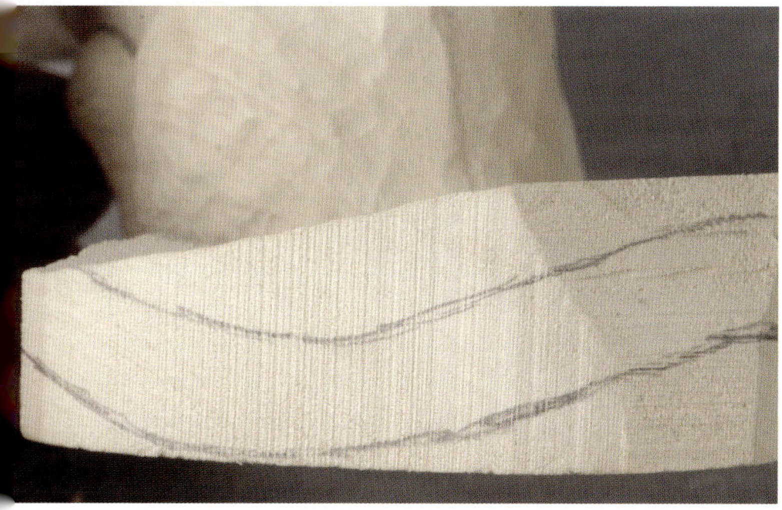

Figure 77. You can get wild and crazy with the undulation of the tail because there is sufficient wood in the pattern to do any number of differing contours.

Figure 78. Use the flame Typhoon carbide cutter to remove the excess wood off the top and the bottom of the tail until it is a consistent thickness. Make sure that you support the tail when roughing it out as part of it is cross-grain and might break. If you are working on the top surface, then support it on the bottom and vice versa.

Figure 79. Narrow up the attachment of the tail to the body to 0.6" and round all of the four corners.

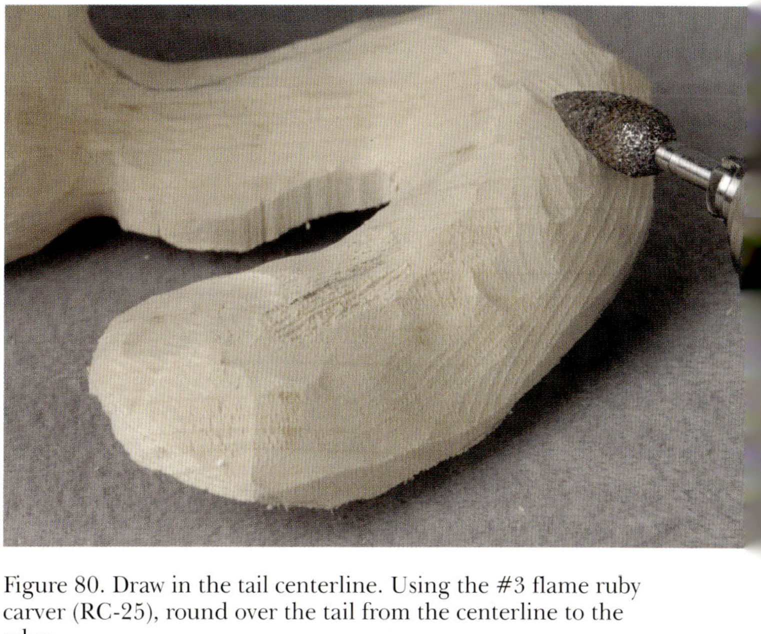

Figure 80. Draw in the tail centerline. Using the #3 flame ruby carver (RC-25), round over the tail from the centerline to the edge.

Figure 81. Slightly concave underside of the tail using the #3 flame ruby carver. Do not make the tail too thin. It should measure 0.3" from the rounded top and straight across the bottom. The concave part should measure approximately 0.25". The texturing and burning will reduce the thickness a little. You do not want the tail so thin that you texture or burn right through it.

Figure 82. On the topside of the tail, drag the #2 flame ruby carver from the center of the tail out toward the edge to break up the surface in preparation for texturing. Try not to do a regular pattern. Throw some short strokes in every now and then.

Figure 83. On the underside of the tail, do the same thing, but, because it is slightly concave, use the small pointed ball ruby carver (RC-16). Drag the bit and do not use the point.

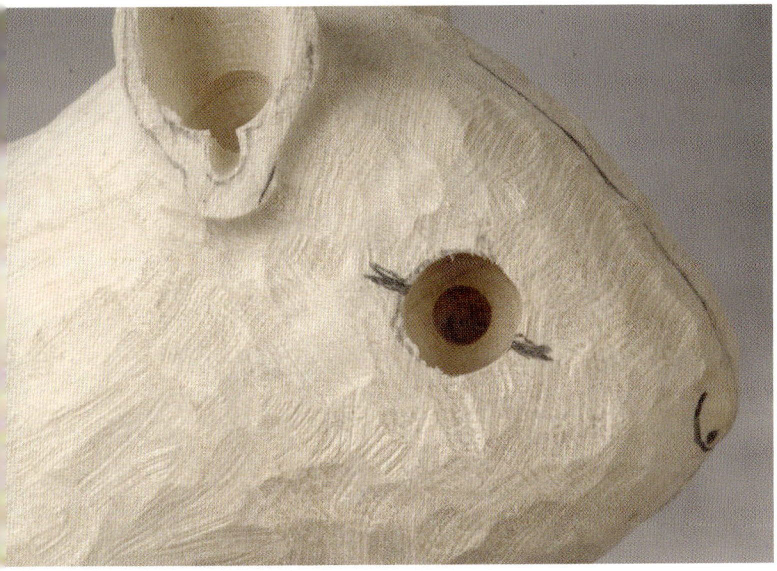

Figure 84. Draw two dashes in the front and back of both eyes. These are the dividing points between the upper and lower eyelids. They should point from the base of the ear to the nose.

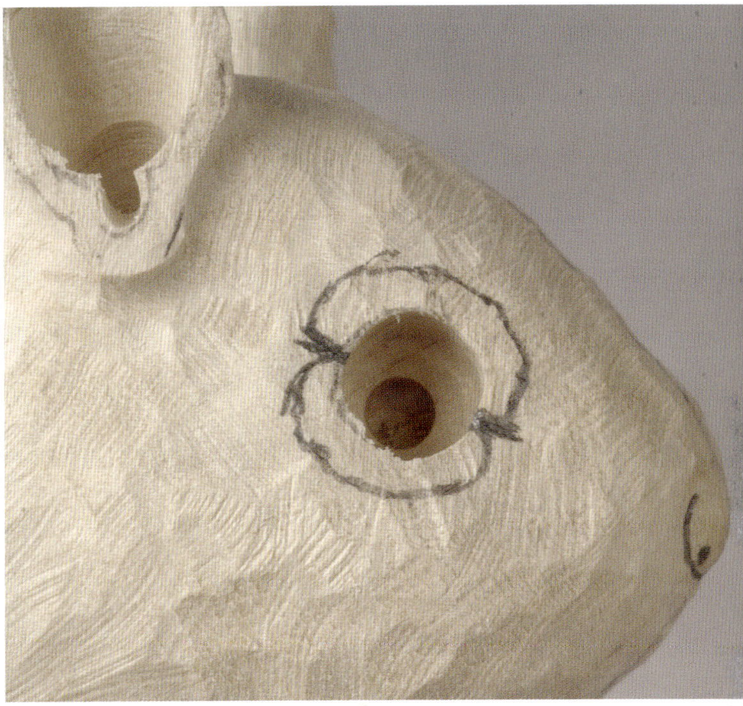

Figure 85. Draw in the upper and lower eyelids meeting at the dashes.

Figure 86. Draw in the nostrils bilaterally on the bottom of the nose.

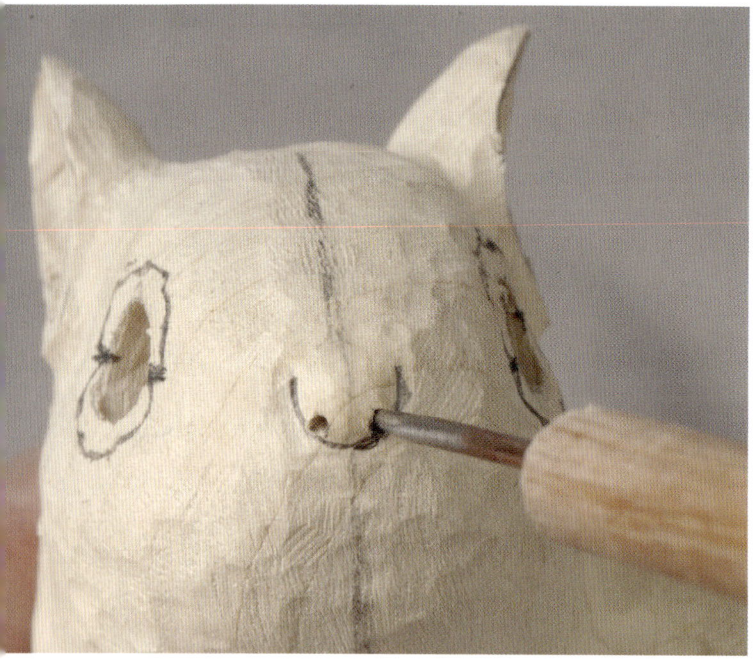

Figure 87. Use the sharp end of the eye tool made in the bunny chapter to poke in the nostril holes.

Figure 88. Underneath the middle of the nose is a short "V" channel/slit dividing the muzzle. Draw in this short dividing line and draw in the mouth with a slight curve at the back of both corners.

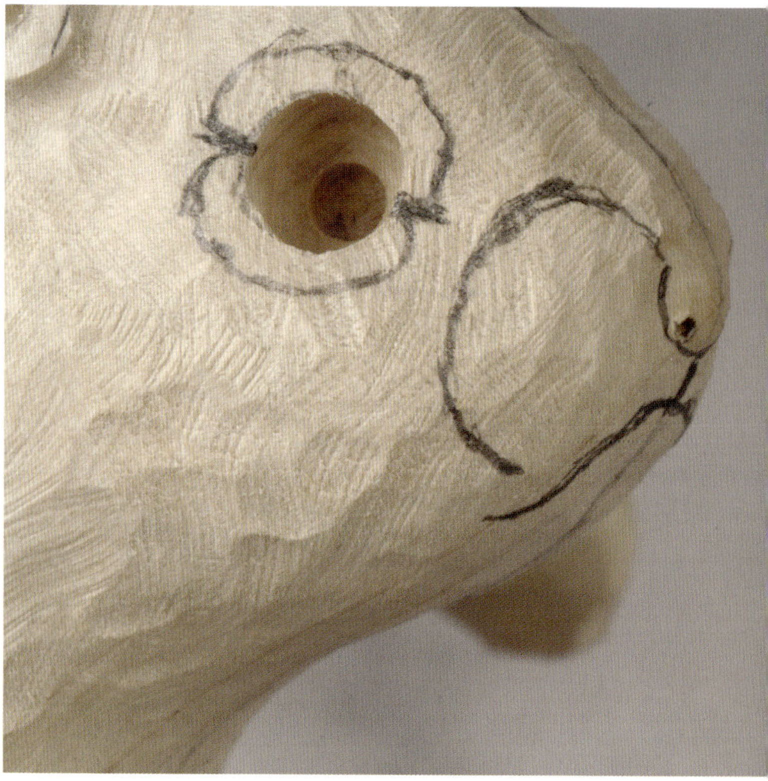

Figure 89. Draw in the whisker pad starting at the top back of the nose and circling around in the shape of a "C" on the right side. On the left side, the whisker pad is a backward "C" shape.

Figure 90. Make sure the whisker pads are balanced and symmetrical on both sides. Note that they do not come right to the mouth.

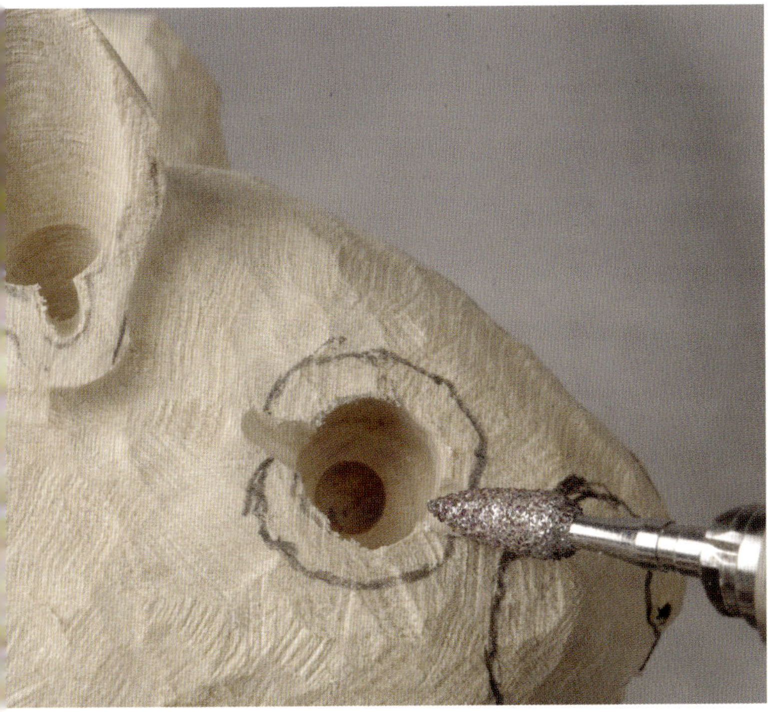

Figure 91. With the #1 flame ruby carver (RC-19), cut in the division slits between the upper and lower eyelids on both eyes.

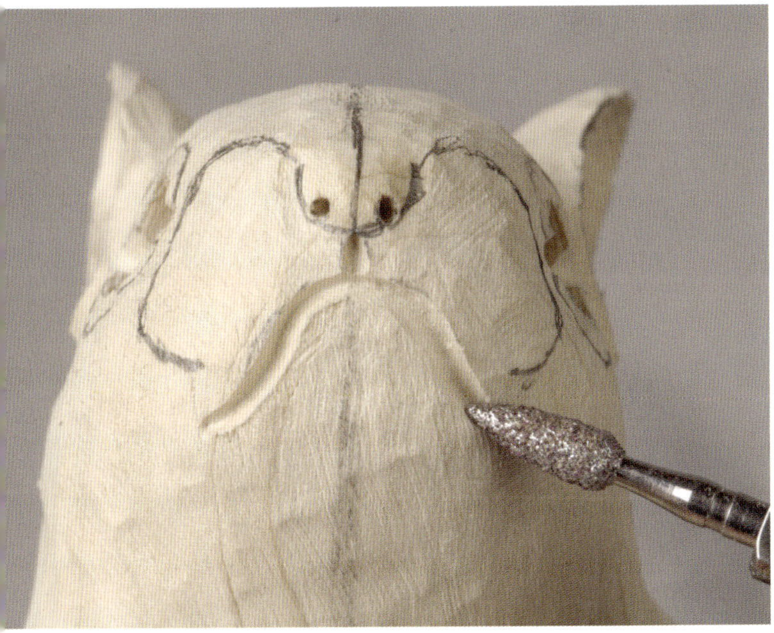

Figure 92. Draw the tip of the #1 flame down the little slit under the nose and around the mouth line.

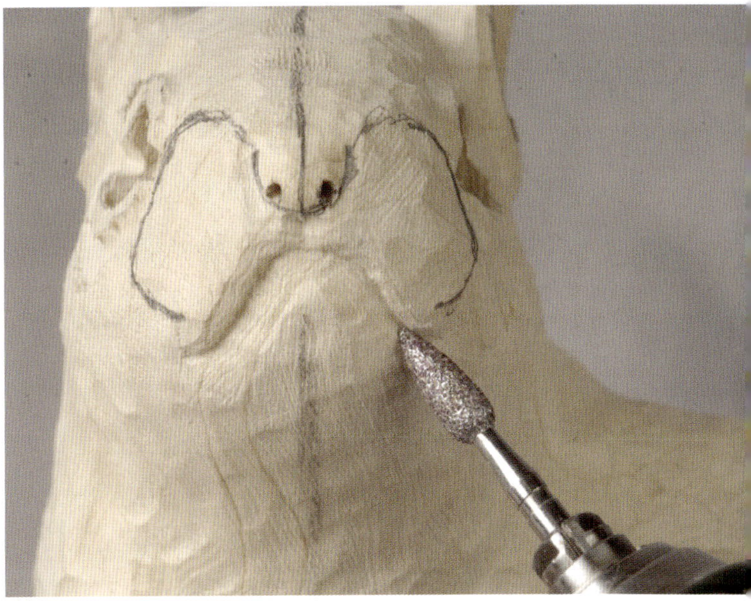

Figure 93. Roll the lower lip down to the bottom of the "V" channel and take the sharp edge off the upper lip.

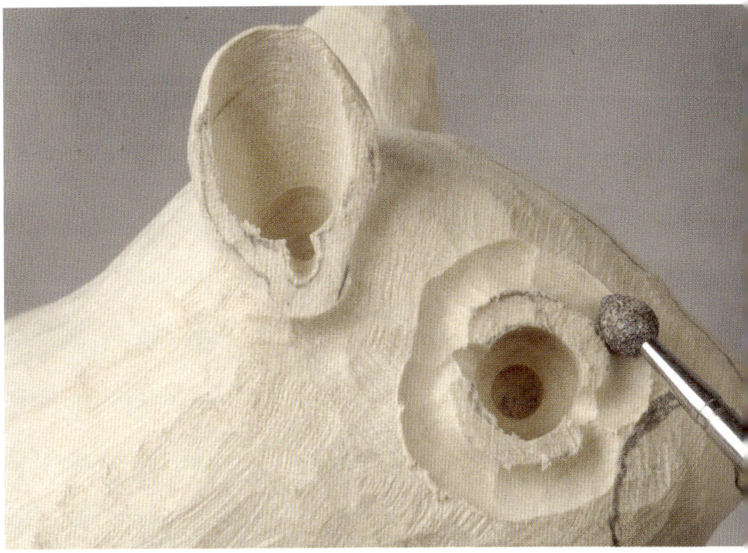

Figure 94. Channel around the eyelids by dragging the small pointed ball ruby carver (RC-16) and using the diameter of the bit to do the channeling.

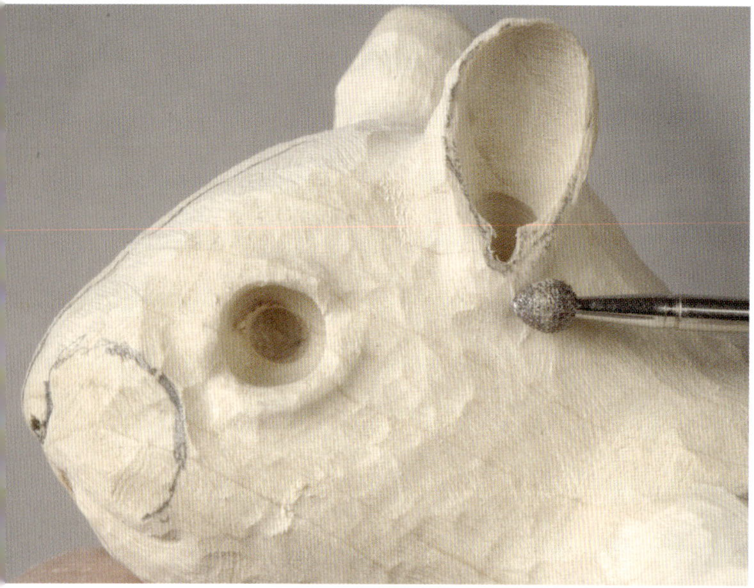

Figure 95. Flow the channel out around the eye except for the front toward the whisker pad line. Round over the upper and lower eyelids inside and outside their contour. The eyelids should be angled down to the bottom of the slits in the front and back of the eye. While you have the pointed ball in your machine, go ahead and round over the bottom ear flange.

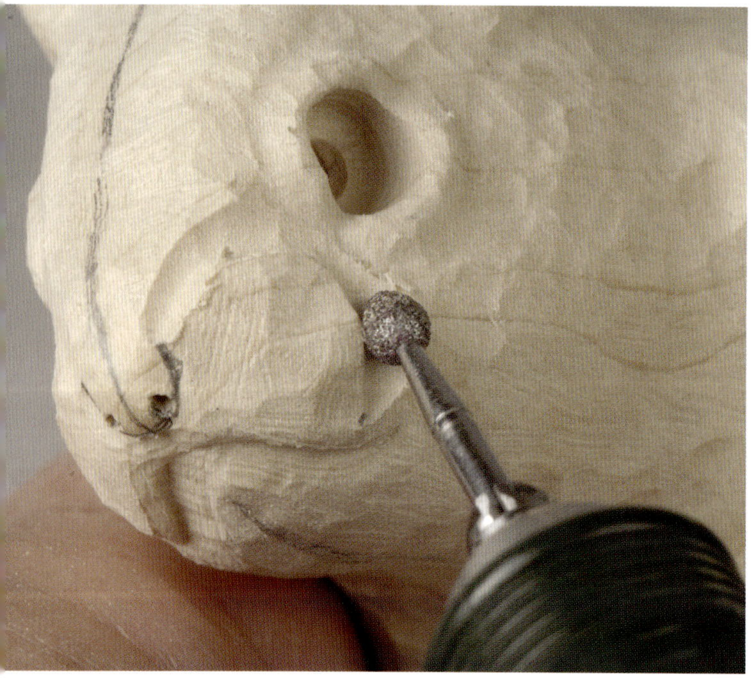

Figure 96. Use the small pointed ball ruby carver to cut the whisker pad channel. Lay the bit down and drag in around on the line. Do not use the point. The back of the whisker pad channel should fall in the same channel as the front of the eyelids.

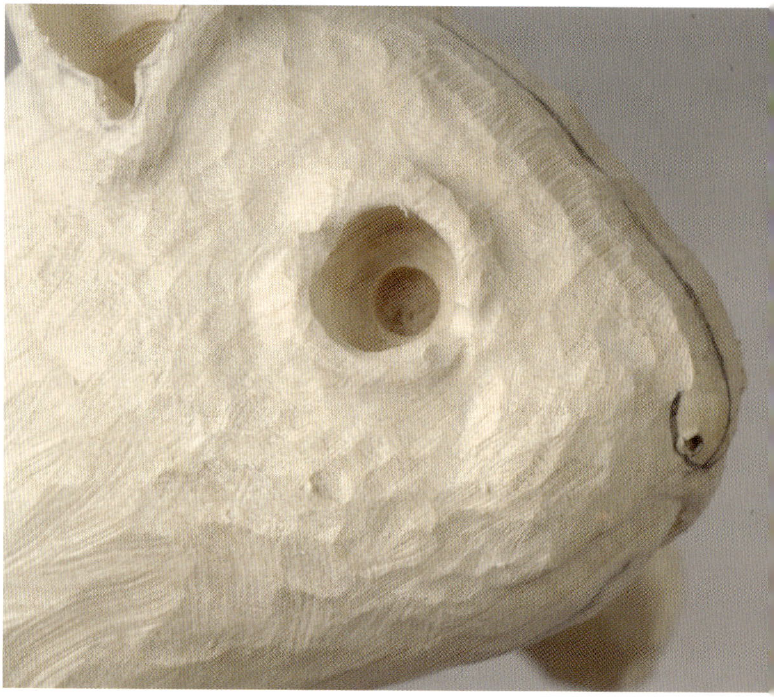

Figure 97. Flow the whisker pad channel out on to the surrounding areas. Round over the whisker pad down to the bottom of the channel. Check both sides of the head to make sure that every thing is flowing out to the surrounding areas and that everything is balanced and symmetrical. Check for balance and symmetry from all views.

Figure 98. Sand and smooth the inside of the earflaps with a stone. Check the ears from all views to make sure that they are even and balanced.

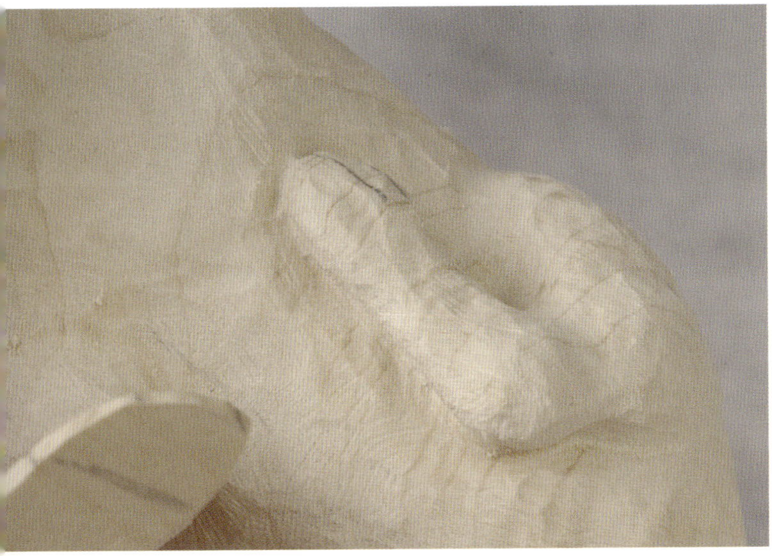

Figure 99. Before drawing in the toes on the scratching hind paw, undercut the bottom of the foot and ankle with the #3 flame ruby carver (RC-20). Make sure that you flow the channel out onto the belly and lower chest.

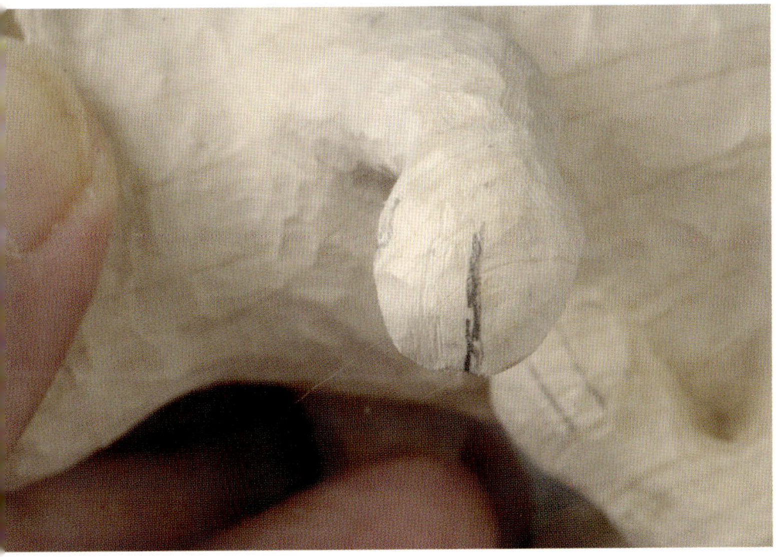

Figure 100. To draw in the toes on the raised front paw, draw a centerline down the middle of the paw.

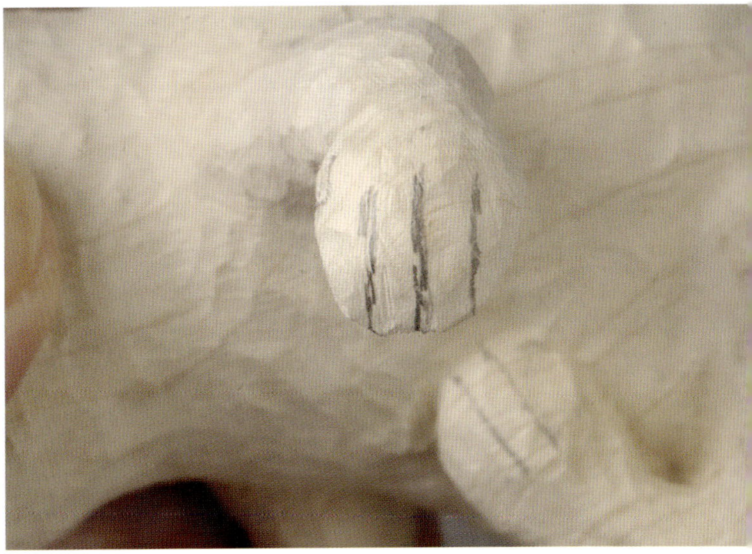

Figure 101. Divide the wood to the right of the centerline equally and put a line, and do the same on the left side. Three lines will create 4 toes.

Figure 102. Also on the raised front paw, the chippy needs a little nubbin of a thumb. Draw that in on the inside of the paw slightly above the length of the digits.

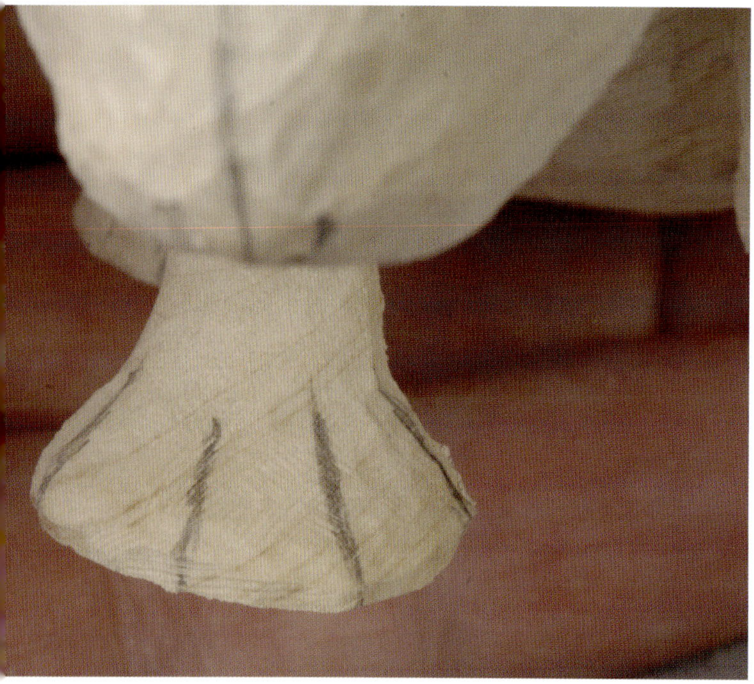

Figure 103. To draw the toes in on the down paw, draw 4 lines representing the middle of each digit.

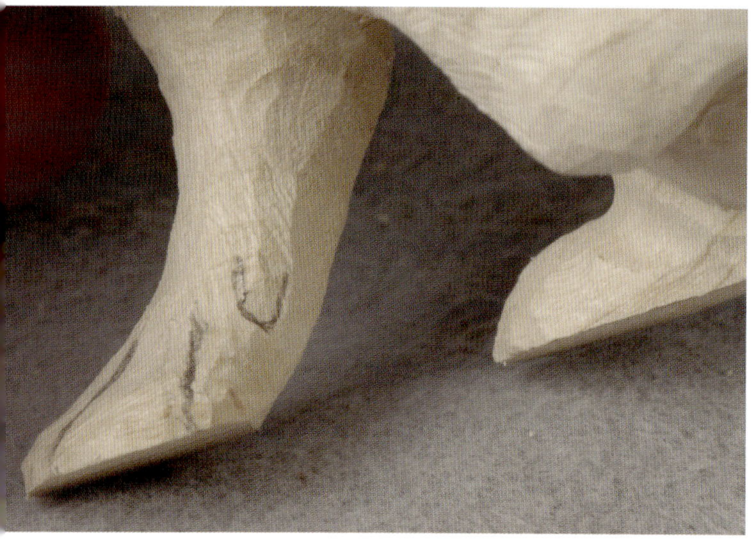

Figure 104. Draw the thumb on the down paw.

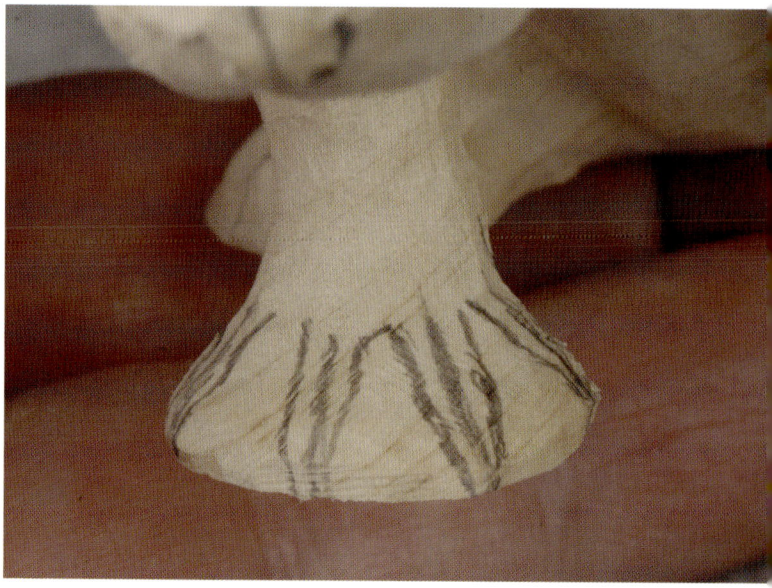

Figure 105. Draw a line on both sides of the digit line. The space in between each toe is going to get cut out.

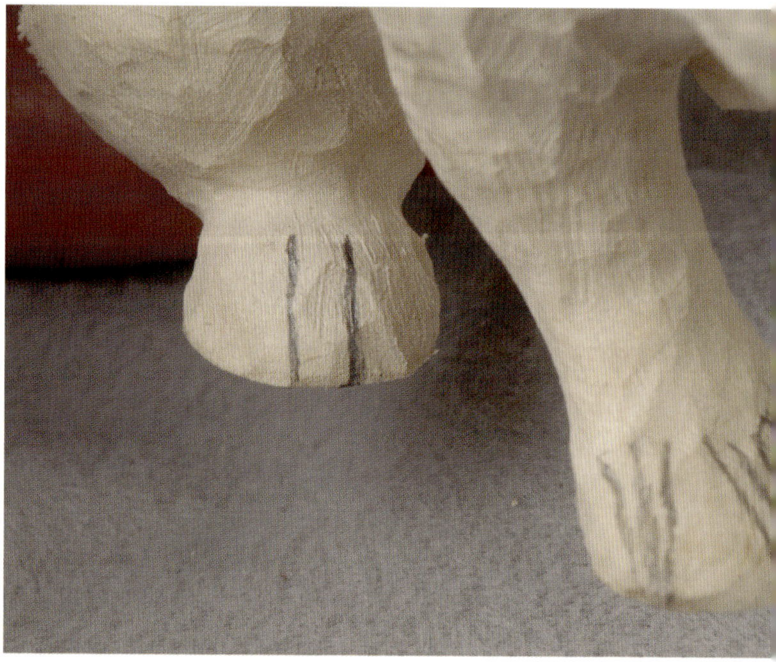

Figure 106. On the right hind paw, draw two parallel lines down the middle of the paw 0.1" apart.

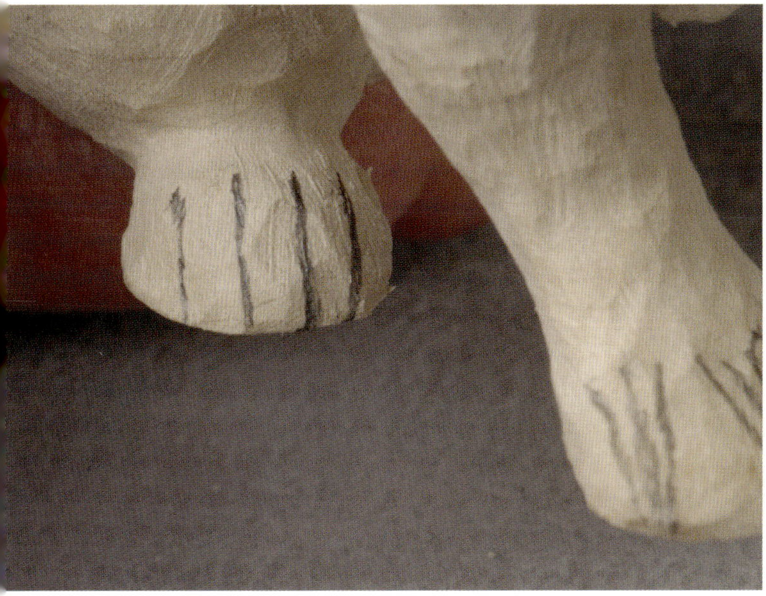

Figure 107. Divide the space to the right in half and put a line and do the same on the left half. Four lines will create 5 toes.

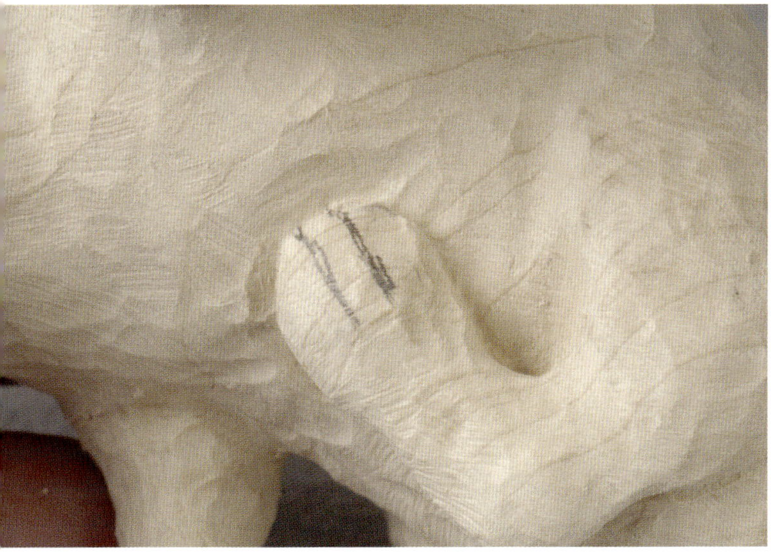

Figure 108. On the scratching paw, put two parallel lines in the middle of the paw 0.1" apart.

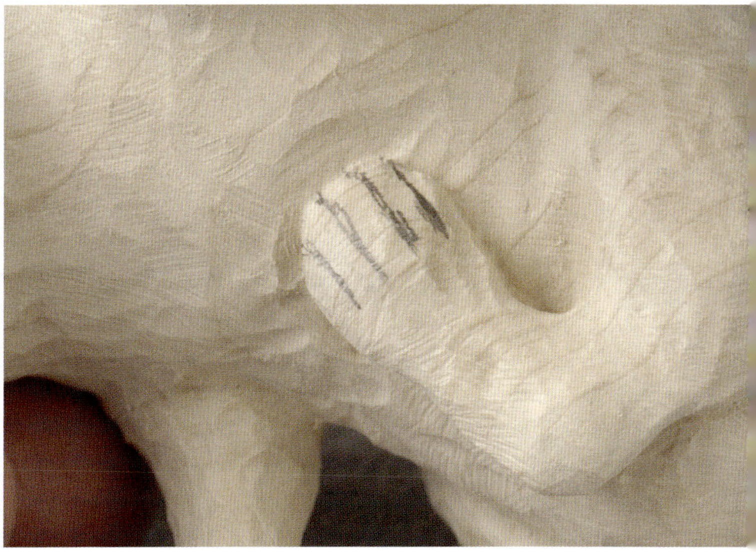

Figure 109. Divide the space to the right in half and put a line and do the same for the space on the left. Four lines will create 5 toes.

Figure 110. The closed paws are all done the same way. Drag the #1 flame ruby carver (RC-19) down each line. Use the point to cut around the thumbs on the front paws. The outer and inner toes on all paws are slightly shorter than the middle ones. The digits need to be carved in underneath the raised paw as well.

Figure 111. Lay the #1 down and roll in on the sharp edges of each toe to round them over.

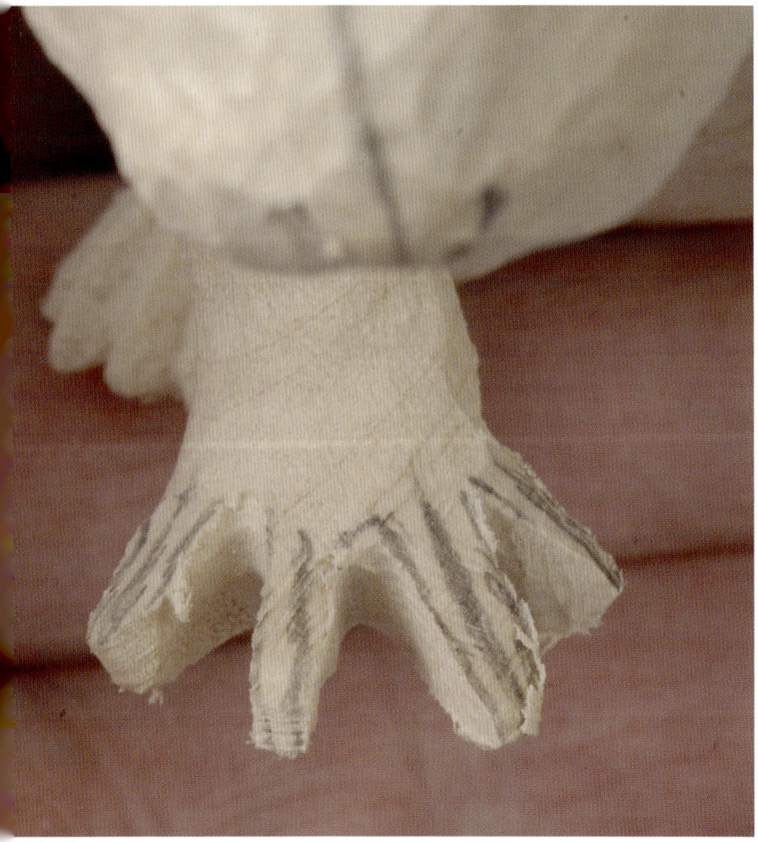

Figure 112. Still using the #1 flame, cut out the excess wood between the toes. Work carefully here, as they are cross-grain.

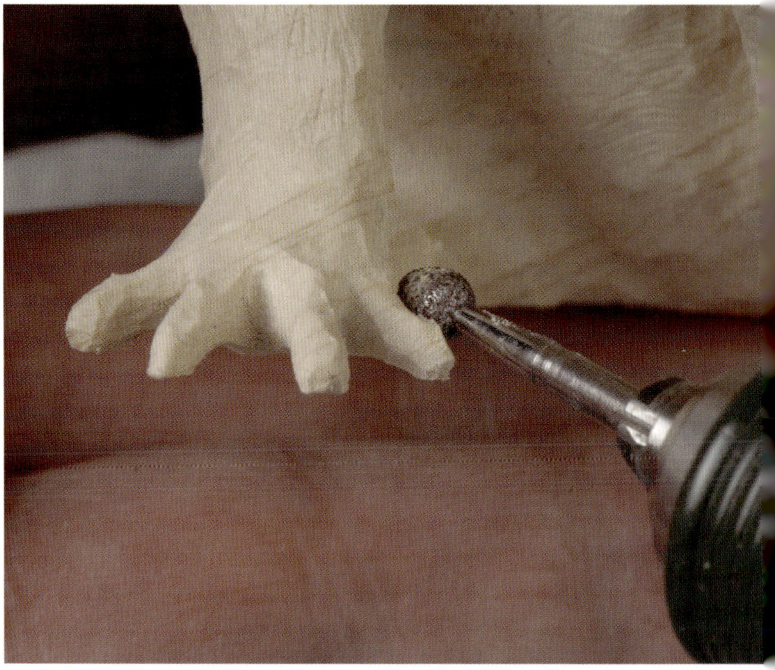

Figure 113. Round over the digits on the down paw with the small pointed ball ruby carver (RC-16). You may need to take some off the top of the paw to get a good transition from the leg to the paw to the digits. Once you get the toes rounded over, they become even more fragile—so handle the chippy with care!

Figure 114. Before we get start on texturing, let's check some dimensions to make sure that your chippy is not too oversized. First, check just above the haunches to make sure that the chippy is somewhere close to 1.5".

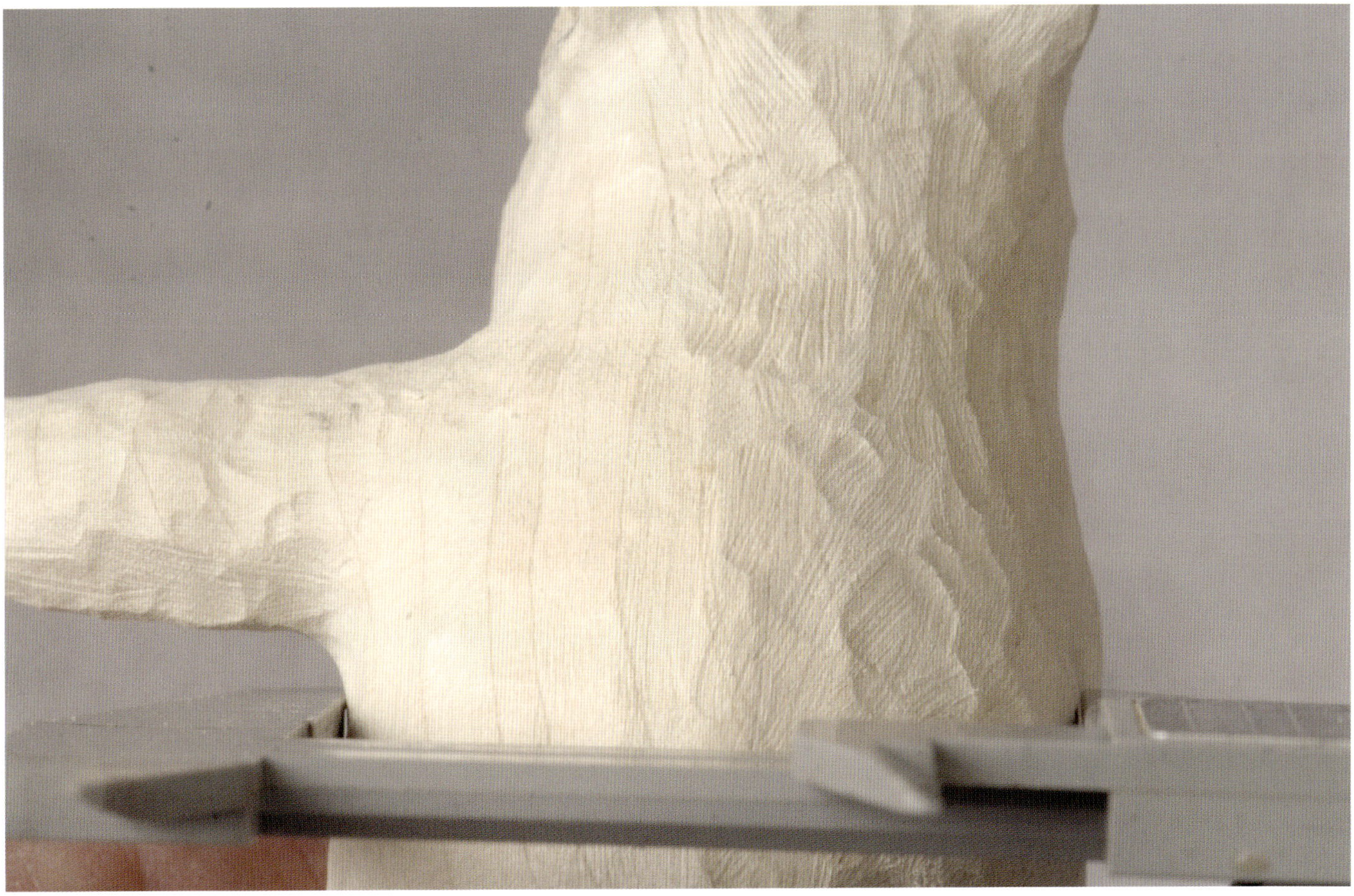

Figure 115. Check the dimension just behind the front legs. This should be approximately 1.5" as well, with a slight bulging of the flanks.

Figure 116. The neck width should be around 1.2".

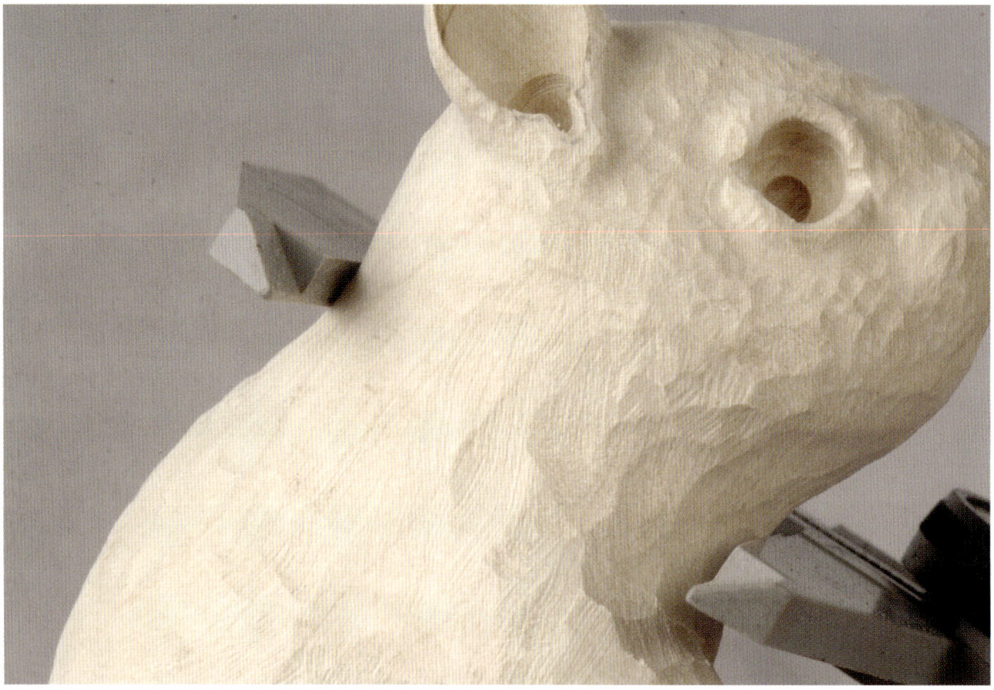

Figure 117. The neck thickness from front to back should be around 1.3".

Figure 118. Basically hair grows and flows from the nose back to the tail. Draw in the flow lines starting at the nose and working back on the legs and body. If you have a question as to the flow, check the hair on your arms, legs, wherever, and the chippy's is the same.

Figure 119. Here you see the flow on the raised paw side. On the toes, the hair flows from the deepest part of the "V" cut out at angle on both sides of the cut.

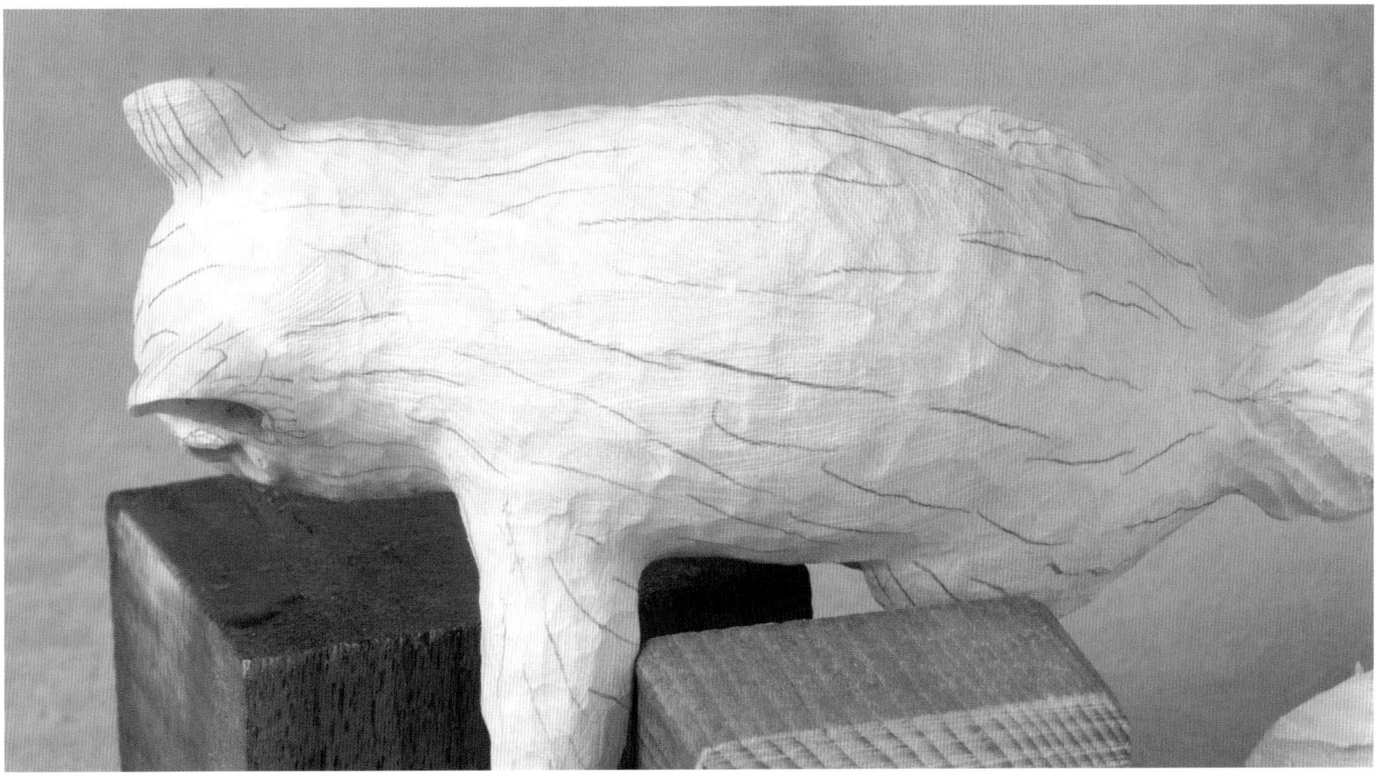

Figure 120. The fur flows straight down the back to the tail. You can see that the hair flows from the base of the ears to the tip. On the front legs, the hair flows straight down the inside surface and then drapes off the back edge.

Figure 121. On the underside, the hair flows from the mouth straight down the chest and belly.

Figure 122. Note how the fur flows back and then down on the whisker pads.

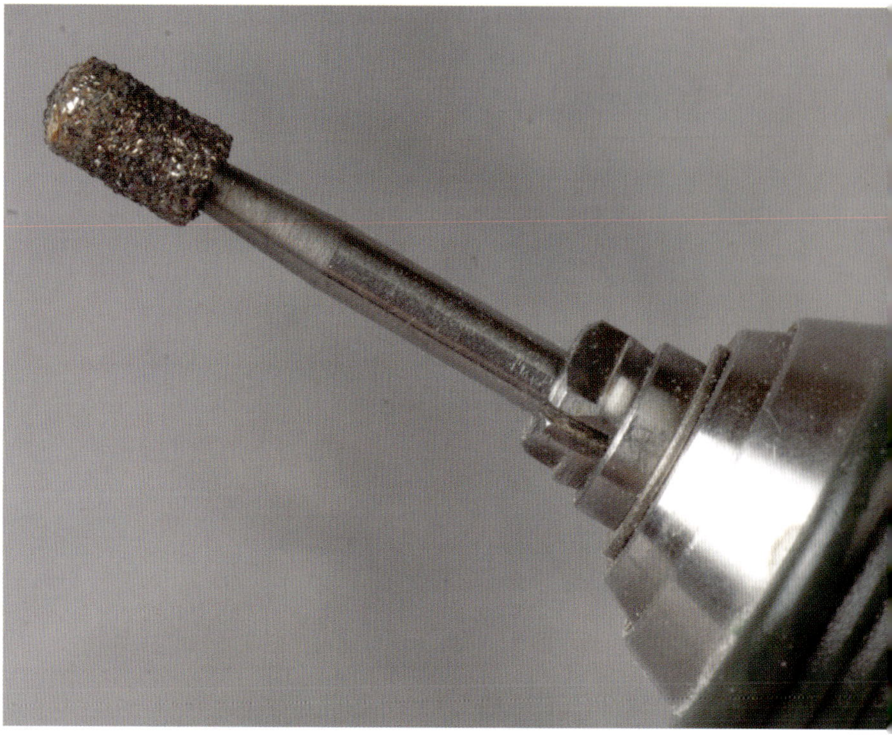

Figure 123. The slightly dome straight-sided cylinder ruby carver (RC-18) is the bit used to texture.

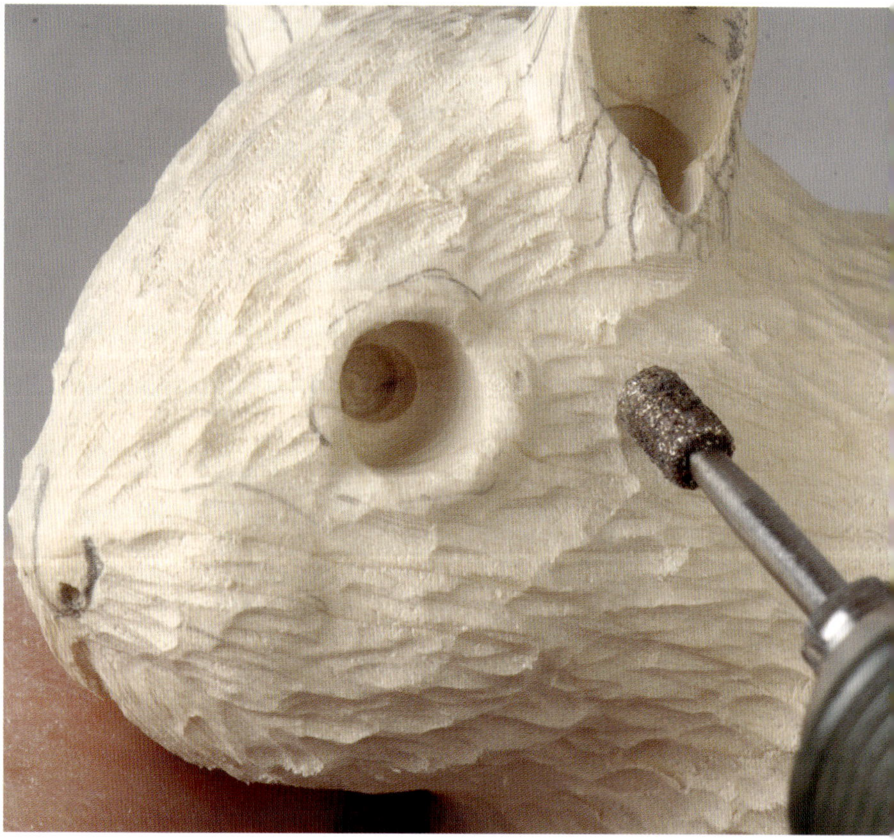

Figure 124. Fur is multi-level. To create that natural fur effect, the surface of the wood needs to be made irregular in heights. Holding the bit at an angle and just using the corner of the bit, begin to texture. Start at the nose and follow the flow lines. The texturing is lighter on the head, a little bit deeper on the body, and the deepest on the tail. Make sure that the texturing strokes are at differing angles and not all just straight. **Do not texture the nose, eyelids, ears, or paws!**

Figure 125. Keep following the flow lines down the paws and body. Leave no area flat or un-textured. Follow the flow lines on the underside as well.

Figure 126. Even though we broke up the surface of the tail with the #2 flame ruby carver earlier, the tail needs more levels of fur. The texturing is the deepest on the tail. Knock the corners of the previous channels off as you are running the cylindrical bit over it. Do the same on the underside of the tail.

Figure 127. Start the burning around the nose and follow the flow lines just as you did in texturing. Each time you put the burning pen down, change the angle of the stroke from the previous one. A medium skew burning tip is ideal for most burning on the chippy. Keep the burning strokes as close together as you possibly can. Try not to dig the point of the burning pen into the wood. Extra time spent burning to make the fur natural will increase the realism of the fur and make the painting infinitely easier! Burn up to and around the eyelids at this point.

Figure 128. To burn the eyelids, start at the front corners of both lids and follow the contour with very short strokes back to the back corner. To burn the ears, start at the base and work toward the tip, changing direction of each stroke.

Figure 129. Concave areas of burning, such as under the neck, are best accomplished with the rounded tip burning pen.

Figure 130. The burning needs to be brushed with the natural bristle toothbrush to get rid of any loose carbon that is created by burning at a high temperature.

Figure 131. Begin to lengthen the burning strokes on the hind and side neck and throat.

Figure 132. Following the flow lines, continue burning the fur down the neck, on to the shoulder area, and down the front leg.

Figure 133. On the underside, work the burning down the neck, chest, and belly.

Figure 134. Continue burning the fur down the back to the tail and over the haunches. You can go back over the burning and deepen some of the areas and make the fur more ruffled and realistic.

Figure 135. To burn in the digits, start at the bottom of the "V" cut and burn at an angle up to the top.

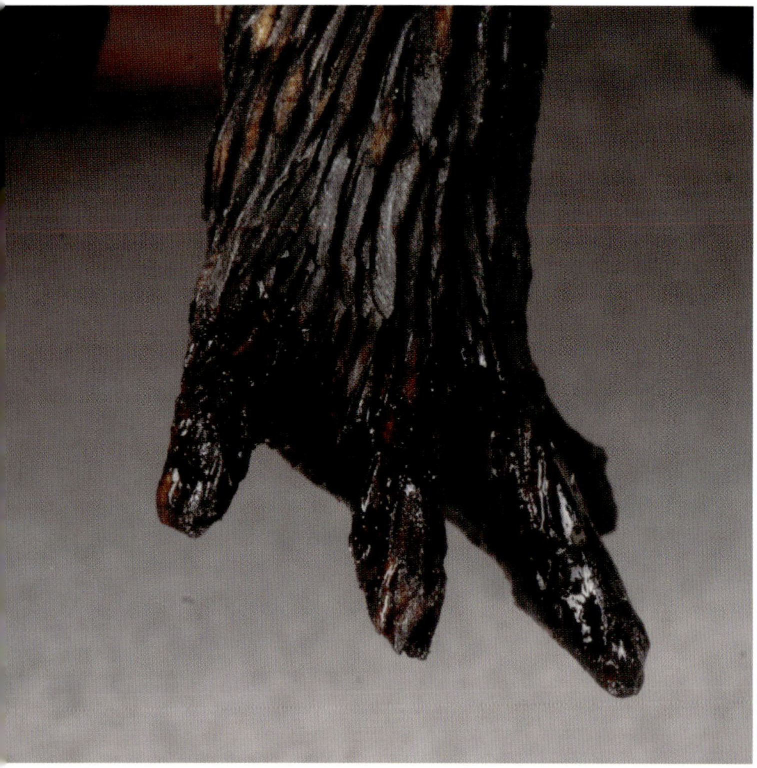

Figure 136. After you burn the fur on the right front paw, apply thin super-glue and let it soak in the underside and top to strengthen the digits.

Figure 137. After the body is done, start on the tail by burning down the middle and flaring the burning out to the edges. Use longer and more curving strokes since the hairs are longer.

Figure 138. Finish burning the top and underside of the tail. While supporting the tail, brush it with the toothbrush to remove any loose carbon.

Figure 139. To seal this project I would recommend dipping it in the 50/50 lacquer/lacquer thinner mixture. Microscopically, wood is a collection of tubes. When the tree is growing there is sap and moisture in the tubes. As the wood dries, the sap and moisture evaporate. Because there are several fragile parts to this carving, it would be safer to fill these tubes with the thinned lacquer, thus making those parts stronger. If you don't have the thinned lacquer, spray two coats of the Krylon Crystal Clear Acrylic Spray, waiting about 10 minutes between coats. Allow the sealer to dry before proceeding in setting the eyes.

Figure 140. Fill the eyeholes almost full of the oily, non-hardening modeling clay.

Figure 141. Cut the eyes off the wires right up next to the back of the eye. Sometimes there is a little glass nubbin on the back of the eye. Do not cut this glass nubbin, as it will likely fracture the eye.

Figure 142. Push the eyes into place with the end of a wooden dowel or something wood. I made the end of an old paintbrush handle concave and use that to push eyes into place.

Figure 143. The eyes do not need to be too deep. You do not want to have to look down into the eyes. When looking from the front view and top view, you want to be able to see a little of the top curvature of the glass.

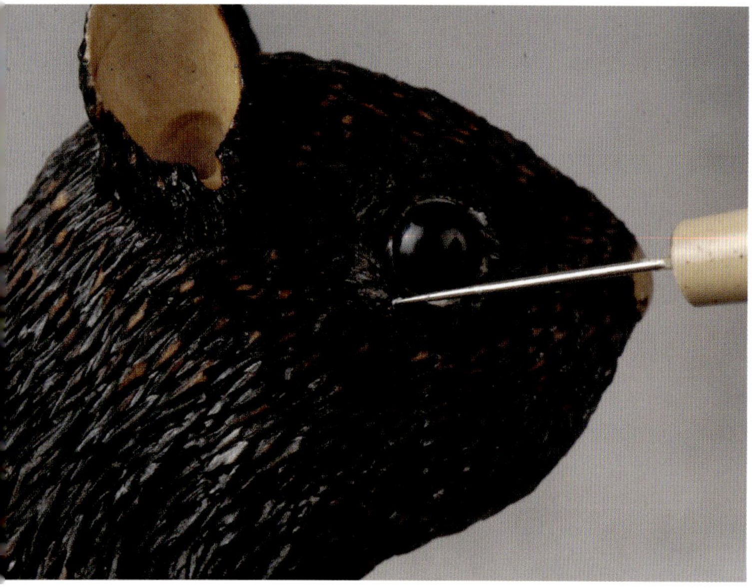

Figure 144. On the other end of the old paintbrush, I inserted and super-glued a portion of the end of a large needle. You will need to clean out the clay in the crevice and this tool is ideal for that. Be careful not to move the eye when cleaning out the remnants of clay.

Figure 145. Use the natural bristle toothbrush to brush any remaining clay out of the texturing. This is when the natural toothbrush just shines. It brushes out clay that the synthetic toothbrushes leave behind. Be sure to get all of the clay out of the texturing. Any clay left will prevent the epoxy putty from sticking. Leave your clay handy so that you can dip your working tool in it periodically to put an oily coat on it, and keep the putty from sticking.

Figure 146. Cut the ribbon epoxy putty straight across. Cut out the center where the two colors have already chemically bonded, and discard this piece.

Figure 147. Mix and knead the putty until it is an even green color. You have about 45 minutes of working time with the putty after it is mixed.

Figure 148. Roll a small diameter worm slightly larger than 1/16". I left the eye tool end, which is 1/16" brazing rod sharpened, in the picture so that you can get some idea of the diameter.

Figure 149. Cut about an inch long piece of the worm, pick it up with the spatula end of the eye tool, and crimp the putty end down into the crevice around the eye. This crimping motion is one in which you will be pressing down and pulling back, all in one motion.

Figure 150. Work the worm into the crevice around the end, leaving a little ridge, which is called the eye ring, raised. Cut off the excess. Continue working the putty into the crevice and making the eye ring diameter as small as you can. The epoxy putty camouflages the edge of the eyehole and forms the little ridge called the eye ring.

Figure 151. Using the poker end of the eye tool, blend the putty down into the texturing of the eyelids. You don't need a quarter inch circle of putty around the eye—you need just enough to fill the crevice, create the eye ring, and blend into the texturing. If the eye ring starts getting too encompassing on the eye, just move it back with the spatula end.

Figure 152. You can use the poker end of the eye tool or the point of a knife to create the corners, front and back, that are at the slits between the upper and lower eyelids junction. Check the eye rings aperture from the front view and make sure they are similar.

Figure 153. Allow 4-6 hours for the putty to harden before painting.

Chipmunk Painting

Note: In color swatches * denotes a little bit

Figure 1. After the epoxy putty has thoroughly hardened, the chipmunk is ready for painting. The first step is to apply white gesso. The gesso acts as a primer on the sealed wood and lightens up the dark color of the burning. Use a stiff bristle brush such as one an oil painter would use on canvas. Wet the brush first and dry most of the moisture out on your dry paper towel. Thoroughly load the bristle brush and wipe some of the excess off on the dry paper towel. Scrub the brush and the gesso back and forth into the texturing.

Figure 2. Coat the entire chipmunk with gesso. Do a second coat of gesso on the under parts that are whitish. Refer to your reference photos. Do the sides of the cheeks, muzzle, throat, neck, inside of front legs, chest, belly and the inside of the haunches. You do not necessarily need to gesso the bottom of the chippy.

Figure 3. If you are doing the scratching chippy, do one coat of gesso all over, dry that, and come back with a second coat on the whitish parts, as in Figure 2.

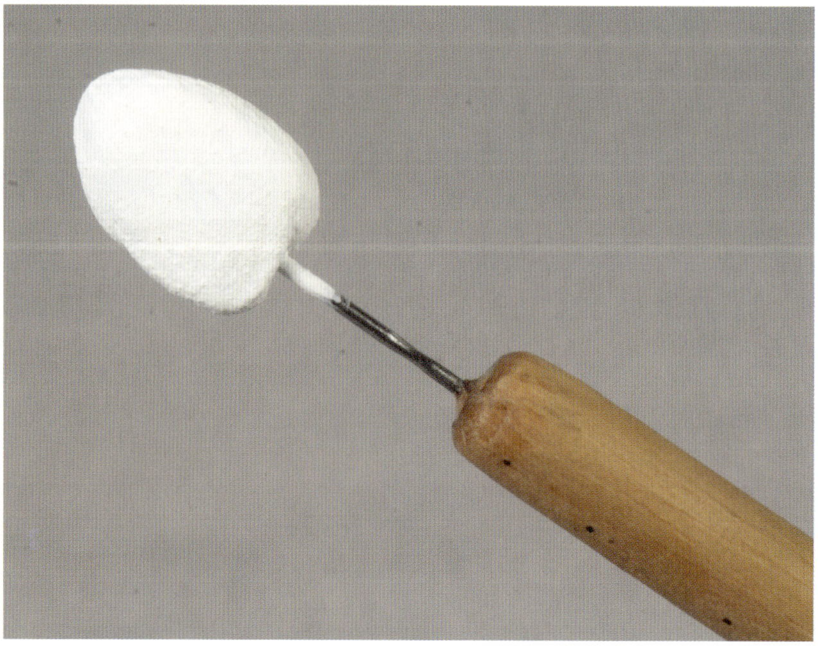

Figure 4. Use a sable or softer brush to coat the sunflower seed with a couple of coats of white gesso.

Figure 5. Carefully scrape the gesso off the eyes. I keep an Exacto knife in my paint box that I only use for scraping eyes. If you use a knife blade that has a nick or burr on it, the glass on the eye may be scratched, and the eye may have to be replaced!

Figure 6. Mixing raw sienna, raw umber, and white gesso, apply several basecoats to the head, ears, neck, the outside part of the front legs and paws, back, haunches, and topside and underside of the tail. You need to do sufficient coats so the initial white gesso coat underneath does not show through. Keep the basecoat mixture thin. By applying several coats, the chippy's fur takes on a very soft look. If you put the acrylic paint on too thick, the fur looks like plastic. Thinner, wetter paint sinks to the bottom of the texturing/burning. Thicker, drier paint stays on the top of the texturing/burning.

RS + RU + W

Figure 7. Take the basecoat on the inside part of the haunches as shown and use a clean, dampened brush to soften the edges of the brownish coat.

Figure 8. If you are doing the scratching chipmunk, basecoat several times to cover the gesso, and use a clean, dampened brush to soften the edges.

Figure 9. Study your reference pictures. There are many variations on the dark striping on chipmunks. There is usually some dark striping through, above, and below the eyes. Mixing burnt umber, black, and just a touch of white, paint in the dark striping about the eyes. Keep your dark striping mixture thin and do several applications on all the striped areas. Also darken the ear canals with this dark mixture.

BU + B + *W

Figure 10. Using the same dark color, paint in the 5 stripes on the back. Note that the middle stripe is the widest and that the space between the middle and the next stripe is wider than the outer two stripes.

Figure 11. Paint in the stripes on the top and underside of the tail. There is an irregular stripe right down the middle and then two outer irregular stripes near but not directly on the edges.

Figure 12. Mixing white gesso and very small amounts of yellow oxide and raw umber to make a dirty white, paint in the eyelids and striping on the eye areas. On some chipmunks, the white areas can go closer to the nose in front and behind the ear. Study your reference photos to decide how much dirty white to apply. You will need to do several coats in order to cover the basecoat color. Using a liner brush, drag the white mixture into the dark striping and vice versa.

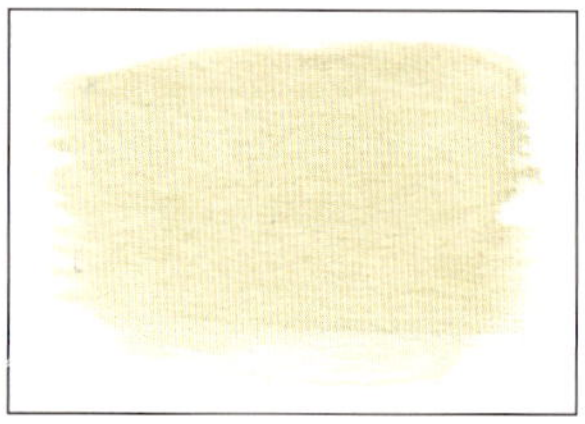

W + *YO + *RU

Figure 13. Using the same dirty white mixture, paint in the white stripes on the back. You will need to pull the dark color of the stripes into the white and the white into the dark. Doing this several times will create a soft look.

Figure 14. The edges of the tail, topside and underside, get tipped with the dirty white mixture as well.

Figure 15. Make a heavy (more paint pigments in the water) wash of black and burnt umber, and wash the nose, top of the head, backside of the ears, hind neck, the middle of the back (excluding the whitish stripes), and the top and bottom of the tail, including the whitish edgings. I use a large round sable brush such as a # 5 or #6 to do this wash. The thinness of the mixture allows it to sink to the bottom of the texturing/burning of the fur, while just lightly tinting the tops and sides. This is a heavy wash and not an actual "coat" of paint.

B + BU

Figure 16. Using a smaller brush and the same dark mixture, streak the haunches, middle of the front legs, between the toes on closed paws, and anywhere you wanted to darken deeper burning.

Figure 17. Mix burnt sienna with small amounts of yellow oxide and burnt umber. Using a small sable brush, load the brush thoroughly with paint and press on the heel to get the brush to flare out. Apply this mixture to the middle and bottom of the haunches. Dry-dab some of the mixture on the dark stripe down the middle of the chippy and both the top and bottom of the tail. On the darker areas, this will create just a hint of the reddish brown color and a very subtle coloration.

BS + *YO + *BU

Figure 18. You will need to refer to your reference photos, or if you have live chipmunks living in your area, check out the variations of color among the ones you know. There are amazing differences in how much of the reddish brown and the golden colors are on chipmunks in general. Use personal preference and artistic license as to how much of the reddish brown and the golden colors you put on them and where they will be applied.

For the golden color, mix yellow oxide and white with a small amount of raw sienna. Load a small sable brush thoroughly with the mixture, press on the heel of the brush to get it to flare out, and apply the mixture to the flanks, tops of the haunches, and dry-ish dabs on the top and bottom of the tail. Again, refer to your reference for other places that the chippy might be a more golden color.

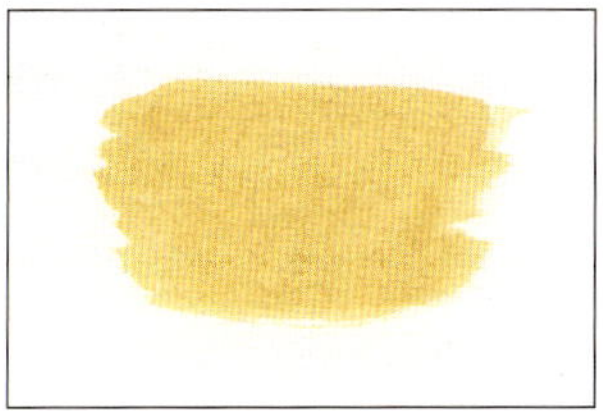

YO + W + *RS

Figure 19. For the whitish under parts, mix white gesso with a very small amount of yellow oxide. Now, yellow oxide is a powerful color; so go easy with how little you add. You want a very light yellowish white. Apply this mixture to the whitish under parts, blending the edges with a damp, clean brush to soften the transition areas.

W + *YO

Figure 20. Mix up the basecoat color used in Figure 6 and use this to further blend the transition areas where the light and the brown meet. Water this mixture down and apply to the underside of the front paws and the edges of the underneath of the front legs.

Figure 21. Mixing white gesso with small amounts of raw umber and yellow oxide, load a small sable brush with the mixture and wipe most of the paint mixture off on a dry paper towel. To get a brush to flare out, press on the heel of the brush. Lightly stroke in the light color for highlights. Dry-brush the highlights on the head, back, front and hind legs, flanks, and top and bottom of the tail. Deposit highlights even on the black striping on the face, back, and tail.

W + *RU + *YO

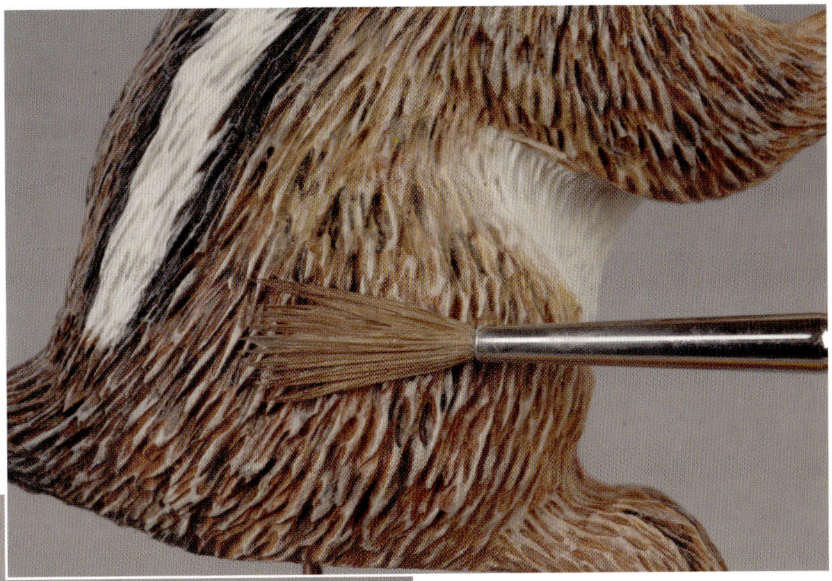

Figure 22. Once most of the paint is gone off the brush, you can actually rub the heel and the bristles across the texturing. The tops of the texturing will pick up some of the residual paint on the brush. If you get blobs of paint, the brush is not dry enough.

Figure 23. Apply a raw umber wash over the areas that are highlighted. Go over the white stripes on the face and back, and then take a clean, damp brush to dilute and remove some of the wash. You want a little of the wash to stay on the stripes to remove the starkness of the white and to sink to the bottom of the texturing to provide more dimensionality.

RU

Figure 24. Darken the ear canals with a mixture of black, burnt umber, and just a touch of white gesso. If you should get any on the inside of the earflap, take a clean, damp brush and remove it. The easiest way to prevent messing up the ear flap is to take a clean damp brush, load the mixed color on the tip of your brush, and apply to the recessed canal. With no paint on the upper part of the brush, it is easier to paint just the recess and not the surrounding flap.

B + BU + *W

Figure 25. Paint the inside of the ear flap and the little slit at the bottom of the ear with a mixture of raw sienna, burnt sienna, burnt umber, and white gesso.

RS + BS + BU + W

Figure 26. Mix white gesso and raw sienna to a light, rosy beige. Using a liner brush, paint in hair-like lines inside the earflap and lighten the flange and entire perimeter of the ear. If you get this too bright, you can always apply a raw umber wash to tone it down.

W + RS

Figure 27. To paint in the toenails, use a liner brush and a mixture of white gesso with very small amounts of black and raw sienna. Scrape the eyes, if you haven't already, and then the chipmunk is ready for whiskers.

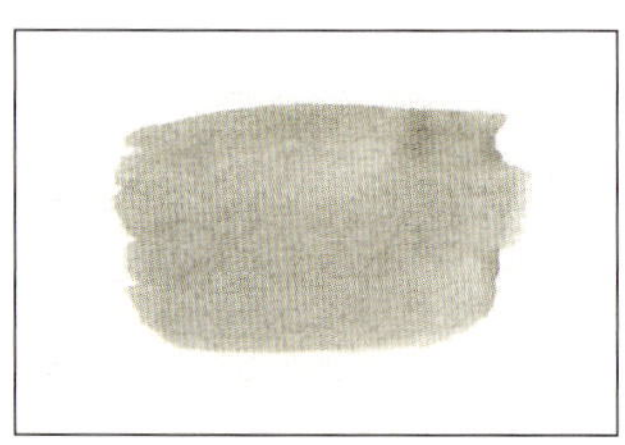

W + *B + *RS

Figure 28. Use a hat pin or needle super-glued into a dowel or paintbrush handle to poke in the eight whisker holes. The first row near the nose has two holes. The remaining two rows have 3 holes in each row.

Figure 29. The top holes in all three rows have a slight upward angle. The middle holes in the back rows are straight in, and the bottom holes of all the rows have a slight downward angle.

Figure 30. First decide what material you are going to use for whiskers. For years, I used the white china bristles in a paintbrush. Over time, I have collected many different swatches of whisker material. For this chipmunk, I am going to use hairs from the hind leg of a porcupine. They are multi-colored and look realistic. The two whiskers closest to the nose are approximately 0.75" and the remaining ones are slightly more than 1". When doing whiskers, you want the tapered part of the hair to be the end of the whisker. Cut each whisker to size, dip the blunt end into the yellow carpenter glue, and insert into the hole.

W + *RU

RU + B + *W

Figure 31. To paint the sunflower seed, basecoat with a mixture of white gesso and a very small amount of raw umber. When this is dry, apply the dark color, which is a mixture of raw umber, black, and a small amount of white gesso. Leave the outside edge light and paint in around some stripes. When this is dry, apply a raw umber wash to the entire seed.

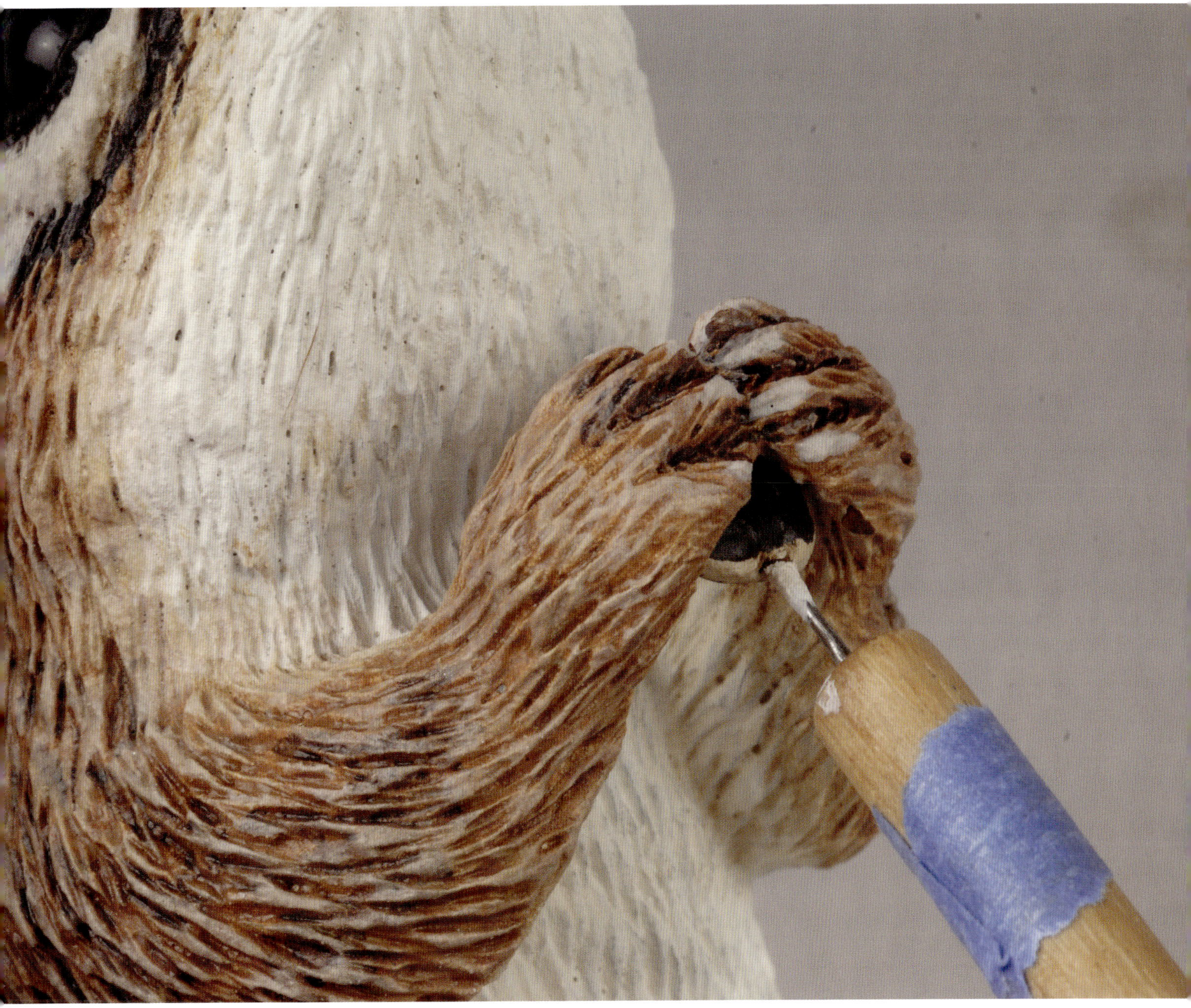

Figure 32. Put a small amount of super-glue on a small piece of waxed or freezer paper. Try the seed in the chippy's paws to see which side of the seed fits best. Dip that side of the seed in the glue and hold the seed in the paws with the needled tool. After a half of a minute or so, the seed should be tight to the wood. You could also use a drop of accelerator here to hasten the glue drying. Attach the chippy to its base.

Figure 33. Finished sitting chipmunk!

Figure 34. Finished scratching chipmunk!

The End of the Book........the journey continues.